EFFECTIVE
GROUP DISCUSSION

EFFECTIVE
GROUP DISCUSSION

fifth edition

JOHN K. BRILHART
University of Nebraska—Omaha

wcb

Wm. C. Brown Publishers
Dubuque, Iowa

Photo Credits: James Ballard: **302, 372;** Robert Eckert/EKM-Nepenthe: **57;** John Maher/ EKM-Nepenthe: **13;** James L. Shaffer: **79, 339, 363;** Jean-Claude Lejeune: **47;** Rohn Engh: **200;** Buick Public Relations: **350**

Library of Congress Catalog Card Number: 85–73361

ISBN 0–697–00359–0

Printed in the United States of America
10   9   8   7   6   5   4   3

contents

preface

As were previous editions, this fifth edition of *Effective Group Discussion* was written to help readers be more productive and satisfied members of small groups. The quality of life is in large part determined by our interpersonal and small group relationships. I believe that if we understand small groups and have a variety of procedures and techniques for making communication in them more effective we will be happier, more satisfied persons.

A major portion of our lives is spent in various kinds of task and activity groups: work groups, committees, task forces, quality circles, and other small groups which have as their objectives the production of goods, creation of policies, and solutions to specific problems. *Effective Group Discussion* is about communication in such groups, but is also applicable to learning and social groups of all types. The text contains a balance between empirically grounded theories of the dynamics of small group communication and specific practical procedures and techniques for improving the functioning of groups. I believe that one must *understand* what is happening before a small-group technique can be introduced with a high probability of being helpful.

Written for the beginning student of small group communication, discussion, and group dynamics courses, this book should also serve well as a reference source for persons appointed to posts of leadership, for consultants, and for anyone active in small groups. Instructors in such academic fields as communication, social psychology, business communication, and education will find it an appropriate and teachable textbook for their small-group oriented courses.

The needs of students were kept uppermost in my mind while writing this new edition. Specific examples are included to compensate for the lack of experience of some undergraduates. Visual illustrations are designed to teach rather than to entertain. A freshman should find the text quite understandable; upperclassmen should find their needs for theory and research summaries well satisfied.

A general model of open systems was used to unify the book. I believe this is the most appropriate paradigm available for understanding small groups. Much of the complexity and jargon of general systems theory was intentionally avoided. Early chapters will help the reader view small groups as open systems of input, throughput, and output variables.

This is not a cosmetic revision. Numerous substantive changes have been made from the fourth edition, while most of what proved beneficial to both students and instructors has been retained. Recent literature on research and theory was consulted, as was my personal experience and that reported by others working with previous editions.

The amount of space devoted to the process of communication has been greatly amplified, from one to three chapters. Chapter six is devoted to explaining small group communication as a dynamic, transactional process involving several persons at once; listening is a major concern of this chapter. Chapter seven is devoted entirely to language in discussions and written records of small groups. Finally, the eighth chapter is given to communication via nonverbal signals during group interaction.

Chapter ten on decision making (as distinguished from problem solving) has been enriched by a summary of techniques for preventing and managing routine conflicts among members. More importantly, a new procedure for dealing with a prolonged conflict which at first appears irresolvable is presented. Some readers will notice some similarities between this procedure and Lee's "Procedure for Coercing Agreement" and the procedure for managing a conflict presented by Adler and Towne in *Looking Out/Looking In*. My procedure for small groups is similar, but different in ways appropriate to contemporary problem-solving small groups. My students and I have found this procedure to be helpful, and believe you will also.

Chapter eleven on problem-solving procedure has been simplified. Students reported difficulty in understanding the different models of problem solving used in the third and fourth editions. I've tried my new "General Model of Problem Solving" with my own classes, who report it much easier to understand and apply than what is in the fourth edition. This model avoids the rigidity found in some small group textbooks. It is inherently flexible, adaptable to the characteristics of any problem. The advantages of "reflective thinking," "ideal solution," "creative problem solving," and "single question" formats are retained without the complexity of four apparently competing model outlines.

Chemers' new "Integrative Systems/Process Model of Leadership" fitted the theme of this book, and includes the most valid perspectives from all previous and more limited concepts of leadership. Classifying leader duties into three categories should help the student understand and remember what might be expected of a small group leader: administrative functions, leading group discussions, and developing the group and its members.

Readers of previous editions know me as an advocate of sharing responsibility, work, and the rewards of small group life. When theory "Z" of management philosophy was published, I found it to represent much of what I believed and knew from small group research on the corporate scene. Just this wcck our local newspaper reported that in 1984 Japanese workers had again exceeded those of other nations in the rate of increase in worker productivity. Much of the fantastic increase in both quality and productivity by Japanese employees can be traced to theory Z in application. I've now included the small group techniques coming from theory Z: the quality control circle and autonomous work groups. Techniques and methods like these will spread widely throughout U.S. organizations. These are not just one more version of consultative management. They represent a fundamental change in worker-manager relations effected through small groups. Every young American needs to understand them.

Conferences and discussions via telecommunication equipment are becoming commonplace. There is now a sufficient body of experience and research to allow giving practical advice to readers who will participate in this form of discussion. I've tried to do so without involving specifics of unique and constantly changing equipment.

Large numbers of students major in organizational communication. A "consultant-observer" role was added to this edition to meet the needs of such students.

Other changes will be noticed throughout *Effective Group Discussion,* but those above I consider especially important. As before, the chapters were written so that instructors need not assign them in the sequence presented in the book. Some teachers may want to address problem solving or leadership very early in a course. Others may want or need to omit some chapters or sections. This should present no problems. More is said about this in the Instructor's Manual.

To understand any field of study, one must acquire the special vocabulary of that field. To this end I have included a list of key terms for each chapter. Study objectives are provided to guide the reader. Lists of supplementary readings and some exercises are provided at the end of most chapters. The Instructor's Manual provides additional exercises and teaching supplements for the faculty member.

Acknowledgments

Appreciation is merited by numerous persons who have made contributions to my work as author of this book; I can name but a few of them. First, I am reminded of how much I owe to such instructors and writers as Robert F. Bales, Ernest Bormann, Elton S. Carter, B. Aubrey Fisher, Kenneth Hance, Alex Osborn, Sidney J. Parnes, J. Donald Phillips, and Marvin E. Shaw. Many colleagues in the study of small group dynamics and communication have expanded my vision through their papers and research reports. My department chairman, Robert E. Carlson, was both encouraging and helpful in providing some release of time from teaching so that I could complete the manuscript.

The critic-reviewers provided through Wm. C. Brown Company were exceptionally helpful: Peter A. Andersen, California State University, Long Beach; Eileen C. Billinson, Northern Virginia Community College; Mary Himmelein, Michael J. Owens Technical College; Gregg L. Phifer, Florida State University; and Mary Wiemann, University of California, Santa Barbara. I have been able to incorporate many of their suggestions, improving the book appreciably. Fellow members of many small groups provided insights as I continued to observe while participating. Students in my small group courses over the past twenty-five years have provided me with a great deal of instruction that has assisted in writing this book. My wife, Sue, gave acceptance and support when preparation of the manuscript diminished our time together. She also assisted with extensive proofreading. To all these persons, and many left unmentioned, my sincere thanks!

J. K. B.

EFFECTIVE
GROUP DISCUSSION

1

the small groups in everyone's life

Study Objectives

As a result of studying chapter 1 you should be able to:

1. Explain why it is important for you to understand the dynamics of small groups and be able to participate productively in small group discussions of many types.

2. Use correctly the terms presented in this chapter, particularly *group, small group, discussion, small group discussion, group dynamics,* and *small group communication.*

3. Classify any small group on the basis of its major purpose and source.

Key Terms

Activity group   a group to which members belong in order to participate in some collaborative activity.

Committee   small group of people given an assigned task or responsibility by a larger group (parent organization) or person with authority.
ad hoc or special—given a specific task to perform, and goes out of existence when this job is completed.
standing—continues indefinitely with an area of responsibility that may include many tasks.

Conference   discussion by representatives from two or more groups in order to find ways to coordinate efforts, reduce conflict, etc.

Discussion (small group discussion)   a small group of people talking with each other face to face in order to achieve some interdependent goal, such as increased understanding, coordination of activity, or solution to a shared problem.

Forum discussion   large audience interacting verbally, usually following some presentation.

Group   three or more persons united for some purpose(s) and interacting in such a way that they influence each other.

Group dynamics   a field of inquiry concerned with the nature of small groups, including how they develop and interact, and their relationships with individuals, other groups, and institutions.

Interaction   mutual influence by two or more persons via communication process.

Learning group (growth group)   groups that discuss in order to enhance the knowledge, perceptions, and interactions of the members.

Panel discussion   a small group whose members interact informally and impromptu for the benefit of a listening audience.

Primary group   small group in which the major purpose is to meet the members' needs for affiliation.

Problem-solving group   a group that discusses for the sake of devising a course of action to solve a problem.

Public discussion group   a small group that plans and presents before an audience a discussion-type program such as panel, interview, or symposium.

Public interview   one or more interviewers asking questions of one or more respondents for benefit of listening audience.

Small group   a group of few enough members for each to perceive all others as individuals, who meet face to face, share some identity or common purpose, and share standards for governing their activities as members.

Small group communication   the scholarly study of communication among small group members, among such groups, and between them and larger organizations; the body of communication theory produced by such study.

Small groups constitute the basic fabric of social life in the last part of the twentieth century. We do not exist as humans alone, but as members of families, work groups, clubs, and circles of friends. We dramatize the life of lonely pioneers and mountain men, but this is the age of communication—no one really lives or works alone today. Most of us spend a major portion of each day involved as members of various small groups. We hear a lot about large organizations, both corporate and public, but an examination of any large organization reveals many interdependent small work groups, task forces, committees and boards. Looking toward the year 2000, communication futurist Robert Theobald foresaw a political order with innumerable decision-making groups in which citizens would serve for definite periods of time. From this he argued that

As the diversity of age and style in decision-making groups increased in the eighties, all those involved needed to develop a far more conscious understanding of the basic communication styles that are required if decision-making groups are to function successfully.[1]

Vital to such groups, he said, will be abilities in communicating with larger constituencies of the small groups that make decisions, development of mutual perceptual patterns, and knowing how to work together so that groups are not merely a "conglomeration of individuals acting out of their narrow motivations, and clashing . . . in their behavioral patterns." The higher a person goes in any organizational hierarchy, the more time the person spends in meetings of small groups and the greater the need for the skills and abilities Theobald described.

Communicating in small groups is so much a part of our lives that most of us take it for granted, failing to perceive and understand what is happening in these groups or how to make them more effective. We need to understand how to communicate more effectively in them, or we are doomed to unsatisfying and ineffectual discussions *ad nauseum*.

I think you will find it highly illuminating to list all the small groups in which you participated during the past week, regardless of how brief the time spent with the group. How satisfied are you with how these groups function, and with your part in each of them? Students in my college classes have listed from two to twenty-four groups, with a typical response being about eight to ten. If your list does not contain the names of at least eight groups, probably you are unaware of much of the fabric of communication in your life. Does your list resemble one of the following examples? A factory worker: quality control circle, union bargaining committee, family (3 groups), fishing trio, church building committee, bowling team. A student: family, Bible study group, sorority, executive committee of sorority, discussion group in psychology class, volleyball team (intramural), car pool, clerks in women's wear department. A faculty member: family, collective bargaining team, arrangements committee for professional convention, research team, executive committee of state historical association, steering committee of AAUP, two committees of academic department, gourmet club, two graduate student committees, and numerous informal discussions among groups of acquainted faculty members and students. These are not exceptionally long lists.

The amount of time spent in *formal* groups alone can be overwhelming. Kriesberg found that executives spend an average of ten hours per week in formal committee meetings.[2] Goldhaber found that at the University of New Mexico the average tenured faculty member served on six committees simultaneously, with eleven hours per week spent in committees and other scheduled meetings.[3] Add to these figures the amount of time spent in informal discussions, and you can see that the importance of small group discussion in our lives cannot be overstated.

It would be delightful if we could say that most of the talk in these ubiquitous small groups is productive of personal satisfaction for the participants, achieves the purposes to which the discussions were addressed, and makes for a sense of unity among the members. But it is hardly so. Our folklore contains many sayings that indicate something is less than adequate in the way many small groups communicate: "The way to kill anything is to give it to a committee." "Committees are groups that keep minutes and waste hours." "A committee is a group of people none of whom is capable of doing anything about the problem deciding collectively that nothing can be done about it." "A group can make a mess of anything." Both popular and scholarly journals carry numerous articles about serious problems in families and other primary social groups, and how vital these are to our personal and societal well-being. As Giffin and Patton wrote,

Since the individual today is experiencing a growing dependency on groups of all descriptions, it is important that people be familiar with the dynamics of group interaction. Once a person has acquired an understanding of the nature of groups, the bases of their development, and their interrelationships with individuals and other groups he has the basis for prediction and control.[4]

We humans need membership in small groups for many reasons. First, we need them *to meet distinctly human needs*. Schutz summarized these as needs for *inclusion, affection,* and *control:* the need to belong or be included in groups with others, a need for love, and a need for power in relation to both other persons and our environment.[5] Second, we need small groups because they are *more effective problem solvers in the long run* than are the individuals. Group members can see the blind spots and biases in each other's thinking, eliminating many faulty solutions and leaving as a remainder an idea that is better than any one member alone could devise. For many of the decisions we must make there is no "correct answer at the back of the book"; only the judgment of our peers arrived at through consensus can guide us in choosing among alternatives. Third, participation in work planning or problem solving has been proven to be a great motivator of effort. People work harder and better when they have helped decide what to do. No plan of action is good if the people who must carry it out don't like it and work halfheartedly. A long line of investigations has shown that groups are powerful persuaders of their members, leading to more personal change than study, lectures, or a one-to-one pitch. Even our self-concepts and personalities are largely formed by interaction in small groups.

You may have studied small groups in a sociology course, especially their role in establishing and maintaining social organization as the link between the individual and society as a whole. In psychology you may have studied how the small group modifies the individual's personality and self concepts, and how various types of small groups can be therapeutic for their members. In the field of speech communication and in this book we focus on the process of communication among the members of small groups, especially how you can influence this process to make the groups in which you participate more satisfying to the members, efficient, and productive of quality decisions. Findings from scholars in many fields will be reported and applied, but throughout the book the central objective will be to help you understand what is happening as members talk and work together, and how to make your own communicating as productive as possible.

Small group discussion, the talk among members of a group, cannot be reduced to a set of formulas; it is far too complex for any simplistic prescriptions or rules. In *Effective Group Discussion* I have used the concept *system* to help you understand how groups develop and function, with numerous guidelines but no absolute prescriptions for success. *System* implies interdependence among components in an ongoing process. In a small group this means that everything that happens in any part of the system makes a difference in every other component of the group. Because the only person you can directly influence and control is yourself, this book is designed to help you develop an awareness of your own behavior in small groups and its implications for other members of the groups in which you are an active member. Put another way, we will aim at developing the art of communicating effectively in a variety of types of problem-solving and learning groups.

Before going further some definitions are needed. Misunderstanding of what I have written, of your fellow students, and of your instructor is likely to be frequent if we do not use certain key terms to refer to the same kinds of events and behaviors. Learning any new subject is to a large degree a matter of learning the special language of the field of study. Throughout this book lists of *key terms* are included at the beginning of each chapter. To start off you need to understand how I have used several terms found throughout the pages that follow.

Discussion and Related Concepts

Group is the first term we must consider. Groups have been defined by various writers with reference to members' perceptions, goals, structure, interdependence and interaction among members. The following definition was chosen as the one most suited to a study of small group communication:

A group is defined as [three] or more persons who are interacting with one another in such a manner that each person influences and is influenced by each other person.[6]

This definition emphasizes interaction and mutual influence. Interaction implies *communication,* the exchange of signals between or among persons who belong to the group, and that at least some of these signals are perceived and responded to in such a way that each group member makes some difference in how each other member acts in the future. By this definition, persons collected in one place would not constitute a group unless and until there was reciprocal awareness and influence. Group members could be widely scattered geographically, interacting through formal channels such as newsletters, telephone conversations, closed circuit TV, or radio, and never see each other face to face. Each member would have some reason(s) for belonging to the group and a sense of membership, but the reasons could be widely different from member to member.

This brings us to a very basic concept in this book: *small group.* Many attempts have been made to define the small group on the basis of the number of members, but this has never worked. *Small* is at best an imprecise relative term, yet a word with which we seem to be stuck when talking about the basic social unit of a few persons who perceive themselves as an entity. The essence of a "small" group is not the precision of some number such as *10* or *15,* but *perceptual awareness,* the upward limit being the number of persons one is able to include in awareness and recall. Studies of human perception have shown definite limits on how much information we can take in at a glance and keep organized in memory.[7] At one glance most of us can perceive a number of similar units from one to about eleven at the maximum. When that number of units is exceeded, we have to begin counting, as "one, two, three . . ." or "three, six, nine. . . ." Attempts to develop category systems for instantly observing and classifying behaviors of people in face-to-face discussion groups revealed that with considerable training most people can learn to handle up to about 12 or 14 categories, but not more.[8] In this sense, the *small group* is one in which members can perceive at least peripherally all the members at once, with some awareness of who is and is not in the group, and the role each is taking. I have arbitrarily eliminated the dyad (two persons) from specific consideration in this book, for there is a lot of evidence that dyads function considerably differently from groups of three or more members. Perhaps the most usable definition of the small group was formulated by Crosbie: ". . . a collection of people who meet more or less regularly in face-to-face interaction, who possess a common identity or exclusiveness of purpose, and who share a set of standards governing their activities."[9] I will also use the term *small group* to refer to groups that meet only once, provided that a sense of shared

Figure 1.1   "Groupness," like "cubeness," is a pattern property.

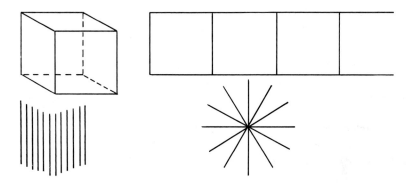

purpose, face-to-face interaction, and some standards for governing their activity also exist within the group.

Small group indicates what is often called a "pattern property" or non-additive dimension. "Groupness" emerges from the relationships among the persons involved, just as "cubeness" emerges from the image of a set of planes, intersects, and angles in specific relationships to each other. One can draw a cube with twelve lines (try it), but only if they are assembled in a definite way. Any other arrangement of the lines gives something other than a cube, as illustrated in figure 1.1. A collection of several people in one place does not constitute a small group. For example, a robber and three police officers may interact orally, but they do not form a small group (lacking an interdependent purpose, shared norms, and procedures). For a small group to exist, the members must share some "promotively interdependent purpose," meaning that all members succeed or fail together in the accomplishment of that purpose. The success of each is dependent upon the success of all; each member promotes the success of each other member. Lacking some sort of interdependence in purpose, a small group simply does not exist even though several people may *look* as if they formed a group. Calling several people a group just because they happen to have been thrown together by time and circumstance does not make them such, regardless of how we label the collection.

Discussion is another key term in this book. "Discussion" has been used in a variety of ways: the "discussion" section of a research report in which inferences and conclusions are drawn; the "body" or major part of a public speech; any oral interaction among persons, including even a verbal fight; and interaction among several persons following some preselected procedure. In this book, *small group discussion* refers to *a small group of persons talking with each other face to face in order to achieve some interdependent goal, such as increased understanding, coordination of activity, or a solution to a shared problem.* This definition implies several characteristics of small group discussion:

1. A small enough number of persons for each to be aware of and have some reaction to each other (from three to rarely more than fifteen; typically from three to seven).
2. A mutually interdependent purpose so that the success of each member is contingent upon the success of the entire group in reaching this goal.
3. Each person has a sense of belonging, of being a part of the group.
4. Oral interaction, involving speech communication via both verbal and nonverbal symbols. This interaction is continuous during a discussion so that the members are constantly reacting, adapting, and modifying their actions in response to each other. Impromptu speaking, rather than prepared speeches, is the essence of small group discussion; in common terms, discussion entails "give and take."
5. A sense of *cooperation* exists among the members. There may well be disagreement and conflict over information, ideas, and activities, but all members perceive themselves as being engaged in a search for a group outcome that will be as satisfactory as possible to all. Argument is viewed as a means for testing ideas so the best ones can be selected, rather than as a way of winning. Thus it is possible for representatives of competing groups to discuss if they seek means to coexist in peace rather than defeat each other.

The term *small group communication* will be used in this book to refer to the study of interaction among small group members, and to the body of communication theory produced by such study that can be used to produce more effective discussion among the members of small groups. Later in this book we will take up a detailed study of this body of theory and principles.

Group dynamics is another term that you may have heard in conjunction with the study of small groups. Although to the layman this term may imply a set of tricks or gimmicks to stimulate interaction, in this book "group dynamics" will be used to refer to a field of study much broader than that of small group communication: ". . . a field of inquiry dedicated to advancing knowledge about the nature of groups, the laws of their development, and their interrelations with individuals, other groups, and larger institutions."[10] We must examine the knowledge gained by scholars of group dynamics if we are to understand the communication going on in small groups, and thus make our discussions as effective as possible.

Being an effective discussant in a variety of types of small groups calls for an understanding of the dynamics or forces at work in the group, both an understanding of and skills in the processes and means by which communication is effected, and a personal involvement or commitment to the group as well as knowledge relevant to the purpose of the group. One could be an effective public speaker, but a poor member of the small groups, and vice versa.

Types of Small Groups that Discuss

Discussions among members of small groups are held for many purposes. The student of small group communication and discussion needs a simplified scheme for classifying both small groups and the discussions in which they engage. A set of classifications (and terms) is helpful when observing, analyzing, or talking about discussions. The classification scheme presented in this section of the book is based on the *purpose* or major objective of the group. It has been useful to many students of the arts of discussing. You will need a verbal definition and mental image of the characteristics of each major type of discussion group so that you can communicate efficiently about groups with your instructor and fellow students of small groups.

Primary Groups

These are groups of people who are together to satisfy human needs for inclusion (affiliation) and affection rather than to accomplish some specific task. All primary groups are long-term. Examples include a nuclear family, roommates, several friends who meet daily around a table in the student center, four women who eat lunch and often attend movies together, co-workers who regularly share their coffee breaks, and white-collar workers who regularly drop into each other's offices for a chat. Such groups *may* take on specific tasks and often make decisions, but more often they provide personal support, chat about a variety of topics, "let off steam," and generally enjoy each other. Their talk will often be disorganized and informal—for talk is not the means to an end so much as the end in itself, a part of human companionship. Universal human needs to symbolize and share experiences and for attention of other humans are met by discussing informally in primary groups. More than any other force in our lives, primary groups socialize and mold us into the people we become; their importance is **tremendous.** However, primary groups are not the major focus of this book, though most of the information and advice for making communicating within small groups more effective applies to them. *Effective Group Discussion* focuses on such secondary groups as problem-solving or decision-making committees and task forces, work groups, and learning groups. The study of communication in primary group relationships is usually addressed directly and extensively in books and courses about "interpersonal" communication.

Secondary Groups

"Primary" and "secondary" are not totally distinct; rather, they represent poles of a continuum of purposes, ranging from almost totally primary to almost totally secondary (task oriented). The purest secondary group would be organized to produce some change on the environment without having any impact on members' needs for belonging or affecting them as persons, whereas a purely primary group would exist solely for the socializing of its members. All groups initiated to accomplish some task are thus more secondary than primary, though many task groups do help members achieve primary human needs for socialization and affiliation.

Therapy and Encounter Groups

All therapy and encounter groups are called collectively "personal growth" groups. They are composed of persons who have come together to develop personal insights, overcome personality problems, and grow as individuals from the feedback and support of others—to engage in personal learning and growth. Some examples are local chapters of self-help groups (i.e., Alcoholics Anonymous, Lost Chords, Gamblers Anonymous), gay-rights support groups, and outpatient groups for clients with personal adjustment problems. Members of such groups do not choose each other, nor are they appointed; they join to help themselves with problems that are both highly personal and social. In this regard they are like members of most learning groups. Most therapy or personal growth groups have an expert professional present to guide and facilitate the interaction. No *group* goal is sought; the group exists because members believe they can gain help from each other. Most such groups have a relatively limited term of existence; in some, membership changes gradually but the group continues. At times your class in speech, discussion, or group dynamics may become this sort of group. It is formed in much the same way as an encounter group: several persons with a desire to learn for individual reasons but needing others for such learning to occur, come together under the guidance of an authority figure probably called the "instructor."

Study or Learning Groups

These groups are similar to encounter and therapy groups to the extent that they are formed as a medium for the learning and growth of the participants. If you are reading this book for a course concerned with small group discussion, your class may be organized into several learning groups. Such groups, rather than seeking growth in the personality as the primary end (although that may be one objective), primarily meet to understand a subject more thoroughly by pooling their knowledge, perceptions, and beliefs. While they are exchanging information the participants also gain practice in speaking, listening, critical thinking, and other communication skills.

I hope you have participated in learning groups in such courses as literature, social science, and philosophy. I have had the pleasure of being in innumerable such groups. As a breeder and trainer of hounds, I have learned an immense amount from discussions with friends while driving to field trials for our dogs. Much of my appreciation of painting came from extensive discussions with others of what we saw in paintings. On my campus, posters advertise the Women's Resource Center, inviting any interested person to drop

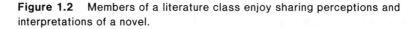

Figure 1.2   Members of a literature class enjoy sharing perceptions and interpretations of a novel.

in for "rap" sessions to explore feelings, beliefs, and values about sex roles in our society. Other posters announce Bible study groups, meditation groups, philosophy discussion groups, and many others.

The "round table" is a type of learning group sometimes sponsored by organizations as a way for people sharing some common interest to come together to exchange information and ideas. Churches, libraries, colleges, and many volunteer organizations produce such informal learning groups.

Problem-Solving Groups

Problem-solving groups vary widely in their composition and functioning, but all of them are formed to help alleviate some unsatisfactory condition (problem). A problem-solving group may go through a complex procedure that begins with exploring the problem and ends with some definitive physical action, or it may be limited to choosing among alternatives or giving advice to someone with authority to decide and take action. Primary and learning groups at times tackle problems, and thus for a time may engage in problem-solving discussions, but that is not their originating purpose. A problem-solving group is so classified because it was *created* to solve a problem or problems.

There are many sub-types of problem-solving groups. Much of the rest of this book will deal with four major categories of problem-solving groups, two of which are relatively new to the American scene: committees, conference groups, quality control circles, and autonomous work groups.

Committees. Committees are groups which have been given an assignment to do some work for a parent organization or some person in a position of authority in an organization. A committee may be formed to investigate and report findings, to recommend a course of action for the parent group, to formulate policies, or to plan and carry out some action. All such tasks require discussion among the members. Boards, councils, and staffs are special types of committees. For example, the board of directors is often called an executive committee. Such groups represent a larger organization, often with very extensive power to make and execute policy.

Committees are usually classified as either *ad hoc* or *standing.* The *ad hoc* or special committee has a defined task to perform, and when that has been accomplished the committee goes out of existence. Many times a special committee is referred to as a "task force" of an organization, with members appointed from various departments of a corporation or segments of a political body. Usually a task force or special committee holds numerous meetings before its defined task has been accomplished; as soon as it has reported its action or recommendations, an *ad hoc* committee ceases to exist. Special committees do such things as evaluate credentials of job applicants, draft bylaws, hear employee or student grievances, plan social events, conduct investigations, devise plans for controlling drug usage among employees, advise governors on what to do about statewide problems, and evaluate programs and institutions.

Standing committees are usually established through the constitution or bylaws of an organization to deal with some class of problems or part of the organization's functions. Such groups continue indefinitely, even though the membership may change periodically. Frequently some portion of the members of a standing committee are replaced on an annual basis, so that the committee has both experienced members and members with a fresh perspective. The most important standing committee of most organizations is given a name such as "Executive Committee," "Board," or "Steering Committee." This committee is generally charged with overall management of the organization, and can function for the entire organization when general membership meetings are not possible. Other commonly encountered standing committees go under such names as "membership committee," "personnel committee," "parking and traffic committee," "program committee," and the like. Standing committees tackle a variety of problems which lie within the area of their responsibility, often doing some work toward resolving a number of problems at a single meeting.

Conference Groups. "Conference" is widely used to refer to almost any type of face-to-face communication; for example, a secretary may say that her boss is "in conference" when she is talking with one other person in her office. At times "conference" is used to refer to a large gathering of persons who hear speeches, study various issues, and perhaps engage in several small group discussions.

In this book, *conference* will be used to refer to a meeting of representatives from two or more other groups; since every large organization contains

Figure 1.3   A committee of nurses preparing a recommendation.

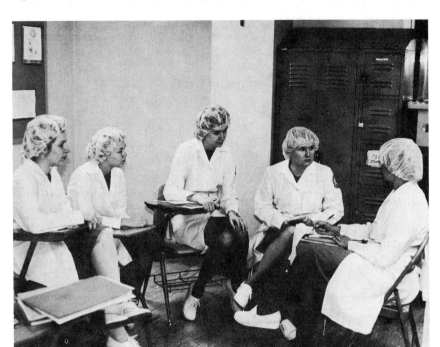

within it many small functioning groups, conferences are very important for coordination within and among organizations. The conferees communicate information from one group to another, perhaps coordinating their efforts. Intergroup conflicts and competition must be mediated to work out a solution acceptable to all groups represented. For example, representatives of various charitable organizations meet to coordinate the efforts of their respective groups and to exchange information and ideas. The various crew heads, designers, and directors must confer periodically to plan and coordinate the efforts of the many people involved in producing a play. Conferences between delegates of the Senate and House of Representatives attempt to resolve differences in legislation bearing on the same issue. Representatives of business and labor meet to decide on wages, working conditions, and fringe benefits. Conferences are frequently held with representatives from the various campuses in a university system to resolve differences in policies, coordinate academic programs, etc. Such conferees must often report their decisions for approval by the groups they represented.

Quality Control Circles. Workers in a production or service company volunteer for membership in a Quality Control Circle. The "circle" meets periodically (often weekly) on company time to develop recommendations for improving the quality of finished products, efficiency, worker safety, etc. Supervisors leading such groups must be trained as problem-solving discussion leaders, and upper management must be committed to respond to all recommended solutions. A few conditions are essential if the Quality Control Circle procedure is to work: workers must share in benefits of their cost-saving ideas, job security must be guaranteed when efficiency is increased, discussion leaders must be open minded toward all ideas suggested, and top management must be willing to act upon suggestions or explain why they are being delayed or rejected. The typical QCC has from five to seven members.

Autonomous Work Groups. Groups of workers are given a defined area of freedom to manage their productive work (autonomous here is somewhat misleading, as all such groups of employees are given strict limits on their freedom to decide). AWGs elect their own leaders rather than having appointed first-line supervisors. The group may decide such managerial issues as in what order to do their assigned jobs, who will do what tasks, and schedules. Coordination by appointed managers is at the group level rather than at the level of the individual worker. After workers have been given such authority it is very hard for management to take it back from them. The claim is advanced that a group can more effectively allocate resources than can a somewhat distant manager, that employees with some say in their work are more committed and productive than workers given less choice, and involvement in decision making meets the psychological needs of the employees without reducing the technical quality of their work. The need for training of the workers who will be involved in AWGs was recently pointed out.[11] Without arguing for either Quality Control Circles or Autonomous Work Groups, with confidence I can predict that employees of the future will be involved in *more* group problem-solving discussions than were their predecessors, and that sensitivity to group phenomena and skills in discussion leadership will be increasingly important.

Activity Groups

These are groups formed to enable members to engage cooperatively in some activity, often both for the sake of doing the activity and for the affiliation provided by doing the activity with others. Members of such groups must invariably solve problems and make choices among alternatives about such matters as when and where to meet, how to pay for their activities, how to conduct the activities, and all the other decisions that must be made in coordinating the efforts of several persons. A few examples may clarify the concept of "activity groups": a dinner group of people who meet at intervals to eat together at a new restaurant; game-playing groups, such as bridge, poker, backgammon, pinochle, and chess clubs; a road rally club; dog, cat, or other animal interest groups; and hunting groups.

Public Discussion Groups

Public discussion groups are created for the stimulation and enlightenment of a listening audience, members of which may become participants in a large-group discussion (forum). Small-group public discussions provide a number of perspectives or beliefs about an issue or problem, permitting listeners to make direct comparisons of the merits of differing beliefs, values, and policies.

Panel Discussion. A *panel discussion* is a public presentation in which a small group of persons representing varying perspectives discusses informally a few issues on which a question of importance to a listening audience hinges. For example, a panel might discuss abortion laws, solutions to congested parking on campus, the pros and cons of quality circles, or the responsibility of society to victims of crimes. A *moderator* coordinates the discussion so that it does not ramble and so that all points of view are given a relatively equal airing. Participants need to be both knowledgeable about the question under discussion, and articulate in expressing their knowledge and opinions. Although panelists need an outline of questions to follow, their speaking should be relatively impromptu, made in response to comments by other panel members rather than as prepared "speeches." The panel discussion is an excellent format for developing an overview of different points of view bearing on an issue of public concern. Public television and radio stations carry many panel discussions. Your instructor may assign groups in your class to prepare and present panel programs. Panel members need not agree on anything except which issues to discuss; the lively argument which ensues can make for an intellectually stimulating program.

Public Interviews. A *public interview* may be conducted by one or more interviewers of one or more interviewees at a time. You may have heard such interviews on public television, "Meet the Press," "The Donahue Show," or other public interview programs. So-called "press conferences" and "presidential debates" are interviews conducted by news correspondents. Interviewers and interviewees may agree in advance on a list of major questions or topics to be discussed, on the range of topics for discussion, or the program may be entirely spontaneous. The interviewer's responsibility is to represent the audience by asking questions he or she thinks they most want or need to have answered, and to help the respondent clarify answers. Obviously, the interviewee is selected because of a special role or knowledge.

Forum Discussion. *Forum* refers to a period of time in which members of an audience are invited to ask questions or express opinions. Frequently a forum follows a panel or interview program; a forum may also follow a film, speech, or other presentation. Members of an audience should always be told that a forum will follow the panel or other program so that they can think of (and possibly write down) questions to ask or comments to make. This term is also used to refer to a discussion held by a large gathering of people, such as a hearing on a proposed change in zoning laws or a public hall meeting in which a political official or administrator goes before all interested persons to discuss with them any of their concerns about the office or agency he or she represents. Mayors, legislators, county commissioners, and other officials schedule "town hall" forums in many communities.

Summary

In this opening chapter we have considered the vital roles small groups play in our lives—the very source of our identity, the vehicle for satisfying many of our most basic human needs, and a means to decision making and problem solving in a complex society. Yet there is much evidence that small groups are frequently ineffectual and frustrating to their members. Understanding the basic dynamics of small groups and the available theory about communication within them is essential if one is to be effective in the arts of small group interaction.

Key terms in the study of small groups and discussion have been defined to facilitate communication. Finally, a scheme for classifying small groups according to purpose and source was presented: primary versus secondary groups; therapy and encounter groups; study or learning groups; problem-solving groups, including committees, conference groups, quality control circles, and autonomous work groups; activity groups; and public discussion groups, including panel discussions, public interviews, and forums.

With your understanding of these key terms and concepts we can now proceed to a more detailed consideration of the dynamics of small groups. Chapter 2 explains the small group as an open system, completing the overview of small group theory. The second section of the book treats the inputs which become the group system: members of the group are considered in chapter 3; and in chapter 4, setting and purpose as input variables. The rest of the book is devoted to the study of group processes and procedures which facilitate desirable outputs: chapter 5 explores the development of a group; chapter 6 establishes the concept of communication as a receiver phenomenon, followed by a study of language in chapter 7 and nonverbal signals in discussion in chapter 8. Chapter 9 develops the concepts of leader and leadership, and provides advice on how to discharge the many responsibilities involved in leading group discussions. Chapter 10 describes a variety of means by which decisions are made in groups and how conflicts among members can be managed productively, followed by a detailed study of problem-solving procedures in chapter 11. Chapter 12 presents methods for facilitating learning through group discussion, and techniques especially useful in production and service organizations. Finally, chapter 13 presents techniques and tools for observing, analyzing, and evaluating small group communication.

Exercises

1. For one week keep a list of all the small groups in which you actively participate during the week. See if you can classify these groups

according to the scheme for doing so in this chapter. Next, rate your personal satisfaction with each group, from "1" (very dissatisfied) to "7" (very satisfied). Compare your list with those made by other members of your class. What do you conclude? Use the format below:

Name or description of Group	Type of Group	Satisfaction
1.		
2.		
etc.		

2. *Icebreaker.* This exercise is designed to help you get acquainted with classmates and to reduce tensions and formality that exist within a collection of strangers. The entire class should sit in a circle for this exercise, so that each member can see each other face to face. While doing the exercise, each member should have his or her name on a card or name tag large enough to be read across the circle.
   A. First, complete the following sentences with the first thing that comes to mind. Each person should answer question 1 before proceeding to question 2. Begin each set of answers with a different person; your instructor will indicate who should lead off, then proceed clockwise until all have answered.
   The three adjectives that best describe me are __ , __ , and __ .
   Three persons most important to me are __ , __ , and __ .
   When I meet someone I like, I _____ .
   When I meet someone I initially dislike, I _____ .
   Being in a small group makes me feel _____ .
   I'm taking this course because _____ .
   Ten years from now I see myself as _____ .
   My favorite place in the whole world is _____ .
   My favorite activity is _____ .
   The thing I am most proud of about myself is _____ .
   B. Briefly discuss the following:
   Who is most like you?
   How do you now feel about your class?
   Who impressed you most? Why?
   What have we learned from this exercise?

Bibliography

The bibliography at the end of each chapter provides sources you may want to consult for more detail about concepts or ideas presented in the text of the chapter. These bibliographies are purposefully limited to the few writings likely to be most interesting and helpful to you as a student.

Cathcart, Robert S., and Samovar, Larry A., eds., *Small Group Communication: A Reader.* 4th ed. Dubuque, Iowa: Wm. C. Brown Company Publishers, 1984. The opening section and first few articles present an excellent explanation of the concept "small group."

Nixon, Howard L., II. *The Small Group.* Englewood Cliffs, N.J.: Prentice-Hall, 1979. Chapter 1 explains the primary-secondary group continuum particularly well.

Shaw, Marvin E. *Group Dynamics: The Psychology of Small Group Behavior.* 3d ed. New York: McGraw-Hill, 1981. On pp. 12–14 Shaw answers the question "do small groups really exist?"

Theobald, Robert. "The Communications Era from the Year 2000." *National Forum* 60 (Summer 1980):17–20.

References

1. Robert Theobald, "The Communications Era from the Year 2000," *National Forum* 60 (Summer 1980):20.
2. M. Kriesberg, "Executives Evaluate Administrative Conferences," *Advanced Management* 15 (1950):15–17.
3. Gerald Goldhaber, "Communication and Student Unrest," unpublished report to the president of the University of New Mexico, undated.
4. Bobby R. Patton and Kim Giffin, *Problem-Solving Group Interaction* (New York: Harper & Row, Publishers, 1973), 6.
5. William C. Schutz, *FIRO: A Three-Dimensional Theory of Interpersonal Behavior* (New York: Rinehart, 1958).
6. Marvin E. Shaw, *Group Dynamics: The Psychology of Small Group Behavior,* 2d ed. (New York: McGraw-Hill, 1976), 11.
7. Robert S. Woodworth and H. Schlosberg, *Experimental Psychology,* rev. ed. (New York: Henry Holt and Company, 1954), 90–94.
8. Robert F. Bales, *Interaction Process Analysis* (Cambridge, Mass.: Addison-Wesley, 1950).
9. Paul V. Crosbie, ed., *Interaction in Small Groups* (New York: Macmillan Company, 1975), 2.
10. Darwin Cartwright and Alvin Zander, *Group Dynamics: Research and Theory,* 3d ed. (New York: Harper & Row, Publishers, 1968), 7.
11. Charles C. Manz and Henry P. Sims, Jr., "The Potential for "Groupthink" in Autonomous Work Groups," *Human Relations* 35 (1982):773–784.

2

the small group as a system

Study Objectives

As a result of studying chapter 2 you should be able to:

1. Consciously and intentionally adopt a participant-observer perspective when engaged in discussions.

2. List and explain the major input, throughput, and output variables in a small group as an open system.

3. Describe the characteristics of an ideal discussion group.

Key Terms

Feedback   some part of the output of a system put back into the system to influence or control future operations of the system.

Environment   the context or setting in which a small group exists.

Input variable   an observable source of energy and "raw material" to any open system; resource from which a system is formed and on which it operates to produce outputs.

Interdependent goal   an objective shared by members of a small group in such a way that achievement of it by any member is dependent on achievement of this goal by all members.

Norm   a rule, usually informal and unstated, which governs behavior of members of a small group.

Open system   a system in interaction with its environment requiring constant adjustment and balancing with external forces.

Output variable   any observable consequence or change resulting from the functioning of a system, including changes in the inputs, the components of the system, products it creates, and its environment.

Participant-observer   active participant in a small group who is at the same time observing and evaluating its processes and procedures.

Process variable   see "throughput variable."

System   a structured complex of interdependent components in constant interaction requiring adaptation among its parts to maintain its organic wholeness.

Throughput variable   also called *process* variable; a characteristic of the *functioning* of a system as it modifies inputs in order to adapt to its environment and achieve goals.

Variable   an observable characteristic or dimension of any phenomenon, the magnitude or quality of which can change from time to time.

"Why should I study how small groups work?" you might ask. After all, group dynamics is a complex field of study with bibliographies that contain thousands of books and articles concerned with research and theory. My answer is very simple, and would apply to almost anything—chemistry, gardening, fishing, basketball, or automobile engines, for example. The better you understand how something works, the more control you are able to exercise so that it becomes productive for you. In short, the more you understand small groups the more effective you can make your role in the many discussions of which you will be a part. Since small groups are ubiquitous, inevitable, and vital in our lives, we certainly need to understand them and develop personal skills as members. The purpose of this chapter is to provide you with a view of small groups as open systems so that you can understand what is happening and why in your groups, then adjust your behavior to achieve desired outcomes for self and group.

The Participant-Observer Perspective

A major purpose of this book, and of the course for which you may be reading it, is to develop a *participant-observer* perspective.

The participant-observer is a regular member of the group, engaging actively in its deliberations but who at the same time is observing, evaluating, and adapting to its processes and procedures. A participant-observer directs part of his or her attention to participating in the group and part to studying how the group is functioning, trying always to be aware of what the group needs at the moment. Such a member makes a conscious effort to be aware of the adequacy of both group inputs and processes in relation to desired outputs. This sort of member can supply needed information, ideas, procedural suggestions, and interpersonal communication skills *when needed,* or seek them from other members of the group who may not realize what is needed at the moment. Lacking such an orientation, the member may be a drag on the system, like a parasite, or an inconsequential appendix that the group could well do without.

Some "members" of groups are participants in name only. They add almost nothing to the inputs of the group, though they may detract little from its energy and resources. Such is the observer who watches and listens, but does little or nothing. This may be the result of lack of knowledge and abilities relevant to the purpose of the group, lack of skills in communicating within small groups, or a lack of sophistication in small group processes and procedures. Doubtless you can think of examples you have known of observer-like members: the committee member who adds nothing to solving the problem assigned to the committee, the classmate in a group discussing a short story who has not read the story, or the knowledgeable classmate who doesn't speak up.

Some members are valuable because of their personal knowledge or skills, but have little understanding of process variables in a small group. So long as the group is operating well they can make a real contribution when asked to do so, but they are of no help in resolving conflicts, reducing misunderstandings and confusion, coordinating the work of others, and helping out when the group gets into trouble.

In contrast, members with extensive knowledge of small group dynamics and communication techniques may be of great value in establishing harmonious relationships among members, verbalizing ideas to unite the group, calling attention to process variables reducing the effectiveness of the group, and suggesting procedures and discussion techniques. To be an all-around valuable member of the group one must have both a participant-observer focus and information and ideas that are needed by the group to achieve its objectives. For example, if members of a group are meeting to develop a traffic plan for a large campus, there will undoubtedly be wide differences in the beliefs about what is desirable and what ought to be done. These differences could lead to destructive conflicts within the group or to the sort of argument that can lead to a truly outstanding solution to their problem, *if* members have the necessary information about the traffic on campus and about small group processes and communication.

Throughout the rest of this book we will be examining the major variables in the small group as a system so you can become a more knowledgeable participant-observer member; gaining the resources of knowledge and skills needed to accomplish the task of the group in which you participate will be up to you. At this point as a beginning student of small group discussion you need an overall image of the "ideal" small group, which you can begin to use at once as a standard against which to compare the groups in which you participate and as a general framework on which to assemble all the experiences and information you will be gaining in this course. For these reasons I have presented an example of an exceptionally productive small group, then developed a model of the small group as an open system, and finally established a standard of excellence for each major small group variable.

An Example of an Ideal Problem-Solving Group

From the hundreds of small groups in which I have participated or which I have observed as a researcher, I have selected one as an example to give a sense of reality to the ideal model presented later in the chapter. This was a committee comprised of five faculty members of a college of Arts and Sciences who had been elected by their colleagues and charged with the task of preparing a draft of a constitution for the college. The college is a component in a large university. It previously had no constitution, but a new bylaw of the board of regents of the university authorized colleges to develop constitutions for their internal governance. The five committee members each came from different academic disciplines. The dean of the college acted as chair *pro tem* at the first meeting to explain what he understood the charge of the committee to be, than asked the committee to elect a chairperson. The group then discussed the duties of that position such as calling meetings, seeing that detailed records were kept, providing tentative agendas for meetings, seeing that multiple copies of all the writing the committee had done were prepared, and providing equal opportunity for each member to speak. Following that discussion a secret vote was taken, and Professor Orin Miller elected. The dean then left the meeting, asking that if possible a completed constitution be presented to the faculty of the college at a meeting to be held six months later.

Fortunately, all members of the new committee were acquainted with each other from having served together on other committees over the previous several years. They had chosen the chair wisely; Orin was accepted completely in the way he filled the role of chair. He suggested efficient procedures, clarified and summarized progress, encouraged, organized, and generally coordinated—but never dominated or forced.

Soon after the dean had left, Orin asked the group how they viewed their assignment and how they might go about producing a constitution. The following discussion ensued:

Paul Steiner: This is a tremendous opportunity to create a model of democratic academic governance. We've never had anything like this at our university, so the constitution we write will be a ground-breaking thing. We have a great challenge, and a great responsibility.

Joan Brightly: Amen! I really feel that this is important, and that we must and can do a great job. If we do our job well, the faculty will adopt the constitution we propose, and it will serve them well.

Tom Mulbach: Yeah, that's how I see it, too. I'm not much of a lover of committees, but this one matters. I can't think of a finer group of people to work with on drawing up our first constitution.

Ray Stone: And how—this is the cream of our faculty. I'm sure we can work well together, and do a fine job. But I think we ought to plan out how we will go about this.

Orin: I'm pleased that we all feel that our task is so important, and that we have such a fine group. Okay, Ray, why don't we discuss what the problems are that we face in writing a constitution, then how we might go about it, and come up with a general plan for our meetings.

Group: Fine. Yes. Good. Let's do it. [etc.]

Orin: Well, then what do we need in a constitution? I suggest we make a list of all the things we think need to be addressed in it.

Ray: Definitely it must state the purpose of the faculty as a group such as setting standards, approving degree programs, examining courses and evaluating them, advising the dean on recommendations for promotion and tenure of faculty, and similar academic matters.

Joan: It will need a committee structure, with the purposes, selection, and organizing of standing committees to do all these things.

Paul: And a section on how the constitution is both adopted and amended as needed at a later date.

This listing of possible component sections of a consitution for the college went on for about twenty minutes, with the chair asking a few questions to clarify ("Do you mean have the departments represented on a rotating basis?"), asking if there was anything else anyone could think of, and writing everything down. Then:

Orin: "Well, that's quite a list! Let me read it all over to you, and see if I've left anything out. Then we might discuss whether this is all we need, and if we need it all. Before we end this discussion, I think we should decide how to proceed from here.

Following nods of approval, Orin read the list, thus summarizing the group output to that time. This summary provoked further discussion:

Joan: We don't have anything about membership. We need to define how one qualifies for voting in the faculty.

Paul: Right.

Orin: Okay, it's added to the list. I think we've made a good beginning on setting our goals. I'll have this typed, run off, and send each of you a copy so you can think it over and maybe suggest additions or deletions at our next meeting. Also, I guess we should put these in some order. Would anyone be willing to try that?

Joan: Well, I've done a lot of work on constitutions in the past, so I guess I could do that. But now I'm anxious to get to talking about what we need to do and how to go about it in the months ahead.

Others: Yes. Me, too. Let's.

Orin: Okay, I think one of the first things we ought to do is draw up a list of similar institutions, then divide up the list among us and everyone write to several of them for copies of their constitutions, then note things we have overlooked as possible topics in our constitution, and sections that especially impress you.

Tom: Good idea. We sure ought to write to Iowa State and Penn State.

Ray: And Michigan State and Western Michigan. I heard they have a fine setup there.

Orin: Those all sound like good places to get examples, but before we get further into that I think we should plan out our long-range agenda, the general procedure to follow through our meetings. Is that all right with all of you? [Nods of agreement from all.] First, when should we meet and how often?

Ray: This is as good a time as any for me. How about the rest of you?

Paul: Well, I can make it, but because of having no classes on this day I'd rather keep it free for research and writing. How about another time? Could we all compare schedules?

The group members then did so, and chose unanimously to meet every Wednesday from 2:00 P.M. until as late as necessary.

Orin: We have an awful lot of work to do, so I think we ought to meet every week, at least at first, until we are sure we will have a draft ready for the faculty meeting in April. What do the rest of you think?

Paul: I agree wholeheartedly, but I think we should skip a week or two until we get back the copies of constitutions we request and have time to analyze them.

Joan: I guess I agree Paul, but I think we should meet next week to finish up our list of possible topics and maybe write a sort of preamble to help us get our sights set and our values in order as to what we want to achieve from or through a constitution.

Paul: Yeah, I hadn't thought of that, but you're right.

Orin: Is that agreeable to you fellows [to Tom and Ray]?

Both replied that it was.

Orin: Why don't we each write down what we think is the purpose of our constitution, and what we think the preamble ought to say about those things?

Group: Fine. Okay. I'll do what I can. That's a good place to start.

Orin: Now let's get on with our long-range plan. We get a list of schools, then divide it up and write to them for copies, then revise our outline of a constitution and take it up a section at a time, one or two sections per meeting, being sure we have time to go over it as a whole and get it prepared before the faculty meeting. How does that strike you as a procedure?

Paul: That sounds good to me, but I've noticed how easy it is if we begin in a group with something to shoot at. So why don't we form one- or two-person sub-committees to write tentative drafts of the various articles and sections?

Joan: I think that's a good way to proceed, if we can choose what sections we begin work on and agree that each of us is to do about the same amount of work.

Tom: That's fine by me, if we can write other tentative sections than those we are assigned when we don't agree with what has been presented to us.

Ray: Yes. I think it is vital that we be very open with each other on what we think and believe, and that we don't have to agree with what someone wrote. It's too important not to bring out all the pro's and con's on each issue.

Orin: I certainly would hope we examine everything we propose from all angles. How do the rest of you see that?

There was general consensus expressed that this was necessary, and that they could disagree openly, yet remain friends, working in cooperation. The committee then set up its list of schools from which to request copies of constitutions.

Throughout their entire eighteen meetings this group followed the general procedure and agenda laid out at the first meeting. Sometimes a proposed article would be accepted with minor revisions, sometimes it would be argued in depth and with strong feelings, but never in the approximately fifty hours of discussion did any name calling occur. Orin sent out an outline agenda for each meeting, along with a copy of articles to be considered at the meeting so members could look them over in advance. At the next to last meeting the following discussion occurred:

Orin: I think we now need to talk about how we introduce this constitution to the faculty and get them to vote for it. I'm really proud of us and the constitution we have drafted, and don't want it to get chopped up or beaten down by people who don't understand it so well as we do.

Joan: Right, Orin. As chairman, you will make the motion for adoption, and explain what we designed it to accomplish, and why.

Paul: Yes, and now I think we should consider all the things people might raise as objections, or what they might want to change, and how we can argue against those.

Orin: Do you all agree? (everyone did, so they proceeded, dividing up the main responsibility for thinking up rebuttals on each section).

At the final meeting of the group:

Orin: I'm really sort of sad to see our "Ben Franklin" committee come to an end, though I can sure use the time to get back to some research I had to put aside. This has been the finest group to work with I've ever been in. As chairman, I can't thank you enough.

Tom: I feel the same—we've been a great group. But, Orin, you've been a model chairman, by far the best I've ever seen.

To this there were strong expressions of agreement, a tribute to Orin, and to themselves for how proud they were of their work. The college was given the constitution, discussed it in great detail section by section, made two relatively minor amendments to it, and then adopted it by a unanimous vote, something very exceptional for a group of 160 people with strongly held beliefs from a wide divergence of backgrounds. This constitution is still in effect, with some amendments over the years, and is regarded as the best college constitution in the university where I am employed. This was, I think, the finest problem-solving group I ever observed. Why? The dynamics and components are many, but especially important were the sense of commitment each member brought to the task, the availability of needed resources (information in the form of constitutions from elsewhere and many informal polls of fellow faculty members; ideas; writing skills; members' skills in cooperation and communication;

an ideal setting in which to work—a quiet, comfortable conference room with chairs in a circle around a table—and a systematic procedure that all had helped to develop. All decisions were made by consensus, which helped build the sense of teamwork throughout. Orin never acted bossy or dogmatic in his role, but he worked very hard to keep the group following its procedures, to see that all points of view were heard and respected, and that consensus was reached. Tom was especially skilled at bringing a sense of good humor and calm to the group when anyone seemed to get upset over a conflict of ideas. As the group succeeded on each different part of the document, that success added to their enthusiasm and ability to work well, including being open about any doubts or disagreements they held. The final products included not only a fine constitution and ready adoption by the faculty, but also a sense of unity and satisfaction among the members. Orin made a statement of tribute to the whole group, saying they deserved the credit for what was accomplished for the faculty, not he. This committee manifested to an exceptional degree the characteristics of an ideal small group as an open system with optimal inputs, throughput procedures, and outputs. With the example of this very real group as a ground, we are now ready to consider the meaning of the statement that "a small group is an open system."

The Small Group as an Open System

You have probably noticed that when a new person joins a group there is a major change in the group, not just a simple addition of a new member. This illustrates the idea of a "system." The small group can best be understood as a system of interdependent components and forces. General systems theory is built on an analysis of living things, which attempt to remain in dynamic balance with an environment by constant adjustments throughout the entire organism. Any system is active, "living," dynamic—constantly changing. No system is ever static: a change in any part of an organism or its immediate environment reverberates throughout the entire system. For example, a "head cold" affects your whole body and its functioning to some degree, not just your head. High blood pressure, as a response of your body to some stress experience with the environment, affects everything in your body, including how you feel, your thinking, and all you do even though the changes may not be immediately perceptible.

One benefit of thinking of the small group as a system is that this emphasizes the notion of multiple causation, which is to say that whatever happens is not the result of a single simple cause, but the result of complex interrelationships among many forces. Another benefit of the systems perspective is that it leads us to look for multiple outcomes of any change in the group. With a systems perspective, we are more likely to consider all of the characteristics of a group when trying to understand and improve its functioning, rather than look at only one or two of them and thus possibly miss what is most important.

The *variables* ("characteristics" or "dimensions") of a small group (or of any system) can be classified into three broad categories: **input** variables, **throughput** (process) variables, and **output** variables. "Input" variables are the components from which a small group is formed and which it uses to do work: *members* of the group, the *reason* for forming the group (for instance, the "charge" to a committee, or the individual needs which members cannot meet acting alone), *resources* such as information and tools, and *environmental conditions* and forces which influence or become part of the group's functioning. "Throughput" variables include the *structure of relationships* among members and their *roles, rules* (norms) which emerge, *procedures* followed, *communication* among members, and all the other things which are part of the processes of a group functioning to achieve some goal(s). "Output" variables are the results of the group's throughput processes, especially tangible *work* accomplished (such as items built, policies developed, judgments made, and recommendations given to some larger organization), *changes in the members* themselves, *effects* of the group *on* its *environment,* and *changes in the group's procedures* themselves. As you can see, these classes of variables are not separable; as was stated previously, everything influences and is influenced by everything else in the small group *system.*

Figure 2.1 is a diagrammatic model of some of the many variables in each of the three categories—input, throughput, and output. The "hopper" at the top of the figure represents inputs into the throughput "machinery" of the system, where the inputs are processed and changed. The exit channel at the bottom of the diagram represents the "outputs" of a small group system. The "tube" on the left side which loops from output to input represents the *feedback* channels through which a small portion of the output is cycled back into the system to modify future operations and processes of the group. For instance, a sense of accomplishment becomes a source of greater unity among members, and the procedures which led to that accomplishment are then used again and again, perhaps with modifications. A simple illustration of this can be seen in a successful basketball team. The output of repeated winning will produce more enthusiasm and commitment to the team by the players, a continually more polished way of performing together, more liking of the members for each other and their coach, greater attendance at games, the likelihood of more funds and better equipment, and so on.

This model of a small group is an *open* system model, meaning that the group interacts with its environment rather than in social isolation. Gross described four characteristics of any open system that apply to the small group[1]:

1. the membership may be changed, but the group continues to exist as a group even though some outsiders become members and some former members become outsiders;
2. members are also members of other groups that may produce conflicting loyalties, demands on time and energy, or even lead some members to leave the group;

Figure 2.1   A model of the small group as an open system.

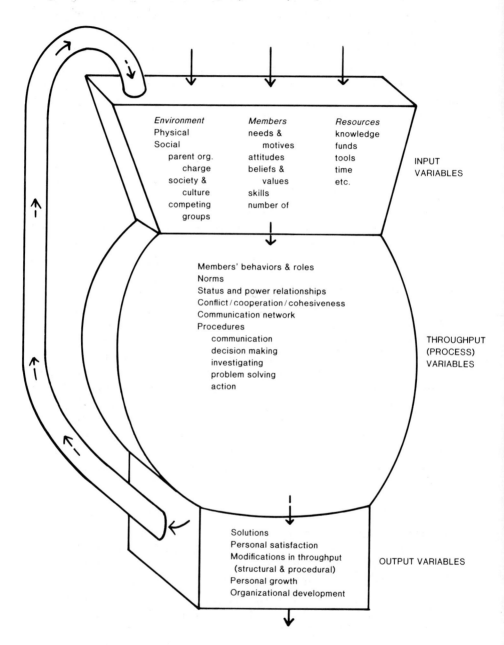

Environment   *Members*   *Resources*
Physical   needs &   knowledge
Social   motives   funds
    parent org.   attitudes   tools   INPUT
    charge   beliefs &   time   VARIABLES
    society &   values   etc.
    culture   skills
    competing   number of
    groups

Members' behaviors & roles
Norms
Status and power relationships
Conflict / cooperation / cohesiveness
Communication network
Procedures
    communication   THROUGHPUT
    decision making   (PROCESS)
    investigating   VARIABLES
    problem solving
    action

Solutions
Personal satisfaction
Modifications in throughput   OUTPUT VARIABLES
    (structural & procedural)
Personal growth
Organizational development

3. resource exchange, which means that resources are used and changed by the work of the group, and outputs are produced that will become further resources to the group or to other individuals or groups with which it interacts;
4. reciprocal influence between the members and outsiders to the group.

With the understandings acquired by examining an outstanding committee and the notion of small groups as systems, we can now proceed to create standards against which to evaluate the major input, throughput, and output variables of any small group in which we might participate.

Standards for an Ideal Discussion Group

The quality of any discussion group can only be determined from its outputs, its effectiveness. The very title of this book is indicative that it is about how to achieve desired outputs (see figure 2.1). Of course, outputs can only be evaluated by comparing them with what the group set out to accomplish, in relation to environmental restraints on goal accomplishment. For example, no matter how skilled a team of veterinarians may be, if they are trying to treat a disease of unknown origin for which there is no therapeutic procedure (such as rabies) they cannot be expected to cure the victim. A realistic goal would be to eliminate as much suffering as possible for the patient. No matter how informed and skilled the members of a committee may be or how excellent their throughput processes, the organization which created the committee may have limited what it can do. The interdependence of all components of a system is demonstrated as we seek to define the characteristics of an *ideal* discussion group. Since "discussion" is the name of the communication process when a small group meets, the emphasis in the abstract descriptions of an ideal discussion group which follow is on the throughput variables shown in figure 2.1 rather than on input or output variables. Of course, most small groups will not measure up to the standards presented any more than most small groups will function as well as the constitution committee I described earlier.

Input Variables

1. **Members**—members share basic values and beliefs relevant to the purpose of their being a group and toward each other. For instance, if one member believes deeply that abortion is a mortal sin and another member believes it is an excellent way to prevent children from being born into a situation likely to be damaging to them, the group is not likely to reach consensus on what the law should be governing abortions. Ideally, members' attitudes toward the group and toward each other would *at least* be described as positive. Each member expects that the others will do a fair share of the work, has something important to offer the group, places trust and confidence in the

statements and actions of the others, and has a spirit of inquiry toward the goal (no pre-determined belief about what the group must do, or what is the "truth" about the subject of learning). The members expect to cooperate and compromise. None has a need to dominate or win over the others. They have the skills needed to think systematically and logically from evidence to a conclusion, and to communicate so that mutual perceptions are developed through their speaking and listening.

2. The **number** of members is small enough for all to be active participants and perceptually aware of each other as unique individuals, yet large enough to supply the variety of knowledge and skills needed to achieve high-quality outputs. A divergence of backgrounds and perspectives will characterize an ideal discussion group, yet a similarity in goals and values will make it possible for all members to support group decisions. For example, five persons with similar values might agree on a goal, yet bring five largely different sets of information about the problem and possible solutions to it. Thus they could consider many different interpretations of what is causing the problem and solve it better than a group of ten people with very similar knowledge and ideas. The five can communicate more informally and efficiently than the ten. Even a group of three persons who can't agree on basic values and goals (for example, what should be achieved by a policy on public prayer) can accomplish little despite the small size of the group.

3. **Resources** to achieve the objectives of the group will be available. Reliable *facts* are known or accessible to members, and they have or can generate reasoned opinions and ideas about the topic or problem. They have physical resources of tools, communication media, funds, and any other needed objects. For instance, one group of which I was a member could not do its work until a highly detailed set of data on computer tapes was made available from a government agency, and a member with computer programming skills was added to the group. We also had to gain access to computer time and that required money to pay for the time.

4. The ideal discussion **group's relationships to other groups** are such that the mission of the group is clear and realistically achievable with the available material and human inputs and, if there are competing groups, it has relatively equal or superior power to them in effecting decisions. For example, an advisory group of workers whose suggestions are never accepted and acted upon is meaningless.

5. To function optimally, a discussion group must have **a place to meet** that provides for members' needs and allows the discussion process to occur without disruption. A committee that has no adequate room in which to meet regularly will expend much energy just finding and changing meeting places, and trying to get members to those places. A committee assigned to decide which of several candidates for a position

to hire could not function in a room where secrecy was compromised by the constant coming and going of strangers.

6. **The group's purpose is clearly defined and accepted by all members.** There is adequate perspective on the external structure, including an understanding of the area of freedom. The group makes constant adaptations to the changes in conditions facing it. All members give the group goal priority over personal goals or needs not in harmony with the group objectives. Members whose personal values are at odds with a group's charge will interfere greatly with efficiency in group process (i.e., one juror opposed to capital punishment on a jury considering the penalty for a convicted serial murderer). If members think the purpose of belonging to a religious study group is to convert others, whereas some other members believe the purpose is to understand each other's beliefs, then the group will have great difficulty.

7. The group has sufficient **time** in which to do its work. If research is needed to understand the problem, group members have enough time to do it thoroughly. Enough meetings can be held to work through all phases of the problem-solving procedure, or to digest and process information and ideas. In short, members both have and commit enough time to do their work as a group, and do it well. They do not try to find a solution to congested parking on an urban campus in a forty-minute meeting!

Throughput Variables

1. **Behaviors of members are predictable to each other.** A member who undertakes an assignment can be counted on to carry it out, such as gathering certain needed information, typing up and distributing a report, or doing something as part of the application of a solution to a problem. Members can be counted on to attend scheduled meetings, or notify the group if this is not possible.

2. **Roles of members are relatively stable, mutually understood, and accepted by all members.** Each finds satisfaction of personal needs and motives in his or her role. Although there is sufficient role definition to permit members to predict each other's behavior, there is also sufficient flexibility to permit anyone to make any needed contribution to the task or group maintenance. The leadership position has been settled in the minds of all members, and the leader has a group-centered orientation. Leadership functions are optimally shared by all members.

3. **Members have relatively equal status,** so that all can exert influence based on their contributions of knowledge, skills, and ideas, not on the basis of status in groups or organizations external to the discussion group. Teamwork is evidenced by sharing of rewards, mutual support, and decision making by consensus. Members expend their energy in

achieving the goals of the group, not in competing for power and position over each other. Thus cooperation is maximized and conflict is limited to the evaluation of ideas in a search for the best possible solutions.

4. **Norms (rules) and the values underlying them are understood and adhered to,** or else discussed openly and changed when found not to be productive. The group has a culture of beliefs, values, and standards that encourages thorough searching for and testing of facts and ideas, open conflict over the merits of ideas, and displays of affection, support, and solidarity.

5. **The flow of communication reveals an all-channel network,** with a high proportion of remarks being directed to all members, and few cliques or dialogues between two persons. Members are skilled in expressing their knowledge and ideas in ways that evoke similarity of understanding of facts and ideas, without inducing defensiveness (threat) in each other. Statements are formulated in ways to make the relationships among statements by different members readily apparent.

6. In an ideal group, **all members understand and share procedures that are efficient, prevent overlooking important issues and facts, and lead to goal achievement.** In a problem-solving group, this means that all members understand and follow a procedure that is based on scientific methods of problem solving. They share in exercising control over this procedure; procedures are decided upon by the group, not imposed on it. Specific discussion techniques appropriate to the purpose of the group are known and accepted by all members. In learning groups, the sequence of issues is decided by the group, with changes made only by consent of all members.

Output Variables

1. **The purpose of the group will be perceived by all members as having been achieved.** Decisions (and solutions to problems) will be supported by members as the best possible, and all will demonstrate an affective commitment to enact decisions made by the group. Solutions decided upon will achieve the desired results and be accepted by most or all affected persons. If the group met for personal growth of members, they will accomplish the things they set out to do by joining the group.

2. **Members will experience personal satisfaction** with their respective roles in the group, the ways in which the discussion process and group work occurred, and their relationships to the other group members.

3. **Cohesiveness will be high,** with each member having a strong sense of identification with the group and giving it high priority among competing demands for his or her time and energy. Affectively, members will have a sense of "we-ness" and so express their attitudes

toward the group both in action and word. A high degree of interpersonal trust exists among members.

4. **There is consensus on the role and leadership structure of the group.** If asked independently, each would name the same person(s) as leader of the group, and as choice for leader in the future. Procedures have been developed which worked to the satisfaction of all members, and will be used in the future if the group continues to deal with similar problems.

5. **The parent organization** (if any) **has been strengthened** as a result of the small group's work. The organization is more productive and viable in the world in which it exists.

Probably few groups you experience will measure up to these standards so well as did the constitution committee described early in the chapter. But you should now be able to determine at least some of the sources of difficulty in any group not producing satisfactory outputs.

Summary

In this chapter the small group was described as an open system with input, throughput (process), and output variables. Input variables include such items as members, skills, knowledge, and other resources. The group as a system processes these resources via interaction among members which involves speech communication as the primary medium, and produces outputs of physical products, solutions to problems, recommendations, perceptions, and changes in members and the group's procedures and cohesiveness. A model of an ideal group was formulated as a standard by which to evaluate any secondary small group. In the next chapter we will examine group members as a type of input variable.

Exercises

1. Discuss the following issues with a small group of classmates, or with the entire class sitting in a circle.
    A. How important is it to develop a participant-observer focus?
    B. How could you tell if a discussion group member had such a focus?
    C. How might we develop such a focus while doing the work of this class?

2. Compare a small group as a living system to a living animal as a system; to a hive of bees, pack of wolves, or other group of social animals with which you are familiar. Identify the smallest and largest living systems you can think of.

3. In this chapter a number of input, throughput, and output variables of small discussion groups were identified. What others do you think

should be included, and why? Your answer should include a modification of figure 2.1.

4. Write a brief description of the "best" small group of which you have ever been a member. Why do you think it was the best? What characteristics of its process and components seem to have made a difference? Now compare your ideas about what made for an outstanding group with those of your classmates.

5. Study carefully the script of excerpts of the discussion from the constitution committee presented on pages 25 to 29. What are the characteristics of the variables that seem to have made this a highly productive, satisfying, and cohesive group that achieved a consensus end product? Compare your answers with those of classmates.

Bibliography

Andersen, Martin P. "A Model of Group Discussion," in *Small Group Communication: A Reader.* 3d ed., Cathcart, Robert S., and Samovar, Larry A., eds. Dubuque, Iowa: Wm. C. Brown Company Publishers, 1979, 43–54. A detailed model of the process of small group discussion.

Barker, Larry L., Cegala, Donald J., Kibler, Robert J., and Wahlers, Kathy J. *Groups in Process: An Introduction to Small Group.* 2d ed., Englewood Cliffs, N.J.: Prentice-Hall, 1983. See chapter 2, "A systems approach to small group communication."

Johnson, R. A., Kast, F. E., and Rosenzweig, J. E. *The Theory and Management of Systems.* 3d ed., New York: McGraw-Hill, 1973.

Tubbs, Stewart L. *A Systems Approach to Small Group Interaction.* Reading, Mass.: Addison-Wesley, 1978.

Von Bertalonffy, Ludwig. *General System Theory.* New York: George Braziller, 1968.

References

1. Bertram M. Gross, *Organizations and Their Managing* (New York: The Free Press, 1964), p. 113.

3 the members of the group

Study Objectives

From your study of chapter 3 you should be able to:

1. Describe behaviors which characterize an attitude of responsibility for a small group, and the importance of such an attitude.

2. Explain how a positive self-concept contributes to being a productive small group member, assess your own self-concept, and name three techniques for enhancing it.

3. Explain why having assertive members with a strong desire to communicate is vital to group discussions.

4. Describe an authoritarian attitude and why it is harmful to most groups.

5. Explain the importance of an attitude of trust in other members.

6. List five components of "rhetorical sensitivity," and explain how such an attitude is likely to facilitate small group communication.

7. Explain the contrasting attitudes of "skeptical inquiry" and "dogmatism" toward information and ideas, and how members characterized by each are likely to behave during discussions.

Key Terms

Assertiveness   behavior that manifests respect for both one's own rights and those of others, as opposed to aggressiveness and nonassertiveness.

Attitude   a complex of beliefs and values held by a person toward some concept or class of objects, producing a tendency to react in a specific way toward the concept or an object of the class.

Authoritarianism   tendency to accept uncritically the information, ideas, and proposals of high status persons, and to prefer strong, dominating leaders.

Communication apprehension   anxiety or fear of speaking in any type of social situation; reticence; shyness.

Dogmatism   a tendency to hold rigidly to personal beliefs; closed-mindedness to evidence and reasoning contrary to previous beliefs.

Encounter discussion   group interaction in which members describe honestly and openly their reactions to each other.

Homophily   a high degree of similarity among group members in such attributes as attitudes, values, and beliefs; "heterophily" is the opposite.

Prejudice   a belief based on partial information about the object of the belief; an attitude toward a class of objects based on experience with one or few members of the class accompanied by a strong tendency to reject any contradictory evidence.

Principle of least-sized groups   formated by H. Thelen, states that a group should be no larger than necessary to include among the members all needed information, skills, and other resources necessary to achieve group goals.

Skeptical inquiry   an attitude of cautious searching for new information and ideas, frequently called "open-mindedness," characteristic of the discussant who is willing to change a point of view when acceptable new evidence or reasoning is presented by others.

The familiar saying that "A committee is a group of people none of whom is capable of doing anything, deciding that nothing can be done" expresses in folk language what many of us have learned the hard way: having a group with members who are incompetent and unwilling is worse than having no group tackle a task. On the other hand, if you have been fortunate to be part of an outstanding athletic team, a highly productive committee, or a warm and supportive family you know just how productive a group of the "right" people can be. Coaches recruit at great expense and trouble to combine needed skills and attitudes, for they know that an outstanding team can come only from the right combination of members—people with both winning attitudes and winning skills. In this third chapter we will examine some of the knowledge available about what it takes to have a winning combination of people for a committee, task force, or other sort of small discussion group.

Attitudes toward Self and Others

The most important resource to a small group is its members: their knowledge, attitudes, and skills. How well they can work together to achieve an interdependent goal depends on the attitudes they hold toward the purposes of the group, toward each other, and toward ideas and information.

An *attitude* can be defined as a complex of values and beliefs held by a person toward some concept that produces a tendency to respond in a specific way to that concept or perception. The more alike or *homophilus* members are in attitudes the more easily they will be able to understand each other and cooperate. *Homophily* refers to the degree of similarity, among persons who interact, with respect to personal attributes, attitudes, beliefs, values, etc. Researchers have shown that a high degree of homophily leads to accuracy in message transmission, whereas a high degree of *heterophily* (difference) leads to inaccuracy or misunderstanding and conflicts.[1] Thus if members value the task alike they are likely to communicate efficiently and effectively in working on it, but if some think the job important and others believe it to be relatively trivial, understanding each other and cooperating will be difficult or impossible. If they differ considerably about what standards should be applied when judging among alternative courses of action, irresolvable conflicts and unrelieved tensions are likely to occur.

An attitude cannot be seen or measured directly. It can only be inferred from what a group member says and does. In this sense attitude is a "blackbox" term, or something that we presume to exist within a person based on what can be observed. We can measure beliefs with opinion scales (frequently called attitude scales) on which a person indicates a position of relative agreement or disagreement to some statement. We can hear what persons say during discussions, and observe how they behave as members of a group. How much value they give to an idea, concept, or thing can be determined by asking them to rank items and by observing what they do and what they don't do. From such observations we can infer if the attitude of a member toward some concept, action, or thing is positive or negative, and to what degree. Thus although "attitudes" remain somewhat vague in concept, they are vital to a group. I have described certain attitudes that are especially important to the dynamics and processes of a small group's discussions. Collectively these attitudes have been called a "group orientation."

Responsibility for the Group

A whole set of constructive attitudes can be summarized in the phrase *a sense of responsibility for the success of the group.* The constructive discussant feels a personal responsibility to see that the group achieves its goals, and will do what he or she reasonably can to help. Likewise, such a person will encourage others to manifest the same types of responsible behaviors. Such a person cannot "let George do it"; this participant is George.

The kind of group commitment that leads to consensus decisions has been related to the pronouns used by group members. Research has shown a significantly higher ratio of self-reference pronouns (I, me, my, mine, myself) to other or group referent pronouns (you, your, yours, we, us, our) in groups that failed to reach consensus than in groups that did. A discussant's use of pronouns will indicate the degree to which he or she is responsible to the group. I advise you to be wary of persons in a group who refer to the group as "you" instead of as "we," who speak of "your" instead of "our." It may pay to ask how committed they feel to the group.

A responsible member can be depended upon to do an assignment that she has accepted and on which the group depends. If she agrees to bring certain information to the next meeting, it will be there. If she agrees to arrange a meeting place, she will do so without fail. If such a member cannot attend a meeting at which her participation is vital (and in a very small group it always is), she will let the group know of this in advance and as soon as possible.

This responsibility to the group continues after the discussion. The ideal discussant supports the group's decisions. He speaks of "we" rather than "I" and "they." He accepts a full share of the blame for any group failure, and no more than his share of credit for group success. He carries out any task that he accepted as a representative of the group, never accepting any responsibility that he cannot or will not discharge. This discussant respects the confidence and trust of other group members, not revealing what they have stated in confidence during a discussion.

Persons who are responsible to the group are active participants, not the passives who fail to speak up or carry out work. Burgoon, Heston, and McCroskey describe such an attitude of commitment:

The good group member is willing to commit himself to the group process and product, whatever the outcome (assuming it doesn't violate his personal ethics). He is willing to devote time and energy to the group's activities. He gives as well as takes. This is basically a question of loyalty. Prior to any particular group meeting, each member should determine for himself if he is really committed to the group's membership and activities. The individual who has no initial commitment to a group, whose entering attitude is one of "wait and see," is not likely to be an asset. In times of stress, he is more likely to "abandon ship" than to address the problems seriously. If a person voluntarily chooses to be a member of a group, he has an obligation to maintain a commitment to it in return for the benefits he gains by membership.[2]

Shaw concluded from a number of studies that persons high on "dependability" are ". . . likely to emerge as leaders and to be successful in helping the group to be effective in accomplishing its task."[3]

Occasionally project groups formed in a class in small group communication have a member who wants credit for the work of the group, but is not willing to do a fair share of the work. Such irresponsible behavior is the greatest single source of friction among members of such student groups and of poor quality projects. It is advisable to bring up your dissatisfaction with the lack of contributions and/or dependability of a fellow group member as soon as you feel it, rather than hope he or she will change before the deadline for the group to complete its work. By then a norm of "the members need do very little work" has been established, and change is unlikely. Unless this conflict is dealt with the group cannot be cohesive.

In short, the valuable group member has an attitude of personal responsibility for the success of the group in achieving its goals, as manifested by commitments of time and energy, dependability in carrying out assignments, and loyalty in times of stress. If you lack such an attitude of commitment and responsibility to the group, it will be better for the group if you are not a member.

Attitudes toward Self

There is a consensus among writers about human relations that only persons who hold positive and objective self-concepts can relate openly, honestly, and objectively toward others. The self-attitudes essential to being a productive group member are summarized by Harris and others as "I'm okay."[4] One must like and trust self before it is possible to like and trust others. Although none of us can have a perfect and complete image of self, the more fully we understand our own motives and needs and accept them, the more openly we can communicate and work with others in a group. Members constantly worried about how their remarks and behaviors will be seen and reacted to by others will not likely speak up to test information and ideas advanced by others, no matter how poor those ideas may be. Thus they will withhold information and ideas the group needs to do a good job. Also, they will be more stinting in giving positive support and rewards to others, the kinds of statements and acts that make discussion rewarding and pleasant to participants.

Objectivity and acceptance of self can be enhanced in a number of ways. There are a number of scales and tests that you can take to gain a clearer picture of your self-attitudes. Your instructor may use some of these in your small group course, or they may be taken at almost any counseling and assessment center, such as most colleges and universities provide for students. Many such centers can provide individual or small group personal growth therapy such as "assertiveness training" or "cognitive restructuring," which can lead to a new level of realistic self-acceptance and liking. You may want to take advantage of these resources if private reflection or feedback from friends indicate a problem.

Sharing feelings and experiences with others in encounter discussions can be helpful to many students with a low self-concept. Disclosing your doubts, fears, and attitudes about self in company with others can lead to greater self-acceptance and acceptance of others, provided the sharing is objective, honest, and reciprocated.[5] *Encounter* means that the group members explore their reactions to each other and their personal feelings openly and honestly. When done in a supportive and positive way under the guidance of a skilled facilitator, encounter discussion can lead to much greater openness while participating in other small group discussions. As fellow group members give you feedback about how they are perceiving and responding to you, your self-images are greatly enriched. How we perceive ourselves is largely due to how we think other persons evaluate us, but often we do not know how others are responding and so cannot make adjustments in our behavior even if we want to. The feedback from other members in an encounter group can fill in many blind spots in self-concepts. Emphasis on the positive can greatly increase our level of self-acceptance and feelings of closeness to and trust of others. Negative feedback will let us know what to change and how, thus leading to more positive feedback and a more positive self-concept. As we discover that others have similar self-doubts and fears, self-acceptance grows and thus the positive self-image essential to being a fully functioning group member is developed.

Attidues toward Others

As has already been indicated, attitudes toward self and attitudes toward others are inextricably interrelated; we can separate them only for emphasis and analysis.

Desire to Communicate

Various theorists have developed scales to measure related attitudes toward communicating with other persons that I have chosen to call collectively an attitude of a "desire to communicate." Reticence in speaking (Phillips), communication apprehension (McCroskey), and willingness to communicate (J. Burgoon) are the major concepts applicable to participating in group discussions. While the degree to which one desires to communicate with others in a group could be called a personality trait, it manifests itself only in potential interaction situations, and so reflects both an attitude of self-concern or doubt and of fear or defensivenss toward the reactions of others to what one says and how it is said.[6] The highly apprehensive communicator will typically avoid group interaction, and when such a person does speak the remark is likely to be irrelevant to preceding remarks and the purpose of the discussion. Such a person is unlikely to disagree, for disagreeing calls for explanation. The apprehensive member is unlikely to make his or her information and ideas available to the group, though intelligence and knowledge may be very high.

If you are currently enrolled in a small group course your instructor may choose to have you complete a scale for assessing your degree of apprehension about speaking in general or about participating in small groups. If you score high on such apprehensiveness, there are a number of courses of action that may be helpful to you. For one thing, a norm of accepting each other's right to hold different beliefs and opinions without receiving ridicule or instant rejection can increase the security apprehensive members feel when expressing a belief or an opinion. A habit of *expressing* support for others' ideas when they are voiced may also help some apprehensive members to open up (assuming the support is honestly felt). Some small groups need a designated leader to enforce such norms and encourage the more reticent members. A simple appeal for fair play may help establish a desirable norm, such as: "When I said 'I don't think the evidence we have heard justifies that position' you cut me off and claimed I was wrong. All I want is an equal chance to have my ideas considered, and not have them interrupted by you. I don't think you even bothered to understand the implications of what I said." The more you speak up and are listened to, the more comfortable you are likely to be in a group— and the more active. If that doesn't help, you might try reporting investigations you make for the group. Such reports could be in the form of written memos; then all you would have to do at the meeting is distribute the memos and answer specific questions others might ask to clarify. You might even try writing out specific solution proposals and submitting them for group consideration.

If you have a general tendency not to speak as indicated by a series of observations or a scale measuring your apprehensiveness about speaking out your college or university may provide some training programs to assist you. They are often available from the department offering a course in small group discussion, or from a counseling center. They may include the technique known as "systematic desensitization" in which you learn to relax systematically and control your tension level, or the technique of "cognitive modification" in which you learn to replace negative self-messages with positive ones. Perhaps you often say something like this to yourself (silently, under your breath); "Nobody wants to hear what I have to say"; "I know I botched up how I said that"; "That's a dumb idea, so I won't say it"; "They'd just laugh if I offered that suggestion"; "That probably doesn't matter, so why say it"; "If it really

Figure 3.1   The desire to communicate shows during group interaction.

is any good, someone else will suggest it." Training and practice in making positive self-statements can increase one's openness in communicating and value as a group member. If you do not have access to special training for communicative apprehensives, making a list of all such statements you make to yourself, then in actual discussions stopping yourself the instant you begin to think one of them (or say it) and replacing it with a positive message may be of real help: "They need to hear this"; "My ideas are as good as anyone's"; "If they laugh at this, they are missing the important point, for this could be a great idea for our group"; "I've got to get this out, for no one else may suggest it"; "The group needs this now, so I'll say it." The instant you find yourself thinking about how you are doing, and especially of what others may be thinking of you, try to refocus your attention on the issues being discussed and your apprehensiveness may drop greatly. Much apprehension about speaking up in discussions comes from thinking about how you are doing instead of what the group members are talking about, so changing your "internal talk" in this way can help much.[7]

Figure 3.2   Assertiveness lies between aggressiveness and nonassertiveness.

Aggressive	Assertive	Non-assertive (passive)

Assertiveness

The productive discussant can be described as *assertive* when communicating
within a small group. An assertive attitude reflects respect for both oneself
and for other members of the group. Many people confuse the terms "assertive" and "aggressive"; it is important that you distinguish between these; you
will need to be *assertive* to protect your rights as a person and group member
from persons who are *aggressive*.

Assertiveness as a way of relating to others lies on a continuum between
aggressive communicative behavior and *nonassertive* or *passive* communicating. An aggressive person attempts to force ideas and practices on others.
An assertive person demonstrates equal respect for both personal rights as a
group member and the rights of all other members. A passive, nonassertive
member fails to stand up to aggressive members, but "goes along" with domination rather than get involved in confrontation or conflict. Figure 3.2 illustrates the continuum of aggressive to passive attitudes toward others. This
figure also shows that most people will fall somewhere between these pure
types, combining some assertive and some aggressive behavior, or perhaps
acting assertively at times although generally passive in the face of aggression.
In fact, most of us vary in our degree of assertiveness in different situations,
although we have a strong tendency to be primarily aggressive, assertive, or
nonassertive in groups.

The person with aggressive attitudes tends to act autocratically, dominating, demanding, and generally pushing others around. An aggressive
member attempts to force ideas and practices on other members of the group.
Name calling, innuendos, insults, threats, and commands all characterize an
aggressive member's attitude. Sarcasm and ridicule are other common aggressive tactics. By talking loudly, pounding the table, and making exagger-
ated gestures, aggressors stop other discussants from talking. Such discussants
are emotional bullies. They interrupt without apology, change the subject, and
hog attention as if it were a commodity to be hoarded. "Do it my way or we
fight" seems to be the aggressive small group member's motto.

The discussant with a *nonassertive* manner toward others "goes along
with" others' opinions or proposals rather than argue, even though inwardly
disagreeing with the proposal. Such a person does not speak up when personal
rights are violated by an aggressor who interrupts in mid-statement, smokes
in a small meeting room without asking if anyone objects, or speaks as if a
personal belief were the only acceptable interpretation of evidence. Nonassertive discussants avoid all direct conflict and confrontation. An extremely
nonassertive person would not speak up when a discussion leader asked, "Does
anyone disagree?" (unless others had previously disagreed), despite a strong

Figure 3.3   Passive "yessers" do not express disagreement.

"All those is favor say 'Aye.' "

            "Aye."   "Aye."   "Aye."
                         "Aye."   "Aye."

belief that the idea or action proposed was wrong. The stereotyped "yes-man," illustrated in figure 3.3, epitomizes passive, nonassertive attitudes. Nonassertive persons tend to make far less eye contact than do assertive or aggressive members, speak too softly for others to hear when they do speak, and to speak in a rather disembodied, "feelingless" way. It's as if they would rather die than raise a fuss!

Some nonassertive group members engage in what is called "passive-aggressive" behavior, or "indirect aggression." They attempt to manipulate subtly, to control or to get even without ever expressing clearly and directly what they believe or want. They sabotage rather than confront an aggressor. A nonassertive member may indirectly express disagreement, disgruntlement, anger, or other negative reactions by being late with an assigned report, "forgetting" to carry out an assigned task, failing to show up for a meeting, neglecting to do a fair share of the work for a group project, being late with a report, or complaining about another member's aggressive behavior (possibly only assertive) to sympathetic friends *outside* the group. Such behavior results in the rights of all being violated: the nonassertive person's, the aggressor's, and all the indirectly affected members of the small group. You can probably recall examples of group members who displayed passive-aggressive behavior, avoiding direct clashes with the aggressive acts of members, yet fighting them indirectly.

In contrast to both aggressive and passive persons, an *assertive* discussant has a positive attitude toward both self and others—"I'm OK and you're OK." The assertive group member's attitude is a sort of golden mean between aggression and nonassertion. If interrupted, such a member is likely to say something like "I had the floor; please let me finish my statement," or "I wasn't finished speaking when you interrupted me just now. I want to continue." An aggressive person might say when interrupted, "Damn it, don't interrupt me!" or simply shout to drown out the interrupter's voice. A nonassertive person would speak no more, but accept the loss of attention, suffering in silence. Cotler and Guerra describe the assertive person as one who ". . . can protect himself from being taken advantage of by others; can make decisions and free choices in life; . . . and can verbally and nonverbally express a wide range of feelings and thoughts. This is accomplished without experiencing undue amounts of anxiety or guilt and without violating the rights and dignity of others in the process."[8] The assertive discussant will not try to dictate to others, and will not allow dictation from peers. The assertive member expresses ideas as directly and clearly as possible, and looks for a new alternative or compromise when other group members have competing interests or ideas. In a learning group, a member with an assertive attitude insists that others listen to understand his or her interpretation of an issue, and is likewise an outstanding listener who tries very hard to understand the differing views of other members. In a problem-solving group, such a member will not insist on a personally preferred solution not supported by others, nor conform for the sake of unity. Rather, the assertive person will make a sincere effort to arrive at group consensus through careful exploration of all relevant information and points of view. Shaw summarized research concerning ascendent (assertive) persons this way: "They attempt leadership, participate in group activities, are assertive, and are creative. They tend to emerge as leaders, promote group cohesiveness, influence group decisions, conform to group norms, and are popular."[9]

Authoritarianism

Partially overlapping the concept of "aggressiveness" is an attitude syndrome called *authoritarian,* in that the authoritarian person is likely to be very dominating when in a formal position of "leader." However, high authoritarians have other characteristics which distinguish this attitude from simple aggressive behavior toward others. Indeed, in many relationships a highly authoritarian person will act nonassertively. Authoritarianism is characterized by an uncritical acceptance of ideas or information from a source identified as an authority, and doing what a person in a position of authority orders without examining the implications of such an action. A group of high authoritarians will seek an autocratic person as leader, one who will tell them what to do. They do not make much distinction between a chairperson of a small committee of peers and a work supervisor. Appoint such a person to chair a committee and he or she will most likely begin to give orders, say what the group should do or recommend, and generally act as if the rest of the group members were subordinates, under the absolute control and authority of the "leader" as boss. When appointed a member of a committee or task force, high authoritarians usually act subservient, waiting for the designated leader to say what to do or give an opinion about what is the best course of action. Then the authoritarian member supports that position uncritically. One danger from authoritarian attitudes was demonstrated by Milgram, many of whose research subjects were willing to give dangerous electrical shocks to other persons when told to do so by an authority (an experimenter in a lab coat).[10] Janis describes how acquiescing to the beliefs of high-status leaders or large majorities leads to poor decisions.[11] Haiman relates the authoritarianism trait to the functions and style of leadership seen as appropriate in small discussion groups.[12] The authoritarian tends to be preoccupied with power and dominant leader styles, to either take charge or follow someone who does so in an autocratic way. Haythorn and associates find that groups of authoritarians show less "positive affect" toward each other, do less asking for the opinions of others and make more "directive" remarks than do groups of egalitarians.[13] The high authoritarian, then, is likely to be bossy and autocratic if in a formal position of leadership, or a passive, servile follower to any person in a leader position. He or she may rebel against a democratic leader for not being "strong" enough. Such an attitude is highly detrimental to teamwork among a group of peers.

Interpersonal Trust

Cooperation depends on trusting others. Without trust, effective group discussion is literally impossible. Persons who are low in trustworthiness are likely to see others as untrustworthy, and so cannot work well in group discussions. Rotter and associates developed an Interpersonal Trust Scale, with which they have constructed a considerable body of knowledge of how trust affects interpersonal relations. Rotter defines trust as a general expectancy that ". . . the word, the promise, the verbal or written statement of another individual or group can be relied on."[14] Trust, he believes, results both from one's past experience with a type of person and situation in general, and from a specific relationship. Thus a man might develop a distrust of women in general, but still trust his own mother whom he believes is an exception to the rule that women can't be trusted. In general, though, Rotter believes persons display a stable attitude of generally trusting or distrusting others, with serious consequences for relationships among small group members. Persons who are trusting of others tend to be regarded by those others as more trustworthy and dependable. Persons who measure low in trust on the Interpersonal Trust Scale are not only perceived as less trustworthy and less trusting by others, but are also actually more likely to lie, cheat, and steal. High-trust college students have fewer personality conflicts and are better liked than low-trust students. Indeed, both high-and low-trusters liked high-trusters better than they liked low-trusters. Yet high-trusters are not more gullible or more likely to be taken in by deceptions than are low-trusters. In effect, the high-truster opts to trust a stranger until that person gives evidence that he cannot be trusted, whereas low-trusters opt to distrust a newcomer until there is clear evidence that he can be trusted. Many police studies have indicated that con artists are most successful with persons who are themselves dishonest and distrusting, rather than with honest and trusting persons. What seems to be called for in a small group—if discussions are to be productive of satisfaction, cohesiveness among members, and quality decisions—are persons who make positive assumptions about each other, trusting initially (at least until proven wrong), and who believe that the other participants want to arrive at a reasonable outcome in a reasonable way. Otherwise, the climate of the group is going to be one of distrust, suspicion, and little sharing of information and ideas, a competitive dog-eat-dog relationship.

Rhetorical Sensitivity

"Let it all hang out" and "tell it like it is" became popular sayings in certain quarters during the later 1960s. Prior to that was a period of conformity at the price of self to succeed in the corporate world, manifested in the phrase "the man in the gray flannel suit." Some writers advocated virtual aggressiveness in "looking out for number one." In reaction to such extreme advice, Hart and Burks (among others) advocated a rhetorical attitude as necessary to effective social discourse. They said that the rhetorically sensitive person would be constantly weighing the potential impact of different messages before uttering them.[15] Carlson subsequently developed a scale for measuring one's attitude toward communicating face to face with others, the Rhetsen Scale. The desired attitude of *rhetorical sensitivity* was described as "an attitude toward encoding spoken messages" that involves ". . . thinking about what should be said and then a way of deciding how to say it."[16] This mindset is said to have five constituent parts that are all relevant to encoding in small group communication:

1. *Acceptance of personal complexity,* which means that the speaker views persons as having many selves, only some of which will be involved in the role(s) taken by a discussant in a particular group.
2. *Avoidance of communicative rigidity,* which implies that the person is free from rigid ways of encoding and interacting, and so is free to speak and act in a variety of ways in different group situations.
3. *Interaction consciousness,* which is a high degree of awareness of the process of interaction leading to avoidance of either sacrificing one's own ideas and feelings in order to please or placate others, or rampant egoism leading to speaking without regard for the needs and feelings of

other participants. Thus the rhetorically sensitive person communicates neither aggressively nor nonassertively.

4. *Appreciation of the communicability of ideas,* indicative that not *all* of our ideas and feelings ought to be uttered in a given discussion even if to express some of them might make us feel better temporarily. The criterion for utterance by a rhetorically sensitive person would be "will communication of this feeling or idea facilitate achievement of my personal goal and our group goals at this moment?"

5. *Tolerance for inventional searching,* which suggests that the speaker realizes that there may be many ways to express an idea, and so he or she consciously searches in mind for the most effective way to evoke a desired response from fellow discussants before speaking.[17]

The rhetorically sensitive discussant occupies a position midway between two extreme attitudes toward verbal encoding: "noble selves" who "see any variation from their personal norms as hypocritical, as a denial of integrity," and " 'rhetorical reflectors' who have no Self to call their own. For each . . . situation they present a new self."[18] Thus the rhetorically sensitive discussant would be one who neither says just anything and everything that comes to mind ("let it all hang out") nor one who tries to figure out the position of the majority (or high status members) and reflects that without personal conviction (the "yes-man" type).

Developing an attitude of rhetorical sensitivity, especially of interaction consciousness,will help you to encode in ways that are both true to your self and yet clear and palatable to fellow group members. Being rhetorically sensitive should help you contribute to mutual understanding and such output variables as group cohesiveness and consensus decisions.

Attitudes toward Information and Ideas

Skeptical Inquiry

Truth does not exist apart from the minds of persons who know and believe. We cannot transfer knowledge from person to person, but only signals from which each can create personal knowledge and meaning. There can be no meaningful problem solving or decision making by a group until the members have achieved a similar awareness of events and similar beliefs about these events and their implications. To achieve such perceptual congruity requires not only highly sensitive speaking and listening, but also an attitude of *inquiry* toward information and ideas. *Dialectic,* the search for truth (in the sense of the best possible answer to a question), depends on the attitude of inquiry as opposed to certainty or a dogmatic stance on what is and should be. Small group discussion implies a form of dialectic by a group.

Persons who have made up their minds cannot honestly engage in a decision-making or problem-solving discussion. They can only seek to persuade others of the rightness of their prior positions by practicing persuasion; they cannot engage in dialectic. In problem-solving discussion, attempting to persuade others is a very important process, but must be reciprocated by a willingness to be persuaded by others in a search for the best possible answers. Likewise, learning discussions are blocked by the out-and-out persuader; the intent of discussants must be to share, to explore differing conceptions and to foster mutual understandings out of which common values, images, and actions can emerge among equals. In this regard, debate and persuasion are diametrically opposed to discussion. If one is not interested in understanding and exploring opinions, values, and ways of doing things different from one's own, one cannot engage in learning discussions, and if one has reached unalterable conclusions one cannot engage in decision-making discussions—only "pseudodiscussions." Such a participant will either subvert other participants, stymie group progress, or be excluded from the group after much friction and loss of time. To join a discussion group with one's mind closed on the issues facing the group, unable to suspend judgment and undergo the process of cognitive dissonance, is no less than a breach of morality. It demands of others what one is not willing or able to do oneself—change position.

This is not to say that argumentation has no place in discussions, that no one should take a strong stand, or that "giving in" is advised. Careful weighing of evidence, evaluation of all reasoning, detecting and testing assumptions, and constructive debating of different points of view can contribute greatly to the quality of group decisions. Open and honest conflict is a sign of cohesiveness and stability in a group; concealing differences of opinion and negative feelings indicates a lack of unity. Conflict over ideas and decisions reflects real concern and involvement. The best forge for testing ideas is to bring in all contrary evidence and arguments. Decisions based on avoidance of conflict or contrary evidence, or consisting of vague statements and platitudes, do not work; the details of solutions are not settled and the problem continues. Rigid adherence, conformity for its own sake, and dogmatic rejection of information or reasoning must be avoided.

Dogmatism

The opposite of an attitude of skeptical inquiry toward information and ideas is a high level of *dogmatism,* or closed-mindedness. The more dogmatic a person, the less willing he or she is to listen in order to understand new ideas, to listen to and accept evidence that contradicts presently held beliefs, and to base conclusions on the total pool of evidence available to a discussion group.[19] Arguments based on evidence and logical reasoning are likely to fail to influence highly dogmatic persons; their decisions are based more on internal needs, feelings, and drives than on a desire to achieve a logically consistent conclusion.

The degree of dogmatism in members of a small group is highly important to the discussions held by the group. Unless group members can persuade each other with evidence and reasoning from it when they hold different beliefs about a problem and what ought to be done to solve it, much time and effort will be spent in discussion but no consensus will emerge. The group is likely to suffer from high levels of tension and unresolved conflict, and either a split may occur or others finally give in to the dogmatists, producing poor decisions and solutions to problems.

As one famous cartoon character put it, "It ain't what people don't know hurts 'em so much as what they know that ain't so." Lee calls this attitude the "mood of allness" in which a person indicates "he wishes to go no farther, to talk no more about something which is to him impossible, unthinkable, wrong, unnecessary, or just plain out of the question. He has spoken and there is little use in trying to make him see otherwise."[20] He may declare, "We've done it another way and we just aren't going to try something new and dangerous. I refuse to listen to such nonsense." "How naive can you be?" or "Let's not waste time with that one." Such comments indicate what Phillips calls the game of "It Can't Be Done," in which a speaker may even give a tightly reasoned argument to show the apparent impossibility of solving a problem ("the best minds have failed to solve it") or of implementing a proposal.[21]

Perhaps you have had the experience of talking with persons whose minds are made up. I recently discussed the relative merits of collective bargaining with a number of highly educated persons, and was dismayed to have some of them manifest extreme closed-mindedness with such statements as "I'm just against unions in principle. They're wrong. I wouldn't even consider joining one." Others said something like this: "Unionism is good. Management just doesn't care about us who do the real work." No evidence, no reasoning, no exceptions allowed for—just an extreme position, unqualified, and in one case even the statement: "There is no sense in discussing it. There is no place for a union here or in any university."

Often dogmatic persons conclude the very opposite of what others conclude from the same evidence. For example, Dwight Eisenhower was almost universally regarded as highly patriotic and loyal. To reactionaries, this was strong evidence that he was a Communist dupe. Most of us like to think that we are open-minded, but careful analysis of many statements from discussions indicates that many discussants' minds are more closed than open. Your mind is closed to the degree that you (1) consistently and absolutely reject ideas that you disbelieve; (2) you cannot distinguish among beliefs different from your own but see them as the same; and (3) you can see no similarity between your own beliefs and disbeliefs.[22]

A special type of closed-mindedness is called *prejudice*. The term prejudice indicates a judgment that is unreasonable, an opinion that is formed without full and sufficient inquiry. In a very real sense we can never know all that could be known about anything, so we constantly need to be open to new and different evidence. How this matters in discussions is stated quite pointedly by a leading researcher into the mechanisms of prejudice, Gordon Allport: "Attitudes become prejudices only if they are not reversible when exposed to new knowledge."[23] It would be nice if we humans were always rational and open to new ideas and information. But such is not the case—all of us hold prejudices.

If you have this problem, what can be done to replace closed-minded behavior and prejudice with an attitude of inquiry? First, accept your own tendency to act dogmatically and prejudicially as normal, and then be on guard for any tendency in yourself to reject information that contradicts personal belief, regardless of where you got the belief. Try to give such new information or reasoning special attention, no matter how hard that may be. Try stating it aloud to the satisfaction of the person who uttered it. To do so will not be easy, but it will make it possible for you to offset your own prejudices with an attitude of inquiry, and thus your group may find agreement on the basis of evidence rather than remain deadlocked due to unalterable beliefs. Second, you might try asking for points of view other than your own. In a continuing group it would be well to tackle the problem head-on by discussing the attitude itself with the group. An effective way to do this is to discuss specific cases of persons acting with a mood of dismissal. Few persons will persist in making allness statements if they are aware that other group members perceive them to be closed-minded. Taking the short form of the Dogmatism Test and discussing the results may have a positive effect on the members of a group inclined to dismissal and dogmatic statements.[24] It may help to keep reminding the group that mutual respect must be given if group cooperation is to be possible.

Group Size

The **number** of persons comprising a small group has a major impact on the group's resources, processes, and discussions. The abilities, knowledge, and skills available to the group increases somewhat for each added member, increasing the potential for problem-solving effectiveness. But this apparent gain is offset at some point by the increased complexity of the organization required to coordinate behaviors of the members and the increased likelihood of internal conflicts.

As group size increases, the complexity of interpersonal relationships increases geometrically. For example, if we consider only the two-person relationships possible, the rate of increase is indicated by this formula: Number of 2-person relationships $= N(N-1)/2$, in which N is the number of members. Thus in a two-person group there is only one two-person relationship possible, in a group of three members there can be three such relationships, in a group of five members there can be 10 dyadic relationships, and in a group of 10 members there can be 45. The complexities of who interacts with whom

Figure 3.4   Large groups tend to be more formal, structured and frustrating than small groups.

are much greater than even the simple formula above indicates. Consider a four-person group with members A, B, C, and D. Each can speak to each other, to each possible combination of two persons, or to all three other members—a total of twenty-eight initiating interactions. For an eight-person group the possibilities are 1,056! In a group of four members the expected ratio of one-to-one messages as compared to one-to-group would be 3/1. However the interactive behaviors Bostrom found in his experimental groups of different sizes were not distributed at all like this:

Most comments in groups of four or five members were addressed to either one person or the group as a whole (roughly 95%). As group size increased from three to four to five, the percentage of one-to-one comments increased steadily from 46.8 to 58.2 to 64.7. Conversely, the percentage of messages addressed to the rest of the group as a whole decreased.[25]

As the size of a group increases, the opportunity for each member to participate in discussion decreases, but the effect tends to be something different from a simple reduction in average number of minutes available per member. There is some evidence that the total amount of talking tends to be less as group size increases.[26] More importantly, the distribution of participation gets more and more uneven as the number of members increases. A few members tend to dominate the discussion, with others participating relatively less. The amount of participation in groups of three or four members was found to be relatively equal, but as groups increased in size up to eight members the difference in the percentage of remarks by the most and least active members became greater and greater.[27] There is a tendency for one central person to do relatively more and more of the talking.[28] Thus the degree of structure and centralization of leadership in one person increases as does the number of persons who compose a group. Speeches tend to become longer, often including several points not pertinent to the issue at the moment.

Lower individual rates of participation are closely associated with lower satisfaction with a group. In student learning groups, increased size resulted in lower satisfaction with the discussions.[29] Such increased frustration is associated with decreased cohesiveness, hence less power of the group to influence its members and to maintain their loyalty. I have repeatedly had students participate in learning discussions in groups of from fifteen to eighteen members, in groups of five or six members, and in groups of two or three members. Afterward they are asked to rate how satisfied they are with the discussions. Every time the average rating has been much higher for groups of five or six. Although the size of two or three permits more opportunity to speak, it is also rather stifling to divergence and the amount of information and ideas is so limited that the students tend to find these groups less than ideal.

As group size increases, more centralized control of procedures is both expected and needed. Leadership roles become more specialized and formal. Great demands are made on designated leaders to keep order, to keep the discussion organized, and to control the flow of ideas. Large groups usually rely on formal rules of parliamentary procedure, with the general rule being that the larger the group the more the "rules of order" need to be detailed and followed rigorously. It is easier for an autocrat to dominate a large group than a small one.

Other effects commonly occurring when group size increases include greater difficulty in establishing criteria or values, more time reaching a decision, lowering of cohesiveness (attraction to the group), and a tendency for cliques to develop within the group.[30] Small wonder, then, that students who have become proficient in discussing in groups of five to seven persons often flounder in confusion when the class as a whole tries to engage in discussion with the same sort of informality and loose structure used in smaller groups.

How large should a discussion group be? The answer depends in a large part on the purpose of the group and its organizational setting. As early as 1927, Smith demonstrated that groups of three were more efficient in solving problems with "easy" solutions than groups of six members, but groups of six were more efficient with problems requiring that a number of solutions be considered and poor ones promptly rejected.[31] Slater found that experimental problem-solving discussion groups of four to six members were most satisfying to the participants, whereas groups larger than six were felt to encourage too much personal aggressiveness, inconsiderateness, competitiveness, centralization, or disorganization into cliques. Participants in groups of less than four reported being too tense and too constrained to express their attitudes and feelings openly.[32] Groups with even numbers of members tend to have more trouble reaching agreement than do odd-numbered groups. Studies of committees have shown the most *common* sizes to be five, seven, and nine.[33]

Keeping the results of such studies in mind, and that maximum personal involvement is essential for high productivity and efficient use of human beings, the group should be large enough to accomplish its goals and at the same time insure members of satisfaction through opportunity for frequent participation. Thelen's "principle of individual challenge in the least-sized groups" is applicable. Thelen declared that to secure maximum motivation and quality performance, we should establish the *"smallest groups in which it is possible to have represented at a functional level all the social and achievement skills required for the particular required activity."*[34]

Other factors being taken care of, the ideal task-oriented discussion group seems to be five, which is small enough to promote an all-channel network and to permit informality and ease in reaching decisions, yet large enough to bring the many types of information and varied points of view needed for wise decisions. For learning groups, the size may range from as few as three to as many as fifteen or more. If the purpose is to encourage individual questioning and thinking, choose a small group. If the purpose is to expose participants to as many points of view as possible, a larger group is better.

Summary

In this chapter we have considered group members as inputs, especially their attitudes toward self, others, and information and ideas. The number of members was also identified as an important variable.

Positive member attitudes toward the group, self, other members, and information and ideas are major resources from which group goal achievement can be predicted. A high degree of responsibility and dependability toward the group, self-acceptance, willingness to communicate openly and honestly, an assertive manner, low authoritarianism, a tendency to trust others, and rhetorical sensitivity are attitudes which must be present if members of a problem-solving or learning group are to make it highly productive. Attitudes of skeptical inquiry and open-mindedness (as opposed to dogmatism) toward information and ideas are equally important if the group is to achieve sound, logical conclusions.

To function well, a discussion group should have enough members to encompass all the skills and knowledge needed to accomplish group objectives, yet be small enough to keep the level of interpersonal and organizational formality low. As a guideline I have suggested Thelen's principle of "least-sized groups." If all other factors are taken care of, an ideal size for discussion groups seems to be about five. Serious changes in group process occur in connection with increases in the number of members: decreasing equality of opportunity to participate, satisfaction, cohesiveness, and sharing in the leadership of the group.

Members with such positive attitudes as have been described in this chapter are essential, but they must also have a clear purpose, a setting conducive to thoughtful deliberation, and a fund of information and ideas relevant to the purpose of the group. In the next chapter we will consider in detail these inputs which must be available if the group process is to be productive.

Exercises

1. Discuss the following with your classmates, first in small groups, then as an entire class: How much can we trust each other to be truthful and to carry a fair share of the work in small groups we form in this class?

2. In what kinds of small groups (if any) might authoritarian persons be beneficial to goal achievement? Under what conditions are such persons likely to be detrimental to the group's purpose?

3. In a small group of fellow students discuss each of the following questions in turn. One person should record any agreements reached by the group, and report these to the entire class.
   A. What sorts of behavior indicate that a discussant is highly dogmatic? Open-minded?
   B. What has been the impact of dogmatic persons on groups to which we have belonged?
   C. What differences are there in how you usually feel when a fellow group member speaks dogmatically and when the member speaks in an attitude of inquiry?

4. How would an assertive discussant act differently from an aggressive member of the same group? From a nonassertive member? With which of these three types of communicative attitudes are you most comfortable? Why?

5. Observe a small discussion group. When you finish observing, rate each discussant on the scale below.

10	0
very responsible and committed	totally irresponsible and uncommitted

Then write a brief paragraph describing the basis for your judgment of each member. Compare your ratings and observations with those of two or three classmates who independently observed the same group. How well do you agree? What seem to be the behavioral differences on which you judge a group member to be relatively responsible and committed?

6. Clip three or four examples of dogmatic or closed-minded statements about some issue, object, or class of people. You can often find these in letters to the editor of a daily newspaper. Next, revise each statement so that the writer manifests an attitude of *inquiry* while still expressing an opinion.

7. List three or four prejudices you once held, but have now abandoned. Describe how you changed each. Then see if you can identify two or three prejudices you still hold, and describe how you will have to behave differently to manifest an attitude of inquiry in each of these cases.

8. Observe interaction among members of a number of groups of different sizes, from three to large groups of fifty or more members. What differences do you notice? Do other members of the class report the same differences?

Bibliography

Adler, Ronald B. *Confidence in Communication: A Guide to Assertive and Social Skills*. New York: Holt, Rinehart and Winston, 1977. An excellent book to help you develop effective attitudes and skills.

Burgoon, Michael, Heston, Judee K., and McCroskey, James. *Small Group Communication: A Functional Approach*. New York: Holt, Rinehart and Winston, 1974.

Lee, Irving J. *How to Talk with People*. New York: Harper & Row, Publishers, 1952.

Rokeach, Milton. *The Open and Closed Mind*. New York: Basic Books, 1960.

Shaw, Marvin E. *Group Dynamics: The Psychology of Small Group Behavior*. 3d ed. New York: McGraw-Hill, 1981, ch. 6.

References

1. E. M. Rogers and K. K. Bhowmik, "Homophily-Heterophily: Relational Concepts for Communication Research," *Public Opinion Quarterly* 34 (1972): 194–213.

2. Michael Burgoon, Judee K. Heston, and James C. McCroskey, *Small Group Communication: A Functional Approach* (New York: Holt, Rinehart and Winston, 1974), 159.

3. Marvin E. Shaw, *Group Dynamics: The Psychology of Small Group Behavior* 2d ed. (New York: McGraw-Hill, 1976), 182.

4. Thomas A. Harris, *I'm OK—You're OK* (New York: Harper & Row, Publishers, 1969).
5. For more detail on this subject and an explanation of how such reciprocal self-disclosure can help, see Gerard Egan, *Face to Face: The Small Group Experience and Interpersonal Growth* (Monterey, Calif.: Brook/Cole Publishing Company, 1973); and David W. Johnson, *Reaching Out: Interpersonal Effectiveness and Self-Actualization* (Englewood Cliffs, N.J.: Prentice-Hall, 1972).
6. James C. McCroskey, "Oral Communication Apprehension," *Human Communication Research* 4 (1977): 78–96.
7. Maxie C. Maultsby, Jr., *Help Yourself to Happiness* (New York: Institute for Rational Living, 1975).
8. Sherwin B. Cotler and Julio J. Guerra, *Assertion Training* (Champaign, Ill.: Research Press, 1976), 3.
9. Marvin E. Shaw, *Group Dynamics,* 2d ed. (New York: McGraw-Hill, 1976), 180.
10. Stanley Milgram, "Some Conditions of Obedience and Disobedience to Authority," *Human Relations* 18 (1965): 57–76.
11. Irving L. Janis, *Victims of Groupthink* (Boston: Houghton Mifflin Company, 1973).
12. Franklyn S. Haiman, "A Measurement of Authoritarian Attitudes toward Discussion Leadership," *Quarterly Journal of Speech* 41 (1955): 140–44.
13. William W. Haythorn, Arthur Couch, D. Haefner, P. Langham, and L. F. Carter, "The Behavior of Authoritarian and Equalitive Personalities in Groups," *Human Relations* (1956): 54–74.
14. A concise summary of this research is provided in Julian B. Rotter, "Trust and Gullibility," *Psychology Today* 14 (October 1980): 35–42, 102.
15. Roderick P. Hart and Don M. Burks, "Rhetorical Sensitivity and Social Interaction," *Speech Monographs* 39 (1972): 75–91.
16. Roderick P. Hart, Robert E. Carlson, and William F. Eadie, "Attitudes toward Communication and the Assessment of Rhetorical Sensitivity," *Communication Monographs* 47 (1980): 2–22.
17. *Loc cit.*
18. Donald Darnell and Wayne Brockriede, *Persons Communicating* (Englewood Cliffs, N.J.: Prentice-Hall, 1976), 176–78.
19. Milton Rokeach, *The Open and Closed Mind* (New York: Basic Books, 1960).
20. Irving J. Lee, *How to Talk with People* (New York: Harper & Row, Publishers, 1952), 46.
21. Gerald M. Phillips, *Communication and the Small Group,* 2d ed. (Indianapolis: The Bobbs-Merrill Company, 1973), 145.

22. Dale G. Leathers, "Belief-Disbelief Systems: The Communicative Vacuum of the Radical Right," In C. J. Stewart, D. J. Ochs, and G. P. Mohrman, eds., *Explorations in Rhetorical Criticism* (University Park, Pa.: The Pennsylvania State University Press, 1973), 127–31.
23. Gordon Allport, *The Nature of Prejudice* (Garden City, New York: Doubleday, 1958), 9.
24. V. C. Troldahl and F. A. Powell, "A Short Form Dogmatism Scale for Use in Field Studies," *Social Forces* 44 (1965): 211–14.
25. Robert N. Bostrom, "Patterns of Communicative Interaction in Small Groups," *Speech Monographs* 37 (1970): 257–63.
26. R. M. Williams and M. L. Mattson, "The Effects of Social Groupings upon the Language of Pre-School Children," *Child Development* 13 (1942): 233–45; B. P. Indik, "Organization Size and Member Participation: Some Empirical Tests of Alternatives," *Human Relations* 18 (1965): 339–50.
27. Robert F. Bales et al., "Channels of Communication in Small Groups," *American Sociological Review* 16 (1952): 461–68.
28. E. F. Stephan and E. G. Mishler, "The Distribution of Participation in Small Groups," *American Sociological Review* 17 (1952): 598–608.
29. James A. Schellenberg, "Group Size As a Factor in Success of Academic Discussion Groups," *Journal of Educational Psychology* 33 (1959): 73–79.
30. See bibliography for research sources that support these generalizations.
31. E. B. Smith, "Some Psychological Aspects of Committee Work," *Journal of Abnormal and Social Psychology* 11 (1927): 348–68, 437–64.
32. Philip E. slater, "Contrasting Correlates of Group Size," *Sociometry* 21 (1958): 129–39.
33. Clovis R. Shepherd, *Small Groups* (San Francisco: Chandler Publishing Company, 1964), 4.
34. Herbert A. Thelen, *Dynamics of Groups at Work* (Chicago: University of Chicago Press, 1954), 187.

4 purpose, setting, and information as input variables

Study Objectives

As a result of studying chapter 4, you should be able to:

1. Explain the concept "interdependent goal" and why such a goal is vital to effective group discussion.

2. Give examples of "parent" organizations and their committees, and explain the relationship between them.

3. Detect the absence of a clear group objective or charge, and help any group lacking such to establish one.

4. Explain the impact of such environmental features as room size, decoration, and seating arrangements on small group members and communication among them.

5. Make physical arrangements facilitative of effective group discussions.

6. Explain and follow a systematic procedure for locating, gathering, evaluating, and organizing information needed for productive small group discussions.

Key Terms

Area of freedom the scope of authority and responsibility of a small group, including limits on that freedom.

Assumption a belief that is taken for granted, and used in reasoning as *if* it were a statement of fact without checking for evidence of its truthfulness.

Bibliography a list of sources of information bearing on a given topic, problem, or issue; a bibliography includes books, journal articles, magazine articles, newspaper stories, interviews, etc.

Charge a statement of the purpose or goal for which a parent organization has created a small group (committee or task force), usually given to the group by an officer or administrator of the parent organization.

Fact, question of asking for description of specific observations; as such, not discussable.

Fact, statement of a *description* of a specific event observed by some person; the statement includes or implies a method of observing by which the statement could be tested for accuracy.

Goal question the goal of a group expressed as a question to be answered through the collective efforts of the members.

  Question of interpretation question asking for judgments or opinions about the meaning of a fact or body of related facts.

  Question of policy question asking for general solution or plan of action.

  Question of value question seeking a judgment about the goodness, merit, or worth of something; special type of question of interpretation.

Hidden agenda item a goal some member or subgroup hopes to achieve through participation in a small group, unannounced and differing from the "surface" or announced agenda of the group.

Implication a statement that is a logical derivative, extension, or conclusion drawn from a belief or opinion.

Inference, statement of   any statement that includes more than a
description of some event, involving some degree of uncertainty and
probability; cannot be checked for truth or falsity by observation.

Interdependent goal (purpose)   a group goal of such a nature that all
members succeed or fail in achieving it together; success of any
member implies the success of all members.

The purpose for creating a group, the physical setting in which it finds itself, and the information and ideas available are vital to both the process of group discussion and the outcomes of it. In chapter 4 we will consider these three sets of input variables and what is needed from each for a group to have effective discussions.

Purpose of the Group

Unless there is some purpose shared by all members, a small group cannot even be said to exist. Of course the individual members have personal needs and purposes for belonging to a group: need for affiliation, need for sharing thoughts with others, need for affection, need for social esteem, need for self-development and actualization, and so on. Many of these personal needs can be met by belonging to a small group without interfering with the group's central purpose in any way. However, the group members must have some *interdependent* purpose: an interdependent goal means that achievement of it by any one person is dependent on achievement by all. Interdependence is the basis of the kind of decision we call *consensus*. A balanced tug of war illustrates interdependence. For any person to win, all on the team will win, and for a team to win, each member must want to win badly enough to exert the maximum effort he or she is capable of. It takes several persons to plan a successful luncheon dance or prom. If the members of the conflicting teams during labor negotiations really want to avoid a breakdown (with a possible strike), such a common interdependent purpose may be enough for them to overcome their conflicts in a spirit of compromise that produces an agreement both teams of negotiators can accept as "good." Thus in a strong group there is a clear sense and understanding that all are needed to succeed, and the members share a common fate of relative success or failure as a group. Any conflicts among the members are subordinate to the interdependent goal, which calls for the best possible collaborative and cooperative behavior.

The first thing members of any newly formed small group need to accomplish is to determine, clarify, and achieve agreement of all members to the purpose of the group. Before setting out on a journey, it is absolutely essential to know where you are trying to go and why—only then can you plot out a course to follow, whether as an individual or group. The group members must ask and get answers to such questions as:

Why have we formed (or been appointed to) this group?

What are we to do? What exactly is our goal? What will be the nature of the output we are to produce? How will we know when we have produced this output and are finished?

What will happen to our group output? Will it be our personal growth and development? A set of understandings to be tested later by an instructor? A report of findings and interpretations to be submitted in

writing to some parent organization or administrator? A
recommendation to be submitted to someone? A program to be
presented to our class or some other audience? Some concrete product
we will produce, such as a barn, a dinner-dance, or a set of bylaws?

Only after the group purpose has been understood alike and accepted by all
members can a small group design procedures for doing its work, begin to
explore its situation in detail, design possible courses of action, decide what
to do, and do the actual work to achieve its goals. Although individual members may have somewhat different personal objectives in belonging to the group,
these must contribute (or at least not detract from) the group's primary objective if the group is to be truly productive. Members who place a high value
on the purpose of the group will work diligently; members who perceive that
the group is making progress toward its goals will overcome adversities and
remain loyal, diligent, and satisfied.

An assignment to a committee impressed me deeply with the importance
of clear goals that are seen as important by all members of a group. I was
appointed to a special committee to evaluate and make recommendations about
an academic program to the chief administrator of our university. At our first
several meetings no one seemed to know what we were to accomplish or why
we had been picked to serve on the committee. We met only becaue we felt
we had to, but our meetings were apathetic in the extreme and we accomplished nothing. After several months we finally determined what we were
expected to produce, and that it was very important. Some initial investigating
showed us why each of us was needed on the committee, and then our meetings
came to life. In a relatively short time we produced a well-documented report
and set of recommendations, for which we received much praise. But if only
we had been given or insisted upon having a clear charge at the onset of our
committee, how much time we might have saved!

Sometimes a group will be ostensibly working toward one purpose, but
actually working toward another. Many discussion groups (such as standing
committees) lose sight of their original reason for being, yet go on discussing
aimlessly. Such lack of purpose results in inefficiency, dissatisfaction, member
loss, and decay of the group. Groups can be compared to other living organisms in this regard. All types of life are formed of similar elements organized
in some specific fashion. When the organism has begun to decay, it sooner or
later must die. Then its elements break apart and are gradually incorporated
into other organisms. In the same way that we keep our environment clean,
satisfying, and productive by hastening recycling processes and not over-
loading the ecoconversion systems, so we need to help small groups that have
served their purpose either adopt new objectives or end rapidly so they do not
become a drain on society. How many "friendship" groups have you known
that went stumbling along although most of the positive feelings for each other
were gone? How many functionless committees, councils, etc., do you know
that limp along, draining far more energy than their productivity warrants?

Each of us can strike a blow for conservation of the social environment by helping such groups die quickly and with grace.

Even wnen there is something to be done by the group, little may be accomplished because the goal is not understood alike by all the members. I have frequently asked each member of a discussion group to write down the purpose(s) of the discussion, only to find that each person had a decidedly different idea about the group purpose. Lacking a common goal, progress is impossible. Goal clarity is essential for effective group discussion.

Many small groups are created by some "parent" organization. The U.S. Congress and most legislatures have a large number of committees, each of which is responsible for investigating and recommending or killing proposed laws. The constitution of almost every voluntary organization creates certain standing committees. Special committees are created by the membership, president, or executive committee to do specific things. For example, the chapter of the American Association of University Professors to which I belong has a steering committee to work out the general policy of the association and coordinate all its activities, an advisory committee to develop proposed language for a contract to be negotiated with the board of regents, a liaison committee for purposes of recruiting chapter members and carrying information between the steering committee and the members of the entire chapter, and a negotiating team that does the actual bargaining with the board of regents. Other committees are created as needs arise.

The Charge

A **charge** is the assignment given to a subordinate group by a parent organization or administrator of an organization. A major component of the charge is the group's *area of freedom*. In effect, the charge specifies what the group is to do, whereas the area of freedom defines both the authority of the group and limits on what the group may do to complete its charge. Here is an example of a charge to a committee from a parent organization, typical of the charges written for standing committees of the university where I am located. This charge is in a booklet created by a special task force that reported to the chief administrative officer of the university, with advisory inputs from the faculty senate.

This committee shall be responsible for the granting of monies to full-time . . . faculty for the improvement of their instructional capabilities. Such grants shall be awarded, but not necessarily limited to, worthy projects in innovative instructional methods, instructional research, pedagogical applications of new technologies, development of instructional materials, and professional development in accordance with the established criteria.

The University committee on Improvement of Instruction shall make its funding recommendations to the Director of the Center for Improvement of Instruction and shall report its activities to the Chancellor.

The charge makes clear that the committee does not have the freedom to recommend that a faculty member be dismissed for poor teaching, that monies be spent to improve a research laboratory, or that some new instructional program be created. Next is an example of a charge given to a task force created by a large transportation corporation.

The task force shall investigate the extent and effect of drug usage (including alcohol) on employee behavior and performance, determine the various costs of such drug usage to the corporation, and make recommendations for appropriate preventive and correctional programs, accompanied by estimated cost-benefit projections.

The findings and recommendations of the task force shall be given to the President in writing not later than January 1, 1982.

The rest of this charge included an enumeration of the resources in time, personnel, equipment, and money available for doing the work of the task force. It was presented to the newly appointed group in an initial meeting with the president and several vice-presidents of the corporation.

No subordinate group should be created if there is not a real and demonstrable need for it that can be stated as a charge. Confusion, frustration, and waste are the inevitable results when a small group is created without a clear and specific purpose. A graduate student in a seminar on small group communication conducted by me did an unusual and interesting paper on what she called "non-group meetings."[1] She had been able to observe a number of meetings of committees created by statute as part of the organization of a large public medical complex. Certain standing committees were required by the charter of the organization, and each had to meet at designated times. These committees had been given very general responsibility for dealing with certain problems that *might* arise in the management of the hospital complex, including such matters as violations of laws and unethical practices. However, more often than not when they met there was no business to attend to—no one had found anything wrong in their scope of responsibility. The result, she found, was considerable talking in very general and abstract terms, expressions of boredom, and expressions by the members that they were wasting the valuable time of many highly paid professional persons. Yet they met, and said they must, because the charter of the organization required them to do so.

A few years ago I was involved in a major conflict while serving on a committee that heard faculty appeals to decisions made by a dean. We committee members thought the bylaws of our board of regents granted us the power to overturn the administrator's decisions, but the dean believed that we had no power but to *recommend* that he change his decisions. A great deal of professorial time was spent trying to resolve this conflict over our area of freedom. For a period of time we refused to consider any appeals. Finally, the dean agreed to abide by our decision on any appeal to his previous decision, and once again we began to function. In short, it is vital that a group be constantly aware of its charge and the limits on its authority.

Hidden and Public Agendas

Confusion within a small group may result from conflict or competition between the avowed group purpose, its *public agenda,* and *hidden agendas* of individual members or even the group as a whole. The term *hidden agenda* refers to any objectives of individual members, subgroups of members, or even of the entire group that are unannounced, covert, and different from the avowed group purpose. For example, one may join a committee in order to enhance his public image as a means to being elected to a public office. Another may join a group out of sheer loneliness, seeking some sense of belonging and affection through membership in a volunteer group. A member of an inter-campus committee, which was assigned to develop a formula for equitable funding of all campuses of a state university system, kept finding something wrong with every idea anyone presented. Finally he admitted that his real purpose was to keep the present arrangement by which his campus received more money per full-time student than did the other campuses. Hidden agendas may not be at variance with the group purpose and charge, but we must be on guard for evidence of them in behaviors that are detrimental to achievement of the public agenda, the announced purpose of the group. If you suspect that a hidden agenda is interfering with goal achievement, it can be dealt with by making it a public agenda item, asking the group to deal with it openly. It is especially important that the designated leader of a group with an assigned task do all possible to keep the group working to achieve that goal, its public agenda. Whenever you are participating in a discussion among persons who do not seem to be working toward the same goal or talking about the same thing you can often help with orienting behavior by asking a question such as one of the following:

"What exactly is our charge?"

"Why are we meeting here today?"

"What do we think we are trying to accomplish together?"

"What common goal(s) do we share?"

"What do we expect to accomplish through our discussion and work
together?"

"Was our group assigned to produce a report of findings, a suggestion for a
larger parent organization or administrator, or has it power to make
final decisions and act?"

"Is this group seeking to understand a variety of ideas and points of view on
a topic, or do we need to reach decisions to which all members are
expected to subscribe?"

If the answer you receive is unclear, insist on getting a clear answer or else on terminating the group. If members are highly dissatisfied with their group, either the purpose of the group, individual purposes, or group membership must be changed. Persons working toward goals they feel to be meaningless or insignificant—or at variance with their personal goals—work poorly at best.

Classroom Project Groups

Instructors frequently assign projects to be done by groups of students, especially for courses in small group communication and discussion. When you have an assignment to produce some output as a group for a grade, you have been given a charge. Be sure that charge is clearly understood by all group members, and understood as intended by your instructor. What form(s) is the output supposed to take? A panel discussion presented before your class? A dramatization of some principle or theory? An instructional unit, actually conducted for the class? An investigation and written recommendation for possible solution of some campus or local problem, reported in some form to appropriate persons? If the group is to produce a written paper, what sort of content, style, organization, and form are expected? In addition to clarifying the charge, also determine how you will be evaluated and graded in this group project, both as group and as an individual. Will the entire grade be on a group basis, so that each member gets exactly the same grade? Will part of the grade be for your individual work and part for the group's as a whole? Will you be required to produce some sort of paper as an individual student, perhaps describing and analyzing the group from some perspective? If so, what form should that paper take? What records will you need to write it well?

Sometimes groups of students tackle issues that are beyond their area of freedom or competence, such as "What should be our position in arms negotiations with the Soviet Union?" or "How might we get America to place less emphasis on material things and more on spiritual matters?" These goal questions are almost limitless in scope. Groups of experts might work for years on them, and still arrive at nothing very precise and specific. As outputs, student groups could do nothing more than express their opinions—and no one is likely to consider seriously any ideas they would recommend. The most important information on such questions is likely to be classified and unavailable, or in major research libraries, or uninterpretable except to specialists. People with needed resources might provide them to a Presidential Commission, but are unlikely to go to the trouble and expense required to present them to students from a discussion course at Pleasant Valley College. A further limitation is that classroom groups usually have no funds except those of the student members themselves, limited time, and few investigative skills.

Early on you need to decide what is of interest to all members of the group that you can realistically *do* as a group. Trying to impress your instructor by tackling what sounds like an intellectual topic will usually backfire; your instructor will probably detect your motive and be very unimpressed by it. Coming up with a new and defensible solution to a campus problem or a panel presentation that airs thoroughly the issues on a bill being considered by your city council or state legislature may be more than enough of a challenge, and highly worthwhile to the people who receive it. Only when you have a goal that fits your charge and members' interests are you ready to tackle the job of creating a procedure to follow, an agenda of steps to follow up to the time of the final production by your group, its grading, and disbanding.

Frequently some members of such classroom groups begin with hidden agendas detrimental to group accomplishment. They may want credit for the project, but not be willing to attend meetings at inconvenient times or do the time-consuming research required. Some seem to need a social or play group, but not to get on with clarifying and accomplishing the project assigned. Their desire for attention, dominance, friendship, or mates can greatly interfere with goal achievement desired by more task-oriented students. I recommend that you be very serious about the public agenda of the group, and do all you can to keep the group working on it. If you think that hidden agendas of some member(s) are interfering with the public agenda, say so in an assertive (but not aggressive) manner and suggest the group get on with its task. Be sure to describe the observed behaviors on which your suspicions rest. Much of this book can be of assistance to you in making a project group successful *if applied*. If you treat small group communication theory and techniques as something to study but not to use in your classroom groups, it will be of little use to you, now or ever. Your class, the organizations in which you hold membership, your society, and most of all you will be the loser.

Group Goal Questions

Discussion is always a form of inquiry, a dialectical search for answers on the part of group members: answers about how to solve or at least ameliorate personal problems, about the meaning of some object, about the condition or value of something, about what to recommend, or about what course of action to pursue. The charge to a subordinate group can always be stated in the form of a question or questions to which the group seeks answers. For example, "What should the XYZ Corporation do to reduce the effects of employee drug usage on its productivity?" or "How shall funds appropriated for improving instruction at A College be expended?"

Such *group goal questions* have traditionally been classified into three broad categories: questions of *interpretation* (often called questions of *fact*), questions of *value,* and questions of *policy.* You will doubtless engage in many discussions of questions of each of these three types.

Questions of Interpretation

Questions of interpretation (judgment or opinion) are those concerned with the meaning of a fact or group of facts. Such questions ask not what happened, but what the facts mean to discussants. Since the answers are matters of opinion, there is much room for different answers. Many groups have as their goal the answering of such questions. For example, a grand jury collects information, then decides whether or not to file charges against a suspect. A so-called "fact-finding" committee of a legislature first ascertains what has happened, then interprets the meanings of these facts and may even recommend policy actions. The facts about heroin usage in a particular city will undoubtedly be judged as indicating a serious (or not so serious) problem. Examples of this type of question, such as the following, can be found in any discussion:

"Has auto theft increased in our city since 1983?"

"How have the attitudes of college students changed since 1975?"

"What conditions appear to have contributed to the decline in the number of family-owned farms?"

"What is the effect of capital punishment on the murder rate?"

"How do major volcanic eruptions affect the weather?"

"How does legalizing gambling affect the crime rate?"

Questions of Value

Questions of value are a sub-type of questions of interpretation. They call for judgment making about the effectiveness, merit, or goodness of something. A comparison is always involved or implied in the answer to a question of value. The comparison may be made to a standard of judgment, to a basic value shared by group members, to other items of the same class, or to other proposed solutions to a problem. For example:

"Which American political party has done more to improve the living conditions of people living in poverty?"

"Is it more beneficial to humanity in the long run to give food to starving people in over-populated countries, or to teach them birth control techniques, modern agriculture, and management techniques?"

"How well has court-ordered integration by busing achieved the educational opportunity it was aimed at?"

"How important is a well-rounded liberal education to students aiming for careers in technological industries?"

"How effective is Bob Blank as a farm manager?"

"How realistic is Miller's portrayal of the motives of a salesman such as Willy Loman?"

When individual and personal valuations are called for, it is important to remember that there is no need for agreement. There is no sense arguing about answers to such questions as: "Is this a good painting?" "Do you like this poem?" or "Is pork or chicken better?" A learning group has no need to agree on matters of value, but merely to understand what the questions imply and the basis for different answers to them. On the other hand, a group trying to arrive at a solution to a problem, when facing a choice among possible courses off action, must agree on values or criteria in order to arrive at a specific recommendation or plan of action. For such a problem-solving group, arriving at agreement on values may well be essential if it is ever to agree on a solution.

Questions of Policy

A question of policy asks "What should be done in order to . . .?" The key word in this question format is *should*. The group is searching for a solution to a specific problem or a general procedure to follow whenever a problem of a particular type occurs. For example:

"What laboratory science courses should be required of liberal arts graduates?" vs. "What lab courses are required?" or "What is the value of lab science to a liberal arts graduate?"

"What changes should be made in our penalties for acts of unprovoked criminal violence?"

"What should be the national law governing abortions?"

"What should we do to eliminate weeds from our lawn?"

Obviously, answers to such questions that will be acceptable to all members of a group can be found only after answers to questions of interpretation and value have been agreed upon. When communication breaks down in a group trying to agree upon a solution, it is usually wise to raise questions of value, asking what criteria are actually being applied. It may also be necessary to collect more facts and interpret them. The patterns for problem-solving discussion provide for discussion of fact, interpretation, value, and policy in that order. But sometimes the discussion is too sketchy at some stage in the process of problem solving to provide a basis for agreement on a policy statement. In this event the group may need to backtrack to answer questions of fact, interpretation, or value previously overlooked. When initially asking for possible solutions to a problem, it is often better to phrase the question as "What *might* be done to . . .?" in order to encourage a variety of ideas before any discussion of their pros and cons is undertaken.

Even though group members have agreed upon the purpose of their group as highly valuable and appropriate to the social context in which the group exists, and have a clearly worded charge or goal question to formulate that purpose, it is unlikely that meetings will be productive unless the physical setting for the discussions is conducive to uninterrupted dialectical discourse. In the next section we will consider the impact of the physical environment in which a small group meets for discussions.

Physical Facilities and Arrangements

For many years researchers have investigated the general hypothesis that the characteristics of a room influences individual behavior and group interaction. An ugly room with stark gray walls, a bare light bulb, junk lying around, and hard floors evoked such responses as fatigue, headaches, irritability, and hostility. A room with warm beige walls, draperies, windows, comfortable furniture, and adequate lighting evoked feelings of pleasure, importance, comfort, and a desire to remain in the room.[2]

The size of a room has an effect on how closely group members will sit to each other. Sommer found an inverse relationship between room size and distance between conversants: as the size of the room is increased, the distance people choose to have between them decreases.[3] It seems likely from this finding that a small group can meet just as well in a fairly large room as in a small one if the room is attractive, comfortable, and free of distractions. My personal experience indicates that this is so.

It is very important that group meeting rooms be free from distractions and provide privacy. Listening to fellow discussants is taxing enough, without the competing stimuli of a television set in the background, non-members moving in and out of a room, pets, and similar distractions. Numerous students have reported that meeting in each other's homes is often unproductive, for babies, spouses, and pets frequently interrupt their work. Sometimes overstuffed furniture is so relaxing that tired members doze off. Most groups report that meeting in a quiet room on campus or a simple apartment seems to work best for them. Always be sure you have a setting conducive to group discussion *before* you meet.

Seating arrangements are especially important to productive discussions. Hare and Bales found that the way chairs are placed in a room influences the pattern of interaction.[4] When seated in a circle, members tend to talk most often to those opposite them rather than to those sitting on either side. If the group has a very dominant leader, persons will tend to get into side-bar conversations with those seated next to them. At a rectangular table, such as is frequently found in a meeting room, persons at the corners contribute least to the discussion, whereas members of the group at the ends and central positions on the sides speak more often. Many groups expect a designated leader to sit at one end of a rectangular table. In my role as chairman of a small group I once tried sitting in a corner spot, only to discover that almost everyone showed signs of discomfort. I asked if the group wanted me to move to the end of the table; all said "yes," so I did move with an obvious improvement in the discussion. It seems to be a widely accepted norm that leaders should sit at the end of a long table. I once was asked what might facilitate more responses from members of a group of store managers who met periodically with top management to discuss corporate policies and problems they were encountering. They had a meeting room with two long tables arranged in a T, with the top managers sitting at the head table. I suggested putting the tables side by side to form a large square, and removing all corner chairs. Simple and obvious, but the president reported that this made a big improvement in subsequent meetings. One academic department I observed met in a typing room, with small tables in rows. I suggested arranging the tables in a rough circle. Again, the result was a great increase in participation and much more lively discussion from member to member without the chairperson seeming to be expected to remark after each member comment.

What guidelines can we derive from such research and observations? The optimum for private discussion is a circular seating arrangement with members seated close together. In most discussions, each member should also have a writing surface. If the group meets in a classroom with flexible seating, have the participants push chairs into a circle (or a semicircle where everyone can see the chalkboard or easel). In a room with fixed seating, a few portable chairs can be brought in or some participants can sit sideways in their chairs in order to form a rough circle. If you have a long rectangular table, get the persons at the middle of each side to push their chairs out from the table, thus allowing for some eye contact between all members. If possible, do not seat anyone at the very corners of a square or rectangular table. A few small tables can be arranged to approximate a circle. See figure 4.1.

If group members are not well acquainted, each should be given a tag or "tent" on which to write or print his or her name. Satisfactory name tags can be made from 3″ by 5″ file cards, with the name printed with crayon or felt-tip pen, and held in place with a straight pin. Adhesive-backed name tags are even better if available. A plain 5″ by 8″ file card makes a good name tent when folded lengthwise. It is printed on both sides and set in front of the discussant so all members of the group can readily read the name.

Adequate lighting, comfortable temperature, and ventilation should be provided in any meeting room. If smoking is permitted, each discussant should have easy access to an ashtray. However, before smoking begins it is important to determine if anyone is adversely affected by smoke, and if so there should be no smoking. Many persons will not participate in groups where smoking is allowed. This issue should be settled when a group gets underway, at its first meeting.

Although it is not always possible, any problem-solving group can make good use of a chalkboard or easel with a pad of large plain paper for recording information, ideas, and questions. Other necessary equipment or supplies (tape recorder, charts, projector and slides, pencils and note pads, etc.) should be all ready to operate before a meeting begins so that getting it set up or distributed does not break in on the interaction.

Informational Resources

Perhaps because we converse so readily in chance meetings with others, many persons look upon a forthcoming discussion as something for which no one

Figure 4.1   Seating arrangements for small discussion groups.

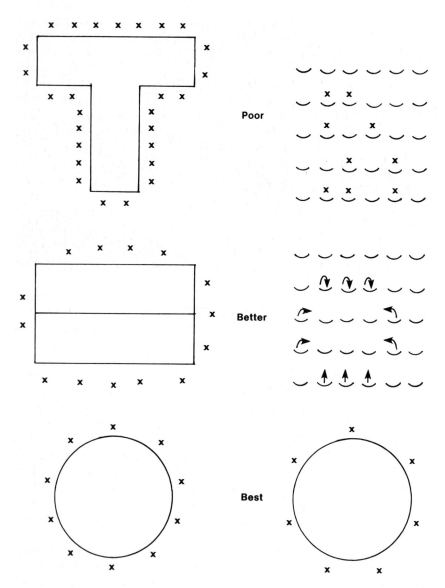

Figure 4.2   All ready for the committee.

(except possibly a designated leader) would prepare. This is a most counter-productive attitude. For most discussions, as in many ventures, to fail to prepare is to prepare to fail. "Garbage in, garbage out" is as applicable to small groups as to computer programs. No matter how skilled group members may be in communicating with each other, the outputs of their discussions will be no better than the informational resources available and used by the group.

Effective discussion grows out of dependable knowledge and clear thinking, which can come only from preparation. Of course there are productive discussions for which nobody seems to have made specific preparations. But appearances here, as in many situations, are deceiving. Participating in such discussions are persons who by nature of their work, life, and study are well prepared: a group of speech communication teachers discussing how to help students overcome reticence, graduate students in public administration talking about reforms needed in the city charter, or a group of dog fanciers talking about how to train their animals. Even the experts can do a better job if they prepare specifically.

Effective group discussion is never a pooling of ignorance. Every dependable conclusion, solution, interpretation, or belief rests on dependable evidence and valid reasoning from the evidence. Half-informed participants can reach only half-informed decisions. The valuable participant has plumbed his subject deeply. Think for a moment of a group of college students trying to intelligently discuss such topics as capital punishment or the control of atomic arms without having first done extensive reading on the subject. Would you place credence in the conclusions of such a group?

How highly group members value the prepared, informed participant was shown in research on emergent leadership in leaderless discussion groups. Geier found that being perceived as uninformed was the greatest single reason why members of leaderless discussion groups were quickly eliminated from any bid for major influence in the group.[5] You simply can't bluff for long in a group that is at all informed and critical of information and ideas. Group members are well advised to make serious individual efforts to be well informed.

Groups are frequently plagued by members who keep telling irrelevant jokes or pulling the group off the topic. Such nuisances are almost always poorly informed. One promotor of study-discussion programs advocated this policy: "If anyone has not read the materials, he is not permitted to speak unless to ask a question." Needless to say, this policy produced prepared participants and satisfying discussions. Many study-discussion leaders report that when the participants have not prepared, the ensuing discussion is listless, disorganized, shallow, and frustrating. Only so much ice-breaking conversation to help members get acquainted is needed. Gossip, storytelling, and shooting the bull may be fun at the time, but they rarely advance a secondary group toward its goal. Many students in my small group communication courses have reported in case studies of their project groups that little progress was made until everyone did the research needed. Then a lot was accomplished in a short time with the needed information now available.

Not only do discussants need information if their groups are to be effective, but it must be relevant, accurate, valid, and as complete as possible. This means that tests of the quality of information must be applied both while preparing for and participating in discussions. The evidence on which decisions are reached may include such nonverbal materials as maps, photos, and objects (e.g., sample products, weapons, tools), and such verbal materials as statements of fact, opinion, and policy. How reliable and valid the information may be is crucial in deciding whether or not to use it—an out-of-date map, a "salted" ore sample, a biased set of statistics, an uninformed opinion, an untested bit of advice, or an outdated concept (e.g., "women belong in the home") can lead to very poor group decisions indeed!

The contrast between being uninformed and informed was discovered by a group of students at a large university. They began attacking the university food service, with a host of complaints about what was wrong and what should be done to improve it. Fortunately, they soon realized that they knew very little about the facts of the subject except for what they had seen and heard as students and customers. Thus, they decided to conduct a careful investigation. The labor was divided among the group members, some studying menu planning, others studying food preparation, others looking into costs, and others investigating food service at other schools. Information was gathered from home economists, dieticians, food service employees, journals, and books. At the next meeting this group of informed students pooled their knowledge, and came to the conclusion that they had the finest food service of any university in their section of the country, that meals were reasonably priced, that menus were better planned than most family diets, and that many of the complaints were due to ignorance or to misuse of the food service by students. The problem soon changed to, "How can we get the students at our university to appreciate the excellence of our food service, and to take better advantage of it?" They also made a few recommendations for minor improvements in the food service, all based on the facts of the case. These suggestions were well received by the man in charge of the service, who expressed his appreciation and put several of the group's suggestions into effect.

Since valid information is so important to productive small group discussion, the question now becomes "What can we do to gather the information we need as a group?" The answer will depend in part on the purpose of the group and the knowledge already possessed by its members. A general procedure for locating information, evaluating, and organizing it is presented next. The steps are presented in the order in which they should be taken for a minimum of wasted effort and time. This procedure may be modified somewhat if you are well versed in the problem area, but none of these steps can be omitted without a possible loss in group effectiveness: (1) review and organize your present stock of information and ideas on the subject; (2) gather needed information; (3) evaluate the information and ideas you have now collected; and (4) organize the information and ideas into a tentative outline.

1. Review and Organize Your Present Stock of Information and Ideas
Undoubtedly you already have some information and experience on the subject, or you would not be discussing it. Taking a systematic inventory of this knowledge can save you much time in preparation, and will enable you to recall what you need when you need to. To begin reading at this point would be wasteful and inefficient.

   a. Place the problem or subject in perspective. To what is it related? What will it affect, or by what is it affected? For example, in trying to plan a scholarship program for a corporation, a task force would consider the corporation's financial condition, long-range plans, obligations to the community, public relations, types of employees, and the like.

   b. Make an inventory of what you know about the subject. An approach that may help you recall is to list courses taken, jobs held, reports, firsthand experiences, articles read, books, ideas, and so forth. Additional headings will suggest themselves as you proceed. These headings can be put on sheets of scratch paper. Then jot down in brief form everything that comes to mind. Let your mind be "freewheeling," without being concerned with the degree of importance, relevance, or even validity.

c. Organize your information into a problem-solving outline. This can be a rough pencil draft. Look over your notes for main issues, topics, or questions about the problem, being guided by a model outline suggested in chapter 11.

d. Look for deficiencies. Your outline of information will reveal what you do *not* know, where specific information is needed, and which ideas or opinions are unsupported.

2. Gather Needed Information

You are now ready to plan research to correct deficiencies in your knowledge and thinking.

Some group members I have observed acted as if once the question or problem had been announced they could just begin looking for evidence in any way and place, and expect to gain the resources needed for effective group work. Whatever the members happened to find in recent magazines, newspapers, and encyclopedias was taken as if it were necessarily valid and sufficient. Further, the group had no system for obtaining needed information and ideas; its "research" was very haphazard. The result of such a haphazard preparation is "garbage in" informational resources and "garbage out" types of conclusions and learnings. A systematic procedure for gaining informational inputs will usually prevent such an undesirable outcome.

A group cannot deal with a major problem or assignment in one meeting. Even if the members have known about the topic or problem in advance, their individual stocks of information and ideas are likely to be very uneven, and their research to date quite full of gaps. Some areas of relevant knowledge will have been looked into by everyone but others totally overlooked. Complicated problems and topics require at least two meetings, and usually several. Recall the example presented in chapter 2 of the committee of professors charged with drafting a college constitution. In addition to clarifying the area of freedom and overall goals of the new group, part of the initial meeting should be devoted to planning how to obtain needed information in the most efficient way possible likely to produce a comprehensive picture of what is known on the subject at this time. The following three-step procedure will help to assure the group that nothing of importance is overlooked.

1. The group should identify *and list* as many as possible of the issues and topics it will need to explore.

2. The group should assess the adequacy of its collective knowledge on the topic or problem, and then determine what information or types of information is needed, thus preparing a list of headings for members' research. As Harnack, Fest, and Jones say, "Groups more often err on the side of too little evidence; but it is important to remember that it is never possible to gather all the evidence there is."[6]

3. The group should assign research responsibilities to individual members. This step is frequently overlooked as a way of preventing gaps in knowledge, delays, and wasting time. Individual assignments will also increase individual responsibility and involvement. The most satisfactory way to make such research assignments is to allow members to voluntarily choose from the list of topics and sources, with the group secretary or chair keeping a list of who has undertaken each task and including this list in the report or minutes of the meeting. A definite deadline should be established for each person or sub-group to report to the group as a whole.

As a general rule, all members should do some common background study and two or more persons should examine every major article, book, or other source on the subject. This will help to offset individual perceptual biases. If each member is a specialist with no one to check his or her findings and interpretations, many errors could creep into the group's understanding of the available information. If a member does not do a competent job of investigating and reporting, the group will suffer greatly from incorrect or inadequate information. Group "experts" also tend to dampen interaction on a topic when they are the only members with detailed knowledge. Of course, while you are looking up the source you have been assigned you may run across other relevant items; record these and bring them to the attention of the group.

Once you have a list of topics or sources, you are ready to begin your detailed personal preparation. We will review only briefly the means for getting information and recording it, for this topic has probably been covered previously in your speech and composition classes.

Information and ideas slip from memory or twist themselves in recall unless we make *accurate* and *complete* notes. Carrying books, magazines, and recordings to a discussion would at best be clumsy, and you might get so lost in the mess that you distract your group.

The best system of note taking is to record each bit of information or idea on a separate 3" by 5" note card. Put a topic heading on the card, followed by the specific subject. Then list exact details of the source, just as you would for a bibliography. Finally, record the information, idea, or quotation. Figure 4.3 shows how to do this.

The note cards provide both accuracy and flexibility. One can arrange them in various groups as one synthesizes and interprets the evidence collected. They can be consulted with ease during discussion without having to leaf through a disorganized notebook. Full reference data permit others to evaluate the credibility of the evidence. It is virtually useless to say something appeared in *The New York Times* or *Newsweek* or "a book by some psychologist." Information may come from many sources, of which three types are most likely to be important in preparing for group discussion: (1) direct observation, (2) reading, and (3) interviews.

Figure 4.3   A note card.

LEADER RATINGS   Affected by Subordinates' Beliefs about Leadership

Martin M. Chemers, "Leadership Theory and Research: A Systems-Process Integration," in Paul B. Paulus, Basic Group Processes. New York: Springer-Verlag, 1983, p. 26.

". . . subordinates ratings of leader behavior may reflect what the subordinate thinks good or bad leaders do, rather than any objective measure of what their leader really does. A number of recent studies . . . strongly indicate that implicit theories of leadership held by individuals affect their ratings of leader behavior."

Direct Observation

Many times information that is needed can come only from some firsthand observation by members of a group, and often firsthand observation is needed to give a sense of realism to the symbolic information available in surveys, tables of statistics, and other print sources. For example, a group that had the goal of developing a plan for making decent housing available to low-income persons might find a plethora of information in print, but still would benefit from direct observation of the actual residences of such persons in the slums and ghettos of a city, and of the kinds of housing available at different prices. In Omaha a commission to look at potential sites for government subsidized housing found it necessary to visit proposed building sites even though they had available maps and reports of what was available. Before discussing how to reduce parking problems on a campus you might need to observe the parking lots over a period of time. A group of students desiring to improve conditions in a self-service coffee shop of a student union spent some time observing what was happening there at various times throughout the day. They recorded the number of persons who did and did not bus their waste materials, the kinds and amount of litter on the floor and tables, the placement and condition of waste containers, and the signs encouraging users to keep the room clean. Another group could get information on how uncut weeds and trees were obscuring traffic control signs only by systematically observing a large number of intersections. A small group can decide if firsthand observation is called for, then assign the task to members most interested in doing this work of information gathering.

Reading

For many topics and problems the major pool of informational resources will be found in books, journals, newspapers, government documents, and other printed pages. Before an individual or small group begins reading and taking notes, it is important to get a perspective on what print resources are likely to yield information on an issue: the number, type, and quality of the sources. To do that, you will first need to compile a *bibliography,* which is a list of published works relevant to a particular topic, problem, or issue. Ideally, you would locate and evaluate all the recent printed information that was relevant before making any final decision about the nature and extent of a problem. That is not always possible, but most certainly you should not limit reading to only one or two sources. Likewise, you would want to read from sources that espoused all points of view, not just one side of a controversial issue. To do so will produce a strong bias in your information, with no way to cross-check the truth and validity of what you read.

To be as efficient as possible in compiling a bibliography, first prepare a list of key terms—"descriptors"—bearing on the topic to guide your search for print items. A reference librarian can often be of considerable help in doing this. Do not hesitate to ask reference librarians for help; my students and I have invariably found them to be exceptionally helpful and courteous. Most major bibliographies, indexes, and compilations of abstracts are now in computer files, each of which has an entire thesaurus of key descriptor terms. Such "data banks" cost money to use, but they make it extremely easy to locate relevant items in print. You may have access to such a service to help your group gain material on a subject. If not, your group or individual list of terms will provide a fine starting point, and as you proceed to gather items from the library other key terms will be discovered. For example, in preparing to discuss "What type of lottery, if any, should our state conduct?" the key words you first used might include: lottery, sweepstakes, gambling, crime, revenue, tax, and betting. As you began to search specialized bibliographies and read articles you might locate other terms to help your search, such as "victimless" and "wagering."

A good library manual, avaiable at virtually every college or university library, is a great help in building a bibliography and locating materials. You may find help in bibliographies of bibliographies, which list special published bibliographies by topic, such as: *A World Bibliography of Bibliographies and of Bibliographic Catalogues, Bibliographical Index,* and *Bulletin of Bibliography and Magazine Notes.* Bibliographies will be found at the end of many books, doctoral dissertations (see *Dissertation Abstracts* to locate these), and research articles. The subject section of the card catalog of the library may reveal books not previously located. You can locate materials in magazines, journals, and newspapers with such special indexes as: *The Reader's Guide to Periodical Literature, Applied Science and Technology Index, The Education Index,* and *The New York Times Index.* Do not overlook publications by federal and state governments. Most libraries have special sections of such material. Most helpful in locating relevant information in these publications is the *Monthly Catalog of U.S. Goverment Publications,* followed by the *Monthly Checklist of State Publications.*

Even while you are compiling a bibliography you can begin reading, and all members of the group should read some of the same things in order to provide a common background. As we shall see in the final section of the book, learning discussion depends on all having read or otherwise shared the same sources. It is especially important when reading for information bearing on a "fact-finding" or "policy" problem that you read efficiently. Often you can read an abstract or summary of an article, thus determining whether or not you need to read the entire thing for details. Instead of reading an entire book, look in the index and table of contents for clues to what is pertinent. Skim rapidly until you find something of value to your group's special purpose. Then read carefully, taking notes of the most important ideas and facts. You may even want to make copies of certain passages or articles to share with other members of your group.

While reading in preparation for a learning discussion of a controversial issue you should read from as many contrasting interpretations or points of view as possible. Before discussing the relative merits of capital punishment, for example, you should study the writings of both those who favor and those who oppose it. *To learn, we must consider that which does not conform to our present beliefs.* We must perceive, accept, and adapt to new information and thinking. This is very difficult to do. We tend to listen to persons who believe as we do and to read only that which supports our present beliefs and values. We tend to be undercritical of such sources, and to be overly critical of sources that contradict us. It has been shown that we tend to forget evidence or beliefs inconsistent with our own.[7]

Interviews

When you can observe only a small part of an entire operation (for example, a nuclear reactor or the operation of a farm) or when you are not sufficiently knowledgeable to observe meaningfully, you may need to interview persons who are trained observers, highly experienced, and have firsthand contact with your subject. Members of the group that observed the operation of the campus coffee shop also interviewed a number of users to determine how they felt about its condition and to ask their reasons for busing or not busing their cups, waste paper, and leftover food. They also interviewed the manager to determine why certain materials that were sources of litter were being used. Members of the faculty constitution committee asked friends at other universities about how they thought their constitutions had worked in practice. Members of the bargaining team to which I belong have interviewed several highly experienced experts for advice not available in print about specific tactics and strategies. However, remember that busy persons who have written down their knowledge and ideas would prefer that you read first, then interview them to clarify or gather only information and ideas not yet publicly available.

If only a few persons need to be consulted, members of a group may want to conduct an in-depth interview with several open-ended questions designed to obtain responses bearing on the problem or topic. Open-ended questions will often elicit unexpected information that the interviewer would not have obtained in response to limited questions. If several group members will be interviewing a larger number of persons, each interviewer should have the same set of questions to ask, with forms on which to record the answers. If the questions have been properly planned the results can be tabulated and easily interpreted. For example, study the questions asked and the summary of answers reported in a newspaper carrying one of the national polls (such as those conducted by Gallup or Harris). One group of discussion students did a project to discover differences between first dates of approximately thirty years ago and today. They selected a sample of interviewees from two age groups, then asked all these persons the same set of questions:

1. Do you remember your first date? Yes _____ No _____

2. How old were you at the time of your first date? _____

3. How did you first become acquainted with the person you dated?

4. Was this a solo or double date?

5. If you remember, what did you do on this date?

6. Did you get a kiss on this date? Yes _____ No _____

It is invalid to generalize the findings from a casual or haphazard sample to a larger population of people. For example, interviews on some public issue with fifty people who walk past a particular street corner will not yield a valid picture about beliefs of all residents of that city, or even of people who happen to go downtown. Interviewing members of a class about some campus issue may yield a very distorted picture if projected to the entire student body. A scientifically designed sample (a representative sample) must be taken if results of interviews are to be projected with accuracy to all members of the population sampled. I urge you not to undertake a sample survey unless some member of your group has been trained as a survey researcher, perhaps in a research methods course. Then let that person design the sampling and interview procedures; other members of the group can follow this procedure when choosing persons to interview.

Other Sources of Information

Useful information may crop up anywhere, anytime. You may hear something important to your forthcoming discussion while listening to a radio or television program. Quite frequently lectures or speeches will be a source of information. An idea may occur to you when you are not consciously thinking about the problem—for example, while riding to work or school. You may be able to direct a conversation with friends to the problem your group is working on and thus get some surprising and helpful information and ideas. Most of us find it helpful to carry some sort of note-taking materials so we can jot down these things when they occur, lest we forget or distort them. The important thing is to be alert for unexpected and serendipitous information, and to record it promptly.

3. Evaluate the Information and Ideas You Have Collected

You will need to evaluate the information and ideas you have gathered in the light of all you have learned through individual research of the problem or subject for discussion. Many of your ideas may collapse in the presence of contradictory evidence. Some of your information may be spurious, from suspect sources, or in direct contradiction to other information. Some will be irrelevant to the problem facing the group. Now is the time to cull the misleading, false, suspect, unsubstantiated, or irrelevant so you will not misinform, confuse, or delay your group.

Distinguish between Statements of Fact and Inferences

It is especially important, both in gathering data and evaluating it during discussion, to distinguish between statements of fact and statements of inference, opinion, advice, preference, or definition.

The major difference between statements of fact and all other types of statements is that factual statements are *true* or *false* in a special sense of these terms. *A statement of fact* is a declarative sentence that refers to an *observation* of some event in the world. The event is described, and the statement includes or implies a method of observing by which the statement could be tested for truth or accuracy. It is a *true* statement of fact if accurate to the observed events, and can only refer to a *past* event actually observed. Facts either exist or do not exist; they are not discussable as such. The truth or validity of such a statement may or may not be directly verifiable. If the statement refers to a presently ongoing situation accessible to the group, it can be verified. If not, only the presence of the statement can be verified (that is, if the statement refers to something that is not continuing or is not accessible to the group). For example, we could not verify that George III occupied the throne of England in 1773—only that records indicate he was king. However, if several independent sources report the same information as fact, you can be more confident than if it comes from only one unverified source. You might not be able to directly verify the population of Australia, but only what the census report at a given date revealed. As benchmarks to help you recognize them, statements of fact:

are limited to description;

can be made only *after* observation;

are limited in the number that can be made;

if primary, can be made only by a direct observer;

are as close to certain as humans can get.

On the other hand, statements of opinion and inference:

go *beyond* what was directly observed;

can be made at any time without regard to observation;

are unlimited in the number that can be made about anything;

can be made by anyone, observer or not;

entail some degree of probability, of inferential risk, or uncertainty.

Statements of advice, taste, or preference do not refer to direct observation, but report a personal liking, choice, value, or taste of someone.

A few examples may help to clarify these differences:

Statements of Fact:
The population of Omaha recorded in the 1970 census was 363,421.
On June 3, 1976, Jack Egrat owned two cats.
The University Library contained 2,437,532 volumes in its catalog on
May 18, 1984.
After instituting lotteries, three states reduced their tax rates.
I-80 runs near both Cleveland and New York City.

Statements of Opinion and Inference:
Omaha is growing rapidly.
Jack Egart likes cats.
The heart of a good university is its library.
We should legalize gambling to reduce the state tax.
You will get to New York from Cleveland by following I-80 (not if you
have a wreck!).

Evaluating Survey and Statistical Data
Factual-type statements including statistics or the results of surveys need to be evaluated with special care for dependability. Surveying is a highly sophisticated operation, and must be done correctly or the results can be very misleading. If the results are not based on a random or other scientific sample,

the results of a survey are quite likely to be misleading. How questions are asked, and by whom, can make a very large difference in the results.[8]

Pay careful attention to statistics. Is the method explained by which the data used in computing the statistics were gathered? Is the method of computing averages or trends described and appropriate? Unless one of your group members is trained in statistical methods, before you accept statistical data as the basis for an important conclusion you should try to get a researcher/statistician to interpret and evaluate such information to avoid drawing erroneous conclusions. Unfortunately, persons sometimes lie when they write up "information," and some writers are not capable of evaluating their own reasoning from limited information.

Evaluating the Sources and Implications of Opinions

Occasionally a student, when first introduced to the differences between statements of fact and of opinion, tends to act as if statements of opinion are unwise or unnecessary in a discussion. Hardly so! As was said before, facts as such are not even discussable, but provide the basis for our discussions of what to do, what values to accept, etc. A group must not only deal with the world as it has been observed, but also determine priorities of value, ethics, goals, and procedures acceptable to all. Inferences must be made as to what will probably happen *if* we adopt each possible course of action. The facts regarding combustion pollution as they affect the environment and the use of resources must be examined, but what to do depends on values, opinions, and judgments acceptable to all if a rational law is to be adopted.

Unexamined opinions are poor guides to belief or action. Statements of inference and opinion cannot be tested for truth or falsity by direct observation as can statements of fact, but they can be evaluated for the degree of probability that they are valid and useful. First, you will want to consider the source of the opinion.

1. Is this person (or other source) a recognized expert on the subject? How do other experts in the field regard the person who expressed the opinion? If they hold differing opinions, how might these be explained?
2. Does the source have a vested interest that might have influenced this opinion? For example, think of the different opinions about whether or not the government should supply special funds to help a large corporation avoid bankruptcy that might be reached by an executive of the corporation, a labor leader of a union whose members work in the plants of the company, a politician trying to impress his constituents with how much he is reducing government spending, and an independent economist.
3. How well does the source support his or her opinion with documented evidence? Is the evidence well organized, with supporting statistics, tables, and clear reasoning?

4. How consistent is this opinion with others expressed by the source? If the statement is not consistent with other opinions and predictions from the same person, is there an acceptable explanation for the change?

Second, consider the *implications* of the opinion. To what further inferences or conclusions does it logically lead, and are these acceptable to the group? For example, a writer may argue that outlawing private ownership of handguns would protect us from accidents and murderers. What are the implications of this opinion? That dangerous devices should not be allowed in the hands of citizens at large? That only unessential dangerous tools that could be used as murder weapons should be restricted? That eventually all potential weapons of murder should be removed from citizens? That less innocent persons would be killed if handguns were taken from the public? Another writer may argue that anyone should be allowed to own a handgun after demonstrating competence in handling it safely and correctly and if the person has no felony record. What are the implications of that opinion? That only convicted felons will use handguns to kill other persons? That most accidents would be prevented if persons knew how to handle guns safely? That handguns are useful to many persons? Still another may argue that legislation controlling handgun ownership is not needed, but that stringent and certain punishment should be meted out to anyone using a handgun in the commission of a crime; that this would solve the "real problem" without creating new problems. What are the assumptions of this position? That the threat of certain punishment is an effective deterrent? That killings by handguns are acts of only criminal "types"? Probably you can detect many implications of each of the above opinions. The point is this—when a group decision depends on opinions, it is most important to *test* these opinions, especially for what they assume and imply. To do so is the essence of discussion. Not to do so is to assure very poor group decisions and policies.

4. Organize Your Information and Ideas

The most efficient and useful way to organize your knowledge is to write a tentative outline, using either a sequence for problem solving (see chapter 11) or one of the patterns for organizing a learning discussion (chapter 12). Ask yourself "What are the questions that must be answered by our group to arrive at a full understanding of the problem or subject?" The answers you are able to give to that question will serve as tentative main issues or points in your preparation outline.

With some tentative major issues you can now arrange your notes into piles, one per issue or possible outline heading. You may be able to further sub-divide some of the piles of notes into sub-headings. For example, information bearing on the nature of a problem might be arranged under the broad topics of "who is affected," "seriousness of the problem," "where the problem exists," "contributing causes," and so on. Organizing your information in such a way will give you a good idea of what is more or less important, suggest how to write your preparation outline, make it easier for you to locate pertinent notes when a topic comes up during the discussion, help you in preparing to ask questions that the group needs to consider, and generally assist you and your group in maintaining an orderly and comprehensive discussion of a complex subject.

When you are preparing for a problem-solving discussion your outline may contain some possible solutions you have found or thought of; doubtless it should. You may have some evidence and reasoning that shows how similar solutions were tried on similar problems. You may even have some suggestions on how to put a plan into effect, how to check to see if it works, and how to make adjustments. However, such thinking and planning is tentative. It is all too easy to become dogmatic on an issue after spending hours preparing to discuss it; it is absolutely essential that your mind be open. The worst sort of preparation is to go to a group discussion prepared to advocate a particular solution against all comers. Just as bad is to feel that one's personal definition and understanding of the problem is the complete problem. If researching and outlining make a participant closed-minded, it is better to remain ignorant. At least an ignorant person will not deadlock the group, and perhaps will listen and learn from others. Remember that the experts in almost any field, the persons at the very frontier of knowledge, are the least dogmatic and sure of themselves. From these persons the discussant who has read widely, thought long, and made a detailed outline should take heed. At the best he or she will now be prepared to contribute some reliable information, some ideas for testing in the forge of the group's collective knowledge and thinking, and perhaps most important, to listen with more understanding, to ask knowing questions, and thus to help shape an image of and a solution to the problem.

When preparing for a learning discussion you may or may not need to prepare an outline. Sometimes a study outline is supplied by a teacher or discussion moderator. For most academic discussions an outline will be quite helpful as a means to pre-sorting and clarifying your knowledge and thinking. Regardless, you will get much more from the discussion as well as be prepared to give more to your fellow learners-through-discussion if you write down the following kinds of items as they occur to you while doing any reading or other preparation:

Significant issues for the group to discuss;
Controversial points of view or policies that the group should examine;
Passages that are unclear, and any questions you want to raise;
How a proposition of a writer relates to his or her personal life and
    experience;
Any other related information or experience that comes to mind.

Summary

In this fourth chapter we have examined three major classes of input variables to the process of effective group discussion: the reason for forming the group, the physical setting, and informational resources.

Only to the extent that group members share an interdependent purpose to which they are seriously committed can small group discussions be productive. Often the purpose of a small group is assigned by some parent organization in the form of a "charge." The charge and the area of freedom it implies must be clear to and accepted by all members, or frustration and some degree of failure are inevitable. Group purpose can frequently be formulated as a group goal question of interpretation, value, or policy. Classroom groups need to be especially clear and realistic when wording their group goal questions.

A meeting place conducive to discussion is free from distractions, comfortable, provides discussants with a face-to-face view of each other, reflects the egalitarian relationship among participants, and includes facilities that might be needed for group recording and individual note taking. A circular seating pattern is ideal.

Clear objectives and ideal physical facilities only set the stage for effective group discussions. Adequate informational resources are the grist on which the mill of discussion grinds; the output can be no better than the information and ideas put into a discussion. Such resources come from discussants who have made the effort to be well armed with information, ideas, and questions. Groups dealing with extensive problems need to devote initial planning to how they will obtain such materials and assign responsibility for their acquisition. Members can begin by reviewing and organizing what they already know. Then they will need to compile a bibliography of sources and to do the observing, reading, interviewing, note taking, and outlining required to obtain, evaluate, and organize information. A preparation outline will usually make it possible to gain perspective on a large mass of information, raise needed questions, and help locate notes when they are relevant to the issues being discussed. To fail to prepare thoroughly for discussions is to prepare to fail in achieving the objectives for which they are held.

Exercises

1. Describe a committee with which you are personally familiar that had trouble because the members ignored their area of freedom, or otherwise violated their charge. How did the parent organization react? If you have a chance to share your example with several classmates, see what guidelines for small group work you can deduce from your examples.

2. To what extent do you agree that an interdependent purpose is necessary for any small group? Explain the reason(s) for your answer.

3. Plan how to arrange your regular classroom (or other meeting room) for a problem-solving discussion by the entire class. Then make a diagram for seating members of your class for three or four simultaneous small group discussions in the same room.

4. Your instructor may give you an essay or a segment of a discussion to analyze for statements of fact, inference, and taste or value. Classify each statement as to type; ignore statements that do not fit into any of these three categories. If you classify a statement as one of fact, indicate whether or not it could be verified, and how such verification could be accomplished.

5. In class, select a topic or problem of interest to all. Then:
   a. Prepare a bibliography of references on the topic, keeping a record of all the bibliographic sources you used;
   b. Prepare yourself to discuss the subject, including a detailed outline and the note cards from all the sources you consulted. These may be submitted to your instructor following the discussion. Be sure your outline contains all the questions you can think of that must be answered by the group to fully understand the problem, arrive at common goals and values, and reach a decision.

Bibliography

Babbie, Earl R. *The Practice of Social Research.* 2d ed., Belmont, Calif.: Wadsworth Publishing Company, 1979, ch. 12. This chapter presents a clear and complete explanation of survey research.

Burgoon, Judee K. "Spatial Relationships in Small Groups," in *Small Group Communication: A Reader,* 4th ed., Cathcart, Robert S., and Samovar, Larry A., eds., Dubuque, Iowa: Wm. C. Brown Company Publishers, 1984, 276–292.

References

1. Mary Ann Strider, "The Non-Group Meeting," unpublished paper, 1974.
2. J. Bilodeau and H. Schlosberg, "Similarity in Simulating Conditions As a Variable in Retroactive Inhibition," *Journal of Experimental Psychology* 41 (1959): 199–204; A. Maslow and N. L. Mintz, "Effects of Esthetic Surroundings: I. Initial Effects of Three Esthetic Conditions upon Perceived 'Energy' and 'Well-being' in Faces," *Journal of Psychology* 41 (1956): 247–54; N. L. Mintz, "Effects of Esthetic

Surroundings: II. Prolonged and Repeated Experience in a 'Beautiful' and an 'Ugly' Room," *Journal of Psychology* 41 (1956): 459–66.

3. Robert Sommer, "The Distance for Comfortable Conversation: A Further Study," *Sociometry* 25 (1962): 111–16.

4. A. Paul Hare and R. F. Bales, "Seating Position and Small Group Interaction," *Sociometry* 26 (1963): 480–86.

5. John G. Geier, "A Trait Approach to the Study of Leadership in Small Groups," in *Small Group Communication: A Reader,* Robert S. Cathcart and Larry A. Samovar, eds. (Dubuque, Iowa: Wm. C. Brown Company Publishers, 1970), 414.

6. R. Victor Harnack, T. B. Fest, and B. S. Jones, *Group Discussion: Theory and Technique,* 2d ed. (Englewood Cliffs, N.J.: Prentice-Hall, 1977), 119.

7. Sir Frederic Bartlett, *Thinking: an Experimental and Social Study* (New York: Basic Books, 1958).

8. If you are interested in reading about scientific sampling and survey procedures likely to produce results representative of a large population (such as the Gallup poll usually achieves), see Earl R. Babbie, *The Practice of Social Research,* 2nd ed. (Belmont, CA: Wadsworth Publishing Company, 1979), chapter 12.

5

development of a group

Study Objectives

As a result of your study of chapter 5, you should be able to:

1. List and explain four phases through which most small groups pass, and describe the activities and processes most prevalent during each phase.

2. Explain the sources, characteristics, and some correctives for both primary and secondary interpersonal tensions among group members.

3. Distinguish between formal rules and informal norms of small groups, and be able to recognize, clarify, and adapt to both in small groups to which you belong.

4. Explain group member roles and how they develop, and the types of behavioral functions which comprise roles.

5. Describe three communication networks common in small groups and the impact of each on both throughput and output.

6. Explain the formation of a status hierarchy and the impact of status differences on group process and output.

7. Use control mode arrows to represent efforts by group members to establish different control modes with each other.

8. Explain cohesiveness, list ways to measure it, and describe six techniques for enhancing it in a small group.

Key Terms

Behavioral function (behavior)   how an act or behavior of a small group member affects the group.

Cohesiveness   the degree of attraction members feel for the group; unity.

Control mode   control or power relationship with other(s) suggested by a group member's statements and nonverbal behaviors, specifically for dominance, submission, or equality.

Fantasy chain   a series of statements by members of a discussion group in which they dramatize a story about other persons in other places and times, in order to create a social reality, norms, and shared values.

Network of communication   the interpersonal channels open to the flow of messages within a small group; collectively, who in the group may (or does) talk to whom.

Norm   an informal rule of conduct or guideline for behavior of members of a group, usually unwritten and unstated.

Phase   stage in the development and history of a small group.

Primary tension   social unease that occurs when members of a new group first meet or at beginning of meetings of a long-term group.

Role   a pattern of behavior displayed by and expected of a member of a small group; a composite of the behavioral functions performed relatively frequently by a member.

Rule   a statement prescribing how members of a society, organization, or small group must or should behave; may be stated formally in writing, or be unstated and informal, as in the case of norms.

Secondary tension   tension and discomfort experienced by members of a group from conflict over values, points of view, and alternative solutions.

Self-oriented behavior   any act of a small group member that is motivated by personal needs rather than the needs of the group.

Social or maintenance behaviors   member acts that primarily serve to reduce tensions, increase solidarity, and facilitate teamwork rather than accomplishing the work of the group.

Status   position of a member in the hierarchy of power, influence and prestige within a small group; initially attributed by other members on the basis of personal characteristics, then earned on the basis of performance as a group member.

Task behavior   any act of a member that primarily contributes to accomplishing the goal of that group.

In this chapter we begin consideration of the *process* or *throughput* variables of small groups. Group characteristics dealt with in this and the next several chapters can be considered as both throughputs and outputs, for the development of functioning processes is one of the accomplishments—outputs—of small group interaction. Our vantage point will be from a *system* level, rather than from that of an individual member; member behaviors will be studied from the perspective of their impact on the processes of the small group as a whole. In this fifth chapter attention will be given to how a small group develops into a functioning system from what was initially a collection of individuals with some common concern. In following chapters, some of the most important group throughput variables will be examined: communication among members and with parent organizations, leadership, decision making, conflict management, and problem solving. But in the present chapter our concern is with how small groups develop through time.

Phases in the Development of Small Groups

Researchers have studied how small human groups develop and change through time. As a general rule there are gradual changes in the way the group system functions, but some very abrupt changes can also be observed. Any demarcation into distinct phases is somewhat arbitrary: the decision of when a group has moved from one phase to another, and even of how many phases there may be, depends on the person doing the observing and classifying of phases or stages. However, all small groups do pass through several stages or phases in their life history, the exact sequence depending on the primary purpose of the group's interaction and other variables. Time is certainly an important variable for understanding any group. A group that is meeting for the first time is no more the same as a group that has functioned for weeks, months, or years than is a small child the same as the teen-ager or adult that child will become.

Single-meeting groups differ from most standing committees and other types of groups which meet for several or more discussions. The one-meeting group has no chance to develop a history, regular procedures and rituals, or extensive rules. Except for stereotypes and previous contacts with other participants in different group contexts, there is little basis on which to predict each other's behavior. Since there is no future for the group, there is no need to build cohesiveness. Models of group development have little relevance. An assigned discussion leader will usually be accepted willingly unless he or she is totally incompetent. With little time to spare, members usually accept the designated discussion leader's statements about the purpose and procedures for the meeting. If the leader has an agenda or outline to follow, the group will likely do so with gratitude.

When members know that their purpose will require them to meet numerous times, they will take time to get organized, moving through a series of phases in the life history of the group. First comes a period of *formation* during which the group will not readily follow any agenda or problem-solving procedure. Even though it may appear on the surface that the discussion is about facts of a problem, objectives, and possible alternatives, the real agenda item will be the development of a group structure: roles for members (especially, who will be our primary leader), status relations, norms to govern behavior, shared values, general procedures for decision making and problem solving, who will interact with whom and in what ways, shared objectives, and so forth. This period of time may seem like aimless milling around to an untrained observer. But after such relational issues have been resolved to some degree, the group will go into a *production* phase characterized by much compiling of information, suggesting of courses of action, and more or less open conflict until decisions emerge. Depending on the degree to which the group achieved a stable structure of roles, norms, and procedures, there may be continual cycling between serious work and problems of interpersonal relations, with the group seeming to have to begin anew at many meetings. Whenever there is some change in membership of a continuing group, considerable reforming must be done. A more stable group will move forward from problem to problem with great dispatch, spending relatively little time on matters of value, procedure, role, and interpersonal relationships.

Invariably there will be some cycling through time between matters of work to be done and group maintenance (socioemotional relationships). Every problem-solving group has both task and social dimensions to be dealt with through discussion. By 1950 Bales had analyzed all group member behaviors as being primarily concerned with either task or socioemotional matters.[1] Tuckman found both issues of group task and formation occupying a group during its formative period. These are not totally separable, but the emphasis will shift from social relations to task as a group becomes more organized through time.[2]

Tuckman reviewed a large number of studies of phases in the development of several types of small groups. From a wide variety of different phases described by observers of therapy, encounter, learning, and problem-solving groups he synthesized a four-phase theory of group development applicable to all small groups. He chose rhyming words to stand for these four stages.[3] The first three phases entail more development of group structure and process than producing as a group.

Phase 1: **Forming**—During the initial stage a collection of people attempts to develop into a group with a sense of interdependence of purpose and membership; also called the "orientation" phase by several writers. While "forming" is going on the discussants are sizing each other up, trying to decide how each will act and react, what the attitudes, skills and competencies of other members may be, and whether or not to make a personal commitment to the group. Collectively, there is likely to be much talking about goals, "where we are going." A structure of norms and roles (including leadership) begins to emerge.

Phase 2: **Storming**—During this phase the interaction is likely to be marked by a great deal of conflict about information, the nature of the task facing the group, and how to achieve it. At a different level this phase involves a struggle for power, influence, and leadership roles. There will be considerable open resistance to influence by other members and what appear to be majorities, with few or no members willing to support the suggestions of others. In some groups the struggle for position may be very brief and subdued. In others it will be lengthy and noisy. It may seem that nothing is being accomplished with so much open conflict, but the groundwork for later cooperation and coordination is being laid. Small groups created by such hierarchical organizations as manufacturing and marketing firms usually test their appointed leaders for suitability during this phase of group development.

Phase 3: **Norming**—In this phase the group works out definite ways of proceeding, guidelines or rules for member conduct, and standards for evaluating their decisions. There is likely to be much open expression of opinions, now marked by considerably more agreeing with each other than in phase 2. In place of strong positions of individuality common in phase 2 are efforts to reduce conflict. If the group is going to be productive, a structure of roles and statuses emerges, along with a high degree of cohesiveness.

Phase 4: **Performing**—Behaviors will now be centered on accomplishing the tasks for which the group was created. Work will be performed, often at a high rate of efficiency. Decisions will be made about what solution to recommend or implement. Actions will be planned and carried out. Little effort will be focused on group formation and maintenance.

The amount of time spent on each of the phases of group development may vary greatly from group to group. Some groups spend a long time forming, and some never seem to get fully organized with a consensus on who is leader. In other groups, storming may be minimal, with a few minor disagreements over such matters as meeting times, agenda items, or procdures for doing something, but the group rather rapidly gets on to the next phase of its development. Norming may go on concurrently with considerable performing. I have participated in and observed numerous groups in which all three of the formation phases were accomplished to a large degree in the first two meetings of a group that held ten, twenty, or even more meetings.

It is important to be aware that these phases in the development of a small collection of people into a group system are not at all related to the stages or steps in problem solving, although some writers have confused the two. Once a group has developed into an operating system (or organism), it may repeatedly go through the problem-solving procedure it developed during the norming phase of its development. Each new problem addressed by the group will see a recycling through the steps of some problem-solving procedure, just as a computer repairperson goes through pretty much the same steps over and over again in solving the problems encountered with malfunctioning computers.

Tuckman's interests as a social psychologist and his objective of finding similar phases in the life histories of groups with divergent major purposes may have led him to label three of the four phases with words concerning social relations. Actually, productive task work, producing the groundwork for a final group solution, may be going on in these phases. In that sense "performing" is occurring to some degree in all phases of the group's life. The important thing for the beginning student of small group dynamics is to be aware that it is *typical* for groups to move through various stages, as it is for all human relationships, from a phase in which identification of common interests and a basis for cooperation and trust is laid down, to an exploration of various alternatives, to a period of time in which there is rapid goal achievement. Long-term groups will tend to spiral somewhat through these phases, going back over the periods of forming, storming, and norming from meeting to meeting, as new problems and members are introduced into the group system, and as other components of the small group system change through time. Such a spiralling through growth and work stages should be no surprise, for it is characteristic of all living systems as the cycles of the season, growth phases, and repeated environmental problems arise. Scheidel and Crowell showed that there is even a spiral-like progression during the time when many groups consider and evaluate each possible course of action as a solution to their problem.[4] This spiralling through phases is illustrated in figure 5.1, showing progressively shorter orientation phases (forming, storming, and norming) and relatively longer performing (task) stages as the group develops. The arrows intersecting the loops of the spiral represent the introduction of something new into the small group system.

Tensions among Members

All of us have experienced many moments of high tension: we feel nervous, irritable, tight, pressured, and strained. Commercials have dramatized the "nervous tension headache" and its accompanying symptoms. The unduly tense person may experience sweaty palms, strained muscles, a lot of twitching, a swinging foot, tapping fingers, looking around instead of at others, etc. Optimal levels of tension (or stress) help us to perform at peak capacity—to run four-minute miles, to speak in public with unusual animation and verve, or to pass a football with an incredible sense of timing. Too little tension and we perform listlessly. Too much tension and we become unproductive, uncoordinated, and unable to think or speak clearly.

Figure 5.1   The process of group development and redevelopment through time.

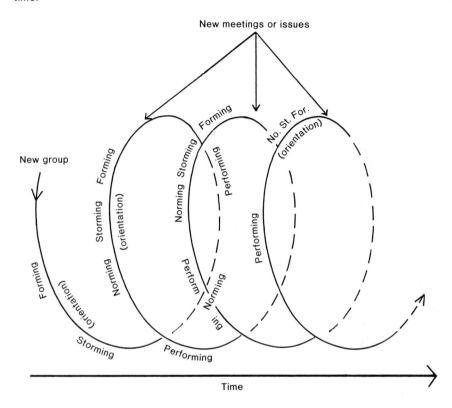

Just as individuals experience varying levels of tension, so do entire groups, with virtually every member keyed up and contributing to a high level of performing, bogged down in apathy, or feeling strained and uncomfortable. Of course the tension is experienced by the individual members, but when all simultaneously experience levels of tension that detract from efficient performing, we have a group tension problem. Levels of group tension vary through time, often in somewhat rhythmic and predictable cycles.

Primary Tension

Bormann first classified distressing levels of tension into two categories: *primary* and *secondary*. *Primary tension* is his name for ". . . the social unease and stiffness that accompanies getting acquainted. . . . The earmarks of primary tension are extreme politeness, apparent boredom or tiredness, and considerable sighing and yawning. When members show primary tension, they speak softly and tentatively. Frequently they can think of nothing to say, and many long pauses result."[5] As you have doubtless concluded, primary tension is the result of not knowing what to expect from persons trying to form a group. This tension will abate as the group forms a structure of roles, norms, and procedures. The need is to learn what to expect of other members, what is and is not safe to say and do, and how to behave. To paraphrase the title of a well-known song, it is a matter of "getting to know us, getting to know all about us." Since the group is as yet largely unstructured, relative power, statuses, and roles are at stake. People realize that they are being judged on how they participate. The apparent boredom and disinterest is only a façade. Virtually every member is vitally interested in how she will be judged, what role she will be given in the group, and what these people will be like to work with. This primary tension must be reduced or the group may get stuck in a mold of formality, hesitancy, and posing, with members not feeling free to speak openly and frankly, or comfortable enough with each other to concentrate on the tasks for which they have been assembled.

There is much that can be done to reduce primary tensions, and to hasten the time when the group functions smoothly with social tension at a minimal level—members at ease, comfortable with each other. This can be achieved even if members are not fond of each other as persons; they can at least know how to predict and relate to one another as parts of a secondary group. Members of one-meeting groups cannot afford the time needed to get well acquainted with each other, but groups that will meet often will be wise to do so. Very early in the life of a continuing group it pays to deal directly with primary tensions: take time to talk about who each person is, ask each other questions, air differences in feelings and backgrounds, chat about hobbies and interests, maybe even have a social hour or party. Joking, laughing together, and finding common ground of interests, acquaintances, and beliefs are helpful in reducing primary tensions—thus developing a sense of togetherness and trust that no one in the group will take advantage of others.

Don't expect members of a continuing group to get to work on the agenda at the very start of each new meeting, either. Even groups with considerable history experience some amount of primary tension at the start of each meeting. Members need to confirm where they stand with each other, to reaffirm their relationships, and that each is accepted as a unique individual. Thus a brief period of "ventilation," chitchat, or small talk is needed before getting down to work, often before the meeting is "called to order" by a designated leader.

Once the high level of primary tension has been reduced so that members can quit worrying about each other, it is time for a task group to get to work. The designated leader should try to sense when this has occurred, and err on the side of focusing on the group purpose too soon rather than too late.

Secondary Tension

Secondary tension results from differences of opinion among members as they seek to do the work of the group. High levels of secondary tension are inevi-

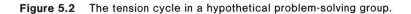

Figure 5.2   The tension cycle in a hypothetical problem-solving group.

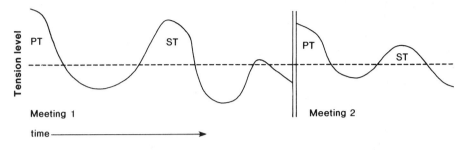

Key: PT—primary tension
     ST—secondary tension
     - - - - level of tension, above which group is inefficient

table as people differ over their perceptions of a problem, disagree about goals and means for achieving them, and criteria by which to evaluate their ideas. Secondary tensions are a direct result of the need to make decisions. Any conflict produces some tension. The phases in group development called "storming," "norming," and "performing" will all entail some secondary tension, likely at unpredictable times to become uncomfortably high and debilitating to group production. The signs of elevated tension from conflicts are quite different from those of primary tension. Voices get loud and strained. There may be long pauses, followed by two or more persons trying to talk at once. Members twist and fidget in their seats, bang on the table, wave their arms, or even get up and pace around the room. They may try to shout each other down. They may at times even call each other names, or aggressively question each other's intelligence or motives. While a couple members attack each other, the rest of the group may sit stiffly and awkwardly by, not knowing what to do.

Throughout its lifespan a group will cycle from periods of high to low tension among members, and periods of high to low productivity. Figure 5.2 represents such cycling in a hypothetical group. Above the dotted line are periods of high tension, while periods of high production are below the line.

Some groups try to ignore secondary tensions because dealing with them is often difficult, uncomfortable, or even painful. A group may dodge the issue of a clash over values or means to a goal. They try to stick to what seems a "safe" area of discussion, doing the job of the group. But as Bormann says, "The problem, however, never goes away, and if ignored or dodged will continue to . . . impede their progress. Facing up to secondary tensions realistically is the best way to release them."[6]

In his analysis of functions performed by group members, Bales determined that three categories of behaviors reduced tensions among members.

He called these types "shows agreement," "shows solidarity," and "shows tension release." *Showing agreement* is socially rewarding to the person agreed with. Agreeing with another member shows support for the person, as if having said "I value you and your opinion." People who have been agreed with show much more confidence than those who have not been agreed with, sticking to minority opinions when they are factually correct much longer than if not given support.[7] The more often people agree and are agreed with openly, the more they relax and communicate positively with each other.

A member can *show solidarity* by any act or statement of commitment to the group. Speaking of "we," speaking well of another member, offering to help, expressing confidence in the group, and speaking of how important the group and what it is doing are to the speaker all show solidarity and encourage other members to move away from the self-centeredness and antagonism. Such statements as "Let's all remember that we are in this together," or "We're *all* trying to come up with the best possible plan," and "Let's not forget how much we've accomplished" can be helpful in the control of secondary tension by enhancing the solidarity of the group.

Many things can be done to *release tensions* when they get too high. Sometimes humor may help, so long as the disagreement producing the tension is not then ignored. Enjoying a joke together and laughing as one often seems to make it easier to listen better and find agreement. In *Pattern for Industrial Peace,* Whyte described how a union staff representative did this repeatedly by using fishing photos whenever discussion among representatives of the steel company and union got overheated with secondary tension.[8] The important principle here is that nobody must seem to win at the expense of the others—losers remain tense.

Groups successful in managing secondary tensions develop high levels of cohesiveness. They can afford to disagree openly with each other, even though disagreements strain relationships somewhat, because they have built strong commitments to each other, a degree of trust in one another as members who will not "pull out" or engage in personal attacks because they do not get their way. Some groups develop procedures for managing the secondary tensions associated with disagreement over goals, values and solutions. Among these procedures are the Nominal Group Technique (NGT) in which decisions are made by anonymous voting, having some member serve as the "devil's advocate" to challenge and disagree with popular ideas, and intentionally inviting in non-group persons who are known to oppose the majority position. Somehow the group must encourage disagreement and open argument in order to test interpretations and ideas, yet limit tension to the threshhold where members can listen well, think clearly, and remain productive in discussions. When conflict becomes intense, it is best dealt with by techniques explained in chapter 10.

Rules and Norms

In order for people to work together there must be rules to guide and govern behavior. For example, we have rules about who can do what, when, and under what conditions in an automobile on public streets. In assemblies of large groups, formal rules of procedure govern how members get the floor to speak, what they can say, when they can say it, how to say it, to whom they may speak, and so on. *Robert's Rules of Order, Newly Revised,* is specified by many organizations as a code of rules governing face-to-face interaction.[9] Robert also developed a code of rules applicable to committees of every organization which adopts Robert's rules as its parliamentary authority; these rules are imposed on any committee of a parent organization which adopts *Robert's Rules of Order.* We create such rules to establish fairness and equity in our discussions with each other, to make interaction more predictable, and maintain order.

A number of parliamentary rules are necessary to accomplish the work of large deliberative groups (25 or more members). But even in large groups, the amount of detail and formality in parliamentary procedure should be adjusted to the size, sophistication, and amount of conflict within the assembly. The member of a committee (or other small group) who keeps uttering "second the motion," "point of order," "question," or "I move to table the motion" may either be showing off or is ignorant of the basic purpose of parliamentary law and of rules of order that apply to small groups.

Committees may have formal rules governing them created in the bylaws or other documents of a parent organization. Any such rule takes the place of any of Robert's rules with which it clashes. Because Robert's rules specifically written for committees are legally in force when an organization has adopted Robert, I have summarized them here for your convenience.

1. The chairperson of a committee may be appointed by the parent organization, that organization can specify that the committee is to elect its own chair, or else the first person named to the committee is automatically the chair, under Robert's rules.
2. A committee meets on call of its chairperson or any two members.
3. The "quorum" (minimum number of members who must be at a meeting in order for the committee to take any legal action) is a simple majority of the number of members, unless specified otherwise by the parent organization.
4. The chairperson is responsible for records of the committee, and writes its minutes or reports unless a separate secretary position is created in the committee. This is quite common in large committees. If a professional secretary from the parent organization is assigned to keep records, the chair is still responsible for these records, and so should supervise and sign them.

5. Members do not need to obtain permission from the chair by formal recognition before speaking or making a motion. They may speak up whenever they want, so long as they do not rudely interrupt another.

6. Motions do not need a second. A motion is a proposal to take some action as a group.

7. There is no limit on how many times a member can speak on an issue, and motions to limit or close discussion are never appropriate.

8. Informal discussion is permitted with no motion pending. In a parliamentary assembly a formal motion must be made before an issue can be discussed. In committee, usually no motion is made until *after* consensus or at least a majority has been achieved through extended discussion.

9. A majority vote (of those actually voting) is required before any decision can be said to be made by a committee. Usually a vote is taken to confirm a decision already sensed by the group, so the decision is actually by consensus. "Straw" votes can be taken at any time to determine if a majority or consensus exists before taking a binding vote. The leader might say: "Let's see how we stand on this. Would all who favor it please raise your right hand."

10. When a proposal is clear to all members, a vote can be taken and the outcome recorded as a decision even though no motion has been introduced.

11. The chairperson can ask if all members "consent" or agree with an idea or proposal. Then if no one objects, the decision has been made and is reported in the minutes—for example, "It was decided by consent that we should have Jean and Bob draft a resolution to present at the next meeting of the club."

12. Committee chairpersons can speak up in a discussion, taking a stand on a controversial issue, without leaving the chair. They can also make motions and vote on all questions as do all other members of the committee. (In some large committees it may be decided that the chairperson will act as if in a large assembly, and then he or she should do so *at all times,* voting only to make or break a tie, and not participating in the substance of the discussion.)

13. A motion to "reconsider" a previous vote can be made at any time, and there is no limit on how many times a question can be reconsidered. Unlike in a parliamentary body, any person who did not vote with the losing side can move to reconsider. Thus a person who was absent or who did not vote can ask for the reconsideration of a previous decision or vote if the action has not yet been carried out.

14. Motions can be amended in committee, but this is best done informally, voting on the proposed change in a motion only if it cannot be decided by consensus in the time available for a meeting.

15. Many of the motions required in an assembly are irrelevant; a member can discuss virtually anything informally in committee sessions, so there is no need for points of order, motions to table, or matters of personal privilege. In short, the bulk of what is called "parliamentary law" is not needed and can even be obstructive to committee deliberations and actions.

16. Formal reports of committees should contain only what was agreed to by a vote of at least a majority of those present at a regular and properly called (notice given each member) meeting at which a quorum was present. Usually the chairperson makes formal reports from a committee in writing. Reports of less formal actions or work in progress may be given orally to a parent organization. If a committee is unable to reach consensus and a minority of its membership wants to make a report or recommendation different from that of the majority, it usually is permitted to do so as soon as the "majority" committee report has been made. This is not a *right* of a committee minority, but of course during debate under parliamentary rules the members who did not agree with the majority position can speak their opposition. However, no one has the right to allude to what happened during the committee's private discussions unless the entire committee has agreed that this is to be permitted.

In summary, only a minimum of rules of order and precedence is required in committees of organizations which have adopted *Robert's Rules of Order, Newly Revised*. Voting is done to show that a legal majority supported all reported findings, recommendations and actions, but not to shut off discussion or suggest that majority is the best way of making decisions by a committee. Any issue within the freedom of the committee can be brought up for discussion at any time, and discussion of it can be quite informal and as lengthy as is needed.

Norms

Not all rules governing social interaction are formally enacted or imposed by the authority of an organization within which a small group exists. Sociologists have for decades studied the nature of informal rules governing social behavior, called *norms*. A **norm** is a rule that is usually not written down or even stated as such, and it certainly is not imposed on a group from above. Rather, as Homans stated well, a norm is ". . . an idea in the minds of the members of a group, an idea that can be put in the form of a statement specifying what the members or other (people) should do, ought to do, are expected to do, under given circumstances."[10] Norms are enforced by "peer pressure," not by authorities. As members of small groups we need to be aware of and concerned about both the rules imposed on the group by some authority (such as a parent organization or governmental agency) and those informal rules—norms—imposed by members on themselves and each other. To be unaware of norms leads to violations by the uninformed member, with consequent punishment, loss of influence, and even exclusion from the group.

Norms reflect cultural beliefs about what is good or bad, proper or improper, wise or foolish. The norms of a small group are the major variable of its unique culture, yet for the most part they will be a reflection of the larger culture (way of life) of the society and organization in which the small group is embedded. As Shimanoff stated, "When group members come together for the first time, they bring with them past experiences and expectations regarding cultural and social rules and rules for specific groups they assume may be similar to this new group. It is out of these experiences and expectations as well as its unique interaction . . . that a particular group formulates its rules."[11]

Norms both guide and regulate behavior of group members. They govern how and to whom members speak, how they dress, where and how they sit, what they talk about, what language may be used, and so on. Indeed, the whole process of communication among members is rule (norm) governed.[12] All norms are evaluative, indicating what ought and ought not be done, what is to be rewarded and what is to be scorned. Rarely do norms specify absolutes, but ranges of acceptable and unacceptable member behaviors. For instance, a norm governing supportive behaviors might indicate that members should *show* agreement with each other when they do indeed agree, but this might be done loudly in words, softly by nodding the head, making the OK sign with thumb and forefinger, or by some other symbol or signal of support for what was done previously.

During the developmental stage of a new small group, norms are developed rapidly, often without the members realizing what is occurring. The first meeting is quite important in establishing norms, especially the first few minutes. At that time, behaviors that are typical of primary tension can become norms if the tension is not released early—speaking softly, being extremely polite, avoiding questioning the sources of another's information, or even opinionated and dogmatic ways of stating beliefs can become norms if not challenged. Members may openly discuss and state rules at initial meetings, but more typically norms evolve through time without any discussion being focused on them. Many norms seem to be below the level of consciousness of most members, yet they adhere to these norms as if they were laws and expect others to comply with them. A norm can be brought to a level of awareness when someone violates it, a new member questions it, or an observer states the norm openly as an apparent rule of the group.

Group norms may or may not be stated openly, but they can be detected by a keen observer. In many cases the observer must infer a norm from behaviors of group members. If all members manifest a particular type of act that is strong evidence that a norm encouraging or requiring such behavior exists. The best evidence of all comes when someone acts contrary to a norm and is then punished in some way by the group. For example, others may frown, fail to respond, comment negatively about the behavior, or even scold the violator: "Let's stick to the issues and not go blaming one another." Every norm has some impact on a group's productivity and member satisfaction. The norms that are counterproductive or reduce satisfaction need to be changed.

Norms may provide expectations about the behavior of either selected individuals (role-specific norms) or all group members. Members of a group share in the expectation that both types of norms will be complied with. Perhaps examples of each type will help you understand them. Notice that these norms are stated as rules, even though not imposed on a group by some parent organization or administrator.

General Norms (applicable to every member of the group)
"Members should sit in the same position at each meeting."
"Members should address each other only by first names."
"Other members should not disagree with the President's ideas."
"No one may smoke during meetings."
"Members may leave the table to get a cup of coffee or soft drink, but
should return to their places promptly after doing so."
"Members need not shake hands during the preliminaries to a meeting."

Role-Specific Norms
"The leader should prepare and distribute an agenda in advance of each
meeting."
"The leader should summarize from time to time, but other members may
do so if the leader does not when a summary is needed."
"Mary may play the critical tester of all ideas, asking for evidence, pointing
out logical fallacies, and otherwise evaluating."
"Mike should tell a joke to relieve secondary tension when the climate gets
stressful from an argument over different points of view."

Adherence to procedural norms is essential if members are to work together. Most discussants will conform to procedural norms of a group. A violation may mean that the norm was not understood by the violator or that she or he disagrees with it. If a procedural norm is clearly understood but still violated by one or more members, this should be called to the attention of the group and some action taken. Continued violation means the member feels the norm is somehow detrimental. Here are two procedural norms typical of effective group discussions: "Members should stick to the agenda, unless all agree to change it." "Members should not interrupt each other."

Most of the norms exemplified above are beneficial to groups which interact according to them. Although it is necessary for groups to have rules which coordinate behaviors, rules—both formal and informal—can be irrelevant or even detrimental to the output of groups. In some groups a norm precluding disagreement with high status members interferes with realistic evaluation of ideas. Groups which have a norm permitting criticism of ideas as soon as they have been proposed may find that innovative, creative ideas are rarely proposed. Groups in which some members are addressed by titles while others are addressed by first names may get little input or productive work from the first-name members. A group in which it is acceptable to belittle or ridicule may find members dropping out or showing very low commitment to the group. It is obvious that a small group needs to pay some attention to the norms that emerge, and be able and willing to change those which appear to be an impediment to goal achievement.

Both formal rules and informal norms may be complied with only to the degree they are enforced. Member enforcement and compliance depends on how well members understand the norms, the relative importance of a specific rule or norm, the value the member places on the group, relative status in the group, and the punishments imposed for breaking a rule. Members generally place more importance on norms which relate directly to the purpose of the group than on those more tangential to the group's purpose. Norms of a fraternity might require members to be friendly and outgoing; however, such behavior would probably be permitted but not required of members of a bomber crew. Accurate reporting will be required of members of a research team, but not likely of a group of fishermen. A student project group literally threw out of the recording studio one member who had not shown up for rehearsals of the radio production it was preparing. A faculty member who misses an office hour will not likely be rebuked by colleagues; one who misses assigned classes will probably receive some negative reactions; one who harrasses students will be virtually excommunicated or even voted out of the department.

Sanctions for rule violations vary with one's status in a group. The higher one's status the more one is free to violate minor rules but the more one must conform to major rules. President Nixon was forced out of office for lying in an attempt to cover up a burglary done by members of his staff, whereas minor officials in government agencies have been allowed to retain their jobs after similar crimes. Only stone-cold sober members of an Alcoholics Anonymous chapter can lead a meeting, but members who have slipped and had a few drinks can attend the meeting. A new member who doesn't yet understand a norm of a standing committee may be taken aside and told gently "We don't do things that way here," then advised about how to act in the future. An old hand violating the same norm might be punished severely.

Compliance with norms of a small group determines one's acceptance and favorable evaluation by other members, how much influence one earns in the group, and how rewards are distributed among members. Thus it is vital to new members that they quickly determine the rules, both formal and informal, when admitted to an ongoing group, and that any member be able to identify norms that are interfering with group goal achievement so they can be discussed and possibly changed. Group norms cannot be observed directly; they are not posted somewhere for all to read. Nonetheless, they can be inferred with confidence by a keen observer.

To help learn the norms of a continuing group, a newcomer can ask old members what the rules are. But many norms will not be part of the awareness of members. You can, however, infer and confirm these rules from observations you make while serving as a member of the group. New members of continuing groups are usually expected *not* to be active participants at first, a norm which allows time to observe and learn the group's norms. There are two types of behaviors to watch for especially:

1. Behaviors which occur repeatedly and with regularity, either by one member or by all members. As Shimanoff pointed out, "Because members usually conform to a group's rules, rule-generated behavior reoccurs."[13] Repetitions of a behavior are evidence that a norm may exist to govern it. Thus you should look for answers to such questions as: "Who talks to whom?" "How do members speak?" "With what kinds of language?" "About what?" "For how long?" "Where do they sit?" "How do they dress?" "When do they move about, how, and for what reasons?" "How is the group brought to order?"
2. Punishment of a member for infraction of a norm (possibly one you have tentatively inferred). The strongest evidence of a norm is negative sanction (negative reaction or punishment) directed at a member who violates it. A somewhat weaker support for the existence of a norm is provided when a violator corrects himself, and this correction is given approval by other members. Thus you want to look for negative reactions to preceeding actions, ranging all the way from a bit of head shaking to forceful negative comments or even threats of violence. Notice behaviors which are reacted to with gestures of rejection, such as head shaking, frowns, tongue clucking, and sidewise glances. What acts do members seem to studiously ignore (as if the person being reacted to were not there)? Listen for negative comments such as "It's about time you got here!" and "Maybe you will have your report ready for our *next* meeting." A negative response from only one person may not be a sanction for violation of a norm, but if more than one person responds negatively you can be almost certain that a norm has been violated, an important rule to that group. When formal rules are violated, such will usually be pointed out by a designated leader of the meeting or by other members with "reminders" such as "We don't need a second for motions in this committee" or "We don't allow members to bring their small children to our meetings." I certainly am *not* recommending that you test a norm's existence by purposefully violating it to see if other members punish you! Groups assume that

good, sane members will obey rules; to deviate from them is likely to lead to your being thought of as "mad" or "bad."[14]

Changing a Norm

You may become aware of rules or norms which seem to you to be detrimental to the coordination and output of a continuing group of which you are a member. For instance, you may think a norm allows members to arrive late for meetings, wasting time and incurring resentment from those members who arrive by the announced meeting time. You may perceive meetings running far beyond the announced time for dismissal, making it impossible for you to stay for the finish and also honor another commitment for that time. You may infer that a rule is inhibiting frank expression of doubts about the wisdom of ideas before they are decided upon, or that the group is wasting time in idle chatter or other diversions. You may find some talk offensive to you, or be bothered by an implicit assumption that every group member is sexist, racist, or ethnocentric like the speaker. In such a case you need not "sit back and take it" but can work to have the group change its rules. A frontal assault on the group in which you become aggressive and demand a change or call the group foolish, thoughtless, inconsiderate, or by some other excoriating term, will likely backfire. In acting that way you will set yourself apart from the group, not speaking as a member but as an outsider whose opinions will carry little weight. First, you must establish an identity as a loyal member of the group committed to its well-being. Secondly, observe precisely what is bothering you. Keep an accurate record of behaviors which reoccur, write out the norm you infer from these behaviors, and then describe the consequence(s) you think follow from that norm. Armed with specific information and an attitude of concern for the group, you are now ready for the third step, constructive confrontation.

Pick an appropriate time, and say that you are concerned with something that seems to be causing trouble for the group, about which you care a great deal. State the specifics of what you have observed, and the norm you have inferred as a group rule. Explain how it detracts from the group's stated objectives. Then ask if other members have questions, or feel as you do. Aside from answering questions to clarify, you have now done most of what you can to help the group. If the norm was subconscious, you have brought it to a level of consciousness, part of the surface agenda of the group. If you are wrong about the norm, the group can now correct you, yet appreciate your goodwill and commitment to the group. If you are right, they will probably appreciate what you have done, decide that some change should be tried, and possibly ask you for a suggestion about a different way of behaving. The group may then make the change—a group decision. Even if the new rule becomes a consensus norm, members may still need reminders of it for some time until it has become habituated, a part of "our way of doing things." An example may clarify how this works. A study group meeting in a small-town library held weekly discussions of similarities and differences in modern Protestant, Catholic, and Jewish theology. The ostensible purpose was to come to an understanding of the major beliefs of these three religious traditions of the Western World, plus an understanding of some more specific articles of faith held by certain members. At times members forgot they were there to *learn,* rather than try to convert each other. The discussion would erupt into an uproar, with several persons talking or shouting at once. One evening just after the meeting had formally adjourned, one member said, "You know, I'm really bothered by our tendency to all talk at once sometimes, and not to listen to each other." Then he turned to me, who had been observing the meeting as a researcher equipped with tape recorder, and asked, "Jack, could some of us hear the recording you just made to see how we must sound to you?" When they heard themselves there were signs of irritation and dismay: groans, "Did we sound like that?" and other indications that people wanted to change the norm that had permitted members to interrupt and try to drown each other out. They left the meeting room in clusters of two and three persons, talking about what they had just heard. At the next meeting the game of "uproar" again erupted, but immediately someone said "Remember the tape recording!" and order resumed. There was no more interrupting for possibly an hour—and then when it occurred it lasted for only a few seconds until every participant sheepishly shut up, with several uttering apologies. That group had a new norm, and no more problems with that sort of counterproductive behavior. In another instance, a new member of a standing committee to which I belonged spoke up at the second meeting to say that several members had smoked at the first meeting he attended. He hated to bring this up, but the smoke made him ill as he had an allergy to tobacco smoke. He hoped we could establish a rule of "no smoking during meetings," or he would have to resign. We discussed this for a few minutes, and decided that would be our rule with the exception that if a member felt an overwhelming urge to smoke, he or she could leave the meeting long enough for a few puffs. That settled the issue to everyone's satisfaction, and the group had a new norm. From then on when a member pulled out a cigarette or pipe, either the person remembered and put it away or another member would quietly give a head shake to the person about to light up. Many groups I have belonged to or observed have tried out new rules to improve the quality of their output after some discussion of the inadequacies of previous norms.

Fantasy Chaining

Norms are based on shared values, beliefs about what is relatively good or bad, desirable or undesirable. Values are frequently explored and tested for acceptance in what appear to be tangents to a group's topic of discussion, in animated sequences of comments that are called *fantasy chains.* The process of group dramatizing or fantasy chaining was first described by Bales in 1970.[15]

Bales claimed that all fantasy chaining relates to *unconscious meanings* or needs of one or more participants. Hence such fantasies have great power to motivate discussants. Usually several persons participate in a group fantasy chain, but not necessarily all members. Consider how this process occurs. Quite often the group seems at a loss for what to say or do. Talking peters out, or perhaps there is an awkward tenseness due to conflict among members. Suddenly someone says something that appears to be off the subject, a tangent about persons in some other time and place.

Interaction speeds up, a pitch of excitement is heard in the voices; often there is some conflict or an edge of hostility. The volume of sound often goes up as the group begins the chain association. Many signs of interest are seen among those who do not participate verbally. Restless . . . movements increase as people try to find a way to get into the conversation. New images and reported events may be rapidly injected, but apparently somehow on the same theme, psychologically . . . for some period—a minute or two, sometimes much longer.[16]

The fantasy is manifestly about persons and events outside the group, that could have occurred in another time (past or future) and another place. At the same time, on a different level, the talk mirrors indirectly the problems of the group at the moment, such as fears, dislikes, loves, jealousies, tense relations between members, relations with other groups, unverbalized hidden agendas, etc. For example, some members of a newly formed project group were interested in creating a panel program on legalizing prostitution in Omaha, but knew that certain other members were devout members of churches which had a history of fighting such things. One person began a fantasy chain to determine if the group could all work on how to legalize prostitution:

Joan: "When I was in Amsterdam I saw these prostitutes sitting in windows inviting passersby to come in, and no one seemed to object. That was a hot section of town!"

Jim (very excitedly, quickly): "Yeah, Boston has a place like that, called the Combat Zone; everyone knew where to go for action, and it kept pressure off people in the rest of the city."

Sally (eagerly leaning forward, excited tones): "That could work great near our Old City area! Hookers could work there and liven it up a bit, and maybe end the silly game of cops and working gals that goes on so much!"

Jan (one of the church activists): "Prostitutes even advertise in the papers in London. Wouldn't that pep up the staid *World-Herald*?!"

Edward: "Yeah—and then the guys and gals who wanted to could get together safely."

Jan: "I see one good thing—I'd know where *not* to go in town!"

The tempo dropped abruptly, and the group returned to discussing what they might do for a panel. Almost at once Jim suggested they take legalization of prostitution in Omaha as their topic, and everyone agreed this was a worthy subject to consider.

Fantasy chains can easily be detected by an observer watching for them by noting sudden changes of pace, levels of excitement, and a sort of electric tension in the air. To interpret the fantasy, Bales suggested that the observer look for a sudden insight into what is going on in the group that has not been openly discussed. Systematic analysis will not work. Through fantasy chains a group establishes a new realm of social reality for its members, a myth that becomes the truth, a sense of unity in a group involved in some dramatic conflict, with shared values and interests.

Role Structure

When you hear the term *role* you probably think of parts in a play or movie. In this sense of "role," a playscript involves a set of interlocking roles, each of which is a character in the cast of the play. You realize that a particular actor may play many different roles in different scripts. Perhaps you have seen Meryl Streep in such diverse roles as a divorced wife and mother (*Kramer vs. Kramer*), a companion (*The Deer Hunter*), a suffering victim of choices (*Sophie's Choice*), and a temptress (*The French Lieutenant's Woman*). In the same manner a person may have diverse roles in the many small groups to which she or he belongs. In one the role may be called "Daughter" or "Son," in another "Father" or "Mother," in another "lead carpenter," and in yet another "church treasurer." In some roles she may be primarily a leader; in others she may play a supporting role. In all cases a person's role is a function of the roles of all other members of the group, just as the actor's role in a play depends upon the roles of other actors in the cast.

In chapter 2 I explained a small group as an open system of interactive and reciprocally influencing components, and presented an "ideal" group as one in which all resources, skills, and functions necessary to accomplish the objectives of the group were present. Thus all the roles necessary to make up a complete group are present, each person playing a role complementary to all the others. There is a division of labor such that each task is performed by the person(s) best able to perform it, and all things needed to achieve group goals are performed. The roles needed to make a highly effective small group always include both "maintenance" and "task" roles. You'll recall that *maintenance* behaviors help develop and facilitate harmonious functioning of members in relationships with each other, and that "task" behaviors are those which primarily do the work-producing outputs for which the group was formed— winning basketball games, building service stations, making judgments about the constitutionality of new laws, searching out information on a public issue and interpreting it for a governor, or designing a suspension system to make the ride in a new car comfortable and controlled. In a fully developed, mature

group, each member has a definite position or *role* worked out through interaction with the other members during the forming, storming, and norming
(developmental) stages of the group.

In order to understand the concept *role* in a small problem-solving or social group, one must also understand the concept *behavioral function*. Every
act of a group member can be called a behavior, but the meaning of an action
to the other group members in relation to their structure and purpose is its
function. Thus I may tell a joke (action), but its function is to reduce secondary tension among members, not solely to entertain them. You may ask a
question, the function of which is to reorient a group in which members have
lost sight of their group goal, or have become confused about the step in problem
solving to which they should turn next. Behavioral function, then, is the impact of member behavior on the social structure (throughput) and task accomplishment (output) of the group. A member's role is the sum of all the
behavioral functions he or she performs, just as an actor's role in a play includes all the actions and lines of the actor during a performance of the play.
Much as each play character has certain primary or defining characteristics,
so each small group member's role is characterized by a predominance of certain functions. Some functions may be shared widely among all members of
a group (such as providing information); others may become almost the ex-
clusive domain of one member (such as initiating discussion and keeping records).

Role Emergence

Who plays each position in a small group is determined largely by the relative
performance skills of all the members of the group. A discussion group with
the task of problem solving or learning will in time develop almost as definite
a structure of member roles as does an athletic team. This is accomplished
through a sort of trial-and-comparison basis. Although certain socioemotional
and procedural roles are needed in every small group, many of these and most
of the task roles depend on the purpose and environment of the group. While
a new group is forming, much effort will be spent in determining who can best
perform the kinds of behaviors needed to unify and coordinate the activities
of the members, and to accomplish the group's tasks. Some of the informal
roles may change considerably in later phases of the group's life as new demands are made on the members from the environment, different stages of
the problem-solving process, and partial changes in membership.

Some small groups have certain *formal* roles, usually appointed or elected
positions. For example, most committees have a designated chairperson who
is responsible for such duties as calling meetings, planning agendas, coordinating the work of other committee members, and making reports to the parent
organization. A committee may also have a designated secretary. Formally
organized learning groups invariably have a designated leader (or leaders)

responsible for initiating and organizing the discussions. A board of directors will usually consist of the president, vice-presidents, secretary, treasurer, and other officers of its parent organization, each of whom has certain definite functions to perform as a board member (as well as for the parent organization) in the formal role.

For a small group to be effective, a stable set of roles (or division of labor) *must* emerge and be accepted by all members. Then each member can be expected to perform certain types of actions or tasks for the group. This is not to say that everyone plays a role totally different from everyone else, or that two or more members may not perform the same types of functions. Indeed, some behaviors—such as supplying needed information—may be widely shared among the members. But in the mature small group each person has a unique *set* of functions to perform, which combined with those of other members provide for all the group's needs in discussing and doing its work. Any effective long-term group has specialists who can be counted on to act when their skills are needed for summarizing, testing ideas, managing conflicts, and so on. However, the group must not depend too much on these specialists, or else when they are absent or distracted no one else will be able to step in to perform those behaviors vital to the progress of the group.

Ideally, group members have considerable flexibility, and each can provide a wide variety of the behaviors useful to the group. Perhaps the ideal all-around discussants would be those who are so sensitive and versatile that they could diagnose what each group to which they belong needs from them, and perform those actions. But no human being can be all things, so we tend to seek role profiles suited both to our skills and limitations and to the needs of each group. In a course concerned with small group communication you have an excellent laboratory for developing new behaviors to achieve greater flexibility in the roles you can perform in small groups.

The role a person has varies from group to group. For a minute think of several different small groups to which you have belonged—most likely you behaved very differently in some of these groups. You probably have noticed, also, that in some groups your role changed considerably through time as you changed, as new persons joined the group, and as the problems facing the group changed. A major principle of small group theory is this: *the role of each member of a group is worked out by interaction between the member and the rest of the group.* Hence the role structure is unique to each group—I have never seen any two groups in which the roles were the same, anymore than they are in any two plays. What seems to happen is this: a member of a discussion group does something. If others respond favorably, that member is likely to do this sort of thing again, a response to previous positive reinforcement. Soon that type of behavior is a part of his or her role. If other members reject the behavior or do not respond favorably (negative reinforcement), the person will not be likely to act that way again. Gradually, from this pattern of selective reinforcement, a fairly stable set of roles emerges in the group, and members come to expect each other to behave in some ways and not in others. Of course a member who has been reinforced for proposing new ideas may not always be able to do so as the problems change, and members who have not previously been initiators of ideas may suddenly have experience leading them to try idea initiating. If positively reinforced, a new facet has been added to their roles. Roles do change somewhat.

Occasionally conflict over roles may erupt in a group. A chair has been doing the consensus testing and summarizing. A member without a formal role summarizes some part of a meeting, and the designated leader (who has been doing this sort of coordinating) displays visible distress through body movements and facial expression, perhaps saying something like "Yes, Mary, I was just about to sum that up. You should also have included _____ and _____ . Now let's get on to . . .." An appointed secretary would not allow someone else to distribute the minutes unless the regular secretary had asked that person to do so for one meeting in his absence, or the person had been appointed secretary *pro tem* for the one meeting. Such conflict is almost always over formal positions, or the status of leader in an initially leaderless group.

Behavioral Functions

In the study of member behaviors and roles, group researchers and theorists have developed numerous classification systems, all of them oversimplified. Each set of roles or behaviors has some limited uses and inadequacies. For example, the most commonly cited are the *task* and *socioemotional* categories already referred to. But every communicative act in a group discussion has both content (task) and relationship (social) implications. If a member says, "Betty, why don't you get us some coffee?" she is both suggesting a task for Betty to perform *and* that she has a right to expect Betty to do what she asks (relationship). If I suggest that two members who are talking past each other in an excited argument about two different solutions (secondary tension being manifested) should listen more carefully, my statement although focused on their way of relating to each other, may also have a direct bearing on the task achievement of the group. And it not only implies a procedure for them to follow, but also that my role in relation to them is such that I have a right to suggest changes in their behavior. Every act in a discussion, then, can be viewed as having both a *task* and a *relational* aspect, probably with greater impact in one area than in the other. As shown in figure 5.3, an act could have much impact on both dimensions, much on one and little on the other, much on both, or little on either.

A person's informal role in a small group is made up of many behaviors of various types. The complete role of an individual is a sort of summary of these types of behavior, reflective of the relative proportions of each. During

Figure 5.3   Two major dimensions of the impact of discussant behaviors.

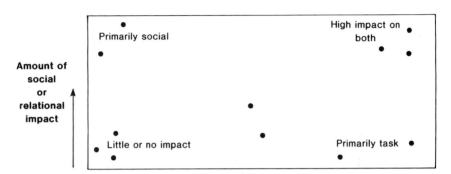

Amount of impact on group task achievement

• Specific act or behavior

a single speech a person may perform more than one of these behaviors, such as both giving information and asking for more information from others. We tend to name a person's role on the basis of the kinds of behaviors he or she most often performs as a group member, but in reality the role consists of an amalgam of those kinds of behaviors that he or she provides most often and in relatively high proportions compared to other group members. Figure 5.4 illustrates the roles of three members of a small group as being composed of the behavioral functions they perform.

What follows is a list of behavioral functions needed by most groups to develop from a collection of persons into a coordinated group that can achieve its goals. Several writers have developed lists of "roles" or functions, but all such lists are arbitrary and none has been tested scientifically. However limited, such a list is useful to help one perceive the dynamics of role emergence and performance. The list below begins with task behaviors, then shifts to maintenance functions.

Initiating and orienting—proposing goals, plans of action, or activities; prodding group to greater activity; defining position of group in relation to external structure or goal.

Information giving—offering facts and information, evidence, personal experience, and knowledge pertinent to the group task.

Information seeking—asking other members for information; requesting relevant evidence.

Opinion giving—stating beliefs, values, interpretations, judgments; drawing conclusions from evidence.

Opinion seeking—asking other members for their opinions.

Figure 5.4   Roles of three members of a small group.

"Idea Leader"

"Procedural Leader"

"Information Specialist"

Clarifying and elaborating—interpreting issues; clarifying ambiguous statements; developing an idea previously expressed by giving examples, illustrations, and explanations.

Evaluating—expressing judgments about the relative worth of information or ideas; proposing or applying criteria.

Summarizing—reviewing what has been said previously in bits and pieces; reminding group of a number of items previously mentioned or discussed.

Coordinating—showing relationships between or among ideas; integrating two or more proposed solutions into one; suggesting how members can work productively together; promoting teamwork and cooperation.

Consensus testing—asking if group has reached a decision acceptable to all; suggesting that agreement may have been reached.

Recording—keeping group records on chalkboard or paper, preparing reports and minutes; serving as group secretary and memory.

Suggesting procedure—suggesting an agenda of issues, outline, problem-solving pattern, or special technique; proposing some procedure or sequence to follow.

Gatekeeping—helping some member get the floor; suggesting or controlling speaking order; asking if someone has different opinion.

Supporting—agreeing or otherwise expressing support for other's belief or proposal; following lead of another member.

Harmonizing—reducing secondary tension by reconciling a disagreement; suggesting compromise or new alternative acceptable to all; conciliating or placating angry member.

Tension relieving—introducing and making strangers feel at ease; reducing external status differences; encouraging informality; joking; stressing common interests and experiences.

Dramatizing—comments that evoke fantasies about persons and places other than the present group and time, including storytelling and fantasizing in a vivid manner; testing a tentative value or norm through fantasy or story.

Norming—suggesting rules of behavior for members; challenging unproductive ways of behaving as member; giving negative response when other violates a formal rule or informal norm.

These are the major types of behavior that are needed to develop a collection of persons into a group, coordinate their efforts, provide and use resources, and thus achieve interdependent goals.

Other types of behaviors that spring from purely personal needs work at odds with the best interests of the group as a whole. Among these self-centered types of acts are the following:

Withdrawing—avoiding important differences; refusing to cope with conflicts; refusing to take a stand; covering up feelings; giving no response to comments of others.

Blocking—preventing progress toward group goals by constantly raising objections, repeatedly bringing up the same topic or issue after the group has considered it and rejected it. (It is not blocking to keep raising an idea or topic the group has not really listened to or considered.)

Status and recognition seeking—stagehogging, boasting, calling attention to one's expertise or experience when that is not necessary to establish credibility or relevant to group task; game playing to elicit sympathy; switching subject to an area of personal expertise.

This list of self-oriented behaviors could be expanded considerably with "special interest pleading," "advocating," "game playing," "confessing," and similar functions. The important thing is for you to be aware of whether a member is trying to contribute to the interdependent group goal, or manipulating and using other members for selfish goals at odds with the best interests of the group as a whole.

Networks of Communication

Concomitant with the development of somewhat specialized roles in a group is the development of a communication network. The phrase *communication network* refers to a pattern of message flow or *linkages* of who actually speaks to whom in discussions. A member who opens a meeting may find the others expecting him to initiate discussion on a new topic or at subsequent meetings. A person who speaks frequently will find others looking (literally) to him or her for some comment on each new issue or when there is a lag in conversation. Infrequent verbal participants will themselves be more and more overlooked and the comments they do make ignored.

Most of the so-called *network* studies of communication in task groups seem to be largely irrelevant to discussion groups in natural (as opposed to laboratory) settings. Persons passing notes through holes in plywood partitions (typical in the network studies) to solve contrived problems imposed on them do not interact any more like persons in discussion groups than do baboons in a zoo interact like baboons in natural clans in a forest or veldt.

Many types of networks have been identified, but the *permissible* as well as the actually used channels must be looked at in any group to fully understand its structure. Usually a group of peers has an *all-channel* network in which all participants are free to comment on a one-to-one basis with all others, and to the group as a whole (see figure 5.5). A *wheel* network is to be avoided in which all comments are directed toward one central person (*leader*) who alone may speak to the group as a whole or to any individual in it. A *Y*, or *hierarchical network*, occurs when an autocratic leader has *lieutenants* with whom he or she interacts directly, and who in turn talk to subordinates. The persons at the ends of the Y rarely if ever interact directly with the leader. In both wheel and Y networks the central person is usually very satisfied with

Figure 5.5 Communication networks.

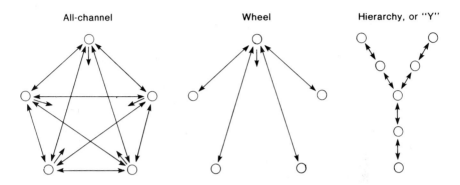

All-channel   Wheel   Hierarchy, or "Y"

his participation and status, but the peripheral members tend to find little satisfaction in participation in the group. Sometimes, however, the central person (*leader*) becomes overloaded with more messages from other group members than he or she can handle, and then becomes frustrated and dissatisfied. The central person is then said to be suffering *information overload*. A wheel or Y network forces some members into a position of low sending, and hence low satisfaction. Interaction in such restricted networks sometimes breaks down into two or more *private* conversations going on at the same time between pairs of individuals during a group meeting. The all-channel network permits rapid communication without having to get clearance from a central gatekeeping authority; everyone is free to say what he or she wants while it is pertinent and fresh in mind. Communication flows freely from person to person. At least half of the comments are addressed to the group as a whole, and all group members can hear and attend to all one-to-one or one-to-few comments. Free feedback of questions and responses is thus encouraged. Many studies have shown morale to be highest when all channels are open, and some have indicated superior problem solving on complex tasks by groups with such networks compared to more restricted networks of flow of communication. To have a functional all-channel network will take some conscious effort on the part of group members, but you are well advised to see that departures from such a completely open net are very brief.

Status Hierarchy

Status refers to the relative importance, prestige, and power of a member in a small group. As group roles emerge, each person is placed in a sort of *pecking order* or *status ladder*. To be high in status is socially rewarding; highs feel important and worthwhile. Other group members defer to high status persons, give them better than average attention, agree often with what they propose, and ask their advice. Persons occupying high-status formal roles may be given special and expensive chairs, large offices and other perquisites, and powers not enjoyed by other group members. Membership in a group that is high in status among all the groups which make up an organization is more attractive than membership in groups with lower esteem. Members of such groups are likely to be more cohesive, hard working, and loyal then average. Likewise, high status members of a group tend to be more loyal to that group and more dependable than low status members. Certain roles in a group carry higher status than others, especially the role of "leader." Designated leaders are often given deference and support, more eye contact, and more attention than other members.

Most of us desire the psychological rewards of high status, so we spend a great deal of time and effort acquiring the symbols of high status in some line of activity or organization—expensive clothing and automobiles, houses in restricted neighborhoods, large carpeted offices, trophies, and titles. So it is in the small group. Members with high status are expected to work especially hard to accomplish the group's goals, and to conform to its norms. To gain high status the members compete directly during the forming and storming phases of many groups. They do so by suggesting procedures and ideas, and trying to win or compel support. Although the group may be talking about its work, the focus of much attention is on status relations, just as chickens put together to form a new flock fight to establish a pecking order. Thus much arguing early in the lifespan of a group is not so much about ideas, procedures, norms, and solutions as it appears to be on the surface, but about who will have what roles and statuses.

Status within a small group is in part *ascribed* by others at the beginning of the group, and in part earned. When a small group begins, status will often be ascribed on the basis of each member's position in the society external to the small group, guided by such benchmarks as wealth, education, work, personal fame, or position in the parent organization of a committee. For example, a committee comprised of a college dean, a professor of biology, an English instructor, two seniors, and two sophomores would initially have that order of ascribed status. But status is *earned* or achieved in the small working group based on each member's perceived contributions to the group's goals, so that order would likely change drastically as functional roles emerged.

Sex has an impact on status and role in a mixed-sex group. Bormann, Putnam, and Pratt reported in 1978 that men tended to resist the leadership of a woman regardless of how well she performed, and resisted her efforts to structure and coordinate work of group members.[17] More recently Bormann and Bormann reported that they found some women resisting efforts of a man to lead groups, largely as a matter of principle.[18] Pratt reported a willingness on the part of some men to have a woman lead groups of which they are members.[19] It seems to me that willingness to support and follow members of the opposite sex in small groups is changing very rapidly, and varies unpredictably from group to group. I still see considerable resistance in some organizations on the part of men to women as group leaders, very little to none in other organizations. Most male university students in my classes seem willing today to have a capable woman lead class project groups. Not many years ago I observed that even the most competent of women took supporter roles (information giver and recorder, for example) in almost all class groups even when the males were far less knowledgeable and organized. Now that more and more women are being placed in such positions as chief executive officer of universities and corporations, Supreme Court justice, and various high-ranking elective offices, maleness may cease to be a criterion for high status in most American small groups in the foreseeable future.

The effects of status differences among members on small group communication are numerous. High-status members talk more often than do low-status members and speak directly to each other more often than do lows; low status members address their remarks more often to highs than to other lows.[20] Low-status members also address more positive messages to high-status members than they do to other lows—another reward of high status.[21] Discussants tend to interrupt and ignore the comments of lows far more than the comments of highs. Highs tend to talk more to the group as a whole than do lows, who express most of their comments to individuals.

Most small groups establish two or three levels of status in their hierarchy. This does not mean that lower status members are not judged to be of value, or that they are unhappy in the group. Cohesive groups value the contributions of each member, and every member knows it. High is not necessarily better, just more influential. Case studies of student groups often contain such comments as this: "Every member of our group played a vital role. Jim, our leader, was most important in the success of our project, but even quiet Norman made a vital contribution with his careful research and by arranging a place where we could meet. He could always be counted on to do his part. I would not change a member of this group even if I could." But when higher status members say "We could have done just as well without Morgan and Jalene on this committee," then low status definitely means "inferior."

Status relations among persons have been called "control modes," an idea advanced by Bateson.[22] We use the jargon of control in everyday life when we speak of being "one-upped" by someone skilled at dominating, or to being "put down." Three categories of relationship types are necessary to understanding control modes:

↑ *One-up,* referring to any attempt to control the behavior of another person, restricting what that person can do as a member of the group.

↓ *One-down,* referring to acquiescing to the one-up attempt of another person, or giving up some freedom to choose one's behaviors; letting other decide for self.

→ *One-across,* when a person attempts to establish equal control relationships in which no one dominates, restricts, or controls other group members, and no one acquiesces.

The arrows provide a coding system for recording how members of a small group relate on the status hierarchy of the group. By putting an arrow beside each comment according to how it seems to function in the context of member relationships one can judge who is attempting to dominate, who is resisting such dominating and seeking in turn to dominate, who is seeking equality with other members in power, and who seems willing to accept the dominance of others. Two one-up arrows would indicate that two members were competing for status over each other, a one-up arrow followed by a one-across arrow would indicate that one person tried to dominate but was responded to by another as a co-equal (not willing to either dominate or compete). A one-up arrow followed by a one-down arrow indicated successful domination. Two one-across arrows indicate that the persons spoke to each other as co-equals.

The most ideal group climate exists when relationships and relative status are somewhat flexible among group members, so that different persons can become more dominant as their knowledge and skills are more pertinent to the issues or problems facing the group at any point in time. At times, in an ideal group everyone might follow the lead of a normally recessive, supportive, low-status person who has just the information or skill the group most needs to organize its efforts at that point. Later, this member might slip back into his or her usually low-status profile of communicative acts, and persons generally more active in the group would again resume their more typical patterns of behavior. In a healthy problem-solving group with relatively high cohesiveness, able to make sound decisions based on thorough analysis and reasoning, there will be periods of conflict (and secondary tension) characterized ↑ ↑, periods of uncertainty characterized by an unusual amount of one-down control behavior ↓ ↓, and periods of working harmony in which consensus emerges among persons of equal status → →.

Cohesiveness

The term *cohesiveness* is used by social psychologists to refer to the common bonds and sentiments that hold a group together.

To say that a group is high in cohesiveness is to say that the relationships among members, on the average, are highly attractive to them; they have a high degree of "stick togetherness" and unity. Defining cohesiveness operationally has not been easy, for we cannot measure the concept directly. How would you observe and measure "the resultant of all the forces acting on the members to remain in the group," a widely accepted definition?[23] Obviously you cannot, but must observe selected behaviors that can be considered an index of how cohesive a small group may be: members' individual assessments of how closely knit they are as a group; how strongly members feel a sense of belonging or affiliation to the group as expressed on a scale; attendance at meetings; favorable remarks about the group to outsiders; degree of conformity to group norms that call for behaviors different from those the members manifest in other social situations; achievement of consensus or lack thereof, especially in expressions of value.

Researchers have shown that groups high in cohesiveness have greater rates of interaction than less cohesive groups, express more positive feelings for each other, and have more satisfaction with the group and its products. The higher the cohesiveness of the group, the greater control over member behaviors the group as a whole will be able to exert.[24]

A high degree of cohesiveness is associated with a high degree of ability to cope effectively with unusual problems, and to work as a team in meeting emergencies. Production groups, if highly cohesive, *can* produce more than low cohesive groups, but may not do so if the members are being influenced by intragroup norms for less production. High cohesiveness is associated with the group's ability to get members to conform to the majority or high status members' desires. Janis has pointed out that conformity in many problem-solving groups contributes to very low-quality decisions, the result of "group-think" that allows for no disagreement with beliefs of high-status members.[25] Deviance from the beliefs of high-status members or the majority may be put down so powerfully that a person holding valid information that negates those beliefs even begins to doubt his own information. As such groups continue through time they become very predictable, less creative, less able to use novel ideas—the "nuts" are silenced or even put out. The very persons who could contribute most to the quality of solutions by pointing out fallacious thinking find the group less and less attractive while the cohesiveness among the majority is growing. Thus we have a dilemma of how to encourage a productive degree of creativity and critical thinking while at the same time maintain a high degree of cohesiveness essential to high potential, personal satisfaction, and loyalty. Specific techniques will be presented later, especially for designated leaders. *Awareness of the problem* is the point here.

However, we do know that a group that accomplishes its objectives, provides members with satisfaction in their participation, offers prestige in belonging, and is successful in competing with other groups, has high attractiveness to its members. This knowledge can be used to offset the strains produced by uncertainty, risk, and deferment of judgment necessary to achieve high-quality work. We also know that cohesiveness is fostered by the degree to which members know and like each other as persons, their frequency of interaction, and the amount of influence exerted by each on the group. Interestingly, open disagreeing has been shown to be more frequent in high-cohesive groups than in low-cohesive groups. A climate of trust in which each member feels secure permits expressions of disagreement on issues, facts, and ideas—provided the disagreement is aimed at arriving at high-quality solutions. But if high-status members resist disagreement as a personal affront, then whatever cohesiveness is achieved by other means will be at the expense of low-quality decision making—*groupthink*. Highly successful and cohesive groups tend to first get well acquainted and interested in each other as persons. They accept the need for secondary tension generated by disagreements, and find ways to reduce these tensions by giving priority to evidence, rational thinking, and compromise. After decisions have been reached, such groups restate the value of the group and of each of its members. Members can be heard saying such things as: "I'm proud of our group, we really thresh out ideas until we arrive at the best, and then we team up." "Even if I disagreed with you, Joe, I'm glad you spoke up. We disagreed openly and honestly, and I learned a lot from you. I like that."

In order to enhance cohesiveness, Bormann and Bormann suggest that a group should consciously do the following:

1. Develop a strong identity as a group and a group tradition or history. This can be done by developing nicknames for the group, insignia of membership, referring to past events with pride and pleasure, ceremonies and rituals, and emphasizing the high quality of accomplishments.
2. Stress teamwork, and give credit to the group. Avoid talking about what you did personally for the group, especially if you are the designated leader. Volunteering to do things for the group, and emphasizing how important the group is to you will help members feel closer to each other.
3. Recognize contributions to the group goal by members, thus rewarding individual members from *within* the group. Low-status members especially need reward and praise from other group members, and *not* criticism, if they are to develop the loyalty that will make them more productive and dependable.
4. Show human concern for the persons who make up the group, providing warmth, affection, and direct attention to personal tensions and problems that members indicate. As soon as personal needs are dealt with, however, the group should get back to the group task.
5. Support both disagreement and agreement, which basically means working for a norm of open expression of disagreement or support for ideas. Highly cohesive groups show more disagreement; open conflict needs to be encouraged, not repressed. When the conflicts are settled, signs of solidarity such as joking, laughing together, compliments to persons who supported rejected ideas that helped build a better group solution, and comments such as "Let's get behind this" are needed.
6. Help the group set clear and attainable goals, which also provide enough of a challenge to yield a sense of pride in group achievement. Continuing groups that fail to reach their objectives tend to display lowered cohesiveness and may even break up. On the other hand,

beating a high school team would not enhance the cohesiveness of a college soccer squad.[26]

Summary

In chapter 5 we have examined seven major process variables: phase developments through time, interpersonal tensions, rules and norms, a role structure developed from individual behavioral functions, communication network, status hierarchy, and cohesiveness. Every group moves through stages of development, usually entailing four phases: forming, storming, norming, and performing, with constant fluctuations in both primary and secondary tension levels among members. Formal rules may guide some behavior of members of groups, especially committees of organizations which adopt Robert's Rules of Order. A set of informal norms emerges to govern other behaviors of members. From their personal behaviors and responses to them, group members carve out individual roles as composites of their typical behaviors in the group, which should be task and maintenance oriented rather than self-oriented. A communication network develops among the members, ideally an all-channel network rather than a wheel or Y. Roles in the communication network are accompanied by different levels of status and power among the members. A high level of cohesiveness among members is both a product and a process variable in the effective discussion group.

In the next chapter we will consider in depth the process of communication by which interaction occurs.

Exercises

1. Observe a small group during at least one discussion; take notes on what you observe and norms these behaviors imply. Then write all the norms you can infer from what you saw and heard, stating each as a rule of conduct about what members (or a specific member) of the group must, should, or may do while acting as members. Briefly describe the observed behaviors on which each norm is based. Finally, indicate whether you think the norm helped the group increase its output (+), had no effect on output (0), or reduced the group's output (−) in relation to its stated goals. Write your report in the three-column format shown below:

Norm	Evidence of the Norm	Impact

2. Select a small group of which you were a member at the time of its founding, and in which you continued as a member for at least several meetings; a committee (or task force) that had at least five or six meetings is ideal. Describe the phases in its development, at least as you can recall them. What phases are you aware of? How could you tell when a new phase of development had been entered by the group? Were the phases distinct or did they overlap each other?

   Share your recollections with several classmates. How well does your collective experience support the phase theory presented in chapter 5?

3. Observe a group with one or more classmates, each observing independently. Using a list of behavioral functions as a guide (see page 376) classify the acts of each member. This will give you a tally of how often each person performs each function. Then write a name for and description of the role taken by each member. Compare your findings with those of your fellow observer(s).

4. Rank the members of the group you observed in number 2, above, according to the status of each in the group. Your ranked list will show the relative amount of power and influence you think each exerts in the group.

5. First, make a list of at least ten small groups in which you have been an active member during the past year (your instructor may wish to change this time span). Then, in a single sentence, describe the role you had in each group. Compare your list with the lists of three to five classmates. What do you discover about a person's roles in different groups?

6. Diagram the flow of communication in a discussion group you observe, using the form shown on page 373. Be sure to record how many times each person speaks and to whom. What is the proportion of the total statements made by each member? What sort of communication network exists in the group?

7. For learning discussion: "What differences have we noticed between small groups which are high and low in cohesiveness?"

Bibliography

Bormann, Ernest G. *Discussion and Group Methods: Theory and Practice.* 2d ed. New York: Harper & Row, Publishers, 1975, chapters 8 and 9.
Nixon, Howard L. II. *The Small Group.* Englewood Cliffs, N.J.: Prentice-Hall, 1979, chapters 4 and 6.
Shimanoff, Susan B. "Coordinating Group Interaction Via Communication Rules." In Cathcart, Robert S., and Samovar, Larry A., eds., *Small*

Group Communication: A Reader. 4th ed. Dubuque, Iowa: Wm. C. Brown Company Publishers, 1984, 31–44.

Tuckman, Bruce W. "Developmental Sequences in Small Groups." *Psychological Bulletin* 63 (1965): 384–99.

References

1. Robert F. Bales, *Interaction Process Analysis* (Reading, Mass.: Addison-Wesley, 1950).
2. Bruce W. Tuckman, "Developmental Sequences in Small Groups," *Psychological Bulletin* 63 (1965): 384–99.
3. *Ibid.*
4. Thomas M. Scheidel and Laura Crowell, "Idea Development in Small Discussion Groups," *Quarterly Journal of Speech* 50 (1964): 140–45.
5. Ernest G. Bormann, *Discussion and Group Methods: Theory and Practice,* 2d ed. (New York: Harper & Row, Publishers, 1975), 181–82.
6. *Ibid.,* p. 190.
7. Stanley Schacter, "Deviation, Rejection, and Communication," *Journal of Abnormal and Social Psychology* 46 (1951): 190–207; and Solomon E. Asch, "Studies On Independence and Conformity: A Minority of One Against a Unanimous Majority," *Psychological Monographs* 70 (1956):416.
8. William F. Whyte, *Pattern for Industrial Peace* (New York: Harper, 1951).
9. Henry M. Robert, *Robert's Rules of Order, Newly Revised* (Glenview, Ill.: Scott, Foresman and Company, 1981).
10. George C. Homans, *The Human Group* (New York: Harcourt Brace Jovanovich, 1950), 123.
11. Susan B. Shimanoff, "Coordinating Group Interaction Via Communication Rules," in *Small Group Communication: A Reader,* 4th ed., Robert S. Cathcart and Larry A. Samovar, eds. (Dubuque, Iowa: Wm. C. Brown Company Publishers, 1984), 36.
12. Susan B. Shimanoff, *Communication Rules: Theory and Research* (Beverly Hills: Sage, 1980).
13. Shimanoff, "Coordinating Group Interaction," 42.
14. Paul Watzlawick, J. H. Bevin, and D. J. Jackson, *Pragmatics of Human Communication* (New York: W. W. Norton, 1967).
15. Robert F. Bales, *Personality and Interpersonal Behavior* (New York: Holt, Rinehart and Winston, Inc., 1970), 105–8, 136–55.
16. *Ibid.,* 138.
17. Ernest G. Bormann, Linda L. Putnam, and J. M. Pratt, "Power, Authority, and Sex: Male Responses to Female Dominance," *Communication Monographs* 45 (1978): 119–155.

18. Ernest G. Bormann and Nancy C. Bormann, *Effective Small Group Communication,* 3rd ed. (Minneapolis: Burgess, 1980), 80.
19. J. M. Pratt, "A Case Study Analysis of Male-Female Leadership Emergence in Small Groups," cited in Bormann and Bormann, p. 81.
20. J. I. Hurwitz, A. F. Zander, and B. Hymovitch, "Some Effects of Power on the Relations among Group Members," in *Group Dynamics: Research and Theory,* 3d ed., D. Cartwright and A. Zander, eds. (New York: Harper & Row, Publishers, 1968), 291–97.
21. Dean C. Barnlund and C. Harland, "Propinquity and Prestige as Determinants of Communication Networks," *Sociometry* 26 (1963): 467–479.
22. Gregory Bateson, *Steps to an Ecology of Mind* (San Francisco: Chandler Publishing Company, 1972).
23. Leon Festinger, "Informal Social Communication," *Psychological Review* 57 (1950): 274.
24. Howard L. Nixon II, *The Small Group* (Englewood Cliffs, N.J.: Prentice-Hall, 1979), 74–76.
25. Irving L. Janis, *Victims of Groupthink* (Boston: Houghton Mifflin Company, 1973).
26. Adapted from Ernest G. Bormann and Nancy C. Bormann, *Effective Small Group Communication,* 2d ed. (Minneapolis: Burgess Publishing Company, 1976), 70–76.

6 the communication process in small groups

Study Objectives

As a result of studying chapter 6 you should be able to:

1. Explain communication as a complex, symbolic transactional process requiring participation of a receiver.

2. Describe how signals are encoded, transmitted, received, transformed, interpreted, and responded to in both intrapersonal and small group communication systems.

3. Differentiate between the content, affective, and relational components of interpersonal messages.

4. Name and describe the fallacy in each of five myths of communication.

5. Demonstrate active listening.

6. Explain and identify each of seven pitfalls to effective listening.

7. Explain how selective note taking and focused listening can improve recall and continuity in discussion.

Key Terms

Active listening   listening to understand what a speaker means, then paraphrasing one's understanding so the speaker can correct or confirm the paraphrase.

Communication   process in which symbols and other signals produced by people are received, interpreted, and responded to by other people.

Complete communication circuit   open interchange system in which both persons send and receive signals, so that a signal from one is responded to by the other, and the response is acknowledged.

Defensive listening   thinking of how to defend some aspect of one's image while apparently attending to the message of another.

Feedback   perception of one's own messages or responses of another to one's messages which leads to change in further message output.

Focused listening   focusing attention on major ideas and issues rather than details of another's message; includes attempting to review and recall those issues with mental and written summaries.

Forcing meaning   listener insisting that speaker meant by some statement what the listener would have meant by the same words even though speaker insists she/he meant something different.

Interpersonal communication   transactional process in which one person's verbal and nonverbal behavior evokes meaning in another.

Intrapersonal communication   process of signal generation, transmission, interpretation, and response within the nervous system of an individual.

Listening   receiving and interpreting oral and other signals from other person (or source).

Message   either a set of signals from one person to other(s), or interpretation and response of listener to a set of signals.

Nonverbal cues   signals other than words to which listeners react.

Paraphrase   restatement by listener in his or her own language of what he or she understood previous speaker to mean.

Pseudolistening   responding overtly as if listening attentively while thinking about something other than the speaker and his/her message.

Referent   that which is referred to by a symbol or message.

Sign   a trace or vestige of something, having an inherent relationship with the thing which it represents to a perceiver; e.g., a footprint, scar, or blush.

Signal   any stimulus which a person can receive and interpret, including both signs and symbols.

Symbol   arbitrary, human-created signal used to represent something with which it has no inherent relationship; all words are symbols.

Communication is the name of the process by which group members share information and create similar perceptions, develop interdependence, coordinate their efforts, reach agreement on ends and means, and forge a collection of individuals into a group. Before we can examine small group communication in detail, we must first develop a shared understanding of the concept "communication." To do that is the purpose of chapter 6.

You may have studied the process of human communication in a previous speech communication course. If so, much of this chapter may be review for you. Even if that is the case, be careful to notice how the key terms and concepts concerning communicating are defined and used in this book. There have been scores of definitions of communication, from very simple to highly complex. Before proceeding further in the chapter, read the following article by King, "The Nature of Communication"; it presents an outstanding and clear definition of communication among group members.

The Nature of Communication[1]
Stephen W. King

Three weeks into a course entitled "Small Group Communication" an earnest student raised her hand and asked, "Now that we know what a 'small group' is, Professor, what is 'communication'?" Many students snickered, thinking the question tremendously naive and trivial.

However, I was apprehensive. Was this student going to force me to deal with the difficult but essential question of definition? I tried to get out of the tense moment by flippantly saying, "What is *not* communication?"

Undaunted, the student pressed her question, "You didn't answer the question; you merely circumvented it."

Trapped! So I said, "Well, Stevens defined it as 'the discriminatory response of an organism to a stimulus,' Miller and Steinberg asserted that communication 'involves an intentional, transactional, symbolic process,' and Samovar and Mills concluded that communication 'includes all methods of conveying any kind of thought or feeling between persons.' "[*]

Gaining confidence the student looked at me and said, "Professor, that was simply a smorgasbord of definitions offering me a great deal of choice but not much clarification."

I prayed for the bell to ring indicating the end of the period. No bell, so I said, "O.K., Miller and Steinberg's definition is the right one. Now, do you understand?"

"No," said the student, "that's the point. You gave me a definition but I don't understand why that definition captures the essence of 'communication' while the others do not. I guess I want to understand 'communication' not define it."

[*]S. S. Stevens "A Definition of Communication," *Journal of the Acoustical Society of America* 22 (1950), p. 689; G. Miller and M. Steinberg, *Between People: A New Analysis of Interpersonal Communication,* Chicago: Science Research Associates, 1975, p. 34; L. Samovar and J. Mills, *Oral Communication: Message and Response,* 3rd ed. Dubuque, Iowa: Wm. C. Brown Company Publishers, 1976, p. 4.

Of course, she was right. Thus, I begrudgingly began a dialogue aimed at understanding communication, its fundamental nature and conceptual boundaries. I invite you to join us on this expedition in search of understanding.

We can begin our expedition with a brief story:

(1) Professor Samuel Withit left the library one morning and saw one of his students across the quad wave to him. He waved back. (2) A few moments later Professor Withit walked by another of his students who gave a friendly "hello" smile. (3) Professor Withit did not see the student and continued to walk to his office without acknowledging the smile. The student, miffed by the rebuff, cut class for the rest of the week. (4) Upon entering the departmental offices, Professor Withit overheard one of his ex-students telling another student, "Professor Withit's class is one of the toughest in this department." (5) Later, Professor Withit dictated a letter to his secretary and requested that the letter be mailed that day. Two days later the letter left the office.

How many of these five incidents would you classify as examples of communication? All five? Two? None of them? Very probably other people would disagree with whatever answer you decided upon. Such difference of opinion is more than just an interesting disagreement; we must ask the question, "Why?" Quite simply, the answer centers on the fact that to decide to call something by a name, in this case "communication," reflects your understanding and, at this point in your study of communication, you *all* probably have different ideas about what is or is not "communication." Let's look at each of these five incidents and try to discover the points at which some of your understandings might differ.

In incident number one (1) no words are exchanged. Because of this, did you exclude this as an example of communication? In incident two (2), a signal— a smile—was sent but not received. Is reception necessary for communication? Professor Withit's behavior in incident number three (3) unintentionally affected his student. Are such accidental effects communication? In incident four (4), Professor Withit was not the intended receiver of the signal sent by one of his ex-students. Did the student communicate anyway? Finally, in incident five (5), the professor's instruction to the secretary was apparently received but not effective. Is the study of communication limited to effective communication?

Possibly your concept of communication allows you to include all the incidents as examples of communication. However, if another person conceived of communication as only those exchanges of ideas through words, incidents one, two, and three would be dropped because words were not uttered. If another individual thought communication dealt only with messages intentionally sent, incidents three and four would not qualify. If success was a prerequisite for yet a third person, incidents two, four, and five would not be included. It is apparent that if we are going to go much further in this study of communication, we must come to a shared understanding of the term.

One way to understand a phenomenon is to identify its parts or components. Accordingly, let's try to decide what the fundamental ingredients of communication are. First, nonverbal communication, which does not rely on words, is a reality. If it is not, why do people get so upset over various hand gestures? Why did Professor Withit's student skip class for a week? Second, to concern ourselves only with successful idea exchange is like calling "teaching" only that which results in the student getting an "A." The result would be that neither education nor communication would ever be improved since no one would have investigated the causes of failure. We must look at both successful and unsuccessful communication. Finally, if we limit ourselves to only those messages intentionally sent, two problems become apparent. First, we have to make some very questionable decisions about what is going on inside a sender's head. Second, and more importantly, we must ignore many messages that do, in fact, have impact, such as Professor Withit's unintentional slight of his student. With these distinctions in mind, let me suggest a description of communication that reflects our understanding of communication to this point: *Communication is a process whereby symbols generated by people are received and responded to by other people.*

Understood in this way we would include all the incidents of Professor Withit's morning except number two (2). In that case the student sent a message, a smile, but it was not received and responded to. Communication was attempted but not achieved. All the other incidents, however, were examples of communication.

Characteristics of Communication

Another way to test the adequacy of our understanding of communication is to see if our concept can accommodate basic truths about communication. Accordingly, let's see if our description of communication fits with five commonly accepted characteristics of communication:

       (1) Communication is a process.
       (2) Communication is complex.
       (3) Communication is symbolic.
       (4) Communication is a receiver phenomenon.
       (5) Communication is transitory.

Communication is a process. This statement implies that communication "does not have *a* beginning, *an* end, *a* fixed sequence of events. It is not static, at rest. It is moving. The ingredients within a process interact; each affects all other others."† Viewed in this way, communication is both dynamic—that is constantly changing—and interactive—at least two actively participating individuals are involved. We can separate the ingredients only if we stop the process to look at it. For example, in an argument between an employer and employee many things are happening simultaneously, each one affecting the others—e.g., the employee thinks his boss hates him, the rebuke confirms that impression, the employee's reaction is seen as a challenge to the boss's authority, other employees giggle at the exchange, increasing the employer's determination to reassert authority, etc. To sum up, the idea of process means that many ingredients—variables—are interacting at the same time to produce results.

Communication is complex. The complexity of communication is reflected in two important observations. First, being a process, it is not as direct and one-way as an injection into the arm administered by a physician. Rather, communication proceeds on verbal and nonverbal levels, in both directions.

---

†D. Berlo, *The Process of Communication,* New York: Holt, Rinehart and Winston, 1960, p. 24.

Second, communication is complex because it involves so many variables, or ingredients. Consider, for example, how many variables are operative during a simple conversation between you and a friend. It is more than just a matter of exchanging ideas with another person; "whenever there is communication there are at least six 'people' involved: the person you think yourself to be; the man your partner thinks you are; the person you believe your partner thinks you are; plus the three equivalent 'persons' at the other end of the circuit."‡ To these six "people" we must add the topic, the communication setting, the goal of communication, and the many other variables that affect any communication event. In addition, everyone has an individual personality, a set of needs, a past history, important personal relationships, and a unique way of seeing the world.

Communication is symbolic. One obvious but important characteristic of communication is that it involves the use of symbols of some kind. Symbols are arbitrary, man-made signs that represent thought. Two important implications of symbol use concern us here. First, a given symbol means something different to everyone. Symbols such as "beauty," "intelligence," and "democracy" illustrate well the many meanings invoked by single symbols. Therefore, communication is not the simple transfer of thought from one person to another. Rather, it is a process in which one individual encodes—translates—his thoughts into a symbol and sends that message via some medium to a receiver. The receiver then translates the message into thought—decodes the symbols. Thought and meaning are not transferred: messages are. Once the student of communication sheds the idea that communication is the transfer of meaning and adopts the view that *communication is an exchange of symbols,* a more realistic conception of the communication process is achieved.

The second important consequence of the fact that communication is symbolic is that not all symbols are words. The peace symbol, "thumbs down," long hair, and sarcastic voice inflection are all symbols that communicate ideas or sets of ideas. Indeed, many researchers contend that more than half of the meaning we gain in face-to-face communication is achieved through these nonverbal cues. The recognition and study of the importance of these nonverbal symbols is a critical aspect of understanding human communication.

Communication is a receiver phenomenon. Remember the second student that Professor Withit met earlier in this essay? That student smiled (an attempt to communicate nonverbally) but the professor did not see the smile. According to the description of communication we developed, the student did not communicate because the professor did not receive and respond to the symbol. This example illustrates an important aspect of communication: "Communication always occurs *in* the receiver."§ Notice how the concept of communication differs from a concept like "love." It is possible to love someone and not have the person aware of it. Even though the object of one's love is unaware of the existence of the feeling, the feeling nevertheless is real. Communication, on the other hand, requires that the receiver be just that—a receiver. Communication

‡D. Barnlund, "Toward a Meaning-Centered Philosophy of Communication," *Journal of Communication* 2 (1962), p. 40.

§L. Thayer, *Communication and Communication Systems,* Homewood, Illinois: Richard D. Irwin, Inc., 1968, p. 113.

attempts that do not reach the receiver, like the attempts of our hapless smiling student, are merely attempts at communication, not communication.

There is another implication we must keep in mind. If communication occurs within the receiver, the intention of the sender is largely unimportant. For example, whether or not Professor Withit intended to slight his student, he did. Whether or not the student whose discussion Professor Withit overheard intended it, his message was nevertheless picked up. Communication occurred because an individual received and responded to a set of symbols.

Third, if communication is identified by receiver response, we ought to examine the types of responses that occur. Let's again examine the episodes with which this essay began. Clearly, one result of the communication was a change in attitudes: the first student probably likes his professor a little more and the second student a little less, or maybe a lot less. Additionally, the professor probably did not think much of his secretary when he found out that the letter was mailed late. Apparently, then, one general effect of communication is that our attitudes toward people and things change. Another type of response was illustrated by the student who skipped class for a week. Obviously, the student's behavior was changed by the communication. By reading this essay, your knowledge of communication will be affected. Clearly, change in knowledge is another general type of response to communication. At this point, we should understand that communication occurs in the receiver and that its potential effects on the receiver are numerous.

Finally, being a receiver phenomenon means that communication occurs when the receiver attaches meaning to others' behavior. As a consequence of the dominant role of the receiver, some researchers have concluded that it is impossible to not communicate. Simply, "one cannot not communicate." / / All behavior, when perceived by another, has potential message value or communicative significance. That is, people assign meaning to other people's behavior or nonbehavior. For example, Professor Withit's failure to respond to one of his students angered the student. Therefore, if *all* behavior can have message value or meaning, it is impossible to not communicate, since you can't stop behaving. Anything you do or do not do *may* have meaning for one who perceives it. A few examples may illustrate this important characteristic of communication.

If you were to ask your roommate a question, is there anything he / she could do that would not mean something to you? What if he / she ignored your question? What if he / she answered sarcastically? What if he / she responded in a very cheery way? What if he / she left the room? No matter what he / she did, you would interpret the behavior as meaning something to you.

When you sit next to a person in the campus coffee shop and he says "hello," he is obviously communicating. Is not the same person communicating when he just looks at his food and ignores your presence. Of course he is! He is saying, "I'm here to eat and not to carry on idle chatter with a person I don't know." Is there anything that person could do to which you would not attach meaning? Probably not.

/ /P. Watzlawick, J. Beavin, and D. Jackson, *The Pragmatics of Human Communication,* New York: W. W. Norton, 1967, p. 48.

The fact that "one cannot *not* communicate" is important. It means that the study of communication must focus on all your behavior and not just on that part of the time when your mouth is open. Furthermore, it increases your responsibility to recognize that what you say and do influences other people.

Communication is transitory. This principle has two parts. First, communication is irreversible. It can only go onward: it cannot back up and try again. This characteristic of communication is best illustrated by the absurdity of the judge's admonition, "the jury will disregard the testimony just given." Impossible! Second, communication is unrepeatable. Even if the message is repeated word for word, the audience has been changed by the first attempt. Therefore, they are different receivers attaching a different meaning to the same message. This principle of communication is well illustrated by the common experience of either telling or hearing a joke the second time; it just is not the same.

So far it works! If we conceive of communication as a "process whereby symbols generated by people are received and responded to by other people" we can account for the observations that communication is a process, is complex, is symbolic, is a receiver phenomenon, and that communication is transitory. Let's test our understanding in yet another way.

Myths of Communication

Another test of the adequacy of our concept of communication is whether it helps us reject myths or misconceptions about communication. Using our description of communication see how it allows us to avoid five of the most common mistaken conclusions about communication.

1. "I understand communication. I've done it for years." Because of this false assumption, people have communicated poorly for centuries. You have breathed for years, driven cars for years, listened to radios for years, and thought for years, and yet you probably realize that knowing more about physiology, engineering, electronics, and psychology could improve your own performance. Many successful salespersons do not understand persuasion. Doing something does not necessarily imply that one understands what he or she is doing.

2. "Communication can be improved simply by improving communication skills." This myth is based on two fallacies. First, it assumes that there are "certain unequivocal laws which, if followed, lead to success, and, if not, to failure."# That simply is not the case. Communication is far too complex a process and our investigation (so far) too unsophisticated for such rules to exist. If such rules were available, they could be printed and distributed at freshman orientation, and all departments of English and Speech Communication could be disbanded.

Second, this myth focuses attention on the speaker, which, according to our description of communication, is stressing the wrong person. Remember, communication is a receiver phenomenon. The study of communication, therefore, should not focus on what the speaker *does to* a receiver (which treats the receiver as a passive, mindless blob), but should

#Thayer, p. 8.

focus on what happens within the receiver as the result of the speaker's behavior.

Communication is not necessarily improved merely by improving communication skills. Indeed, communication is improved "first, by the communicator's understanding of the communication process, then by the communicator's attitudes and orientations; and only then by the techniques the communicator employs."**

3. "I didn't misunderstand him, he misunderstood me." Because of human nature, we are always convinced that we are right and the other person is wrong. For example, I have heard students say things like, "It was John's fault, his speech was so confusing nobody could have understood it." Then, two minutes later, the same student remarked, "It wasn't my fault, what I said could not have been clearer. John must be stupid." Poor John! He was blamed when he was the sender *and* when he was the receiver. John's problem was that he was the *other* person, and that's who is always at fault.

To understand and to improve communication, you have to be willing to accept the idea that communication is a two-way process with at least two active participants and "fault" must be divided between them.

4. "Most problems, from interpersonal to international, are caused by communication breakdowns. These breakdowns are abnormal and easily correctable." Let's look at the first sentence of this most common of myths. In recent years a number of widely discussed, little understood, and generally ambiguous terms and phrases, such as "communication breakdown," "communication gap," and "credibility gap," have been introduced into our everyday vocabulary. These terms have become the dumping ground for many phenomena we can't explain in an easier or more direct way. The fact that college administrators and students disagree is not a communication breakdown. The fact that teenagers frequently argue with parents is not a communication gap. The fact that minorities demonstrate for a greater share of the economic "action" in this country is not a communication breakdown. Calling these problems gaps or breakdowns ignores the psychological, economic, political, and physical realities which caused the symptom of poor or infrequent communication.

The second part of this myth is equally erroneous. Ineffective communication is not abnormal. Communication is complex and poorly understood; is it any wonder that without much knowledge or training in communication we are not very good at it? Further, since communication is so complex, can we expect it to be easily corrected when it is found to be inefficient?

5. "All communication is attempting to achieve perfect understanding between participants." This myth is dangerous on two counts. First, it assumes that "perfect understanding" is possible. Second, it denies an important reality: sometimes the goal of communication is to be misunderstood.

To achieve "perfect understanding" through communication limited to a humanly-devised symbol system is impossible. Our symbols frequently do

**Thayer, p. 8.

not come close to fitting the ideas they are supposed to represent; at best, they are approximations. There is always a very real possibility, indeed probability, that the idea you try to communicate will not be the idea your communication partner decodes from the symbols you have chosen to represent the idea. Recognizing that symbols are inexact, we should try to make our communication as efficient as possible. This, rather than "perfection," is a realistic and attainable goal.

Do you always want to be perfectly understood? Probably not. Have you never answered a test question vaguely to avoid demonstrating ignorance? Have you never sidestepped giving an opinion about a friend's new car or clothing? Often we intentionally garble our messages so as to avoid embarrassment or hide our true feelings. The following selection from an Oscar Wilde play illustrates this use of communication well.

> THE DUCHESS: "Do, as a concession to my poor wits, Lord Darlington, just explain to me what you really mean."
> LORD DARLINGTON: "I think I had better not. Nowadays to be intelligible is to be found out."††

What Is Not Communication

One final test of our understanding of communication is whether we can use such understanding to identify what is not communication. That is, we should be able to answer the question, "What isn't communication?"

We have said that communication takes place whenever someone attaches meaning to another's behavior. It is clear that unless one's behavior is perceived by someone, communication has not occurred. That is, what one does or says in isolation is not communication.‡‡ Furthermore, we must exclude those behaviors which, though perceived, have no meaning or significance for the perceiver. Perceived behavior to which the perceiver does not attach meaning is not communication. Every day we interact with others in ways that result in no significant interpretation or meaning being attached to the perceived behavior. For example, when you jostle your way in or out of a crowded lecture hall, your behavior and that of many others are mutually perceived, but only in the rare circumstances of inordinate rudeness does anyone attach meaning to that type of perceived behavior. Note that this argument retains the focus of our study on the receiver: Does the receiver attach meaning to that which is perceived? Obviously, what is meaningful for one person might be inconsequential for another. For example, you would probably ignore the fact that your friend does not wear a watch, but a psychiatrist may take that to mean something significant about your friend's psyche.

Thus, to answer the original question, behavior that is not perceived by another or to which no significant meaning is attached is not communication. Behavior that is both perceived and meaningful is communication.

You may now argue, "O.K., but earlier you said that communication can't be turned off, and now you say some perceived behavior is not communication. Isn't

††O. Wilde, *Lady Windermere's Fan,* cited by Thayer, p. 306.

‡‡Of course, communication with ourselves can be considered communication— intrapersonal communication. However, this essay has focused on the social or interpersonal nature of communication.

that contradictory?'' Not at all. Not all behavior communicates, but it has the *potential* for communication. The important distinction is that you cannot *avoid* communicating. It is impossible for you to turn communication off as you do a radio. When this point was presented earlier in the essay, I was looking at the sender and forcing him or her to recognize all the ways he or she is constantly giving off communicative behavior. When I say that all behavior need not be communication, I am focusing on the receiver and asking the question—does the receiver actually assign meaning to perceived behavior? Not all behavior actually communicates, but it does have communication potential.

Summary
Are you now ready for a definition? We described communication and then tested our understanding of the thing described in many ways. We found that our understanding of communication helped us identify what is and isn't communication, it assisted in rejecting fallacious myths about communication, and it can accommodate several basic truths about communication. Accordingly, we can now define communication in a way that *reflects* our understanding, rather than merely assert a definition that is separate from our understanding. Simply, we understand communication to be ''a process whereby symbols generated by people are received and responded to by other people.''

Communication Systems

Human communication systems can be studied at any level of existence, from individual to society. You will recall that *systems* were defined as complexes of interdependent components in constant interaction, requiring constant adaptation among the parts of the system, and that every part of a system is to some degree influenced by any part. *Intrapersonal communication* refers to communication occuring within an individual, among various components of his or her organism as electrochemical signals flow throughout the nervous system. Intrapersonal communication includes the study of cognitive processes we call *perception* and *thinking,* as well as sensation, muscle control, and coordination of the entire organism.

    Social systems of communication involve two or more persons exchanging and responding to each other's signals. At the *interpersonal* level the communication process involves two or a few persons exchanging both verbal and nonverbal signals in an interactive process. *Small group communication* refers to interpersonal communication when three or more *persons who comprise a small group as defined in chapter 1* are simultaneously sending, receiving and internally processing, and reacting to signals from each other. The upper level of small group communication occurs at some point when members lose awareness of other members as individuals. At that point a large group may or may not exist, but *public communication,* involving a primary source of verbal signals to other persons not perceived, for the most part, by the signaller (''public speaker'') as persons with unique characteristics, will be going on. The listeners in a public communication system are usually referred to as an *audience*. The most common forms of public communication systems involve public speeches and written or visual messages in a closed-circuit electrical system carrying signals to a limited audience. Public communication becomes *mass communication* when the signals are carred by some medium potentially available to an indeterminately large number of persons—broadcast television and radio, newspaper, pamphlet, book, magazine, film, etc.

It follows from the preceding description of the five levels at which communication can be studied that in the small group intrapersonal, interpersonal, and small group levels are all important to outputs of the group. Indeed, all of what we have previously considered in this book has a direct bearing on the communication process among small group members, and is frequently included in books and articles treating "small group communication": attitudes, personal skills, rules, roles, and so forth. Communication is the process by which the components of the small group system influence each other.

Intrapersonal Communication Systems

In the past few decades scientists have greatly expanded our knowledge of intrapersonal communication, especially knowledge about the nature of the sensors, signals, brain and other central nervous system (CNS) operations, and how we interpret signals. The science of intrapersonal communication is highly complex and includes far too much for inclusion in this book. For our purposes as students of discussion within small groups of persons, I will describe only in the general way needed to appreciate what is likely to go wrong when members of a group interact.

As illustrated in figure 6.1, any given intrapersonal communication episode begins with a signal from some source that impacts on a sensor of a person, in this case "Jane." The signal can come from inside or outside the body: a rise in heart rate, pressure on a toe, a gas bubble in the stomach, a flashing light, a sudden roar from a steam valve, a voice. The moment a sensor reacts to a signal an episode of intrapersonal communication has begun in Jane. Assume that Jane's entire information processing system is intact. The sensor(s) emits signals into an afferent nerve that carries it into the central nervous system of the spinal cord and brain, where various switching operations occur, sending signals to one or more divisions of this great central information processor. Based on Jane's physical and psychosocial needs, the condition of Jane's systems, past experiences and knowledge, values, beliefs, expectations, and many other variables, the CNS will respond in some way—a decision is made and action taken. The "decision" may or may not be at a level of consciousness. For example, the filters of the CNS may decide that no action is appropriate at the time, and "kill" the signal—thus the response is no *overt* response. This happens often when you are sleeping and do not waken to a voice that

Figure 6.1 An intrapersonal communication system.

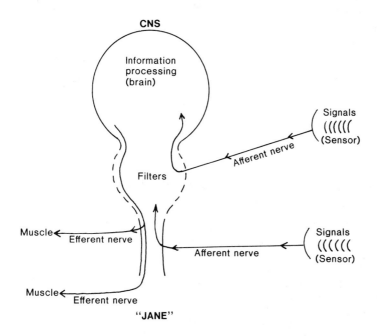

has impinged on the ears and energized the auditory nerve so that signals are carried to the brain. Sometimes the response to such a signal is to weave it into a dream. If the signal to the ears is interpreted at a level below consciousness as being especially important, or is of sufficient power, you will waken, consciously try to interpret the sound, and respond in some overt way. Thus a mother of a very young infant may waken at its slightest cry, rise from bed and go to the baby, but she may sleep through a much louder sound from adults talking nearby, or an auto horn. In the small group, a person who has previously had very little to say or is considered a low status member of the group may not even be perceived at a conscious level by the more active members when he or she does finally speak up, unless the speaking is exceptionally forceful.

Of the multitude of signals constantly coming into Jane's CNS from sensors, only one at a time can be the focus of attention; the rest are either dealt with by the autonomic nervous system below the level of consciousness, serve as a background to signals focused upon, or are ignored. To reach the threshold of awareness, a signal must be of some minimum strength and duration. Thresholds vary from sensor to sensor, time to time, and person to person. Thus one person may not be aware of what another member of the group says, while a third member listens quite well. Often one must expend considerable energy vocally and nonvocally to have his or her signals become the center of attention by other members.

Interpersonal Communication Systems

Like the term "communication," the phrase "interpersonal communication" has been defined many different ways. Some writers use this phrase to refer to any incident when symbols generated by one person are received and responded to by another; some use the phrase to refer to all dyadic (two-person) symbol exchanges. Still others limit "interpersonal" communication to exchanges in which each person is involved as a unique individual, not just as the occupant of a role. For instance, if when talking with an attendant at a gas station you are perceived only as a customer and you perceive the attendant only as a functionary, the exchange would not be classified as interpersonal.

All small group communication involves interpersonal communication, since to become a *group* the members must perceive each other's strengths and weaknesses in relationship to their objectives, at least to some degree. Awareness of each other as unique individuals is part of the definition of a *small* group. Since communication among the members of a small group is at an inter*personal* level but as part of the small group process and involving awareness of several others, I have incorporated further explanation of interpersonal communication with the explanation of small group communication systems. Unlike most textbooks about interpersonal communication, *Effective Group Discussion* does not consider in depth such topics as development of a self-concept, self-disclosure, expression of feelings, and perception.

Small Group Communication Systems

Small group communication occurs whenever three or more members simultaneously emit and respond to signals from each other. Figure 6.2 represents communication among three members of a small group, A, B, and C. The process by which they interact is called *transactional*, for each is both sender and receiver, influencer and influenced, and each creates a personal meaning for the signals to which he or she responds. Of course signals from other members are selectively received by the sensors and transformed into nerve messages, then interpreted in the CNS. The *response* signals must be converted from electrochemical signals in the nervous system of each to some form that can be conveyed in the media that link the discussants. The most important signals in discussions are carried by air and light waves. Each person reflects light waves that then carry the reflected visual signals to the eyes of other members who are looking. When these light waves impinge upon the retinas of the other discussants, they are transformed by a chemical process into afferent nerve signals (electrochemical) that are carried to the CNS for processing as described at the intrapersonal level. Movement, dress, gesture, body

Figure 6.2   A small group communication system.

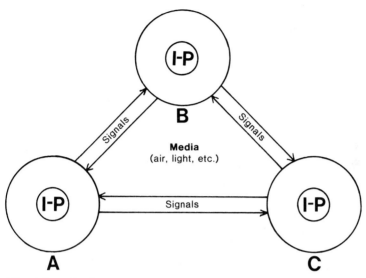

I-P = Information Processors

form, facial expression, eye focus and pupil opening size, and distance are among the many types of important light messages received by discussants that can be interpreted and responded to as meaningful signals. At the same time, air molecules are moving in waves in response to the actions of each discussant's speech mechanism (vocal folds, lips, jaw, palate, etc.). These air waves may be encoded words, or such nonverbal signals as coughs, wheezes, sighs, and whistles. Thus what originated as a *meaning* in one person has been transformed into signals in efferent nerves, then into muscle actions, then into air and/or light waves, then into some sensor activity, then transformed again into electrochemical signals in the receiver's afferent nerves, processed in the CNS, and given meaning as a *perception,* thought, or mental image. The only characteristics of a message that can remain unchanged during all these transformations is the arrangement or structure of bits of energy.

In the preceding article, King stated that the process of communication was highly complex. Now you can understand a little more clearly just how complex it is, and can readily understand that in any discussion involving this process much can go wrong that will evoke misunderstanding.

It will require great attention and effort if we are not to have many serious misunderstandings among members of a small group, leading to perceptual dissimilarity, low cohesiveness, dissatisfaction, and poor solutions to problems. You will recall from reading the article by King that communication involves an exchange of symbols and signs, not of meanings. Each member of the group creates meanings from signals sent by others based on what is actually received and how it is interpreted. Achieving similar understandings among the members of a small group can be very difficult; it can never be taken for granted.

The Complete Communicative Transaction

To verify one's understanding of another's meaning during discussion requires a *complete* transaction. Recall King's statement that "communication is a receiver phenomenon." For a validated interpersonal transaction to occur there must be an overt response to an initial message and an acknowledgement of that response so that both parties to the interchange know that they have communicated as desired. Thus if member A says, "What happened in the student center that everyone is talking about?" (Initiation), B might say, "A big fight broke out between members of two fraternities" (Response), to which A would possibly nod or say "Oh, I see" (Acknowledgment). In the case of a small group, each speaker addressing the group as a whole needs a response of some perceivable sort from each other member (maybe only a nod or a frown), and needs, in turn, to acknowledge that response. The speaker may find that he or she has to correct or revise the original message because the response indicates he or she was not understood as intended. Or the response may be the lack of response—in which case the speaker has two choices: to give up or to restate in a more forceful or different way. Nothing is more dampening to cohesiveness, interest, and enthusiasm than a lack of perceivable response—*feedback*—denying the speaker's very existence by indicating "you matter not at all; you are not worth responding to." To be unresponsive during group interaction is to be a very negative force. Passivity displays an attitude of rejection of others, and of noninvolvement in the group.

Notice if there is a difference in the amount of response to each other by members of groups in which you participate. With which do you find yourself most comfortable—those who react openly and clearly, or those who give little response? I suggest that you monitor your own response behavior, and change it if you find that you are a discussant who fails to respond actively to speakers; in short, don't break the communication circuit. Many student journals have had statements like this: "Even though Jean didn't say much, I was able to tell where she stood. You could tell from her face and movements that she was involved. Ed was another story. It was hard to tell how he felt, and I never could trust him."

The Message Sent

"Message" can refer to either a set of signals from some person to others, or to the interpretation and response of a discussant to a message received from another. A "sent" message consists of both verbal and nonverbal signals. A sent message might consist of a short speech by a group member: all the words, and all the nonverbal signals accompanying those words, such as gestures, vocal tones, pitch changes, and eye movements. Another message sent might consist of only nonverbal signals, such as a mix of facial expressions and a shift in posture. In this case, the message *received* by a person who perceived and interpreted those nonverbal cues might be something like "Charles is not interested in what I have to say." Notice that the response in this transaction is *verbal* at the intrapersonal level. An entirely nonverbal or entirely verbal human communicative transaction is quite rare in small group discussion. Every verbal statement has its nonverbal elements, and responses to entirely nonverbal signals always include words in the mind (intrapersonal level) of the receiver. To illustrate this principle, look at another person with whom you have some involvement but who is saying nothing, then see if you can avoid *thinking* with words while you interpret what you see. It can't be done! In the next two chapters we will focus first on verbal and then on nonverbal signals in small group discussions, but in practice they are not separable.

In addition to its verbal and nonverbal elements, every verbal message has direct and indirect implications of at least three types: content, affective, and relational. The *content* level is what is often called the *denotative* aspect of words, or what the speaker is talking about. Thus someone might say "Eighty-four persons were murdered in Central City last year according to the police department's annual crime report," denoting the statistic and what it represents in criminal behavior. The *affective* level of the message is how the speaker feels about what has been denoted; his or her manner while speaking might be interpreted as showing great concern, or being rather neutral to all these deaths. The *relational* implication of the statement concerns how the speaker sees his or her relationship to the listeners, usually conveyed in nonverbal signals. Thus the speaker's manner while speaking may indicate to the other participants that he or she wants to be taken as an unchallengeable authority (↑), sees the other participants as equals (→), or feels very subservient to them (↓). Attitudes of arrogance, dominance, submissiveness, distrust, superiority, neutrality, or concern are not often stated directly as such, but listeners interpret them from nonverbal cues—such are the *relational* aspects of interpersonal messages among small group members.

Because communication is a receiver phenomenon, it is especially important that we consider the listening behavior of group members. Communication among group members can be no better than their listening skills permit. The rest of this chapter is devoted to listening well and responding appropriately to signals from fellow group members.

Listening and Responding during Discussions

Mutual understanding among members of a small group depends even more on how they listen and respond to each other than it does on how they speak. Listening has been defined as a "selective process of attending to, hearing, understanding, and remembering aural (and, at times visual) symbols."[2] "Hearing," the reception by the ear of sound waves and transformation of them into auditory nerve signals, is only a part of listening. Listening includes hearing, and much more—especially the *interpreting* of signals heard. During a discussion a listener must first hear, then assign meaning to aural signals in order to have listened. A person with acute hearing may be a poor listener because of how she interprets and responds to others' statements, whereas a different person with considerable hearing loss may be an excellent listener during small group discussions where some hearing loss is not a serious impediment if one really wants to understand other members of the group. A good listener with reduced hearing acuity will attend extra closely, ask others to speak louder if necessary, and interpret very accurately despite the hearing loss.

It is much easier to detect that a fellow communicator is not listening well in a dyad than in a small group. In a group of several persons one member can avoid speaking for relatively long periods of time. Only when the person speaks do other participants have a basis for judging the adequacy of his or her listening, for one can fake the outward signs of listening. Irrelevant comments and obvious misunderstandings of a previous speaker are the evidence that poor listening was going on.

Few, if any, persons think of themselves as poor listeners. Do you? Yet the evidence is that most of us are pretty poor at getting information from listening, at interpreting accurately others' meanings, and at retaining what we have listened to in long-term memory. At times some discussants are not even aware of what is being talked about by other members of a small group. Berg found that topics were switched approximately one time per minute in discussions he observed. It seemed as if hardly anyone was listening to and responding to what previous speakers had said in these discussions.[3] This sad finding has been confirmed by several other investigators observing groups in a variety of cultures and situations.[4] Nichols reported that students listening to lectures on which they knew they would be tested retained even for a short time only about fifty per cent of the new information presented by the lecturer.[5] I've found that when small group members (whether in college classes or corporate personnel in training groups) are required to paraphrase a previous discussant's point of view to that person's satisfaction, about half the time observers report that listeners were unable to do so. Even when they know they will be required to demonstrate accuracy in listening, most people can get approval from the previous speaker for how well they understood only half the time. How much, then, must group discussants misunderstand when they are *not* on guard and trying their utmost to listen well!

The cost of poor listening is high. In the work scene many jobs are done incorrectly, people are hurt or killed because they did not understand what was intended, shipments go awry, and both time and material are wasted. In meetings of small groups the costs are also high. Much time is wasted while repeating ideas for persons who weren't listening or misunderstood what could easily have been understood by listening well. Needless personal conflicts frequently arise producing high levels of secondary tension and distress. Chopra observed that when group members did not respond to and reinforce one another, retaliation, withdrawal, and defensive behaviors increased.[6] We all want to be understood when we speak; not being responded to with some sign of an attempt to understand irritates us.

Pitfalls to Listening Effectively

We all tire at times, grow preoccupied with things deeply worrisome to us, or suffer from an overload of information and noise. On such occasions we cannot listen well; that is understandable. But even when we are not troubled by illness, exhaustion, or a personal problem which has no immediate relevancy to the meeting in which we are participating, we may still listen poorly as a result of personal habits, insecurities, and behavioral patterns we have acquired. What follows are several patterns of behavior which interfere with listening well. Persons who engage in these behaviors often do not realize that they are either not listening at all or doing so very badly.

1. **Pseudolistening.** Pseudolistening refers to faking the real thing by giving an appearance of listening to understand. Pseudolisteners nod, smile, murmur polite responses, look the speaker in the eye, and may even give verbal support such as "Right" or "Good idea." Behind the mask the pseudolistener is not listening to understand, but is off on some personal train of thought: a daydream, a personal problem, sizing the speaker up as a target, or just thinking he has heard this before. When their behavior is pointed out, most pseudolisteners say something like "That stuff he was saying is boring," when in truth they had dismissed the topic in a stereotyped way without giving the speaker a chance.

2. **Silent arguing.** Many persons listen selectively to information which confirms their views and to arguments they already agree with. Instead of listening well to contrary evidence and arguments (necessary if one is to help a group find the best possible course of action), the selective listener ignores these or carries on a silent argument. Without adequate understanding, he or she argues that the other is wrong.

   One cannot both listen to self and to a fellow discussant. You cannot listen well enough to understand another accurately if at the same time you are thinking of how to respond. Only one item can be the center of attention at a time—if one's own thinking, then not the speaking of another. If you listen primarily to find flaws and argue them in your mind you are very unlikely to perceive and understand the idea adequately, or the evidence and reasoning supporting it. This silent arguing is closed-mindedness in action. Such is *dogmatism,* opposed to searching and inquiring after the best possible alternative or idea. If you are aware of your biases, and of when you start silent arguments, you can consciously stop it. Try to compensate for this bad habit by extra effort to understand what another is saying from his point of view so that you could express it to his satisfaction. After all, that is the purpose of listening during a cooperative group discussion—to arrive at mutual understandings. Only after you have understood another's meaning as intended are you in a position to disagree and argue validly against the other's position.

3. **Premature replying.** This can take two forms. Most common is preparing mentally to make your own remark before fully understanding a question or statement by another member of the group. You'll recognize at once that this behavior is similar to silent arguing, but "premature replying" need not involve disagreeing. Group members who know each other fairly well often think they know what the other will say long before she has finished a statement, jump to a conclusion, and then get ready to reply without allowing time to listen to the full statement (including the important nonverbal cues that accompany the words). The result is a lot of misunderstanding and disjointed discussions in which the subject seems to be constantly changing. In many instances the premature replier shifts the topic to her favorite subject, or to an aspect of the problem she is most familiar with, regardless of whether the subject addressed by the previous speaker has been adequately discussed to resolve it. Such switching of the subject with a premature reply is sometimes called "stagehogging," a most appropriate label.

4. **Focusing on irrelevancies and distractions.** Instead of keeping attention focused on what other members are saying or signalling nonverbally, some members let themselves be distracted and attend to background noises, furnishings, statements made by persons not in the group, or other less-than-ideal environmental conditions. Some will pay undue attention to a speaker's dialect, appearance, or personal mannerisms, and thus miss his or her meaning. As one woman from Georgia said to group members, "Damn it, listen to what I have to say, not to how I speak. I can't change that now. It makes me really mad when someone says 'Oh, how you talk is so cute I just can't pay attention to what you are saying.' "

5. **Sidetracking.** Another discussant mentions some experience or idea, and you begin a reverie as you recall some past experience that the statement triggered. Meanwhile, something else has been said that you missed. Watch out for the tendency to sidetrack into your personal storehouse of memories while others are still speaking.

6. **Listening defensively.** When we feel that the image and role we are trying to project in a group are being threatened, we are likely to become defensive. Defensive persons do not listen well, at least in the sense of listening to understand another as that person wants to be

understood. When we feel defensive about an idea or self-concept, we usually quit listening in order to invent ways to defend self and attack the other. This is, however, the very time when we need most to understand the perception and values of the other person which we find irritating. There may be a real clash in values, the speaker may be trying to assume a one-up position of dominance, or perhaps only has a different way of verbalizing a belief or value that I as listener actually share.

It is especially important to watch for "emotive" or "trigger" words so that you do not miss the other's point in a burst of negative reaction to a word. For instance, if someone refers to a person you respect as a "bastard," it may be all too easy to attack the speaker instead of discovering why she or he dislikes that person. Some persons have very strong negative reactions to terms such as "nuclear energy," "abortion," or "right to life"; they fail to listen to what the speaker means, and why. When you get too emotionally involved it is time to take a deep breath, back off, and try to understand the meaning of the speaker to whom you are responding with such vigor. Take another look! Check your understanding.

7. **Forcing meaning.** This behavior is not common in small group discussions, but when it happens the cost is high. Forcing meaning refers to the listener who insists that the speaker meant by a statement what the listener would have meant if he or she had uttered those words. "Oh, yes, I know what you meant. I heard what you said," says the meaning forcer, insisting that his interpretation is correct, despite protests of the speaker. Underlying this behavior is the faulty assumption that words have meanings in and of themselves. It also stems from a rigid, dogmatic bent of mind that will not entertain two or more apparently contradictory ideas.

You have probably noticed that in all of these types of nonlistening or poor listening behaviors there is an element of evaluation or judgment. The listener is so busy judging the speaker and the speaker's ideas that he or she does not take time to understand empathically, without judgment. The sequence is entirely reversed from what it should be, "bassackwards" as a Pennsylvania Dutchman might say. First, we need to understand each other's ideas; then and only then are we able to judge appropriately. As Kelley put it, we need to be "empathic" listeners who try to understand what the other means from his or her point of view, with the motivation to receive information being greater than the motivation to evaluate and criticize.[7]

Often in the early stages of a new group's emergence and development not much effective listening may be in evidence (especially while members are struggling for roles and status). If this nonlistening continues at length, something must be done or the group will get little work accomplished and may disintegrate. Most of all, each of us needs to become aware of how she or he listens, and to assume the responsibility for changing our own bad habits of poor listening. What you can do is explained next.

Active Listening

Effective listening is an active process requiring every bit as much effort as speaking. We refer to the listener who is trying hard to understand and recall as an *active* listener because in such a person the heartbeat accelerates from what it would be at rest to a rate similar to that when the person is active, engaged in physical effort. Heart rates of poor listeners frequently go down toward the level of sleep! Active listening takes an act of will or determination, a decision to apply one's self to understanding before judging, and to select what to recall and then behave mentally in ways likely to insure that memory.

A good test of how well you have been listening is a technique called "active listening." This technique virtually forces the listener to understand a speaker before replying or adding to a discussion. What you do is restate, IN YOUR OWN WORDS, what you understood the previous speaker to mean, and then ask for confirmation or correction of your paraphrase. It is very important that the listener paraphrase, not repeat word for word. A small child or tape recorder can repeat, but that does not demonstrate understanding. A paraphrase in the listener's own words gives the speaker a good basis to judge if a statement was adequately understood, if the listener failed to get part of the intended message, or if it was misunderstood. The original speaker can then reply to the feedback by stating acceptance, adding what was left out, or making a revision of what was originally stated and asking the active listener to once more try a paraphrase. Only when the original speaker is fully satisfied that the listener has understood what was intended does the discussion go forward with agreement, disagreement, elaboration, some different point, or whatever the active listener wants to say. The following examples will clarify the active listening technique:

Ed: "Requiring landowners to farm in such a way that topsoil is not lost is absolutely necessary if we are to protect the earth as a habitation for our descendants." (opinion)

Gail: "If I understand you, you think we should require that farming practices prevent as much as possible the erosion of topsoil, for such erosion destroys the earth for growing things." (paraphrase of Ed's opinion)

Ed: "Right, Gail." (confirmation and acceptance of paraphrase)

****

Mike: "If every college graduate were required to demonstrate some competence in using a computer that might be helpful right at graduation, but computers are changing so rapidly that grads would be no better off than if they had no such training in a few years unless they kept up-to-date or had to use a computer all along." (opinion)

Charles: "Do I understand you correctly? Are you saying that a computer science course should *not* be required to get a degree?" (attempted paraphrase of Mike's opinion)

Mike: "No, just that it should be more than just how to use a computer; you ought to understand computers, what they do and don't do." (rejects the paraphrase and attempts to clarify)

Charles: "So you think there should be a requirement for a graduate to be able to explain what computers can and can't do, as well as to be comfortable with a computer."

Mike: "Yes, more than a course as such." (confirms paraphrase)

Charles: "I agree with that idea, and think we should also have a requirement for ability to investigate, organize, and write a term paper." (his paraphrase confirmed, Charles now has added his opinion, a new topic, to the discussion)

Although every idea advanced in a discussion should be evaluated, only when you are sure that you understand another's point on an issue should you even *attempt* to evaluate it. So the procedure is to listen actively and confirm your understanding of another's idea before expressing your evaluation of it, either affirmative or negative. Then, and only then, is evaluative, critical listening in order. Then it is appropriate to comment on whether or not the statement was pertinent to the previous theme of discussion, if there is sufficient basis in evidence and reasoning for the idea, if it reflects some prejudice or stereotype, etc. Productive listening during discussions entails first understanding what another meant and confirming that understanding, then evaluating the significance and validity of the comment.

A slowdown in the pace of interaction and many questions for clarification are likely to be side effects of active listening. If you are not used to listening actively, for a time you may find yourself with nothing to say for a moment after the other finishes speaking. But keep practicing active listening; soon you will find yourself making spontaneous responses in place of strategically preplanned remarks or irrelevant statements which sidetrack the discussion. Cohesiveness and cooperation are likely to increase in your group.

A part of active listening during discussions is to be an open responder. This was previously explained in "The Complete Communicative Transaction" (p. 152). Only overt feedback can provide the speaker with the responses he or she needs. Positive feedback indicating that a message has been received and understood can take the vocal form of an "um-hum," "gotcha," or "yeah," or such nonverbal gestures as head nodding, smiling, frowning, changing of body angle, or hand gesturing. More expansive forms of these cues usually indicate agreement. Of course, you will be careful not to engage in "pseudolistening" where you send responsive signals but are not actually listening to understand—just trying to be "polite" and accepted. Pseudolistening is often more damaging to trust and cooperation than is argumentative listening, for the speaker at first thinks the responder understands and agrees, then later realizes he cannot place confidence in nonverbal responses from such a person.

When an active listener cannot hear adequately or is not confident of her understanding, she will say so quickly, asking for a repetition or clarification. Once understanding has been established, such a person is open about her agreement, desire for more information, skepticism, or whatever may be her response.

Focused Listening

A disorder plaguing many problem-solving groups is that members seem not to have much functional memory of the important issues or ideas that have been raised and agreed upon. During the excitement of exploring a new idea or argument it is very easy to forget vital information about the problem, ideas presented as possible solutions, or goals/criteria accepted earlier by the group. A skilled coordinating leader or group secretary would have a written record of these items, but only during an occasional summary might the other participants be reminded of them. So it is necessary for each participant to remember what is the issue of the moment, what has previously been discussed and dismissed, and what has been decided upon if the discussion is to be efficient, moving in an orderly fashion toward the group goal. *Focused listening* for such recall is important for all discussants. We can remember only limited amounts of information in a given period of time. Further, we remember information in groups or sets of related items; we remember poorly lists of unorganized bits of information, whether these be examples that are unrelated, nonsense syllables, phone numbers, or ideas for solving a problem. You probably have read about this principle of memory in your basic psychology textbook.

I've observed that the members of highly productive problem-solving groups maintain considerable perspective on the discussion as a whole by focusing their listening. They attend to and recall the *main points* of the discussion. They listen for issues, rather than for specific facts and opinions, except as these relate to and support major issues and proposals. They keep a note pad on which they record important information presented by others, criteria, and especially all ideas presented for consideration as possible solutions. It is a rare person who can trust random access memory for such details; we remember more of the details if they are related to major issues or points. You will recall far more of a discussion if you keep a mental summary of the main issues (questions) discussed and how each is settled than if you try to remember specifics; you can keep a written account of "facts," if needed. Such listening will help you keep on track, and allow you to reorient a group when someone switches the topic before the group has reached a decision on an important issue. In all too many discussions no one seems to realize that the group is flitting from topic to topic with no closure on any of them. The focused listener maintains a perspective on the entire discussion. A group plagued by constant shifts of topic has often been helped by a nonparticipating process observer who pointed out the problem and encouraged members to listen well. By doing that the members were able to maintain perspective on the group's purpose and the content and progress of their discussion.

Summary

Human communication is a complex transactional process that involves the generating of symbolic signals, many transformations of those signals as they are exchanged, received, and interpreted, and numerous sources of interference and distortion. To be an optimal discussant, one needs to understand that process as it occurs at intrapersonal and interpersonal levels during small group communication. Intense attention to both encoding and decoding are required if members of a small group are to achieve similar perceptions. Productive discussants are active listeners who frequently check their understandings with paraphrases. They avoid the pitfalls of pseudolistening, silent arguing, premature replying, focusing on irrelevancies and distractions, sidetracking, listening defensively, and forcing meaning. They maintain their focus on issues and ideas of the discussion, supplemented by mental reviews and notes.

Exercises

1. For small group discussion: "In what ways and in what parts of a small group communication system can interferences occur in the process of communication?"

2. Practice the rule that "each discussant must rephrase in his own words his or her understanding of the previous speaker's meanings (ideas *and* feelings) to that speaker's *complete* satisfaction (as indicated verbally or by a head nod) before he or she may have the floor and add anything to the discussion." If the paraphrase is not accepted, the original speaker may then clarify, the rephraser may try again, or someone else may try. One member of the group should not participate, but keep an accurate count of the number of times paraphrases are accepted and rejected. Be sure to count each attempt to rephrase. Discuss the implications of listening, how to improve communication, and how you felt during this project.

3. Prepare a chart for recording observations of listening behaviors and responses of members of a discussion group. The chart should have four columns headed as follows: Active Listening; Premature Replying;

Sidetracking; Forcing Meaning. With several classmates observe either a live discussion or a recording of one. As you observe, note each instance of these types of behaviors.

Now compare your observations with those of your fellow observers. What do you conclude about the listening-responding behavior of the discussants? Were there apparent instances of pseudolistening, silent arguing, defensive listening, or focusing on irrelevancies and distractions? What seemed to be the effect of group members' listening behaviors on group outputs?

Bibliography

Cathcart, Robert S., and Samovar, Larry A., eds. *Small Group Communication: A Reader.* 4th ed., Dubuque, Iowa: Wm. C. Brown Company Publishers, 1984, section 5.

Steil, Lyman K., and Barker, Larry. *Effective Listening: Key to Your Success.* Reading, MA: Addison-Wesley, 1983.

References

1. Reprinted with permission from Wm. C. Brown Company Publishers and the author, Stephen W. King, "The Nature of Communication," in *Small Group Communication: A Reader,* 4th ed., Robert S. Cathcart and Larry A. Samovar, eds. Dubuque, Iowa: Wm. C. Brown Company Publishers, 1984, 214–223.
2. Larry L. Barker, *Listening Behavior* (Englewood Cliffs, N.J.: Prentice-Hall, 1971), 17.
3. David M. Berg, "A Descriptive Analysis of the Distribution and Duration of Themes Discussed by Task-Oriented Small Groups," *Speech Monographs* 34 (1967): 172–175.
4. Earnest G. and Nancy C. Bormann, *Effective Small Group Communication,* 3d ed. (Minneapolis: Burgess, 1980), 97.
5. Ralph G. Nichols and Leonard Stevens, "Listening to People," *Harvard Business Review* 35 (1957): 85–92.
6. Amarjit Chopra, "Motivation in Task-Oriented Groups," *Journal of Nursing Administration* (1973): 55–60.
7. Charles M. Kelley, "Empathic Listening," in *Small Group Communication: A Reader,* 4th ed., Robert S. Cathcart and Larry A. Samovar, eds. (Dubuque, Iowa: Wm. C. Brown Company Publishers, 1984), 296–303.

7

the language of discussion

Study Objectives

As a result of studying chapter 7 you should be able to:

1. Describe the nature and function of each of the three major components of a language.

2. Explain the concept "symbol" and why it is so important to understanding the process of small group communication.

3. Describe the nature and disruptive effects on discussions of bypassing, abstract and ambiguous language, and emotive words, and at least one way to prevent or correct each of these types of disruptions.

4. Express your ideas during a discussion so that your statements are organized, unambiguous, and relevant to preceding remarks.

5. Distinguish among the purposes of the six major types of questions raised during discussions.

6. Write minutes or summary reports of small group meetings that are accurate and in an easy-to-read format.

Key Terms

Abstract   general, nonspecific; a word lacking a specific referent is said to be abstract.

Ambiguous   any word which can plausibly be understood in two or more senses is said to be ambiguous.

Bypassing   misunderstanding resulting when two persons do not realize they are referring to different things by the same words, or have the same referents for different words.

Cliché   a trite, stereotyped phrase or saying used to explain some event.

Code   a set of units of a particular type and level used in a language, symbolic in nature, such as the sounds, syllables, and words of a spoken language used by some definable society or population.

Concrete words   low-level abstractions, referring to specific objects, experiences, relationships, etc.

Emotive words   "trigger" words which connote more than they denote, associated with highly pleasant or unpleasant experiences.

High-level abstraction   word or phrase commonly used to refer to a broad category of objects, relationships, concepts, etc.

Minutes   written sequential report of every item dealt with during a group meeting, including a record of all motions and decisions.

Question   verbal request for a response; interrogational statement.

Answerable   one for which an answer can be provided from some sort of observation or interpretation of observations.

Information seeking   request for specific statement of fact.

Opinion seeking   request for judgment or opinion; may be for interpretation of a body of facts, value judgment, relative merits of proposed solution, or personal appraisal of any issue.

Orientation seeking   solicits answer to help define context, direction, or goal during a discussion.

Policy seeking   request for general position or plan of action.

Procedure seeking   request for suggestion of procedure which group can follow; appeal for structure or coordination.

Relational   seeks answer describing how members relate to each other, relative statuses, rights and responsibilities, or description of any socioemotional dimension of the group.

Referent   that which is referred to by a symbol; the object denoted by a word, sentence, or statement.

Syntactic rules   rules governing the appropriate usage and arrangements among code units of a language, such as in phrases and sentences.

Although there is no such thing as strictly verbal or nonverbal communication among group members, the communicating of *ideas* is effected primarily through the use of language. In this chapter we examine verbalization as a means to small group communication; in the next chapter the focus of attention is on the role of nonverbal signals in small group communication.

When you observe a small group you are likely at once to be aware of the spoken messages which flow from member to member. "Discussion" implies verbal messages—lots of words being exchanged. For any learning or problem-solving group to achieve its objectives requires communicating extensively via words. In this chapter I present an overview of the nature of language, some ideas on what can go wrong when we speak words to each other, how sensitive and informed word choices and arrangements can facilitate group progress, how verbalization relates to group formation, and how written verbal messages can be used to enhance group output.

Language

A language such as Spanish, English, or Russian consists of a *code* or codes of symbols, rules about how and when to use the words in the code, and some assumptions about the nature of the world. We will look at how each of these components of language enters into the quality of a discussion.

The **code** is the set or sets of signals used in the language. In a spoken language the codes are sets of sounds (phonemes) and words along with the patterns in which they are uttered. In the written version of a spoken language, we have the alphabet code and the code of all written words in the language. There are also the codes of punctuation marks. Each language has some code units unique to it, and may have many sub-languages or dialects. Each community of language users develops its own unique sub-code. For example, every corporation develops some unique words and usages which are signs of membership in the corporation, every family has some idiosyncratic uses of certain words and may develop a few words all its own, each craft or professional group has its own jargon, and so on. Thus professors of geology use a special version of English different from that used by scholars of education, and car salespersons develop their own dialect or jargon. One's membership in a continuing group is contingent upon learning and using the special language accepted by and used among the members of the group.

Each literate person has somewhat different codes or vocabularies for reading, writing, listening, and speaking. Most of us have a much larger reading code than we have for writing. Most of us also have a much more extensive vocabulary for writing than we do for speaking. Speaking allows little time to reflect and seek just the "right" word. We can interpret many words others may speak to us, even though we may rarely or never utter these words. Furthermore, we have learned different codes for different functions and relationships. None of us would write a love letter in the same code we would write a letter of application. We must use words in a code shared by other group members if we are to be understood by them. We must use a code perceived as appropriate to the context and group, and even a code appropriate to the subject, or others may be annoyed and distracted from the purpose of the discussion.

Informal rules govern all language usage. There are rules about what code units are acceptable in various groups and contexts, for what subjects, and with whom. The same group of persons would probably use considerably different language when meeting in a church or synagogue from when collected around a van in a parking lot just before a football game. When in a patient's room most health-care personnel use different words to describe the patient's condition than those they address to colleagues in a conference room with no patients or family members present.

Syntactic rules govern the arrangement of code units. In English one would not say "Out the lights put," but that arrangement of words types would conform to the rules of some languages. Another rule of syntax indicates that modifying words should be adjacent to the words modified ("the red dress in the closet" rather than "the dress in the closet red"). We have extensive rules governing where to place verbs in sentences, uses of connectives, sentence length, and so on. If others understand us as intended, violation of syntax rules has little effect on group accomplishment, but such violations may lower one's credibility and status in a group of well-educated persons.

In addition to codes and syntactic rules, every language also has built into its code and structure some assumptions about the nature of the world and of human perception. For example, in English we speak as if characteristics we perceive in some object are inherent in the object, are relatively unchangeable, and exist apart from our perception. Thus we might say "The lizard is green," implying that the greenness is part of the lizard, not a function of how we perceive it through a unique pair of eyes and nervous system. But to a person with blue-green colorblindness, "green" is a meaningless term just as it is to an animal lacking retinal cells which respond to different wave frequencies. If the lizard belongs to the chameleon family the greenness may disappear when the background color changes. A more appropriate statement would be "Greenness is occurring as I perceive the lizard," or "To me the lizard looks green at this moment." Such statements are not only in accord with what we know about perception and the physical world, but also leave room for others to perceive and interpret differently.

Of all the characteristics of language, none is more important to understand and keep in mind while discussing than that all language is *symbolic.* Words have no inherent meanings, but are used in conventional ways by a community of users to represent specified items and classes of experiences. *Signs,* unlike symbols, are directly connected with whatever they represent to us. For example, a blush is a sign of stress, a track in the snow is a sign that

Figure 7.1 Many words, one referent.

Referent

Words (symbols)

Chair (English)
Chaise (French)
Stuhl (German)
Sedia (Italian)
Silla (Spanish)
Stol (Swedish)

a rabbit hopped past, and profuse sweating is a sign of an increase in temperature. *There is no meaning to a word apart from the person using and responding to it.* Different languages use different words to refer to the same objects, further demonstrating the principle that *meanings are not in words, but in the users of the words.* Figure 7.1 shows some of the different words used by persons to refer the same object. The object or experience referred to by a symbol is called the *referent.* Only if speaker and listeners have approximately the same referent for a word will they have perceptual similarity. In figure 7.2, Joes says "I have a lot of junk in my room." His reference includes two balls, magazines, a fishing rod, an old trophy, a broken tennis racket, and a box of things left over from a party piled in one corner of the room. Herbie is thinking of some marijuana and other dope, and he is wondering if Joe is a pothead or a pusher. Mary envisions the litter on top of her dresser, and she suspects Joe is as careless as she is about cleaning up after preparing for a date. Obviously Joe's words had very different meanings to these three persons. By social agreement we may communicate effectively with symbols only when we have similar referents for them, and similar symbols for the same referents. If you say "There is a frog on the floor" what might you mean? My dictionary lists many different uses of the word *frog* discovered by the persons who compiled the dictionary: some of them are an amphibious animal, a decoration around a button hole, a railroad track crossover, shoulder braid on a dress uniform, a throat irritation, and an object to hold flowers in a vase. If you propose to a group "Let's get done early," meaning by 4:00 P.M., but another member thinks of 2:00 P.M., a problem for the group results. It is important never to forget that symbols have no inherent and certain meaning.

Figure 7.2   One statement, different referents.

Disruptions from Language Choices

The understanding that symbols (including all words) have no absolute or certain referents can help prevent a variety of misunderstandings and disruptions common in discussions. Especially be on guard for bypassing due to different word uses of speaker and listeners, misunderstandings and disruptions likely to result from highly abstract or ambiguous language, and the potential impact of emotive words.

Bypassing

Two discussants bypass each other when they have different references for the same word or phrase, but think they have the same meanings. Each hears the same words, but the images each creates are so different as to represent a serious misunderstanding. They are "talking past each other." For example, I once listened to a group discussing religious beliefs argue for about half an hour (wasted time!) about whether or not man had free will. The group formed sides, led by an atheist and an avowed Methodist. After listening to a tape recording of the discussion and getting to specific cases they realized that they were actually in agreement! Each side had been using the term "free will" to refer to a different phenomenon. They were able to see that all believed man had free will (Type 1, some ability to make conscious choices among alternatives), but did not have a free will (Type 2, much of what happens in life is beyond our control and is determined by the converging of forces within and without). In a very simple case of bypassing, a young nurse reported this: "I left a pan of water, soap, washcloth, and towel with a new patient, telling him it was time for his bed bath. When I returned in half an hour I found him scrubbing his bed with the cloth, but personally unwashed. He was not supposed to get out of bed!" In another instance a man whose car battery was too low to turn over the engine told a helpful motorist who had stopped that because he had an automatic transmission she would have to push him about thirty-five miles per hour. You guessed it—she backed up and rammed into his rear bumper at thirty-five miles per hour, doing $300 damage![1] I have watched members of many groups go on talking blithely as if they understood each other when any careful observer could tell that members had very different meanings for some key term. This usually results in conflict at a later date, especially if the misunderstanding is over some course of action to be taken by the group. Tempers flare, individuals go on the defensive, and time is wasted—and sometimes serious damage is done—as a result of bypassing.

Bypassing results from two myths about language: (1) "Words have meanings in and of themselves," or *right* meanings, and (2) "A message encoded in words can have one and only one meaning." Both of these myths are patently false in light of our understanding of how communication occurs, but *we often act as if they were true.* We sometimes behave as if we thought anyone who doesn't understand what we mean when we utter words is somehow foolish, stubborn, or wrongheaded. We seem to forget that two or more persons can communicate effectively through symbols only if they use the same code or definitions—they must be in agreement on the referents for their words at a given time. Just as in playing poker we must agree on the value of each chip color, so we must have a shared understanding of the "values" or referents for the words we use to play the communication game. For optimal verbal communication we must never forget that a key term may be used differently by different group members, and that people can refer to the same experience or object with different words. With these principles in mind, we can often determine what a speaker means from the context of the remark, what we know about the speaker's background, and from nonverbal cues which accompany the utterance. Even when we are cautious in our use of words and other symbols we can still come up with meanings considerably different from each other when we speak and listen.

Abstractness and Ambiguity

In discussions of ideas, many statements are necessarily highly abstract, lacking specific referents. As one moves away from terms referring to specific and unique items, the degree of abstractness and ambiguity increases. Consider the following set of terms, each of which is higher in level of abstraction and thus more vague than the ones preceding it:

Jantha Whitman, freshman at Booker College

freshman students at Booker College

college students

students

women

humans

mammals

living things

When the first term is used between persons both acquainted with Jantha, the picture in the speaker's head is likely to be similar to the picture in the head of the listener, and the listener could pick out Jantha from a group if asked to do so. But when we talk of "students," "politicians," "democracy," or "environmental problems" the pictures and feelings speakers and listeners experience will often differ greatly. Only terms that name unique objects are likely to be free of any vagueness. For example, one discussant said: "Lecturing is a poor method of teaching." Another responded: "Oh, no it isn't." An argument ensued until a third discussant asked for some examples (lower order abstractions). The speakers were then able to agree on specific instances of effective and ineffective lecturing, especially when some quantitative research data were introduced. The vagueness reduced, the group reached agreement on a less abstract statement: "Lecturing, if well organized, filled with concrete instances, and done by a skilled speaker, can be an effective means of presenting factual information and theoretical concepts. It is usually less effective than discussion for changing attitudes or developing thinking skills."

Leathers studied the impact of abstract statements on discussions. He found that the abstract statements consistently had a disruptive effect on subsequent discussion, and that the degree of disruption increased as the statements became more highly abstract. His groups contained "plant" discussants who were trained to say things like "Don't you think this is a matter of historical dialectism?" After such a statement, most of the other discussants became confused and tense, and some just withdrew from further participation.[2]

Ambiguity results from phrases that could plausibly have either of two types of meanings to the listeners. For example, "I just can't say enough that is good about his effort for the company." What does the speaker mean? That the employee being discussed made such extensive contributions that it is impossible to describe them all, or that he did so little that the speaker cannot give the kind of recommendation the listeners want for a possible candidate for a new position? In such a case, even vocal cues may not clear up the ambiguity.

Ambiguity can also result from a "mixed" message, one in which the words seem to imply one meaning but the vocal cues indicate something different. For example a speaker might say "That seems like a great idea" in a flat pitch with little emphasis, thus implying with her voice that she does not really care about the idea. Or a speaker might say "Take as long as you like to think this through" while glancing at his watch. Such ambiguous messages are highly disruptive to a discussion.

What can we do as group members to prevent the confusion, tension, and serious misunderstandings which are often an output of abstract or ambiguous language? When you hear an abstract or ambiguous statement and realize that the speaker could mean more than one thing by it, ask the speaker to clarify. Ask for specific examples or descriptions. A description or detailed explanation will usually reduce or eliminate misunderstandings or uncertainty. Use active listening—paraphrase and ask the speaker to confirm or correct your understanding reflected in the paraphrase. As speaker you can use concrete examples to illustrate and limit the possible interpretations of your own abstract statements. Choose terms you think others in the group would probably use to refer to what you have in mind, and use synonyms for key words, such as "an appeal, that is to say a request for a retrial," "a vapor barrier, plastic sheets that water vapor can't penetrate." When possible use specific descriptions or measurements instead of comparative terms such as "tall" and "cool."

Occasionally a discussant will try to enhance personal status or conceal ignorance by using technical jargon not in the code of other group members. The resulting "snow job" may intimidate other group members into accepting the jargon-user's opinions without challenging them for supporting evidence and reasoning. Thus the intimidator does not have to answer probing questions about personal study of the issue, research findings, and assumptions on which the conclusion depends. By using technical jargon the speaker has assumed a priestlike status, one that is hard to challenge. Few people dare to question the testimony of physicians, dentists, or psychiatrists when they speak in technical codes during discussions. When someone uses such language in a small group discussion, you can be pretty certain that the speaker is trying to evade or cover up a lack of evidence. Ask him to explain in terms you are familiar with, and insist that the *group* understand and not allow the "expert" to decide or dominate a decision by means of a smokescreen of ambiguous language.

Occasionally a discussion hangs up on a *cliché,* stopping objective evaluation of a proposal or belief linked to the cliché. All clichés are highly abstract, and though they may be true in a very general way, they never fit any two specific situations in exactly the same way, since each event or object is somewhat unique and different from every other. To stop a proposal to spend money for a cost accounting program that could control waste and inefficiencies, someone may say something like "Let's not spend more money. A penny saved is a penny earned, you know." And all the steam goes out of the people proposing the idea of spending now to save a lot in the long run—their valuable idea has been clobbered by a cliché. Conventional truths embodied in clichés are often out of date, or they may be instances of "common sense" based on superstition or intuition, such as the common-sense belief that you can't stop a massive train with air (brakes on trains and eighteen-wheelers are operated by compressed air). Often no one thinks to ask how the cliché fits the present situation. The group's machinery for creating and processing possible solutions grinds to a halt on the monkey wrench of a cliché. (I hope you detected that cliché!) Here are a few of the most common "idea killers":

"Nothing ventured, nothing gained."

"Let's act now. Don't put off 'till tomorrow what you can do today."

"No one does it that way anymore."

"He won't change. You can't teach an old dog new tricks."

"A watched pot never boils."

"It can't be done. There's no way to get there from here."

"That's a tail wagging the dog. We're too small for that idea."

If someone uses one of the trite high-level abstractions we call a cliché, what can you do? First, be on guard for such easy answers as proverbs or clichés and their stupefying effects on creative thinking. When you spot a cliché, point it out as such and suggest that the group examine the specifics of the situation to see if the cliché fits. Ask how the present problem might be *different* from others like it. Sometimes you can stop the negative impact by giving a contradictory cliché; for example, "You can't teach an old dog new tricks" might be offset with "But you're never too old to learn. Now let's really evaluate . . ." "We tried that and it didn't work before" might be counteracted with "We're not the same now as before. You never step into the same river twice. Let's see if Bryan's idea might work in our situation."

Opinions uttered in sentence fragments or in an evasive manner increase the ambiguity and vagueness level of a discussion. It is quite common for spontaneous participants to utter sentence fragments; they mention a subject, but never finish making a point about it, at least not in words. Sometimes a non-verbal signal is used to complete the utterance, but anyone not watching will not have much chance to get the point and nonverbals are notoriously ambiguous. Incomplete sentences occur in any spontaneous group interaction, but fragments like the following add to the confusion in the minds of even attentive discussants:

"Uh, I'm thinking that we might—well, what is going on here, anyway?"

"Maybe we should divide . . . there seem to be a lot of issues . . . a lot of confusing bits and pieces . . . will make for a poor solution."

"You know what members of that sorority are like (here a roll of the eyes, smirking twist of mouth, and toss of head to left)."

All these statements could easily enough have been uttered directly and unambiguously, leaving little doubt in attentive listeners' minds about what the speaker was referring to, as indicated in the following revisions:

"I think we might improve our understanding of what made it possible for a mechanic to steal so many auto parts if we ask the head of the motor pool how inventories are kept and revised."

"Maybe we should divide our discussion of what to do to improve the registration procedure into component topics of advising, enrolling in a course, departmental assignments of faculty to courses, sources of cheating on enrollment, and the drop-add procedure. Otherwise we may get all these mixed up, overlook some problems, and have a long discussion characterized by unrelated bits and pieces of dialogue."

"I think members of Lumba Dumba Sorority are vain and snobbish. They rarely speak to women in Gamma Raya Sorority, who may not come from such wealthy homes, but seem friendlier to me and have far better grade point averages."

Another type of abstractness leading to disruption of discussions results from expressing opinions as ambiguous or loaded questions. The form of the utterance is that of a question, but the function is to express a judgment. Such verbal constructions often leave the responder in a double-bind where any plausible reply can be attacked. The classic example is "When did you stop beating your wife?" instead of saying unambiguously "I think you were a spouse beater." Even the common "Isn't this a nice day?" is an indirect way of saying "I think this is a nice day" or (with different inflection) "I hate this kind of weather." "Who made you the boss?" is probably an evasive way of saying "You're not going to tell me what to do. We all have equal authority in this group." Statements that have been called "rhetorical questions" are not questions in intent; these are the so-called "leading questions" that suggest an answer, yet the speaker can deny making a suggestion. For example: "Wouldn't it be a good idea to brainstorm this question?" "Why don't we recommend that the school buy a bus to transport debate teams?" or "Don't you think prostitution should be legalized?" When a discussant hears a rhetorical question he or she can often clarify or prevent confusion by restating it as a declarative sentence, such as: "You seem to think we should brainstorm this issue. I agree." "You are recommending that the school buy a bus for the debate team." "You seem to favor legalizing prostitution."

To increase your sensitivity to the vagueness that results when discussants seek to avoid responsibility for clearly worded value statements or other opinions, you may want to try the "question dialogue" game with a classmate or other acquaintance. During the period of the game only statements in the form of questions can be spoken; each should reply to the other's previous question with another question, and keep that up as long as possible. The result may sound something like this:

A—"So, how are you feeling today?"
B—"Do you think I have some unusual feeling today?"

A—"Don't you?"
B—"What makes you ask?"

A—"Does it matter why I ask?"
B—"How many of your feelings do you like to share with me?"
(and so on)

Emotive Words

Some words are mostly used to evoke strong feelings; these "connotative" words have been associated with highly pleasant or unpleasant images and experiences in our culture. They have little denotative impact on most listeners compared to their blockbuster connotative impact. They primarily *evoke* rather than indicate. Such are the "fighting" or "trigger" words to which many people have "signal reactions"—unthinking, instantaneous reactions in which the person responds to the word as if it were the actual, ugly thing. Many persons react to emotive terms like trained dogs salivating when a bell is rung even though no food is present. Such powerful physiological reactions to words with highly negative connotations may be normal, but they do involve nonthinking responses to words as if they magically had become things the *listener* would have referred to by symbols. Some of the more common trigger words are racial and ethnic slurs, sexist terms, and other epithets. In all cases there are alternative denotative terms which to most people seem neutral or even positive. For example:

Negative Connotation	**Neutral or Positive Connotation**
egghead	intellectual
broad	woman
manipulative	persuasive
jock	athlete

When a discussant (or something he or she likes) is called one of these negative terms, the response is usually highly defensive. Constructive, inquiring discussion ends. The group problem-solving process is disrupted, as counterattacks fly back and forth.

Discussants need to be sensitive to current usage and to the meanings and feelings of other group members if such defensive spirals are to be avoided. For example, a white group member with no prejudicial intention may say "colored," and a black group member may respond defensively—to the listener "colored" indicated that the speaker was a racist acting in a superior manner. One discussant might say "Nebraska has socialistic power generation and distribution," meaning that such facilities are owned by the public and managed by a board elected by voters. Some Nebraskans would react to such a statement in a very defensive way, stopping progress of the group to wrangle about "socialism." Or perhaps one discussant expresses a judgment or suggests a solution, and another replies: "Why that's nothing but _____ !" "You're proposing _____ !" "That's _____ !" In the blanks may go any word or phrase used to label something strongly disliked or feared, and for which the respondent has a highly unpleasant connotation: *communism, fascism, federal control, racism, childishness, chauvinism,* or other words used in derogation. The speaker has now been identified with something ugly or fearful. He or she may clam up, deny and argue, or call the speaker some name. The group will likely get caught in a sidetrack of whether the subject of discussion should be called by the stigmatic term. The goal is forgotten, harmony is lost, feelings are hurt, and members lose face. Even if the group gets reoriented, residual antagonism is likely to hamper cooperation: "Nobody gets away with that!"

The use of sexist terms is a major problem for many groups. Terms that were once used interchangeably to refer to all people and to males specifically are now rejected as biased against women. For instance, the word "man" has been used in the past when the person referred to could be either male or female (patrolman, chairman, businessman, postman). Some words have a special ending to indicate a woman, but no such ending to indicate a man: usherette, actress, Jewess, and poetess are examples. Much preferred are the root forms that do not imply the sex of the person referred to: usher, actor, Jew, and poet. Many persons resent any word that implies an inappropriate sex criterion for filling any role or performing any task, and this resentment will often disrupt a discussion. Most certainly if you view women as inferior beings who should be "kept in their place," you are in for some serious relearning. Consciously eliminating all sexually stereotyping terms from your speaking vocabulary may be necessary if you are to avoid being disruptive in many discussions.

The worst form of stigmatizing is out and out name-calling. Adrenalin rises and physiologically we prepare to fight when called by such names as "pig," "male chauvinist," or "nigger." Such behavior is almost certain to turn attention from the issues before a group, reduce trust, and evoke defensive reactions.

What can you do to prevent, reduce, and alleviate stigmatizing? First, recognize that persons have feeling about everything, and these feelings are not to be rejected. When a person or her beliefs and values are challenged, her concept of self is also challenged and must be defended. Next, be aware that your feelings and evaluations are just that—YOUR feelings and opinions—not characteristics of some objective reality outside yourself. Some labelling and stigmatizing are likely to occur when persons express how they feel about things. We can reduce it in ourselves, using phrases to remind others and ourselves that our judgments are our judgments: "*I* don't like . . ." or "It seems to *me* that . . . ," for example. When someone expresses a stigma or "trigger" term, another participant or designated leader can reduce the danger of direct and wasteful conflict or defensiveness by inviting contrasting feelings and points of view, first restating the stigmatic statement in unloaded terms. For example: "Joe has called the ACTION program phony and fascistic. That's one point of view. What are some others?" "Okay, Helen's belief is that public power is socialistic. Are there other ways of looking at it?" A statement that "Scientists who use defenseless animals for research are brutes" might be rephrased: "Ed believes that it is brutal to use animals in laboratory research. What do others of us believe on this issue?" By replacing the stigma term with a more denotative one and obtaining expressions of different evaluations and feelings toward the denoted object, the group is now in a position to examine the idea objectively, in a mood of skeptical inquiry, basing conclusions on more adequate information than was previously available.

If no one is ready or willing to express a point of view contrary to that of the stigmatizer, the designated leader can sometimes help remove the block to objectivity by playing the devil's advocate. He or she expresses a point of view contrary to that of the stigmatizer, indicating that it is one that ought to be considered in order to objectively weigh the proposal from all points of view and on its own merits. For instance, he or she might say: "Joan has called the loan fund socialistic. Let's consider another judgment of it that I've heard expressed by . . .. They say it helps students develop independence."

All of this points to the importance of trying to develop group norms against the use of stigma terms, and for an objective examination of all evidence and points of view. A periodic examination of the values and norms implicit in the language we choose and the ways we express our feelings and beliefs can be quite constructive in a group plagued by language barriers to communication.

Improving Communication by Organizing Remarks

In addition to choosing words with care, how you put them together can make a great deal of difference in the responses others make to your messages. A useful comment does not come at random, nor is it randomly organized. Outstanding fluency—the ability to speak smoothly and with apparent ease—is not essential to being a valuable discussant, but clarity is. How you organize your remarks can make a great deal of difference in how easy it is for others to interpret your remarks as you intended.

The syntax of your remarks should be conventional and clear. For example, to say "Year last of all automobiles percent seventeen recalled from the past five years were" would call attention to your unusual word arrangement in the sentence (syntax) and away from the content of the remark. The words are the same, but syntactic structure gives very different implications to "ate the rabbit" and "the rabbit ate." "It no way won't work somehow" would leave everyone confused. Conventional sentences that are simple, direct, and clear, will facilitate mutual understandings. Clarity thus results both from choosing words likely to have similar referents for both you and listeners, and from arranging them by the syntactical rules of English. Thus you would say "Last year seventeen percent of all autos made in the past five years were recalled," or "There are two features of this plan that probably will not work."

Speak concisely. If listeners appear bored or restive, you may have spoken at too great a length. Try to state your ideas as simply and briefly as possible. Some participants restate every point several times, or take two hundred words to say what could be stated in twenty. This reduces the opportunity for others to participate, and often results in the long speech being tuned out by others. If you notice that others restate your ideas more briefly than you uttered them, you should work for a concise style. For instance, the length of the following sentence makes it confusing: "Although I have no doubt about the possible efficacy of the operations of this proposal, there remain unresolved complications about it that might eventuate at some indeterminate point if untoward circumstances tending toward time slippages were to arise and signal-exchange operations were conducted." To be concise and clear one could say "This plan would fail if someone received a late signal or was not prepared to act when he got the signal."

State one point at a time. This is not an inviolable rule, but generally speaking, you should not contribute more than one idea in a single speech. A several-point speech is definitely out. A group can discuss only one idea at a time; confusion is likely to result if you try to make several points at once. A comment in which you attempt to give all the data on an issue or present a series of points is likely to be too involved to be grasped and responded to. How would you respond to this? "Many persons are injured when bumpers fail. Furthermore, I think brakes need to be designed to prevent fading, and then there is the problem of ignition systems that stop the car when powerful radio signals hit them." One person might begin to reply about brakes, while another was thinking about how the ignition systems could be perfected, and another was thinking about a wreck when his or her bumper failed—confusion! As a rule, address one issue or idea at a time, unless you are setting up an agenda for discussing several items, and you say so.

Relate your statement to preceding remarks. A useful comment does not come at random, nor is it randomly expressed. A general pattern to follow is this: relate the contribution to what has already been said by another; state the idea; develop and support it; connect the contribution to the topic or phase of the problem be.ng discussed. You will notice that this format provides an answer to the three basic questions to be asked when evaluating any extended contribution: What is the point? How do you know? How does it matter at this time? For example:

Helen, you said many magazine articles have been cut out. I also found that every encyclopedia had articles removed from it. The librarian told me it costs about $1,000.00 per year to replace damaged encyclopedias. So we can see that a serious part of the problem is the loss of widely used reference materials.

Improving Communication by Asking Appropriate Questions

Every affirmative statement is an answer to some question, whether or not the question has been actually asked by someone. It has often been said that "Being educated means that you know how to ask the right questions, not that you have all the answers." The process of dialectic—a search for truth through discussion—is a search for the best possible answers to questions. Very important to effective and efficient group discussion is the asking of a variety of types of questions when each is appropriate, and asking them in a way that makes them answerable and suitable to the complexity of issues groups deal with. Being able to ask or recognize the various types of questions, and when each is needed, will make you a valuable member of any goal-oriented group.

Characteristics of Questions

Two characteristics of the way in which questions are formulated are of special importance. First, all questions can be classified as either *answerable* or *unanswerable*. As Weinberg pointed out, just because we can put a question mark after a string of words does not mean we have asked a meaningful or answerable question. If "answers" are given to an unanswerable question and we are unable to choose among them on any objective basis, there is no way to tell which is the correct or best answer.[3] To illustrate, consider the following: "What is the population of China today?" "What was the population of Omaha according to the 1976 census?" "How fast can a greyhound run?" and "Why did God punish the Martins by burning their house?" Most persons would agree that a factual answer, based on specific methods of census taking, could provide an objective answer to the first question even though such an answer may not now be available. Thus it is *potentially* answerable, but not answerable at the moment without extensive nonverbal activity. The second is readily answerable; records will give a specific incontrovertible answer to what the report says. The third question is ambiguous because it contains variable terms—it can only be answered when specific conditions are stated naming the dog, and such conditions as time and place. Thus it could be made meaningful by asking, "How fast did Diamond Jack run in the third race at the Atokad Greyhound Race Track on July 3, 1973?" The fourth question is meaningless, because it refers to nonobjective concepts, unobservables. That question assumes some personal force called God, and that this God took direct causative action. To answer it, what would we observe? Under what conditions? How? Such a "question" cannot be answered by any known means, so there is nothing to be gained by discussing it except confusion and conflict. You can help a group by pointing this out, and suggesting that the question either be dropped as meaningless or else be rephrased in a meaningful way that provides for some sort of observational answer (e.g., "What beliefs do each of us have about why the Martins' house may have burned?"—our beliefs can at least be stated and observed *as our beliefs*).

Second, all questions can be classified as *limited* or *open-ended*. Limited questions ask for a specific, brief answer, such as information, or seek to discover if another person agrees or disagrees with some proposition. Such questions do not encourage elaboration or different points of view. A limited question implies that there are only one, two, or a very few possible responses. Once a short answer has been given, there is no room for further response. For example: "How old are you?" "Do you think age is related to wisdom?" "Did you like that movie?" "When must we submit our report?" or "Which side do you think is right, the students or the administration?" Especially be wary of questions that suggest a one- or two-valued orientation. Although there are useful two-valued ways of classifying things, in most cases such thinking leads us to overlook matters of degree. Few things are either all good or all bad, all black or all white. If something were pure black, no light would reflect from it. But even lampblack reflects some light. Digitalis is poisonous in some quantities, but a powerful medicine in other quantities. To ask, "Is this painting beautiful?" is to imply that it is either all beautiful or all ugly. As a rule, phrase questions in terms of degree, not as either-or.

Open-ended questions imply a wide variety of possible answers, encouraging elaboration and numerous points of view. They imply more than a one-word or brief answer, with room for many responses. For example: "How beautiful do you think she is?" "What did you like about the movie?" "What are the relative merits of both the students' and the administration's points of view?" "Can anyone tell me more about that?"

Types of Questions

Questions asked during the course of a discussion can be classified according to the function of the answer sought. In other words, each type of question implies that the answer should contain a particular type of content in the reply. Questions may be concerned with group orientation, procedure, relations among members, information, opinion, or policy. The first three types are about matters of group process; the latter three are about the group's task.

Orientation-Seeking Questions

Early in the discussion of a problem or subject it is vital that the group determine the purpose(s) of the discussion, the area of freedom of the group, and the type of output the discussion is to achieve (such as understanding, findings, advice, a plan, some recommendation, or thing). Questions seeking information and opinions about group goals are especially helpful in providing orientation if asked early, but they may be needed at any time when the group seems to have lost direction and purpose in its discussions. Consider the following examples:

"What are the purposes of this meeting?"

"How many nominees are we to report for each position to be filled?"

"Should we be trying to reach an agreement on what is the best policy regarding capital punishment, or just understanding the arguments for various proposed policies?"

Often a discussion can be improved greatly by asking the second-order question, "What question are we now discussing?" Getting someone to clarify the issue under discussion by stating it as a question will often reveal that a group has gotten off track, or is cycling rather aimlessly among issues. From the frequency with which themes or topics are switched in many discussions it appears that often no one knows quite what the issue is—a major problem in group communication, and one that must be resolved if discussion is to be productive, more than an aimless "rap" or bull session. Many discussions ramble so badly that they could be described aptly as a series of disorganized answers looking for questions.

People need expressions of human warmth, but not rambling, unfocused interaction. Discussants bothered by aimless talk often avoid pointing this out for fear of being labeled as heavy, all-work types. When you sense that an initially purposeful discussion has degenerated into a bull session, ask "Where are we and what are we trying to accomplish by this discussion?" This question may be all the jolt the group needs to stop, take a bearing, and orient their verbal exchanges toward a shared goal.

Procedure-Seeking Questions

Questions asking how to proceed as a group are needed relatively infrequently, but they are vital if teamwork is to be achieved. The procedural question asks such things as how to coordinate activity of members, what techniques to use for organizing interaction, in what sequence to take up items for consideration, how to make a decision, how to outline a problem-solving procedure, or simply what to do next. Unless all members of a small group are following the same general procedure, their efforts will be uncoordinated and ineffectual. Here are a few examples of procedure-seeking questions:

"What is our agenda for this meeting?"

"How shall we organize this discussion?"

"What procedure do you think we should follow?"

"How can we get our recommendations written up and reported to Vice President Garfinkle?"

Hirokawa found that effective problem-solving groups spent significantly more time discussing and agreeing upon procedural matters than did ineffective groups.[4] When no procedure for the group to follow has been agreed upon (or announced), or if you do not understand what to do next or who is to do what for the group, that is a good indication that a question of procedure will facilitate group productivity.

Relational Questions

Relational questions seek clarification of the socioemotional status of the group, especially how well members are relating to each other as persons. They seek information about how members are feeling toward each other and toward the group. Sometimes they may ask who is responsible for a particular task or type of task, such as keeping records, or what members want in their relationships with each other. If a group member's nonverbal behaviors seem to indicate annoyance, anger, boredom, frustration, or alienation from the rest of the group, a question about what the person is feeling might help to bring the tension out in the open and thus permit the group to deal with it before a serious interpersonal clash occurs or a potentially valuable member is lost to the group. When you feel some negative or positive affect toward the group, asking if others feel likewise may help the group correct a previously unrecognized problem with its goal, procedures, or way of interacting. Contrariwise, a socioemotional question might get members to express positive feelings toward another or the group as a whole, thus heightening the group's cohesiveness. In a continuing group it is almost always more productive to deal with budding tensions and interpersonal conflicts before they become serious, rather than to hope the tensions will go away. The following examples of relational questions illustrate the type:

"Are we all acquainted with each other?"

"Is everyone comfortable with this seating arrangement?"

"How do we feel about working together on this task force?"

"Did anyone feel left out during our discussion this evening?"

"Joan, something seems to be bothering you. Mind sharing it with us?"

"Do you think we're showing enough respect for each other's ideas and
   opinions?"

"Is anyone else angry about anything that has been going on in this
   meeting?"

Such questions about relationships among members can help greatly to get
hidden agendas out in the open, to resolve both primary and secondary tensions, and to prevent struggles over status, power, and control from weakening
or even destroying a group.

Information-Seeking Questions

These ask for specific statements of fact. They may refer to observations of
something that has occurred, factual statements reported elsewhere, what some
group member said earlier, or to a need for clarification of a statement. The
information-seeking question implies an answer limited to a report, without
interpretation or inference about that report. Confusion often arises when a
question seeking information is replied to with a guess, hunch, theory, or pet
belief. An observation or fact as such is not discussable; it can merely be reported and possibly verified by further observation and report. Examples of
meaningful information-seeking questions illustrate the type:

"What factors did the fire chief say contributed to the burning of the
   Martins' house?" (To verify, ask him or ask someone who heard him.)

"How did you do on the English CLEP exam?"

"What did you say, Sally, was the number of abortions in University
   Hospital last year?"

"By 'police' did you mean all law enforcement officers or only uniformed
   ones?"

"What does anybody know about the extent of crimes of violence in our
   city?"

The answers to such questions may be true or false, depending on whether or
not the answer conforms to what happened. The accuracy is discussable, but
a fact itself is not subject to discussion—only to observation. It is important
to determine whether what appears to be a question of information is really
such, or if it is ambiguous or meaningless (does not refer to any observable
event).

Opinion-Seeking Questions

Opinion-seeking questions (also known as questions of interpretation) are those
asking for others' opinions, interpretations, and judgments about the meaning

of a fact or group of facts. What is sought by the questioner is not a description of events but an explanation of what the events mean to the answerer or a prediction about the future. Since the answers are matters of opinion, there is room for different answers from reasonable people. Many group discussions have as a goal a consensus answer to an opinion-seeking question. For example, a grand jury must decide whether the evidence warrants a criminal trial. A so-called "fact-finding" committee of an organization first ascertains what has happened, then interprets the meanings of the facts located. The facts about drug traffic in a city have their meaning in their interpretations by various persons and groups. Examples of opinion-seeking questions, such as those below, can be found in any discussion:

"How good a president was Harry S. Truman?"

"How many family-operated farms are there likely to be in the U.S. in 1995?"

"Is there a need for more interstate highways in the U.S.?"

"What would be the climatic effects of a nuclear war?"

"Why are the bristlecone pine trees dying?"

"Did the writers of the Constitution intend for prayers to be uttered aloud in public schools and legislatures?"

Questions of *value* are a special type of opinion-seeking question. They call for judgments about the merit or worth of something. You probably noticed that the question about President Truman was such a question. A comparison is always implied in the answer to a question of value. This may be a comparison to some specific standard or to a similar type of object or idea. For example:

"Is it more beneficial in the long run to supply food to starving people in over-populated countries, or to help them control their populations?

"Which political party has done more to improve the living conditions of low-income citizens?"

"How well has court-ordered integration achieved the goal of equal educational opportunity for all children in a school district?"

When personal evaluations are called for it is important to remember that there is no need for agreement. There is no sense in arguing about answers to such questions as "Is this a good painting?" "Do you like this poem?" or "Is lamb or beef better tasting?" A learning group has no need to agree on matters of value, but merely to understand what the questions imply and the bases for different answers to them. On the other hand, a group trying to arrive at a solution to a problem, when facing a choice among possible courses of action, must agree on values or criteria in order to arrive at a recommendation or plan of action. Problem-solving groups usually find it necessary to agree on values before they can agree on a solution.

Policy-Seeking Questions

These are questions which ask what should be done to solve a problem, considering all the information found and interpretations of it, and the values agreed upon by members of a group. The word which usually indicates that a question seeks a policy statement as an answer is "should." For example, "How many credits of science *should* be required of liberal arts graduates?" or "What should be done to reduce the damage to waters and forests resulting from acid rain?" When policy-seeking questions are posed, answers that will be acceptable to all members of a group can be found only after answers to relevant questions of information, interpretation, and value have been agreed upon.

When conflict seems unresolvable among members of a group seeking to answer a policy question, it is usually wise to raise questions about values, asking what criteria each member is applying to alternative solutions. It may also be necessary to ask information-seeking and opinion-seeking questions; quite possibly the group got to the policy issue before adequate information bearing on the problem had been shared and interpreted, and before shared values had been expressed as goals and criteria. Productive procedures for group problem solving provide for discussion of information-seeking, interpretation, value, and policy questions in that order. When discussion has been too shallow and hurried at some stage in the process of problem solving to provide a basis for agreement on policy questions, the group may need to backtrack to questions about facts, interpretations, and values before consensus or even a simple majority can be achieved.

Verbal communication among members of a small group is not all oral; members may address memoranda to each other, provide handouts to accompany oral reports of investigations or readings undertaken for the group, and present charts or other visual aids during meetings. But the most important of the written messages which coordinate work of a committee or task force are the official written records of its meetings.

Records of Meetings

Efficient work within a continuing task force or committee depends upon written records of meetings. Such written records serve many purposes: to remind members of what was accomplished at a meeting so they do not repeat it at a subsequent gathering; to provide a reminder to members who have agreed to undertake certain tasks for the group (such as investigations, purchases, and physical arrangements); to provide continuity in discussions from meeting to meeting when a group undertakes the solution to a complex problem requiring many deliberative meetings; to confirm and standardize the images members have of what was decided upon and accomplished at a meeting; to provide a legal record of attendance, decisions, and actions taken by a group that is responsible to a parent organization; to bring members who had to miss a meeting up to date on what the group did; and to keep other interested persons informed about the group's progress.

Although learning groups rarely keep records of their meetings since the outcomes are individual learnings, problem-solving groups always should. Even a single-meeting *ad hoc* group usually benefits from a written report of the meeting, as a reminder to all members of what was discussed and decided, and to assure that all agree with the understanding of the secretary or reporter. Most committees of larger groups are required to keep records of their meetings, and they usually must submit reports not only to all members of the committee, but also to the parent organization (and sometimes to other interested groups). For example, at the university where I work, the committees of the Faculty Senate must write reports of each meeting, and the reports are distributed to all members of the senate and sometimes to selected administrators.

The primary purpose of such written reports is to preserve a record of the important *content* of a discussion, including how decisions were made. In general, the name of the group, the time and place of the meeting, the attendance (including absences), all agenda items discussed, major findings, decisions reached bearing on the group's procedures and task, assignments of members, actions to be taken at a later date, and the signature of the writer comprise the written record. Committee minutes rarely say much about processes or communication, except to report that a decision had a clear majority or was unanimous. Even as the content of the discussion is the responsibility and the property of all members, so is the report. It is usually unwise to report *who* suggested what solution or idea, or who presented what information. Sometimes this could be threatening to the members, and so may stifle creativity if they fear the responses of some superior administrator in an organization (e.g., the Chancellor in the case of a university committee, or the instructor in the case of a class committee). So record all information, all ideas, all accepted criteria, all decisions, and all responsibilities for action—but only in the latter case report the name unless required by some parent organization or authority.

The format and amount of detail included in reports of small group meetings vary considerably, depending on the origins and nature of the group and the circulation of the record. Some organizations have a standard format for their committee minutes. Others do not. Robert's manual on parliamentary procedure says only the following regarding committee minutes: ". . . a brief memorandum in the nature of minutes for the use of the committee."[5] Robert also says that in small committees the chair usually is the secretary, whereas in larger committees a separate secretary may be elected or appointed. Regardless, the chair of a formally appointed committee is responsible to see that written records are kept of meetings and that the group's reports to its parent organization are written and presented properly.

The written record of a task force or *ad hoc* committee may take the form of a summary report to the members, but a standing committee which must take up more than one problem or broad topic per meeting should usually keep minutes very much like those kept by a parliamentary assembly. Items on the agenda (formal order of business) should be numbered in the order in which they were taken up during the meeting. Discussion of problems leading to some action or recommendation to be submitted to a parent body can be organized around the problem-solving procedure followed during that actual discussion. Here is an example of minutes of a standing committee of a university graduate facility.

Minutes of April 12, 1985 Meeting of Committee A

Committee A held a special meeting at 1:30 P.M. on Friday, April 12, 1985 in room 14 of the Jones Library.

Attendance: Walter Bradley, Marlynn Jones, George Smith, Barbara Trekheld, and Michael Williams.

Absent were Jantha Calamus and Peter Shiuoka.

1. The minutes of the April 4 meeting were approved as distributed.

2. Two nominations for membership in the graduate faculty were considered. A subcommittee of Bradley and Trekheld reported that their investigation indicated that Dr. Robert Jordon met all criteria for Membership. It was moved that Professor Jordon be recommended to Dean Bryant for Membership in the Graduate Faculty. The vote was unanimously in favor.

The nomination of Professor Andrea Long was discussed; it was concluded that she met all criteria, and that the nomination had been processed properly. It was moved that Professor Long be recommended for appointment to the Graduate Faculty. The motion was passed unanimously.

3. Encouragement of grant activity. Discussion next centered on the question of how to encourage more faculty members to submit proposals for funding grants. Several ideas were discussed. It was moved that we recommend to President Yardley that:

   a. A policy be established to grant reduced teaching loads to all professorial faculty who submit two or more grant proposals in a semester; and

   b. That ten percent of all grant overhead be returned to the department that obtained the grant for use in any appropriate way.

This motion was approved unanimously.

Sometimes the written record of meetings of a task force takes the form of a summary report of the discussions. Then the group prepares a final report for its parent organization. What follows are two meeting reports of a project group from a small group communication class. Group members were preparing to present an instructional program to their classmates on "The Group

Polarization Phenomenon." Their examples may help you prepare meeting reports which are concise, yet clear.

Report of Second Meeting of Polarization Instructional Group

Date of Meeting: November 22, 1983
Time and place: 3:35 P.M., in our regular classroom, CBA 202
Attendance: Beverly Halliday, Bart Bonn, Hal Darling, and Judy Hartlieb. Bill
        Miklas, absent.

Report of Previous Meeting
    Judy distributed copies of the last meeting's record to the group members. It was approved.

Phone Numbers
    Phone numbers of all members were exchanged.

Test Ideas
    Hal read some ideas for test questions from a book he had borrowed from Professor Brilhart. The group discussed criteria for a test question, and determined that a question that was "close to home" and applicable to the class members should be sought. The issue was to be considered further when the group next met.
    The meeting was adjourned at 3:45 P.M., with plans to see one another on Tuesday, November 29, during class.

Report of Third Meeting of Polarization Instructional Group

Date of Meeting: November 29, 1983
Time and place: 7:30–9:00 P.M.; Room 151C, Arts & Sciences Hall
Attendance: Beverly Halliday, Bart Bonn, Hal Darling, Bill Milkas, Judy Hartlieb.

Report of Second Meeting
    Judy distributed copies of the report of the second meeting to all members. It was approved. It was decided that Judy would be responsible for recording and distributing reports of each group meeting.

Goals
    A suggested outline for problem solving presented by Bart was followed. This led to a discussion of group polarization and to determining the actions to be taken in solving the group's "problem."
    The group goals were identified as (1) understanding group polarization, (2) conducting a presentation on group polarization for the class, and (3) each member being able to write a personal essay about the group experience.

Test Portion of Presentation
    After some discussion of the type of test to be used in the presentation, it was decided that Hal would be responsible for trying to locate a book with sample tests which could be considered by the group at the next meeting. Hal will also have primary responsibility for this portion of the presentation and will see to it that copies of the test are produced and ready for the class. The other group members will individually brainstorm for test ideas, and further discussion of this test will take place during our class meeting of Tuesday, November 22.
    Criteria for a test were discussed. It was concluded that the purpose of the test would be to demonstrate the phenomenon of group polarization at work in the small

group. The test would be divided in such a way that each individual in the class would first take the test alone, and then with a small group.

Leader and Role

The group determined that the leader would be responsible for developing agendas and outlines for future meetings, and would serve as an overall controller and fill-in or back-up person for other group members. Beverly was selected by unanimous vote to fill this role as primary group leader.

Structure of Presentation

A structure and time schedule for the presentation were decided upon:

5 minutes—Each member of the class will take the test individually.

10 minutes—The class is divided into four groups, with four of our small group members serving as observers. Each group of classmates will decide *as a group* how to answer the test.

5 minutes—One member of our group will present a short report on group polarization research to the class. At the same time, the four observers will be finishing their notes regarding what happened in their respective groups.

5 minutes—The four groups will each discuss what occurred in the group. The observer may start the discussion or serve as a guide/reference person, answering questions and offering insights into what happened relative to polarization within the group.

5 minutes—The class as a whole will have opportunity to share what they observed and experienced within their groups. The observers may again start the discussion, and open the floor to any class member's contribution.

Additional Member Roles

Bart agreed to present the five-minute oral report on polarization to the class as a whole.

Bill will be responsible for arranging meeting places, and will serve as back-up to any other member who might be absent. The meeting adjourned at approximately 9:00 P.M. Further planning will take place on Tuesday, November 22, during class time.

Such records as the above will help members recall from meeting to meeting just what facts were presented, what assignments were accepted for research, what progress was made toward finding a commonly accepted solution, and so on. Without such a written report, each meeting of a group tends to "begin from scratch." Much time is wasted, and often members forget what was decided, leading to needless argument and even open conflict. Further, such a report can give a sense of accomplishment to the group and help to foster cohesiveness among members.

Summary

Discussion of ideas is possible only because of the invention of human languages. All languages consist of codes of symbols, rules for arranging the code units, and assumptions about the world being communicated about in the language. Symbols have no inherent meanings; to understand each other, people must use the same codes, and symbols must refer to the very same or very similar referents. We can use language in discussion to facilitate mutual understandings or in ways that lead to misunderstandings and disruptions of group progress. Many disruptions result from bypassing in which discussants do not realize that they are talking about the same thing using different words, or use the same words to refer to very different ideas without awareness of the different referents. Highly abstract and ambiguous language leads to confusion and misunderstanding among group members. Clichés frequently act as stoppers to thinking and the exploration of ideas. Emotive words, especially those used to stigmatize, can evoke defensive reactions and conflicts.

One can facilitate group progress by making concise remarks that are unambiguous, and by relating them to prior remarks and goals. Often asking appropriate answerable questions can coordinate and clarify group talk. Major functions of questions are orientation seeking, procedure seeking, clarifying relationships, information seeking, opinion seeking, and policy seeking. A major leadership service needed to coordinate efforts of members of continuing groups is the writing and distribution of accurate records of meetings, either in the form of minutes or summary reports. Language is a major medium of effective discussion, but misunderstood or misused it can obfuscate and stalemate group achievement of goals.

Exercises

1. Listen to a recorded discussion, or to a discussion among several classmates. Each time someone utters a cliché you recognize, write it down. Then record your impression of any effect the cliché has on subsequent discussion. What did you discover? Share your findings with fellow observers.

2. "Question Dialogue Game." Carry on a dialogue with another student in which you make statements to each other only in the *form* of questions. Leading or rhetorical questions are permitted. The first one to use the form of a declarative sentence instead of a question loses the round. What did you discover in doing this?

3. Describe an instance of misunderstanding resulting from one of the following types of verbalization. Be specific in describing what was said and what happened in response.
      high level abstraction or ambiguity
      sexist language
      ethnic or racial epithet

4. As you listen to a tape-recorded discussion, make a sheet listing each of the *types* of questions, thus getting a frequency count of each type.

Also record each actual question and the appropriateness of the response. Compare your results with those of other members of your group who listen to the same recorded discussion.

5. With others, listen to a tape-recorded discussion. Each time the group seems to be discussing a new question or issue, stop the recorder, write out what you judge the question under discussion to be, and the logical-psychological implications. Compare results with others listening to the same discussion.

6. Following a meeting of a committee, task force, or project group of members of your class, each participant should write up a report of the meeting. Circulate the reports among group members, compare them, and decide as a group on the format and content of the most useful report for the group.

Bibliography

Condon, John C., Jr. *Semantics and Communication.* 3d ed. New York: Macmillan Company, 1985.

Gulley, Halbert E., and Leathers, Dale G. *Communication and Group Process: Techniques for Improving the Quality of Small-Group Communication.* 3d ed. New York: Holt, Rinehart and Winston, Inc., 1977; especially parts 1 and 3.

Hayakawa, S. I. *Language in Thought and Action.* New York: Harcourt, Brace and Company, 1949.

References

1. William V. Haney, *Communication and Organizational Behavior,* 3d ed. (Homewood, Ill.: Richard D. Irwin, 1973), 246.
2. Dale G. Leathers, "Process Disruption and Measurement in Small Group Communication," *Quarterly Journal of Speech* 55 (1969): 288–98.
3. Harry L. Weinberg, *Levels of Knowing and Existence* (New York: Harper & Row, Publishers, 1959), 213–16.
4. Randy Y. Hirokawa, "A Comparative Analysis of Communication Patterns within Effective and Ineffective Decision-Making Groups," *Communication Monographs* 47 (1980): 312–21.
5. Henry M. Robert, *Robert's Rules of Order, Newly Revised* (Glenview, Ill: Scott, Foresman and Company, 1981), 416.

8 nonverbal signals in small group communication

Study Objectives

As a result of studying chapter 8 you should be able to:

1. Describe three major characteristics of interpersonal nonverbal signals.

2. Explain each of the six major functions nonverbal signals perform in the process of small group communication.

3. Name eight types of nonverbal cues presented by discussants, and describe at least two types of contributions each makes to communication among members of a small group.

4. Demonstrate increased sensitivity to both the nonverbal signals you send and those sent by other members of groups in which you participate.

Key Terms

Gesture   an expressive motion of the entire body or some part thereof.

Kinesics   study of communication via movements.

Nonverbal   not verbal; not relying on linguistic signals.

Proxemics   study of human uses of space and territory when relating to other humans.

Within a few seconds after you enter a group you are ready to pass judgments on the other members. You are ready to predict which members will be friends, which will be hard workers, and which trouble-makers. But if someone dared to ask how you made these judgments, you would probably be hard-put to provide an articulate answer. Is it the clothes they wore? The shape and smell of their bodies? How they combed their hair? Maybe it's the way they sat, or where they sat, or how they moved their bodies when they turned to look at you? . . . It's possible that the shape, size, color, or decorations of the room "turned you off."[1]

What do nonverbal signals contribute to establishing cooperative relationships, norms, and procedures necessary to creating a group and getting its work done? How important are nonverbal cues in the process of communication among members of a small group? *Extremely important*—though exactly how important cannot be measured with precision, for the impact of nonverbal exchange varies from group to group, and moment to moment within a group. Studies in teleconferencing (interaction via electronic media of various sorts) have indicated that restricting the *nonverbal* channels has a great impact on relationships and procedural control.[2] Birdwhistle, a pioneer in the study of body movement signals, is of the opinion that only 35 percent of meaning is communicated verbally when people are face to face; the other 65 percent of meaning is evoked in response to nonverbal signals.[3] Mehrabian, a psychologist working in the area of interpersonal communication, put the percentage of meaning derived from nonverbal cues during face-to-face interaction as high as 93 percent.[4] He estimated that on the average, 55 percent was due to facial cues and 38 percent to vocal cues. These percentages are certainly not precise, nor applicable in any specific group situation, but they do make a point we cannot afford to forget if we want to understand and contribute maximally to small group discussions—nonverbal signals and channels are tremendously important in the process of group communication. In chapter 7 we examined the nature and functioning of language in communication. Although language is vital to discussion, much of what goes on in small groups is done by sending and responding to nonverbal signals. In chapter 8 the focus is on the nonverbal dimensions of communicating.

Before we examine nonverbal communication in detail, it is important to realize that among humans in small groups there is little communicating that is totally nonverbal, and none that is totally verbal. In chapter 6 human communication was defined as a receiver phenomenon, requiring the response of a person (or persons) to perceived signals, and including the processes by which signals are created, disseminated, received, and responded to. Conscious human beings invariably interpret signals with words—words in their heads, called "thinking" or "self talk." To illustrate, consider what happens when you notice that an acquaintance is passing you on a walk without any sign of recognition. Inside your head you silently react with words such as "She didn't even notice me," or "She must be angry with me," or "She seems really upset about something." Thus you have reacted to nonverbal signals with verbal ones—in short, the process of communication entails, in most interpersonal situations, both verbal and nonverbal signals. To confirm this principle, try to discover instances where you engage in discussion without words being part of the process of any complete transaction. Most likely you'll find that you use words when attributing meaning to almost every signal coming from other group members.

Nonverbal cues are the most important medium of exchange in establishing feelings and relationships among group members, whereas verbal (symbolic) signals are the primary means of exchanging information and ideas related to accomplishing learning or task objectives. Nonverbal signals supplement the words we utter, providing clues to listeners about how to interpret the words. They are the means of regulating much of the flow of talk. In the rest of this chapter we will first consider some basic propositions concerning nonverbal signals and responses to them in small group communication, then how the functions listed above are performed by various types of signals emanating from appearance, eyes, movements, voice, space, touch, and uses of time.

Codes of nonverbal signals are culture bound. What follows is about mainstream American culture, and will *not necessarily be valid* for persons from countries other than the United States or some subcultures within the United States. For instance, many members of the Omaha tribe would not look you in the eye during a small group discussion—to do so would show disrespect. A person from China might pause at length before answering a direct question, not out of uncertainty or deviousness but as a sign of respect. There are great differences in the distances at which members of different cultures prefer to converse. The moral is clear: be very cautious when interpreting nonverbal signals. Even minor cultural differences can produce widely different signals and responses to them. Even small groups develop slightly unique nonverbal codes through time.

Characteristics of Nonverbal Communication

1. *You cannot stop sending nonverbal signals to other members of a small group.* This is often stated as "you cannot *not* communicate," at least in the sense of emitting signals which others can perceive and interpret. Nonverbal signals go out continuously from us; they cannot be stopped. Your body shape, posture, movements, eyes, clothing and accessories, skin color—these are all signals to others which may be responded to, whether or not you so intend. Even if you choose to sit immobile and impassive, others in the group may notice that and react with distrust, dislike, or worry about what you are up to or what is wrong with you. In a small group, "nothing never happens" with anyone. There is no way to be present with others and not be subject to

constant interpretation by them. You may not be a verbal participant in the group's discussion, but you cannot be present and not be a participant in the nonverbal interaction with has tremendous impact on the mood, climate, cohesiveness, and interpersonal relationships of the group. There is no ducking out of the stream of communication when a group meets. So the question is not "will I communicate?" but "how?" The only way to stop sending nonverbal signals is to leave the group.

2. By themselves, many *nonverbals are highly ambiguous.* To prevent misunderstandings, they can be clarified by verbal explanations. For instance, a smile can signal feelings of friendship, a sense of agreement, a private reverie, acknowledgement of another person, gloating over someone's misfortune, a feeling of superiority, or simple liking. A shake of the head from side to side might be interpreted as disagreement, whereas the head shaker could be feeling disbelief or amazement. Looking at one's watch might be interpreted as being bored, but it could also mean that the person has to take medication on a fixed schedule or has another meeting in a few minutes.

3. *When nonverbal and verbal cues seem to contradict each other, a listener-perceiver will usually trust the nonverbals.* There is good reason for this tendency. Many nonverbal signals come from the physiological and muscular components of emotional states and from one's habitual outlook on life and other persons. These reactions are controlled not by the higher centers of the brain cortex, but by basal structures of the brain which we share with virtually all mammals. The hypothalamus, brain stem, pineal body, and other parts of the brain which control bodily processes, hormone outputs, and feelings, and the autonomic nervous system, are responsible for generating such nonverbal signals. These are subject to little or no conscious control. Few of us can control whether or not we sweat, whether or not our blood pressure rises, the level of tension in muscles of internal organs, how widely our pupils open, the emission of chemicals from pores of the skin, or when and how much we blush, stutter, and have trouble recalling names. Only part of the time are we aware and in control of what our feet are doing, our bodily angles, or the set of the head while engaged in small group discussion. During discussions few of us exercise conscious control over the tonal quality of the voice, the rate at which we speak words, or the modulations of vocal pitch. In short, we can largely control the words we utter, but we have very little control over the nonverbal signals which accompany or stand apart from those words. Thus the nonverbal is relatively spontaneous, and more to be trusted in most cases than the more easily manipulated stream of words.

When conflict arises, we sense threat through nonverbal signals not in harmony with the words they accompany. Say you love me in flat tones, and I'll not believe you. Say to the committee that you want to hear what others think while you proceed to look away, drum the table with a forefinger, and no one will believe you. Speak of how trusting and honest you are while your hand half covers your mouth, and most of us will react with suspicion.

The whole pattern of nonverbals is more significant than any one signal. If some nonverbals appear incongrous with others, we tend to become extra guarded in interpreting them. Such mixed sets of nonverbal signals often result from attempts to conceal or deceive. Sincerity, honesty, total personal integrity as a group member is the best way to prevent sending mixed messages that produce confusion, defensiveness, skepticism, and distrust in fellow group members. You may be a consummate manipulator, a superb con artist, but as Lincoln said, you can't fool all of the people all of the time. Most of us fool few people for long in a small group; our bodies leak signals that we are trying to conceal. Most of all we may fool ourselves into thinking we are fooling others. When sender and receiver have different backgrounds, mixed messages may result despite total sincerity.

Functions of Nonverbal Signals in Small Group Communication

Nonverbal signals serve six major functions during group interaction: supplementing the verbal code, substituting for words, contradicting verbal statements, expressing emotions, regulating the interaction, and indicating status relationships. Being aware of these functions can help you act in ways that will be appropriate when responding to others and make your own signals more clear and unambiguous to them.

Supplementing the verbal. A movement or gesture may effectively *repeat* what is being said, as when a person points to item three on a chart at the same time he says, "now look at the third item on our list of ideas." Such repeating makes the verbal message doubly clear. Other nonverbal messages serve to complement or elaborate what is said. For instance, a discussant might shake his head from side to side while saying, "I cannot accept that suggestion. I consider it immoral," in a voice louder and more strained than usual, or hold up three fingers while saying "There are three things in support of your suggestion."

Some nonverbal signals give emphasis or accent the verbal message. A nod of the head, increased force on a particular word or phrase, and a shake of the finger can all indicate "this is an especially important thought or word I am now uttering." Thus by repeating, complementing, and emphasizing, nonverbal signals can supplement the verbal.

Substituting for words. Many gestures are substitutes for words. You are probably familiar with the American Sign Language that is used for com-

Figure 8.1   Nonverbal signals supplement the verbal ones.

munication among persons who cannot hear speech. A slight back-and-forth nod of the head is often used to indicate agreement or to bid at an auction without saying anything. If the chairperson of a small group asks "Do you want to vote on this?" and then sees one person shaking her head from side to side, no vote will be taken at that time. A finger movement can indicate to another discussant that you want him to lean closer to you, or a circle made with the thumb and forefinger can say in effect "I approve" or "You're okay." Because only one person can be speaking at a time in an orderly discussion, a great deal of the communicating among members is done with nonverbal substitutes for words. Not to be aware of these, or not to consciously look for them, will mean that you are missing many important potential messages among the group members.

Contradicting verbal messages. When something that a person says in a discussion doesn't seem to "ring true," often that is because the nonverbal cues contradict the words uttered. Members of therapy and encounter groups are especially likely to watch for contradictory nonverbal messages, but they occur in other learning and problem-solving discussions when someone is lying, conning, or has mixed feelings. For instance, someone might say "Yes, I'll go along with that," but in such a way that you expect him to give no real support to the idea. When you observe nonverbal messages that seem to contradict what someone is saying, it will usually pay to point this out and ask what the person means. For example, "You said you like your boyfriend, but something about the way you said it sounded as if you really don't care very much for him. What do you feel?"

Expressing emotions. As the previous example indicated, our feelings are communicated more often by nonverbal cues than by what we say. Try saying "I like you" in a variety of ways, and notice how each seems to indicate a very different feeling. Sitting close to another person can indicate more positive feelings for him or her than any words will convey. A smile and nod can signal "I like your proposal." Starkweather reported that some vocal aspects of anxiety were immediately detectable.[5] Davitz and Davitz were able to associate particular voice characteristics with both active and passive feelings.[6]

Regulating interaction. Certain nonverbal messages control or direct the flow of interaction among group members. A designated discussion leader may use nods of the head, eye contact, and hand movements to indicate who should speak next when two or more persons have indicated a desire to do so. Favorable nods encourage a speaker to continue, whereas a lack of overt response or looking away often signals "shut up." Persons will show they want to speak by leaning forward, raising a hand or finger, opening the mouth, and possibly by uttering a nonverbal sound such as "uh." Hand signals may be used to speed up a dawdling speaker, or slow someone who is rushing. So it is that nonverbal cues are the primary means of regulating the flow of verbal interaction in discussion groups.

Indicating status relationships. It has previously been pointed out that sitting at the end of a table may indicate leader status or desire for a high degree of influence in a small group. A feeling of relative superiority is often indicated by staking out a larger than average amount of territory at a table (with books, etc.), suddenly getting very close to another, a penetrating stare, a loud voice, and a patronizing pat or other touch.[7] Relatively high status persons tend to have more relaxed posture than lower status group members. On the other hand, uncrossing arms and legs, unbuttoning a coat, and general relaxation of the body often signal openness and a feeling of equality.[8] Body orientation, the angle at which a participant's shoulders and legs are turned in relation to the group as a whole or another person, indicate how much one feels a part of the group, and often that one is more committed to a subgroup than to the group as a whole.[9]

Types of Nonverbal Signals Exchanged among Discussants

Although we usually respond to a pattern of simultaneous nonverbal signals rather than to a single cue, nonetheless it is important to be aware of the variety of types of such cues in order to avoid overlooking some of them. There are many ways of classifying nonverbal signals. Those which are listed below seem to play an especially important role in communication among members of small groups.

Figure 8.2   Nonverbal signals regulate interaction.

Physical Appearance

Members of a small group that is just beginning to form react to each other's appearance long before they begin to judge each other's knowledge, reasoning, leadership, and other verbal skills. Information about one's sex, race, physique, and height cannot long be concealed. Nonverbals can reveal clues to occupation, self-concept, and attitudes toward others. Financial condition, status in the community, educational background, likes, and how friendly one may be are traits often judged from what can be seen. The judgments may or may not be correct, and may be changed later, but they will be formed initially from nonverbal signals you present.

Height and physique are major physical properties to which others react. Various body builds are interpreted by a majority of people as being more or less easy to get along with, and varying in happiness, dependability, and relative masculinity or femininity. There is much prejudice in America against endomorphs (heavy bodies), who tend to be perceived as lazy, stupid, sloppy, and not very dependable, but as jolly and easy to get along with. Ectomorphs (tall and slim) tend to be perceived as frail, but studious and intelligent. Mesomorphs (athletic types) are more likely than others to be perceived as leaders. Especially important among body characteristics is height. Other matters being at all alike, the taller a man the more likely he is to be literally looked up to as a leader; short persons will have to "try harder" to be perceived and selected as procedural leaders in small groups.[10] Being aware of the prejudices others have against you or that you may have against the physiques of others will, I hope, help you to react to what a person **does** rather than to body type and height.

Dress influences initial judgments of others, as do hair style and items of adornment. Many readers may have seen John Malloy's column, "Dress for Success," which is syndicated in many daily newspapers. In his columns and books Malloy reports many findings regarding the impact of dress and other matters of appearance on one's success in business and professional roles. Jeans, a body shirt, a gold chain and pendant, and an earring would surely reduce one's chances of being accepted as a member of a task force composed of managers from an industrial insurance company. On the other hand, executives of Apple Computer would be regarded as somewhat strange if they dressed like railway executives. One who conforms to the dress norms (code) and other appearance norms of a given corporate setting will more likely be listened to and followed in a small group than will a person whose appearance indicates rejection of values and norms of the organization from which the group was formed. In summary, inappropriate dress and adornment may result in hostility or aggression toward small group members.[11]

Space and Seating

The study of how we use personal space and territory in communicating is called *proxemics*. More study has been reported of this aspect of nonverbal signalling among small group members than of any other. A need to be included as a member is signalled by how we orient our bodies in relation to the group. A person who sits close to other members, directly in the circle in a flexible seating space or close to a circular table, or at a relatively central point on a square or rectangular conference table, signals a greater sense of belonging or need to belong to the group than does a member who sits outside the circumference of the circle, pushed back from the table, or at a corner. Such persons may feel a greater need for privacy or some hesitation about committing themselves to the group. The more personally involved we feel with others the closer we are likely to be to them. Sitting within range of touch indicates that we feel intimately or personally involved, whereas from just outside touch range to several feet away indicates a more formal, business-like relationship.[12] Patterson reported that groups making collective decisions sat closer together than when the same persons were making individual judgments.[13] Of course individuals vary somewhat in the distances they prefer to be from others. Females tend to sit closer together than do males, and to tolerate crowding better. People of the same age sit closer than people of noticeably different ages as do people of the same or different social statuses.

The better people are acquainted, the closer they tend to sit. Thus members of a group that has been in existence for a long time and has developed high levels of trust would be comfortable sitting close together in a small room or around a table, whereas people just beginning to form a group could be expected to desire more space between each other. But we humans are highly adaptable, so when room or other constraints violate our chosen distances from others, we can adapt for short periods of time. But when crowded by others for too long a time, many people grow tense, sweat more, and are inclined in general to be more stressed and defensive. Thus group leaders would be wise to watch for signs of stress from being crowded too closely for comfort or spaced too widely for a sense of inclusion, and attempt to make adjustments by rearranging the room, taking a short break, or finding a more comfortable place for subsequent meetings.

Groups (and society in general) have norms governing appropriate distances among members. Burgoon et al. tested a number of hypotheses concerning violations of the normative distance. Their findings indicate that low-status group members suffer reduced persuasiveness, sociability, and attraction ratings from other group members when these norms are violated. Persons of high status enhance their ratings and influence in the group when they violate distance norms, coming either closer to others or getting somewhat farther away than the norms suggest. This effect was particularly strong when the high status member chose a distance from other group members greater than that suggested by the norm.[14] Thus it seems advisable that unless and until you have achieved relatively high status in a small group you conform to expectations regarding space from other members. If you have achieved a high level of influence, then you may increase this even more by sitting a little apart from the other members.

Leadership emergence in a group is related to space; dominant persons and leaders usually choose central positions in the group. They sit at end positions of a rectangular table, or across from as many others as possible. Often other members avoid sitting next to a designated group leader (e.g., chair of committee, program coordinator, task force leader), so that the circle looks like the diagram in figure 8.3.[15] Such a seating pattern has advantages for the leader, reinforcing the special status of that role and allowing the leader to watch others for signs that some intervention is needed to coordinate and control interaction.

People sitting across from each other speak directly to and in response to each other more than people sitting side by side; at least this is true in most learning and task groups.[16] However, when the group has a dominating leader, "side bar" conversations tend to break out, with persons seated beside each other engaging in conversations. Burgoon reported that students given free choice of seating arrangements in small classes chose to sit in a circular or U-shaped arrangement so eye contact could be maintained with most of the group.[17] Thus we can conclude that most of the time discussion tends to flow across the circle of the group, and that persons in high status or leader positions tend to sit where they can maintain eye contact with many others, facilitating their own active participation in the group.

Figure 8.3 Typical spacing between designated leader and other members of a small task group.

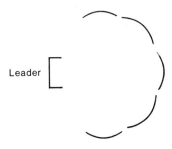

Leader

Eye Signals

For most people, establishing eye contact is preliminary to conversing with another person. This is undoubtedly related to the tendency of group members to respond more often to discussants across from them than to members sitting on the same side of a table or close at hand in a circle. Americans in small groups often use eye contact to seek feedback, when they want to be spoken to, and when they want to participate more actively.[18] In a competitive relationship between two persons, direct eye contact (or staring) may indicate something like "let's fight" whereas in a cooperative group it signifies friendship and cohesiveness.[19] As previously mentioned, eye contact is used to regulate the flow of conversation among discussants. Averting the look from another is usually taken as a sign that one wishes not to speak. Persons who seek and provide eye contact are often regarded as more believable than those who offer limited eye contact.

Eye movements can also signal disgust, dislike, superiority, or inferiority. In short, the eyes provide many important clues in human interchange.

Facial Expression

Facial expression is highly indicative of feelings and moods. Without a word being spoken, you can often perceive anger, support, agreement, disagreement, and other sentiments from facial expressions. Eckman, Ellsworth, and Friesen found that at least six types of emotion could be detected accurately from facial expressions.[20] Some people change facial expression very little—"poker faces." They tend to be trusted less than persons whose expressive faces signal their feeling states more openly. But most persons with rather expressionless faces "leak" their feelings by physiological changes such as sweating, increased heart rate, and blushing.[21] If group members show little change in facial expression, you might watch for signs of physiological changes as clues to their reactions when not speaking.

Movements

The science of how we communicate by movements is called "kinesics." To a considerable degree we reveal our feelings by bodily movements and gestures. We show tension by shifting around in a chair, drumming fingers, swinging a foot, or a twitching eye. Such behavior from several members may indicate that secondary tension needs to be dealt with. Perhaps the annoyed members think that too little progress is being made, or they are annoyed by blocking behavior. The source of the tension so revealed can often be brought into the open and dealt with by pointing out the kinesic signs of tension and asking what is producing them.

How open to and accepting of others a member of a group feels is indicated by body orientation, according to findings of Scheflen.[22] Members tend to turn directly toward others whom they like, but to turn somewhat away from persons they do not like. Leaning toward others indicates a high degree of inclusiveness, a mutual sense of belonging, whereas leaning away may signal a sense of rejection. Group members who sit at angles tangential to the rest of the group may not feel included in the group nor want to belong.

When members of a small group are "tuned in" to each other they tend to imitate each other's postures and movements. This behavior is called "postural echoes," "body synchrony," or "body congruence." Scheflen observed many instances of parallel arm positions, self-touching behavior, and leg positions indicating a sense of congruency among group members.[23] Several studies found that people are more likely to imitate the movements and gestures of persons with high status and power than of low status group members.[24] In short, by noting whose behavior is being imitated nonverbally and what members are engaged in synchronous bodily positions we can get clues to referent power and coalition formation within a small group.

Some work groups are highly dependent on body movements and gestures for coordination of their efforts: work crews at some distance from each other, athletic teams, troupes of dancers, musicians, and actors in a play. Carpenters and concrete workers often watch each other to coordinate their moves. Lifting a heavy wall into place leaves little energy for talking, as does the heavy work of moving concrete flowing from the chute of a mixer truck. Notice how the members of a basketball team work together without talking during a play. The play caller often uses hand and finger signals.

In discussion groups, control of the "floor" for talking is done largely by bodily movements and eye contact, collectively called "regulators." Speakers often signal that they are through speaking through such turn-yielding cues as relaxing and the end of hand gestures.[25] Scheflen reported that a speaker who is concluding a point or argument generally changes head and eye position and makes a noticeable postural shift.[26] A listener can bid for the floor by leaning forward, waving a hand, and opening the mouth simultaneously. In small group discussion the regulating of who gets to talk and for how long is largely done by nonverbal signals.

Vocal Cues

Vocal cues (or "paralanguage") are characteristics of voice and utterances other than words from which listeners interpret meanings of speakers. Included are such variables as pitch, rate, and fluency of utterance, dialectical variations, force, tone quality, and silences (pauses). Listeners tend to agree on the characteristics they ascribe to speakers based on vocal cues, as shown by extensive research since the 1930s.[27] Included are such characteristics as attitudes and interests, personality traits, adjustment, ethnic group, education, anxiety, and other emotional states.[28] The tone of voice has been recognized as an excellent indicator of a person's self-concept and mood. How we react to statements such as "I agree"or "Okay" depends much more on the pitch patterns and tone of voice than on the words themselves. Anxiety about communicating has been related to nonfluencies such as interjections ("uh"), repetitions, hesitations, sentence correction, and even stuttering.

Misunderstanding of irony and sarcasm occurs if some group members are insensitive to the importance of vocal cues which can indicate that the words are being used in a sense almost opposite to that in which they are usually used. A recent study found that only a small proportion of young children understood sarcasm, and that even by the senior year in high school nearly a third of students took sarcastic statements literally.[29] Sensitive discussants will be listening actively for indications of sarcasm, and also for the signals of high levels of arousal such as loudness, high pitches, a metallic tone, and a fast rate of speaking. People who speak very quietly in a low key may have little persuasive impact—they don't seem to have much personal involvement in what they are saying—but members whose voice changes are very extensive may be seen as irrational, not to be trusted as leaders or sources of ideas. Taylor found, however, that excessive vocal stress was judged more credible than was a monotonous vocal pattern.[30]

Nonverbal vocal cues play an important role as responses in some groups. Called the "backchannel," nonverbal vocalizations such as "Mm-hmmm," "uh-huh," "mmmmm," and other nonverbal sounds (along with various movements and gestures) are taken as signs of interest and active listening. Anderson claims that white Americans do not give such backchannel responses nearly so frequently as do blacks, Hispanics, and people of southern European origins.[31] This can lead to friction within a group if members who use the backchannel a great deal think others are not really attuned and listening well, while the less active backchannel responders perceive their group mates as being rude for interrupting so often!

In sum, vocal cues signal how to interpret many ambiguous statements. They reflect feelings and desired relationships. They serve as a major channel for feedback when it is not possible to utter discursive sentences, letting the speaker know that listeners are interested, impatient, seek the floor, agree, or disagree.

Time Cues

How group members relate to each other in time affects their feelings toward each other and their ability to coordinate efforts toward a shared goal. Most Americans are highly conscious of time, treating it as a commodity to be "spent" and "saved." In many cultures time is regarded quite differently; each person may act according to an inner sense of need or feelings rather than by the clock. Dealing with native Americans who have lived primarily on a reservation can be frustrating for the majority of dominant-culture Americans, who have little concept of how to structure group behavior by events occurring naturally around them rather than by the clock. In many Third World cultures clocks are meaningless to many natives. This makes for considerable difficulty when clock-organized Americans and western Europeans try to work in small groups with residents of less clock-oriented countries. In some places work stops when it rains, or when humidity and temperature produce a level of subjective discomfort, or when the sun is at a certain position in the sky. To a lesser degree differences in time orientation can make problems when urban and rural people try to cooperate in group activity. More time to chat, a sense of "we'll get to it when we are ready," and a slower pace of responding are more typical among strictly rural people than among city-dwelling Americans.

In the fast-paced culture of the American business world, being considerate of the time of others with whom you must work in groups is very important. People who come late to meetings (unless due to absolutely unavoidable circumstances) are judged to be inconsiderate, undisciplined and self-centered. It is likewise considered improper to leave a meeting before the announced time for it to end, unless some prior arrangement or explanation of the need to do so has been made. Task forces, committees, learning groups, and even primary groups (such as a family gathering for Thanksgiving dinner) consider those who arrive late and leave early not to be very committed to the group, and to be low in dependability and responsibility. Such persons are likely to be low in influence, never allowed to emerge as leaders, and generally treated as marginal members.

People can talk too much or too little, thus gaining an undue amount of the time "commodity" or too little to carry weight. Summarizing the research, Harper, Weins, and Matarazzo found that persons who talked somewhat above an average percentage of the time for a group were viewed most favorably on leadership characteristics. Those who talked about an average amount of the time were inclined to be most liked. Extremely talkative group members were regarded as rude and selfish, members the group could do better without.[32] Derber refers to excessive talking as "conversational narcissism."[33]

Pacing a meeting of a committee or other task group so that the entire agenda receives some attention and that decisions get made when required is a valuable "clock watching" function. It can help curb the narcissistic tendencies of members to shift the topic so they can exploit it for personal attention. A reminder that we have X number of minutes left for the meeting and two more items that must be settled will often curb unnecessary reiterating of what others have said clearly, get a high proportion of truly relevant remarks, reduce attention-seeking subject changes, and lead to closure on an issue.

Touch

Much important communication in interpersonal relations is effected through touching. Touch is vital to group maintenance in some primary groups and athletic teams. In work groups, committees, and activity groups touch may be relatively minor or almost nonexistent in the array of nonverbal signals. The amount and kind of touching people expect, accept, and enjoy depends on enculturation and the type of relationship. Touch is almost always threatening between strangers (except for a handshake), yet often expected between friends.

Touch among members of a small group may help strengthen cohesiveness and teamwork. Families join hands in prayer or during a memorial service. Football players hold hands in a huddle, or slap and hug each other. The type of touch, as well as the setting, has a lot to do with the reaction. Pats are usually perceived as signs of affection and inclusion. Stroking is usually perceived as sensual, highly inappropriate in small group meetings. A firm grip on an arm or around the shoulders is usually a control gesture, interpreted as a one-up maneuver. Among a group of equals such touches will usually be resented, and may provoke conflict over ideas—a sort of indirect way of saying "Take your hands off me. I'm not your lackey!" A gentle touch *may* be a means of getting someone to hold back, not overstate an issue, or grant the floor to another, but only if the persons involved in the touch are closely allied and trusting of each other.

People vary widely in the degree to which they accept and give touches. It is very important that you touch others in a group only when you sense they are accepting of touch. Andersen and Leibowitz found that people vary from touch avoiders to those who enjoy being touched, and that touch avoiders react *very* negatively to being touched.[34] Although touching the right person can do much to strengthen bonds, it is vital to respect the rights of those who prefer not to be touched, and never to touch unless it is comfortable for you to do so. A forced touch can be detected as such by a sensitive person, and seems phony or manipulative.

It seems appropriate to give a gentle pat as a sign of solidarity to persons who like being touched, even in committee and task force gatherings, if you feel comfortable doing so. But jabbing, squeezing, or holding someone by the shoulders in order to get the floor is likely to be resented by anyone. Inept touches are almost certain to increase tension within a group. My advice is go easy on this channel of nonverbal communication with members of work groups and committees. In primary groups, the norm for touch as a show of warmth and affection can be developed to the benefit of all.

Summary

In this chapter we have seen that nonverbal signs are highly important in communicating emotions and establishing relationships among members of a small group. Nonverbals play a major role in establishing many of the throughput characteristics of the group. Nonverbals perform many other communicative functions, including supplementing and clarifying our verbal expressions, substituting for words, and regulating the flow of talk and attention. There is no way to stop the sending of nonverbal signals when in the presence of a group—they are continuous—and so one cannot *not* communicate nonverbally with one's fellow group members. When verbal and nonverbal signals seem to contradict, most perceivers place greater credence in their interpretations of the nonverbal than the verbal signals.

There is a large variety of types of nonverbal signals that can be interpreted by perceptive group members. Among these, body type, appearance and height, and dress are part of the basis for initial impressions and clues to personality traits, social status, and relative power when a group begins to form. Spatial relations also indicate relative power, and along with body angles indicate how much a person feels included in and committed to a group. Seating arrangement has a lot to do with who replies to whom during discussions. Distances among members reflect both norms, position in the group, and personal liking. Eye contact signals both inclusion and control. Facial expressions are highly revealing of feelings toward the group as a whole and specific others. Body movements (including gestures) are used extensively, along with the eyes, to control turn-taking and to supplement statements. Personality characteristics and moods are interpreted from vocal cues, as well as how serious or sarcastic a speaker may be. Nonverbal voice signals, along with facial expressions and gestures, are used extensively in the backchannel to show interest and support. Vocal cues often clarify otherwise ambiguous words. We Americans regulate our lives by clocks, the time dimension of nonverbal behavior. How we time our behavior in relation to other group members is taken as indicative of our relative regard for these other members versus our degree of self-centeredness. Differences in time orientations due to varying cultural practices can thus lead to severe misunderstandings and mistrust among group members with different time practices. Pacing work by the clock is often necessary in the work of task groups. Touch, though infrequent among members of most groups, can be a means of enhancing solidarity and providing rewards, or of controlling the actions of persons touched. Touch in many primary groups is vital in expressing liking and approval. Touch must always be of the appropriate type and adapted to the preferences and needs of others. At the most basic levels of human grouping, nonverbal signals are integral to the coordinating process we call "communication."

Exercises

1. In a practice session, group discussants should first refrain from giving any bodily or vocal responses to comments of others (i.e., no head nods, leaning forward, hand gestures while another talks, "uh-huh" comments, facial expressions, etc.) for about ten minutes. Then, during the next ten minutes, everyone should react nonverbally (both physically and vocally) as fully and completely as possible. Members should then describe how they felt in each situation, why, and what this shows about group communication.

2. During a fishbowl discussion, any observer may call "freeze" at any time, at which point each discussant should remain motionless without changing even so much as eye direction. Then the observer asks each other observer to comment on what each discussant's posture, position in the group, eye direction, and nonverbal behavior seems to indicate about his or her feelings toward the group. After this, both observers and participants may discuss the implications of these observer comments and the basis for them.

3. This is a test of sensitivity to nonverbal visual cues in small group discussion. Each of the three photographs that follow shows a small group engaged in discussion. Study each photo carefully, then discuss with four or five classmates your perceptions and responses to it. What do you judge each person shown to be thinking-feeling? On what specific nonverbal cues do you base your interpretation of each person? What functions do these nonverbal cues seem to be serving?

Bibliography

Andersen, Peter A. "Nonverbal Communication in the Small Group," in *Small Group Communication: A Reader.* 4th ed., Cathcart, Robert S., and Samovar, Larry A., eds., Dubuque, Iowa: Wm. C. Brown Company Publishers, 1984, 258–275.

Burgoon, Judee K. "Spatial Relationships in Small Groups," in *Small Group Communication: A Reader.* 4th ed., Cathcart, Robert S., and Samovar, Larry A., eds., Dubuque, Iowa: Wm. C. Brown Company Publishers, 1984, 276–292.

Burgoon, Judee K., and Saine T. *The Unspoken Dialogue: An Introduction to Nonverbal Communication,* Boston: Houghton Mifflin Company, 1978.

References

1. Lawrence R. Rosenfeld, *Now That We're All Here: Relations in Small Groups* (Columbus, Ohio: Charles E. Merrill Publishing Company, 1976), 31.
2. Robert Johansen, Jacques Valle, and Kathleen Spangler, *Electronic Meetings: Technical Alternatives and Social Choices* (Reading, Mass.: Addison-Wesley, 1979), 17–25.
3. Ray L. Birdwhistle, Lecture at Nebraska Psychiatric Institute: Omaha, Nebraska; May 11, 1972.
4. Albert Mehrabian, *Nonverbal Communication* (Chicago: Aldine-Atherton, 1972).
5. J. Starkweather, "Vocal Communication of Personality and Human Feelings," *Journal of Communication* 11 (1961):63–72.
6. Joel R. Davitz and Lois J. Davitz, "Nonverbal Vocal Communication of Feeling," *Journal of Communication* 11 (1961):81–86.
7. Erving Goffman, *Relation in Public* (New York: Harper and Row, Publishers, 1971), 32–48.
8. Gerald I. Nierenberg and H. H. Calero, *How to Read a Person Like a Book* (New York: Pocket Books, 1973), 46.
9. Stewart L. Tubbs, *A Systems Approach to Small Group Interaction* (Redding, Mass.: Addison-Wesley, 1978), 185.
10. J. Spiegel and P. Machotka, *Messages of the Body* (New York: The Free Press, 1974); and J. B. Cortes and F. M. Gatti, "Physique and Propensity," in *With Words Unspoken,* L. B. Rosenfeld and J. M. Civikly, eds. (New York: Holt, Rinehart and Winston, 1976), 50–56.
11. L. L. Barker, D. J. Cegala, R. J. Kibler, and K. J. Wahlers, *Groups in Process: An Introduction to Small Group Communication* (Englewood Cliffs, N.J.: Prentice-Hall, 1979), 184.
12. Edward T. Hall, *The Silent Language* (Garden City, N.Y.: Doubleday, 1959).
13. M. L. Patterson, "The Role of Space in Social Interaction," in *Nonverbal Behavior and Communication,* A. W. Siegman and S. Feldstein, eds. (Hillsdale, N.J.: Lawrence Erlbaum Associates, 1978).
14. J. K. Burgoon, D. W. Stacks, and S. A. Burch, "The Role of Interpersonal Rewards and Violations of Distancing Expectations in Achieving Influence in Small Groups," *Communication* 11 (1982):114–128.
15. R. F. Bales and A. P. Hare, "Seating Pattern and Small Group Interaction," *Sociometry* 26 (1963):480–486; and G. Hearn, "Leadership and the Spatial Factor in Small Groups," *Journal of Abnormal and Social Psychology* 54 (1957):269–272.
16. B. Steinzor, "The Spatial Factor in Face to Face Discussion Groups," *Journal of Abnormal and Social Psychology* 45 (1950):552–555.

17. J. K. Burgoon, "Spatial Relationships in Small Groups," in *Small Group Communication: A Reader,* 4th ed., R. S. Cathcart and L. A. Samovar, eds. (Dubuque, Iowa: Wm. C. Brown Company Publishers, 1984), 285.
18. J. McCroskey, C. Larson, and M. Knapp, *An Introduction to Interpersonal Communication* (Englewood Cliffs, N.J.: Prentice-Hall, 1971), 110–14.
19. R. V. Exline, "Exploration in the Process of Person Perception: Visual Interaction in Relation to Competition, Sex, and the Need for Affiliation," *Journal of Personality* 31 (1963):1–20.
20. P. Eckman, P. Ellsworth, and W. V. Friesen, *Emotion in the Human Face: Guidelines for Research and an Integration of Findings* (New York: Pergamon Press, 1971).
21. R. W. Buck, R. E. Miller, and W. F. Caul, "Sex, Personality, and Physiological Variables in the Communication of Affect via Facial Expression," *Journal of Personality and Social Psychology* 30 (1974):587–596.
22. A. E. Scheflen, "Quasi-Courtship Behavior in Psychotherapy," *Psychiatry* 28 (1965):245–256.
23. A. E. Scheflen, *Body Language and the Social Order: Communication as Behavioral Control* (Englewood Cliffs, N.J.: Prentice-Hall, 1972), 54–73.
24. J. K. Burgoon and T. Saine, *The Unknown Dialogue: A Introduction to Nonverbal Communication* (Boston: Houghton Mifflin Company, 1978).
25. S. Duncan, Jr., "Some Signals and Rules for Taking Speaking Turns in Conversations," *Journal of Personality and Social Psychology* 23 (1972):283–292.
26. A. E. Scheflen, *Body Language and the Social Order: Communication as Behavioral Control* (Englewood Cliffs, N.J.: Prentice-Hall, 1972), 54–72.
27. N. D. Addington, "The Relationship of Selected Vocal Characteristics to Personality Perception," *Speech Monographs* 35 (1968):492; and Ernest Kramer, "Judgment of Personal Characteristics and Emotions from Nonverbal Properties of Speech," *Psychological Bulletin* 60 (1963):408–20.
28. Joel D. Davitz and Lois Davitz, "Nonverbal Vocal Communication of Feelings," *Journal of Communication* 11 (1961):81–86.
29. P. A. Andersen et al., "The Development of Nonverbal Communication Behavior in School Children Grades K–12," Paper presented at the annual convention of the International Communication Association, Minneapolis, Minn.; May, 1981.
30. K. D. Taylor, "Ratings of Source Credibility in Relation to Level of Vocal Variety, Sex of the Source, and Sex of the Receiver" (M.A. thesis, University of Nebraska at Omaha, 1984).

31. P. A. Anderson, "Nonverbal Communication in the Small Group," in *Small Group Communication,* R. S. Cathcart and L. A. Samovar, eds., 265.
32. R. G. Harper, A. N. Wiens, and J. D. Matarazzo, *Nonverbal Communication: The State of the Art* (New York: John Wiley and Sons, 1978).
33. C. Derber, *The Pursuit of Attention* (New York: Oxford University Press, 1979).
34. P. A. Andersen and K. Leibowitz, "The Development and Nature of the Construct 'Touch Avoidance,' " *Environmental Psychology and Nonverbal Behavior* 3 (1978):89–106.

9

leading small group discussions

Study Objectives

As a result of your study of chapter 9 you should be able to:

1. Define and distinguish among the concepts of leadership, leader, emergent leader, and designated leader.

2. Explain the major theories and findings of trait, function, and contingency approaches to the study of leadership.

3. Explain five types of leadership power, and how power can be applied democratically through group-centered leadership.

4. Describe characteristics typical of effective discussion leaders.

5. Develop a personal philosophy of group-centered democratic small group leadership.

6. List three major classes of responsibilities expected of small group discussion leaders, and explain both general approaches and specific techniques for providing these services.

Key Terms

Autocratic leader   a person who dominates and manipulates a group, usually for personal goals, using coercion, rewards, and positional power to influence.

Completer, leader as   leader who determines what functions or behaviors are most needed for a group to perform optimally, then attempts to encourage or supply those behaviors.

Contingency approach   study of how outcomes of leadership vary with differences in input or context variables; adapting leadership services to such variables.

Democratic leader   person who coordinates and facilitates discussion in a small group by consent of the group, thus helping to achieve group-determined goals.

Designated leader   a person appointed or elected to position as leader of a small group.

Discussion leader   leader of a group's verbal interaction; coordinator of discussion process and procedures.

Emergent leader   member of an initially leaderless group who in time is named as "leader" by all or nearly all members.

Functions approach   study of functions (behaviors) performed by actual small group leaders.

Leader   a *person* who exercises goal-oriented influence in a group, any person identified by members of a group as leader, or a designated leader.

Leadership   influence exerted through communication that helps a group clarify and achieve goals; performance of a leadership function.

Power   potential to influence behavior of others, derived from such bases as ability to reward, coerce, or supply needed expertise, or from personal attraction and the consent of those who follow.

Pseudodiscussion   going through the motions of discussion when the important outputs have been predetermined by an autocratic leader.

Structuring leadership   behaviors that function to organize and coordinate group interaction and work.

Trait approach   study of personal and behavioral characteristics of both designated and emergent leaders.

It is universally believed that leaders are important to the outcomes of small group discussions. As Hollander concluded, groups with single designated leaders work more efficiently, have fewer interpersonal problems, and produce better outputs than groups lacking such a designated leader.[1] But what *behaviors* provide effective leader services to a small group is not so clear or agreed upon. "Leader" and "leadership" are highly abstract terms that have been used for a multitude of referents concerning personality traits, interpersonal activity, and a great variety of situations. In this book we are not concerned with a general theory of leadership for all types of leader-follower situations, but only with leadership of discussion groups in which all members have a voice in the decisions and actions of the group. Thus we can narrow our study of leadership by excluding, for the most part, such groups as work crews, combat units, athletic teams, large organizations, and mass meetings, except when these groups are engaged in discussion.

To serve others as a leader can be a source of self-esteem, recognition, and appreciation from others. Leading discussions can meet personal needs for control of both situations and other persons. It can provide the satisfaction of accomplishment, the taking on and meeting of a challenge, similar to the satisfaction experienced by a successful craftsperson or athlete. But for every potential reward of a leadership role there is the concomitant potential for failure and disappointment. Although most members of small groups of peers would like to be recognized as leader, many hesitate to take on any formal role of leader, for to do so entails high levels of responsibility and visibility. Perhaps they lack knowledge and confidence about what to do, or fear the possibility of failing and losing face. The sheer amount of work required in some committee leader roles may dissuade many. Others avoid a position of leadership because they think it requires manipulating others.

Before reading further in this chapter, complete the following scale to find out what *you* think discussion leaders should do, and how they should do it. *After* you have completed the scale, turn to page 255 to score your answers and locate your position on the autocratic-democratic dimension of discussion leader philosophy. You may want to discuss the items in this scale with classmates, or compare your score with theirs. As a result of completing and discussing the scale you may be able to understand much of the chapter in a more personal way.

A Learning Activity

Figure 9.1   The Sargent and Miller Leadership Scale. (F. Sargent and G. Miller, "Some Differences in Certain Communication Behaviors of Autocratic and Democratic Group Leaders," *Journal of Communication* 21 [1971], pp. 233–52.)

We are interested in the things that are important to you when you are leading a group discussion. Listed below are several pairs of statements. Read each pair of statements and place a mark in the one you believe to be of greater importance. On reacting to the statements, observe the following ground rules:

1. Place your check marks clearly and carefully.
2. Do not omit any of the items.
3. Never check both of the items.
4. Do not look back and forth through the items; make each item a separate and independent judgment.
5. Your first impression, the immediate feelings about the statements, is what we want.

1. a. _____ To give everyone a chance to express his opinion.
   b. _____ To know what the group and its members are doing.
2. a. _____ To assign members to tasks so more can be accomplished.
   b. _____ To let the members reach a decision all by themselves.
3. a. _____ To know what the group and its members are doing.
   b. _____ To help the members see how the discussion is related to the purposes of the group.
4. a. _____ To assist the group in getting along well together.
   b. _____ To help the group to what you think is their best answer.
5. a. _____ To get the job done.
   b. _____ To let the members reach a decision all by themselves.
6. a. _____ To know what the group and its members are doing.
   b. _____ To let the members reach a decision all by themselves.
7. a. _____ To get the job done.
   b. _____ To assist the group in getting along well together.
8. a. _____ To help the members see how the discussion is related to the purposes of the group.
   b. _____ To assign members to tasks so more can be accomplished.
9. a. _____ To ask questions that will cause members to do more thinking.
   b. _____ To get the job done.
10. a. _____ To let the members reach a decision all by themselves.
    b. _____ To give new information when you feel the members are ready for it.

The characteristics, functions, relationships, and communicative behaviors of leaders have been studied extensively by small group theorists and researchers since the early 1940s. Prior to that time it was widely believed that leaders were specially gifted persons who were born to lead, and that there was little anyone could do to develop leadership skills. Even today, despite research findings to the contrary, persons often speak as if there were some mystical quality of leadership that if possessed makes one a leader in virtually any situation. Generals are assumed to be capable of supplying effective leadership in education or government; football captains are elected to class offices; great teachers are made chairpersons of committees—and sometimes the results are dismal. I still receive forms on which to rate former students as job applicants that contain a scale like this: "Leadership—superior __ ; above average __ ; average __ ; below average __ ."

Persons who keep abreast of research in leadership know better. Leadership is not *a* quality or personality trait; leading requires a wide variety of personal characteristics and communicative behaviors, and varies greatly from situation to situation and from group to group. As Tropman wrote, many people have little idea of how to supply the crucial roles needed in a committee, or of the need for role flexibility as they shift during a day from chairing to member roles in a variety of small groups.[2]

Training persons to diagnose and supply the changing leadership services needed by specific types of group situations has made many organizations more productive. Businesses and agencies constantly search for persons with attitudes and skills needed for specific positions of leadership, and then give them further specialized training in such matters as management theory and practice, human relations, listening, speaking, group dynamics, and conference leadership. Armed forces provide a variety of types of training in leadership skills for officers of all ranks. Unions conduct leadership training programs to develop special skills in their membership. In short, there is a continuing demand for persons with special leadership skills.

Money and time spent on developing discussion leadership skills are invested wisely. As we have seen, discussion is fundamental to democratic organization and cooperation. No discussion group can be effective without appropriate leadership—and that means skilled leaders. Whenever a group has a designated leader (either elected or appointed), that person can almost literally make or break the group. In my own research studies I found that the degree of success in goal achievement and member satisfaction by adult study groups was so closely related to the leader's behavior that I often said: "Let me watch the leader for fifteen minutes and I will predict whether or not the group will be successful." Countless committees and task groups have faltered and accomplished little when the chairperson did not know how to perform as a leader.

But what does it take to lead *discussions* well? In a very real sense, this entire book is an attempt to answer that question: an understanding of the process dynamics of small groups, positive attitudes toward self and others, dependable and relevant knowledge, interest, commitment to the group's goals, sensitive listening and encoding skills, a belief in the potential contributions of all members, a desire for democratic decision making, and skills in systematic problem solving. There are special techniques we can use to supply needed leadership services for the small groups to which we belong. In this chapter we will first consider the concepts of *leader* and *leadership,* then a variety of approaches to the study of leadership, a philosophy of *discussion* leadership, the special responsibilities you assume when appointed or elected discussion leader, and some ways to meet those responsibilities so that both process and output variables of discussion are enhanced.

Leadership and Leaders

It is possible—though quite uncommon—for a discussion group to have no designated leader and yet to have excellent leadership. It is also possible for a discussion group to have a formal leader and yet be woefully lacking in leadership. If these statements seem paradoxical, it is only because the terms *leader* and *leadership* are confusing due to overlapping meanings.

Leadership

Social scientists are virtually unanimous in defining leadership as *interpersonal influence.* Probably the most widely used definition in the area of small group communication is that by Tannenbaum, Weschler, and Massarik:

We define leadership as *interpersonal influence, exercised in situation and directed, through the communication process, toward the attainment of a specified goal or goals.* Leadership always involves attempts on the part of a *leader* (influencer) to affect (influence) the behavior of a follower (influencee) or followers in *situation.*[3]

However, this is a general definition, not limited to small groups. Only attempts to influence behavior in an effort to achieve a *group* goal will be considered leadership in the context of small group discussion, thereby excluding behavior through which one member influences another to do something apart from or contrary to the goal of the group. Excluded would be influence irrelevant to the group's goals, such as one member influencing another to emulate his mannerisms, aid him in an attempt to sabotage the group, or join him for a drink after the meeting (unless that is done to achieve greater harmony within the group).

Influence refers to the exercise of *power,* which in groups of relative equals depends on the consent of other group members to be influenced. The exercise of power to influence depends upon a follower (or followers) perceiving that a leader has a power base that can be exercised, whether or not the power is actually available to the person exercising the influence. If no one follows, there is no leader.

French and Raven identified five bases of power that a designated leader may have in some degree: reward, coercive, legitimate, referent, and expert.[4]

Members may be *rewarded* by giving them special attention, favors, or acknowledgement. Members who resist an attempt to influence are sometimes *coerced* by threats, lack of opportunity to speak, or ignoring them until they comply. A boss or other authority figure may use such power to virtually force acquiescence, but such behavior is not leadership.

Legitimate power stems from an acknowledged position and title. Many small group members will follow directives from a person holding such a position: a private will accept the legitimate power of his sergeant to chew him out, but would not let another private do so. A work supervisor may assign duties, but not a colleague. In the typical committee, most members will attend meetings at the call of an appointed chairperson, and will accept the agenda prepared for a meeting by that person. Most discussants let designated leaders exercise some control over the flow of verbal participation and problem-solving procedures.

Referent power is based on attraction of one person to another, or identification. Such power comes from the desire of group members to associate with a person whose behavior they admire. This type of power is often called *charisma*. The ideal discussion leader models behavior which other members admire and emulate. If you chair a committee or lead a class discussion, your behaviors should be a model for other members in listening, considering all sides of an issue, and keeping remarks clear and orderly. Such behavior becomes admired by others who then allow you to influence them, giving you referent power.

Expert power is attributed by members to another for what he or she knows and can do. A member of a small group who has the knowledge and skills essential to overcome obstacles to a goal will have a high degree of expert power. It may matter little that he or she is not personally attractive, the holder of a position granting legitimate power, or able to either reward or punish. The expert is influential because he or she is perceived as having vital knowledge and skills.

Group-centered leadership entails the judicious use of power to serve the group's interests. Any source of power can be weakened by indiscriminate use or overuse. Members will often resist or rebel if coercive power is employed, come to dislike rather than identify if referent power is used for the personal gain of the leader, or refuse to be influenced and thus remove the base of legitimate power.

The more these five power bases are concentrated in one person, the more that person can dominate a small group, possibly leading to autocracy with decisions being made by one person. The greater the degree to which the bases of power and influence are distributed among the members of a small group, the more likely is verbal participation to be shared, decision making to be collaborative, and the designated leader to serve as a coordinator rather than boss. Sometimes when there is no legitimate leader (by appointment or election), a long struggle for the status of primary leader ensues in a group, with competitors struggling to win followers. Several studies have confirmed that such groups are ineffective unless a stable leadership structure (including a primary leader) emerges. A group undergoing a struggle for the leader position produces poor products, dissatisfaction, and low levels of cohesiveness.[5] The conclusion is clear: someone in a group in which the bases of power are widely shared must emerge as *the* recognized leader or the group will be a failure in solving its problems. But what does it take to emerge as leader or to be accepted as a legitimate designated leader in a discussion group? Certainly the responsibility for leadership functions and influence are shared in successful discussion groups.

When formal organizations appoint persons to positions of control in small groups or someone is elected chairperson or leader, that person must still earn leadership from within the group. The designated leader will be challenged and tested as he or she attempts to coordinate activities of members. If that person is not able to emerge as the natural or chosen leader of the group, another person will do so or the group will flounder.

Discussion leadership is the responsibility of all members of a small group; it will usually be shared by several of them. It is now believed that the tasks that were considered to be the sole responsibility of the leader (introducing the problem, guiding the discussion, probing, spreading participation, clarifying, resolving disagreements, asking questions, etc.) can better be handled by many members of a group. Some persons may have more skills at a certain leadership task, have special knowledge, or sensitivity to what the designated leader has missed. If so, a *leadership team* emerges. If we conceive of leadership as services that help a group clarify and achieve its goals *as a group,* then it must be obvious that everyone in the group has some contribution to make to its leadership. Anyone who does not has no business being in the group!

Leaders

Even though leadership functions may be diffused within a group, the management of a business or governmental organization will hold a designated leader responsible for the productivity of the group. Designated leaders of small groups in other settings are not free from such responsibility either: ". . . group members and outsiders tend to hold the leader accountable for group beliefs, proposals, actions, and products."[6] Thus the role or position of "leader" must be clarified. The term *leader* is used in this book in three ways: (1) to refer to *any person who is perceived by group members as their leader;* (2) to refer to *any person who has been appointed or elected to a position of leadership* such as "chair" or "coordinator"; and (3) to refer to *any person who is exerting influence within a group toward achievement of interdependent group goals.*

A designated leader has a special responsibility to maintain perspective and to see that all needed leadership services are performed. In this regard, Schutz described the function of a leader in a group as a *completer:* ". . . the best a leader can do is to observe what functions are not being performed by a segment of the group and enable this part to accomplish them."[7] As Schutz says, the prime requisites to being a leader are: knowing necessary group functions; sensing unfulfilled group functions; performing and getting others to perform needed functions; and being willing to take necessary action, even if personally displeasing. This concept of "leader as completer" is a powerful guide to anyone who wants to be an effective discussion leader, and emphasizes again the importance of having some image of optimal group discussion such as is presented in chapter 2.

In the second sense referred to above, "leader" is also the name of a special role in a small group. The functions and duties of that role depend somewhat on the person occupying it, the membership of the group (its skills, expectations, and beliefs about leaders), the source of the group, the degree of development of the group as a functioning system, and the goals of the group. The ideal is for leadership functions to be shared so that each member supplies those services that he or she can do best, with the designated leader doing whatever no one else can do as well, and having a special responsibility to monitor the functioning of the group as a system in order to provide leadership services when needed (or encourage others to do so). For example, a designated committee chairperson might take notes and summarize, unless someone else is doing so for the group. The leader's role is determined by an interaction of such variables as the external situation facing the group, the expectations and beliefs of members about the leader role, and the respective skills of all members. For most committees and boards, the "chair" role involves a mix of duties involving discussion leadership, administration, and liaison.

One-meeting groups should almost always have designated leaders. In a one-meeting group the designated leader will likely do most of the organizing, clarifying, summarizing, and other procedural tasks; concomitantly, he or she will probably do little suggesting or evaluating of ideas. In a continuing group, routines will develop with members taking on specialized roles; after a time, the designated leader may be able to participate very much like any other member. As members take on tasks of leadership and develop skill in them, the designated leader's proportion of leadership functions will decline. However, a designated leader will always be expected to serve as coordinator and spokesperson for the group.

Approaches to the Study of Leadership

Several approaches to the scientific study of leadership have emerged, of which three are especially appropriate to the leadership of discussion groups: trait, function, and contingency. Recently an integration of all these approaches has been attempted under the title "Systems/Process Model."[8]

The Trait Approach to the Study of Leadership

Trait studies began with the assumption that leaders are a special class of people, distinguishable from followers on personal traits. Summarizing much of this research, Bird was unable to find much consistency in the reports of "leader" traits, possibly due to inadequacies of measurement, the wide variety of types of groups and tasks studied, varying definitions, and other unspecified variables.[9] From later studies it has been shown that some general traits tend to be related to leadership. Leaders tend to exceed other group members in such characteristics as IQ, knowledge, verbal facility, and flexibility. They tend to be larger physically, and more attractive. They are also more sociable than average, as shown on measures of dependability, frequency of participation, cooperation, and popularity. They show above average initiative and persistence.[10] But as Stogdill concluded from his 1948 review of leadership studies,

A person does not become a leader by virtue of the possession of some combination
of traits, but the pattern of personal characteristics of the leader must bear some
relevant relationship to the characteristics, activities, and goals of the
followers. . . . The evidence suggests that leadership is a relation that exists
between persons in a social situation, and that persons who are leaders in one
situation may not necessarily be leaders in other situations.[11]

Geier studied the characteristics of students who emerged as leaders of initially leaderless class project groups at the University of Minnesota. Members of the groups were questioned regularly to determine which members were perceived as exerting leadership and if a consensus leader had emerged. Both directly observable behaviors of persons who emerged as leaders and traits perceived by fellow group members were examined. In the successful groups, definite consensus leaders emerged; in all groups much energy was spent on a struggle for leader status. A two-phase pattern of leader emergence was found. During the relatively short, conflict-free first phase (forming), participants with three types of characteristics were eliminated in the minds of other members as contenders for the position of leader: members uninformed about the problem facing the group, infrequent participants, and rigid or dogmatic persons who expressed their opinions categorically and were not influenced by other members' opinions. The second phase in the struggle for the leader post ranged from a relatively short to a prolonged period of time. At the beginning of this phase approximately forty percent of the group members still had a chance to become the leader of the group. First, those who were authoritarian and manipulative in their methods were eliminated by fellow members in favor of the more democratic. The final characteristic of behavior eliminating remaining contenders was called "offensive verbalization" by Greier, and included such behaviors as "incessant talking and stilted speech." It is also important to note that in the majority of groups where a leader emerged, another person who had contended for the leader post emerged as a lieutenant,[12] a sort of co-leader and supporter of the emergent leader.

The Functions Approach to the Study of Leadership

As a reaction to the barrenness of the trait studies up to that time, after World War II scholars began to examine the *functions* performed by leaders. This approach examines the services provided by designated leaders contributing to group goal clarification and achievement. Leaders may help get the work of the group done, structure interaction among members, develop and maintain the group as a system, and help members meet personal needs that otherwise would reduce their ability to contribute to the group. Bales divided all leader functions into two broad categories, task and socioemotional. He found that relatively few persons could perform both types of functions equally well, thus indicating the need in many groups for a leadership team of at least a task specialist and a socioemotional specialist.[13]

Stogdill, in a review of the literature, identified six functions performed by leaders:

1. Defining objectives and maintaining goal direction.

2. Providing means for goal acheivement.

3. Providing and maintaining group structure.

4. Facilitating group action and interaction.

5. Maintaining group cohesiveness and member satisfaction.

6. Facilitating group task performance.[14]

It is probably obvious to you that these process functions are important to the outcomes of a group discussion, with the possible exclusion of 6. Performing these functions during discussion requires many specific types of actions. These are described and advice on how they can be provided is given in the last major section of this chapter.

The central function—the one most expected of a discussion leader—is a coordinating one. Maier illustrated this service to the group with an analogy comparing the designated discussion leader's role to that of the nerve ring in a starfish, and the other group members to its rays. When the nerve ring is intact, it connects and coordinates the rays, and the starfish is very efficient in its movements. If the ring is severed, the rays can influence each other's behaviors to a degree, but internal coordination is missing. If one ray is stimulated to step forward (perhaps to seize a clam), the adjoining rays sense the pull on them and also begin to step forward, showing coordinated behavior based on external control. But if opposite rays are stimulated simultaneously, the animal becomes locked in position as each ray tries to move in opposite directions; this can even tear the starfish in two and destroy it. The central nerve ring does none of the moving, but it coordinates the behavior of all the rays. Thus we get the coordinated behavior of a higher type organism rather than the summed efforts of five rays physically together but not coordinated unless one dominates the others. The ring does not do the work, but collects the information from all rays and produces an organismically unified response rather than a collection of individual responses that may or may not be interrelated. Maier likens the function of a group-centered discussion leader to that of the central nerve ring: "Thus the leader does not serve as a dominant ray and produce the solution. Rather, his function is to receive information, facilitate communication between the individuals, relay messages, and integrate the incoming responses so that a single unified response occurs."[15] Coordinating is acknowledged by virtually all writers to be the primary function of designated discussion leaders, but **how** it should be performed is a central question in small group leadership philosophy.

Recently, communication researchers have begun to study the communicative functions of discussion leaders. Knutson and Holdridge found that persons who emerged as leaders in small policy discussion groups were significantly higher than others in the percentage of orienting statements, such as information and summaries.[16] An important leader service may be the verbalizing of a rhetorical vision or image of the basis for unity rather than conflict among group members.[17]

What one does and how one does it as a leader in a discussion group depends in large part on attitudes (degree of authoritarianism, of openmindedness, etc.), which collectively can be called a philosophy of leadership. "Philosophy" as used here refers to a set of beliefs, values, and ethics concerning the relationship between leaders and followers, or how a leader *ought* to act. In this sense a philosophy embraces the entire scope of functions performed by a would-be leader, the purpose of them as primarily serving self or group, and whether decisions are best made by leader or group collectively. One's style in attempting to exert leadership can be called a philosophy in action.

An experimental approach to the functions performed by group leaders was taken in the research conducted by White and Lippett. Their findings indicated that a democratic way of performing leader functions had output advantages over autocratic and laissez-faire leader behaviors.[18] However, the results must be generalized to adult discussion groups with caution for the groups studied were boys clubs organized to construct craft objects with the assistance of assigned adult leaders. Democratic leaders allowed the boys to decide policy issues, with encouragement and assistance from the leader. Laissez-faire leaders took almost no initiative, but did respond to inquiries from the boys. Autocratic leaders made assignments, gave orders, and rigidly controlled all verbal interaction, shutting off boys who did not agree with them.

More germane to the purpose of this book was a finding by Sargent and Miller (who developed the scale at the beginning of this chapter) that democratic leaders encouraged much more member participation in the problem-solving discussion process than did autocratic leaders. Rosenfeld and Plax found that autocratic discussion leaders asked fewer questions but answered more than did democratic leaders, expressed more negative reactions (coercion attempts?), and made fewer attempts to get others to participate actively.[19]

One line of research into the leaders of problem-solving discussion groups has focused on what is called "leadership structuring style," which refers primarily to what I have called "procedural leadership." As Jurma described them, "structuring leaders actively work to organize and coordinate group interaction" by helping to formulate goals and ways to achieve them, clarifying, providing task-related information, and stressing egalitarian behavior.[20] Non-structuring designated leaders participate very little and suggest no structure or procedure, acting in a laissez-faire style. A general conclusion from this line of research is that groups with structuring designated leaders are more effective in problem solving and more satisfying to the participants than are groups with assigned nonstructuring leaders.[21] Independent judges rated discussions led by structuring leaders to be of higher quality than discussions with assigned nonstructuring leaders.[22] In summary, this line of research has produced consistent findings that a leader who organizes group discussions in a democratic manner produces both better task outcomes and higher member satisfaction than does either a nonstructuring or autocratic leader.

The Contingency Approach to the Study of Leadership

The contingency (or situational) approach to the study of leadership in small interacting groups has investigated the general hypothesis that the style of leadership needs to be varied according to contingencies of group purpose, task complexity, organizational context, member characteristics and expectations, and other variables. When we consider all types of small groups, this hypothesis is clearly supported. Fiedler developed a model of three major factors upon which appropriate leadership behaviors are contingent: leader-member relations, task structure, and position power.[23] The central thesis of Fiedler's work is that individuals' personal needs and characteristics would make them suited for leadership only in certain contingencies, and so it is more productive to match prospective leaders to situations than to try to change a person's leadership style. This theory also implies that as a group's situation changes through time different types of persons would be needed in the position of designated leader. Problem-solving discussion groups, according to Fiedler's theory and findings, would generally be served best by a democratic structuring leader with concern for persons, rather than by autocratic or non-structuring leadership. However, in other types of situations, such as supervising police or production workers or leading primary groups, a much more autocratic or a socioemotional style of leadership would be more productive.

It has been demonstrated that what members think of as appropriate leadership functions and style is contingent upon situational variables.[24] Wood used a questionnaire to determine what members of continuing small groups with task, social, and dual task-social objectives expected of designated leaders. She named the three major factors that emerged as task guidance, interpersonal attractiveness, and team spirit. Members of both task and dual-purpose groups rated task-oriented leadership (analogous to structuring) highly important, whereas members of social groups rated interpersonal attractiveness high and task orientation low. A moderate degree of team spirit was expected of leaders in all types of groups.[25] Griffin found that the amount of structuring and directive behavior preferred from supervisors was dependent upon the level of "growth needs" of subordinates. Persons high in growth needs (they prefer challenging jobs) most preferred participative, considerate supervisors, whereas employees with lower growth needs accepted more autocratic supervisors.[26] Downs and Pickett examined contingencies of leader style and member needs. Groups of participants with high social needs were most productive with task-oriented procedural leaders, and least productive with no designated leader. Groups of persons low on interpersonal needs did equally well with designated leaders who provided task-structuring only, leaders who provided both task structuring and socioemotional leadership, and no designated leader. Groups with members both high and low in interpersonal needs performed somewhat better without a designated leader. A complex relationship among members needs, leadership style, and member satisfaction was found, giving support to the general contingency hypothesis of leadership in small discussion groups.[27] Differences in follower traits have been known to influence reactions to different leader behavior patterns: degree of authoritarianism and dogmatism, need for achievement, and locus of control (whether one feels in control of one's life or governed by fate).[28] From the research and theory we can safely conclude that a discussion leader needs to be *flexible,* adapting to situational contingencies, but that in almost all situations a democratic structuring approach will be productive.

Chemers' "Integrative Systems/Process Model" of Leadership

No single approach to the study of leadership has provided a comprehensive explanation of how leadership and group output are related. Chemers created a heuristic model of leadership, integrating the variables studied in all the major approaches to understanding leadership: "The model does assume that leadership process is a multivariate system in which each set of variables is influenced by, and in turn influences numerous other sets of variables."[29]

Chemers' model is a version of the small group as an open system, with emphasis on leadership. Inputs include "leader's personal characteristics," "cultural characteristics," "situational characteristics," "expectations and intentions," and "follower's individual characteristics." Process variables include "leader behaviors" and "follower behaviors." Output variables of the model include "satisfaction," "group performance," and "feedback" influences on process variables through time. Only by viewing all leader-follower behaviors as parts of a complex process system are we likely to develop increasingly valid theories of leadership for either scientific studies or as guides to practical behavior when in leader roles.

Getting practical. Up to this point we have examined theory and research concerning small group leaders and leadership without prescribing any specific role functions or techniques. In the rest of chapter 9, I present a point of view about the personal philosophy that I believe you may want to adopt in order to lead discussions effectively, the functions I think you should be prepared to perform as discussion leader, and specific techniques that can be used to provide those functions. Put another way, up to now this chapter has been primarily descriptive; the rest of it will be more prescriptive. Persons from college freshmen to senior managers in large corporate structures often ask, "How should I act as discussion leader? What will I be expected to do? How can I do it?" Based on the research and theory described above, studies of special techniques, and a great deal of practical experience, I have provided some answers to these questions, answers that I think you will find helpful. These are suggestions. Try them out. *Adapt* them to your specific personality and the situations you face. Use what you can. In time you will develop your own philosophy, a variety of functions to fit group contingencies, and a wide range of skills in providing needed leader services, whether or not you hold a position of designated leader. Do not expect to be an instant success. It may take years of practice to develop into the versatile discussion leader you hope to become. Now is the time to begin.

Group-Centered Democratic Discussion Leadership

I believe that in most situations a designated discussion leader will be most helpful to a group seeking to learn or solve problems if he or she adopts a democratic group-centered role, with primary attention to task and procedural matters and secondary attention to interpersonal relations. The designated discussion leader will serve best who gladly shares the multitude of leadership functions and responsibilities while acting as a monitor of the group's processes, acting as a completer to supply needed functions, and accepting a large share of personal responsibility for the success of that group. An autocrat who seeks to push personal goals, procedures, beliefs, and solutions on a group will in most peer groups or work groups of educated employees produce apathy, poor quality of outputs, low levels of commitment, interpersonal conflicts, and general dissatisfaction.

An autocratic discussion leader seeks to impose his or her will, belief, or solution on the group. The result is a *pseudodiscussion* during which the group goes through the motions of discussion but the end result is predetermined by the leader. Under an autocrat, no one speaks unless permitted by the leader. Everyone's ideas are judged by the leader. The autocrat decides alone on the agenda, and the procedure by which a problem will be discussed. He or she may listen to advice, but when the autocrat's mind is made up, the decision has been made. Power resides in this one person rather than in the group. He or she acts like the dominant ray of a nerve-severed starfish rather than as a coordinating leader. Such a leader rarely announces the agenda of a meeting in advance, nor does this leader often help inform members. Armed with a private agenda and as the only fully prepared person, an autocrat readily dominates the other discussants. For example, an autocrat in the classroom decides just what questions will be discussed, and the "right" answer to each. When such hard-sell tactics fail to gain support, the autocrat may attempt to coerce compliance by actions such as calling the members lazy, stupid, or irresponsible, or by making threats.

If an autocratically inclined leader lacks the power of an absolute head, he or she may use manipulative techniques to seduce agreement. An autocrat is interested in whatever will advance personal ideas and purposes, interrupting and ignoring or arguing with anything contrary, often without trying to understand the other speaker's point of view. A "divide and conquer" approach may be tried, by setting up a one-to-one communication network with a lot of "sweet talk" and politicking with promises of personal rewards to members who give support. Such an autocrat distorts summaries toward a personal purpose and states ideas with highly emotive language, sometimes coercing agreement by preventing the group from making a decision until time for the meeting has almost run out, then pressuring others to accept a solution. The autocrat may coerce participation from a member who prefers not to speak by saying something like "Tim, what do you think of that?" or "Mary, don't you agree?"

On what assumptions would you base your personal style of leadership? An autocratic style rests on the beliefs that a few select persons (of which the autocrat is one) are specially endowed, that the majority of people are incapable or irresponsible, that the way to get most people to act is to give them personal rewards and punishments. Such premises underlie the governing techniques of both political dictators and discussion leaders who predetermine the result that their groups should reach.

A democratic style of leadership is based on the belief that the collective wisdom is greater than that of any single member, and the correlative belief that all persons affected by a decision *should* have a voice in making the decision. In a democratic climate, any attempt to coerce or manipulate is both immoral and impractical. Immoral because manipulation destroys the human capacity to reason and decide for one's self. Impractical because manipulation when sensed leads to apathy, resistance, or even counterforce. A democratic leader participates with the group in making decisions concerning both the procedure and substance of discussions. He or she *serves* the group rather than making it a servant to self-serving ends.

The democratic discussion leader, in contrast to the autocratic leader, seeks to discover the group's will and facilitate its achievement. An outcome of this sort can never be predetermined by anyone, but will be the result of interaction. With democratic leadership, discussants speak when they want to, at least within the procedural norms adopted *by the group.* All ideas are treated as group property, and judging them is the responsibility of the entire group. Authority for decision making resides with the group. Influence comes primarily from information, ideas, and skills in doing what is needed to achieve mutually acceptable goals. When discussion leadership is democratic, everyone has equal opportunity to prepare for discussion. Even establishing the agenda and the procedure for discussing a topic or problem is the prerogative of the group, not a single member (or leader). All power exercised by the designated leader is granted by the group for the group's good. Such a leader may suggest and encourage, but will not compel, coerce, or manipulate. Ideally, a designated leader's approval is no more important than that of any other member. In practice, a democratic leader will suggest procedures, but will not impose them. He or she may *suggest* a plan or solution, but will be quite ready to follow any procedure or accept any solution that the group, by consensus, prefers.

Both autocratic and democratic discussion leaders are in stark contrast to what is often called laissez-faire, which is really an abdication of responsibility for leading. The laissez-faire "leader" does virtually nothing. In practice, he or she may open a discussion by saying: "It's about time we started our discussion," then sit back. Into the void someone must step, or the group will flounder aimlessly. The usual result is either anarchy or a struggle for status. A group of skilled discussants, given this kind of appointed leader, may proceed fairly well, but all too often they waste time or an autocrat takes over. Structure is essential to group process. Even a self-appointed autocratic leader beats chaos.

Many times a designated discussion leader is in a formal position as part of a larger organization, and so may need to exert bureaucratic leadership. As examples: a foreman is charged by his superiors with seeing that certain tasks are accomplished by the work group; a study-discussion leader is partly responsible to the organization sponsoring the study-discussion program (often a university, public library, or great books foundation); the chairperson of a committee charged with some task is responsible to the parent body; a department head is bound by regulations and responsibilities that cannot be ignored. Such leaders must make clear the area of freedom and the limits placed on both chair or supervisor and the group. It is essential for a "head" to make absolutely clear when the decision will be made by the group and when he or she is only seeking information and advice on which to base a decision. Some of the topics to be discussed, the procedures to be followed during discussion, and specific recommendations or solutions to be applied can be determined by the group as a whole.

Designated task leaders (heads of departments, foremen, officers, even committee chairpersons) seeking a group decision often find the group waiting for the leader's analysis of the problem and solution to it, which the group members then tend to accept or reject apart from its merits in fact and logic. For this reason designated leaders are generally well advised to refrain from suggesting solutions, at least until after group members have suggested a number of them.

A remedy may be for a superior to adopt a nondirective style of leading that puts responsibility on the group for directing their activities. The leader would then exercise great self-control, withholding leadership at critical junctures, even letting the group flounder at times, so that participants will develop their own skills and motives. The nondirective leader will call attention to problems facing the group, whether of task or group maintenance, but will not solve them. On some occasions he or she may suggest and invite other alternatives, but will leave the decision to the group. This is not an abdication of leadership. Whereas the laissez-faire "leader" does nothing, a nondirective leader works very hard, listens intently, and reflects observations back to the group: clarifying a problem, supplying information, or summarizing what he or she has noticed, but always asking members of the group if they agree. A nondirective leader will ask many questions and will rebound to the group questions calling for a personal opinion. In time he or she can lead democratically and still discharge all responsibilities to a superior or parent body by making clear to all group members what must be done. Once members are accustomed to accepting responsibility for making decisions that affect them, they will not often want it any other way.

Personal Characteristics of Effective Discussion Leaders

Knowing the characteristics that tend to distinguish effective leaders from less influential group members should be helpful in your efforts toward becoming the best leader you can, or to select wisely whom to support as group leaders. Of course the positive attitudes toward self, others, and information and ideas described earlier as member input variables are important. But from trait and function studies we can enumerate more specific characteristics of effective discussion leaders.

1. *Effective discussion leaders have a good grasp of the task facing the group* (whether the task be learning or problem-solving). They are informed, good at analysis, and have promising ideas for solving

problems. Studies by Maier, Geier, Larson, Knutson, and Holdridge, among others, all indicate this principle.

2. *Effective discussion leaders are skilled in coordinating group members' thinking and encoding toward a goal.* They are above average in ability at systematic thinking and problem solving. To be an effective designated leader, you need to be able to suggest an appropriate procedure or structure for problem solving, and to be skilled in detecting tangents and bringing a group back on track. The leader of a learning group needs to be able to provide some agenda of issues and themes, yet be flexible enough to encourage contributions of relevant issues and themes from all group members.

3. *Effective discussion leaders are active in participation.* They are above average for group members in frequency of verbal participation, yet not excessive talkers. They are never reticent in a small group, implying that such emergent leaders have a favorable self-concept, nor overly defensive or sensitive about being criticized or disagreed with. Morris and Hackman, like Geier, found emergent leaders to be among the most frequent participants in discussion groups (not necessarily the *most* frequent).[30] To be relatively quiet in a group is to have no chance to emerge as a leader, and to maintain the position of leader a member must be verbally active.

4. *Effective discussion leaders encode clearly and concisely.* Ability to speak well has been shown to be important to success in all social contexts. The effective discussion leader can speak to the group as a whole in clear, impartial terms, yet be able to espouse a personal point of view when that is needed. His or her remarks are concise, organized, and pertinent. Such leaders, whether designated or emergent, are rhetorically sensitive rather than tactless, and especially skilled in encoding consensus decisions. Russell found that leaders of problem-solving groups were distinguishable from other members by higher degrees of communicative skills.[31] Lashbrook also found that leaders were perceived as speaking more clearly and fluently than other group members.[32] Discussion leaders are most certainly characterized by special facility in verbalizing the goals, values, ideas, and ideals of their groups.

5. *Effective discussion leaders are open-minded.* I found that study-discussion leaders chosen by participants as future leaders were much more conditional in the way they expressed judgments than were leaders not chosen as future leaders. Maier and Solem demonstrated that a leader who suspends judgment and encourages full consideration of minority viewpoints is more effective than one who does not.[33] I have repeatedly given *dogmatism* and *authoritarianism tests* to students in discussion classes, and found that students most often chosen as leaders by classmates tended to score much better on these measures of

openmindedness. Haiman reported similar findings for his classes when using these scales and an *open-mindedness scale* that he devised.[34] The picture is clear: effective discussion leaders are more open-minded than average participants and can encourage open-minded consideration by participants. They provide excellent models of the inquiring mind by considering all information and ideas, even those contradictory to personal beliefs.

6. *Effective discussion leaders are democratic and group-centered.* This characteristic was developed thoroughly in the preceding section. As Rosenfeld and Plax put it, ". . . people are equals with whom they work, the rewards and punishments are to be shared."[35]

7. *Effective discussion leaders have respect for and sensitivity to others.* Fiedler, of contingency theory fame, reported that discussion leaders of productive groups displayed above average skills in human relations. Rosenfeld and Plax found that democratic discussion leaders made relatively more positive socioemotional remarks and were more sympthetic than were autocratic leaders.[36] To adjust to the changing needs and moods of members of a group, one needs to be tuned in to the nonverbal cues that indicate these. Democratic actions rest on trust in the collective wisdom of the group and respect for the rights of all members. Several case studies have shown that building a team spirit and sense of cooperation often depends on finding and emphasizing common interests and values, which takes a high degree of sensitivity and awareness of others. Kenny and Zaccaro found that leadership depends heavily on one's ability to perceive and adjust one's behaviors to the needs and goals of members.[37] The best discussion leaders are excellent listeners, empathic, patient, and able to summarize accurately.

8. *Effective discussion leaders are flexible in taking their distinctive roles.* Many studies have shown that effective discussion leaders take on roles distinctively different from those of other group members.[38] For example, I found that the most effective study-discussion leaders were those who asked more questions, gave more procedural guidance, and expressed fewer personal opinions than other members. The concept of the "leader as completer" indicates the need for role flexibility, as does Fiedler's contingency theory of leadership. Wood observed that actual committee leaders did show such flexibility from meeting to meeting as conditions changed.[39] You are well advised to practice and develop skills in as many of the task, procedural, and maintenance functions of group interaction as possible.

9. *Effective discussion leaders share rewards and give credit to the group.* They readily praise the group for successes, not taking credit or glory to themselves. They stress teamwork and look for ways to make members feel important to the group.

Still more terms could be used to characterize the behavioral style of effective democratic discussion leaders in groups of peers, but the major findings that have shown up with some consistency in recent research have been described sufficiently for you to form an image of the ideal small group discussion leader: informed, egalitarian, organized, knowledgeable, a skilled problem solver, active and outgoing, democratic, respectful and accepting of other persons, nonmanipulative, articulate without being verbose, flexible, and group-centered.

Responsibilities and Techniques of Discussion Leaders and Chairpersons

A designated discussion leader cannot evade the responsibility for certain tasks and functions. Most adults are members of many small groups, and have neither the time nor the resources available to keep abreast of all details, regulations, and changes in the groups. Often we come rushing into a meeting, literally out of breath, with our minds still occupied by other matters. In this condition we try to orient ourselves to another discussion. If our leaders (or teachers) greet us with, "Well, what shall we do today?" we are likely to be irritated and to get nothing done. Students with five classes a day and businessmen with several conferences a day must place special responsibilities on designated discussion leaders. The leader in such cases has a special job to do, and doing it well will foster group cohesiveness, acceptance of solutions, and acceptance by members of responsibility for the group's success. The group still retains the power to decide within its area of freedom, and can act more wisely because the leader has served it well.

Some persons avoid or even refuse assigned leader roles, such as chairing a problem-solving committee or leading a Bible discussion group, because they believe it will demand more time and effort than they can or are willing to give. Sometimes this may be valid, of course, but usually it need not be if the functions of leadership are discussed within the group and divided up on a reasonable basis. This can produce a leader team of two or more persons who share the major duties often expected of a designated leader, yet one person is still in a position to serve as liaison to other groups and organizations, and as a sort of clearinghouse within the group. This chairperson would typically plan the agenda and outline for a meeting, exert most of the structural and procedural leadership needed to keep the discussion organized, see that summaries and decisions get made, and perhaps watch out for misunderstandings to clarify as needed. A co-procedural leader might agree to take on the primary responsibility of spreading opportunity to participate verbally and watching for signs of tension that need to be dealt with. Someone else might be assigned to act as recorder for the group, writing down important information, interpretations agreed upon, ideas proposed as possible solutions, decisions reached, issues to be discussed at a later date, assignments, etc., and to write up reports and minutes (if needed) for the group. Certainly every member can assume responsibility for leadership services, for such is the very essence of being a productive discussant—to contribute to goal achievement in whatever way one can—and thus all serve as leaders from time to time. In short, *the designated leader's duties in a continuing group need not require much more effort and time than are expected of all group members; indeed, as a rule they should not in groups of equal members.* Still, the designated leader usually will find the duties of office burdensome unless the group deals with this issue openly and cooperatively. Many wise, experienced small group leaders refuse to proceed into the substance of extended group work until this matter has been attended to.

Some study or learning groups handle this problem of overwork by rotating the duties of primary discussion leader from meeting to meeting, but this only works well if all members are relatively equal in ability to perform that role. Co-leadership assignments are often very effective in such groups. There is very little research on how co-leaders function as a team, but there have been limited case studies. Some co-leaders alternate major responsibility for various functions, whereas others maintain about the same relationship to each other throughout the life of a group. The Minnesota studies reported by Bormann discovered that many emergent leaders in initially leaderless task groups had a "lieutenant" who supported and generally assisted the leader in a wide variety of ways. About all we can say is that co-leaders, especially if designated as such, should plan together how they will work to serve the group in the best way possible, and periodically review their relationship.

Surveys of what members of problem-solving and learning groups expect and want from designated leaders clearly indicate that structural leadership is very important. Thus an appointed or elected discussion leader must decide on the amount and kind of structural leadership to exercise. When working with peers, many leaders err on the side of too little control, a few in the direction of too much control or in imposing procedures without the consent of the group. Each designated leader must decide his or her own course, but should constantly review it for needed changes. This can be done by asking other members of the group to discuss how much procedural control they desire, and by using various response forms described in chapter 13. While developing a unique role the leader can experiment to find out what seems to be of most help and what is most acceptable to the group members. Generally it is wiser to supply too much rather than too little procedural control. Considering situational variables can help you optimize your leadership style and functioning:

1. *Group purpose and goals*—learning, personal-growth, and value-sharing groups need far less structure and control than do groups facing complex problems.

2. *Member expectations*—at least initially a designated group leader will need to conform to what members expect of the role, although this can often be changed through group discussion itself.
3. *Specific procedures and group methods often require rather strict procedural control*—brainstorming, buzz-group procedures, problem census, or the Nominal Group Technique require close procedural control, whereas a less complex pattern for organizing discussion will take far less control from a designated leader.
4. *Membership skills and maturity must be taken into account*—members with training and experience in discussion are much more able to share in leadership than are members with little or no training in discussion techniques.
5. *The leader's skill and confidence should determine how he or she acts*—it is decidedly more difficult to share tasks of procedural leadership than to monopolize them. Democratic leadership calls for skills in listening, organizing, summarizing, and timing that may take a long time to develop.
6. *Time urgency may be a factor*—occasionally a decision must be made in a hurry, in which case a group will welcome strict control on its procedures. When time is not limited and members are vitally affected by what they decide, they will need less control.
7. *Highly involved groups require less control*—when members perceive the task is important to them personally, they will often resist close procedural control by a leader. The implication is clear: the designated discussion leader should do all possible to help members realize the importance of their task, and become involved and concerned.

This brings us to specific duties that the designated leader of a small group may be expected to perform, and some ways to perform them congruent with the research findings and philosophy presented in the first part of this chapter. Any group member may perform many of these functions, but the designated leader has a definite responsibility to see that they are provided. To help everyone know what is expected, organizations with boards and committees should have a handbook or manual detailing the general charge to each standing committee, the role responsibilities of chairpersons, and what is expected of committee and task force members. *Every* member of such sub-groups should be given a copy to help create a shared reality in which goals, norms, and procedures are mutually perceived.

Administrative Duties

The role of chair of a committee, board, work-planning group, quality circle, or other task group that meets on a continuing basis involves, in almost all cases, a number of *administrative* responsibilities. These are tasks which must be done for the group if it is to function well in its organizational setting. As

---

Figure 9.2   The agenda for a committee meeting.

Agenda for Personnel Committee

Time and Place: May 13, 1984; 12:30 P.M.; Thompson Library, Room 17

1. Approval of minutes of meeting of April 17, 1984.
2. Review of nominations for Graduate Faculty Membership.
3. Appeal by Professor John Clausen of deferment of nomination.
4. Preparation of slate of nominees for positions in the Graduate Council beginning September, 1985.
5. Decision on proposed revision of Appendix IV of Graduate College Constitution. (see attached documents)

---

administrator, the elected or appointed chair does not *make* policy, but sees that policies decided by the group or affecting its functioning are carried out. Especially important among the administrative services are planning for meetings (including getting out notices and agendas, setting the stage, and providing the needed resources), following up on members' assignments, making needed reports, and serving as liaison with other groups and the parent organization.

Planning for Meetings

Adequate planning and preparation are necessary for productive discussions. The purpose(s) of the meeting, necessary outcomes, member preparation, meeting time and place, special resources, room preparation and possible follow-up should all be considered carefully by the designated leader. Below is a checklist that you can follow to be sure that you have not overlooked something needed to facilitate a productive discussion:

_____ 1. **Define the purpose of the meeting.**
If no purpose is defined, no meeting should be held. "To talk over our coming year as a committee" or "to talk about sexism in company offices" are NOT adequately defined objectives; they are at best vague statements about what the group may do during its meeting. "To establish an agenda of problems for committee actions during the coming six months" or "to establish a procedure and assignments for discovering the types and amounts of sexism in company offices" would give clear purpose to the meetings.

_____ 2. **List the specific outcomes which should or must be produced from this meeting.**
Has the parent organization demanded a report within a week? Must the board of trustees be given a recommendation within two days or the committee will have no advisory input before the

trustees act? Is there a work deadline to be met? Must plans be
made to finish some task?

_____ 3. **Establish starting and ending times for the meeting.**
Frequently committees and study groups meet with strict time
limits imposed by other concurrent meetings, class and work
schedules, or other environmental variables which the group has
no power to change. Volunteer groups, student project groups and
committees, or other small groups not bound by such factors
should know when meetings will begin *and end.* Otherwise,
members cannot arrange transportation, schedule other activities,
etc. Don't run meetings overtime! That will kill member
involvement and attendance quickly. Instead, arrange to use the
time well, plan extra meetings if the entire group consents, or do
only what can be done in the time scheduled.

_____ 4. **Notify members of the purpose or agenda, necessary preparation,
and time and place of the meeting.**
It is the administrative responsibility of the chair to be sure that
members are notified and given ample opportunity to prepare for
a meeting. In large organizations this duty may be delegated to a
staff person such as a professional secretary. Seeing that the
notice is properly prepared and distributed is still the
responsibility of the designated leader.

_____ 5. **If special resource persons will be needed at the meeting, advise
and prepare them for the meeting.**
Small groups frequently need to question specialists with unique
knowledge, skills, or experience. Perhaps a student group needs to
discuss their dissatisfaction with the university president before
making a policy decision; a financial expert's advice could be
invaluable to a committee charged with recommending a position
to a bargaining committee. A learning group might want to hear
directly from a spokesperson for a religion not represented in
their membership. Have such persons been invited and told what
to expect at the meeting, and have the members prepared to ask
informed, appropriate questions?

_____ 6. **Make all necessary physical arrangements.**
Has the meeting room been reserved? If needed, have handouts,
notepads, chalk, charts, ashtrays, and possibly beverages been put
in place? Is the room arranged as a circle or oval for discussion
seating?

_____ 7. **If needed, prepare a procedure by which the group can evaluate its
process.**
If the group needs to consider its throughput processes, an outline
of questions should be developed to assure that important

variables will not be overlooked and little more than a bull session about the discussion occur. Also, have prepared appropriate Post Meeting Reaction forms (see chapter 13).

Following Up on Meetings

Two kinds of follow-up are most often necessary to ensure that group discussion produces something tangible: reminding group members of assignments to be sure they are done, and getting out necessary reports from the group to other groups or individuals. If adequate reports or minutes have been kept of a meeting, most of what needs to be followed up on will be indicated in this written record.

Frequently group members agree to special assignments, both investigative and productive. Someone has agreed to find bibliographic items; someone else to conduct an interview; and a third member to get copies of a state statute—all before the next group meeting. A brief phone call tactfully asking if the member encountered any trouble in completing the assignment will often encourage and remind the member to perform so the group is not handicapped by lack of the necessary information. If members are to purchase items, do certain work, etc., it may also be wise for the group chair to make a tactful call to see that the job has been done as agreed upon. There's nothing like a picnic when the person responsible forgets to bring the recreational equipment!

It is often necessary for a chair to prepare and send actual letters, memoranda, formal reports, notices of group decisions, advice prepared by the committee, etc. to appropriate persons. This includes getting copies of minutes prepared and distributed, but more especially the writing of formal resolutions, the actual sending of advisory policy statements to administrative officers, the calling and conduct of a press conference, or carrying out whatever decisions for action the group has made. The group should have decided *what* to do and *who* is to do it. Very often the *who* is the group's designated leader. Doing so is part of his or her liaison function in many cases.

Liaison

Someone often has to speak for a committee or task group. Usually this is one of the service duties of the chair. Members expect leaders to represent them to other groups and individuals, and will often refer inquiries from outsiders to the chair. In many organizations the chairs of standing committees maintain contact among the working groups that comprise the organization; many corporations have regular meetings of division managers for this general purpose. Whenever you act as a liaison person, remember that you represent the *group* and are not speaking from a personal perspective or position.

When a committee makes a report at an organizational membership meeting or presents a resolution for parliamentary action, the chair almost invariably speaks for the committee. Such reports and all formal resolutions must be approved in advance by the entire committee, but explanatory and supportive comments to encourage a favorable vote may be prepared by the chair alone.

Occasionally committee chairs will be interviewed by public media. If you anticipate this happening, you can be prepared to answer reporters' questions. Whatever a chair says, it must be fair and acceptable to all group members as a statement of the group's work, findings, and beliefs. Any statement which seems to lean to one side of a controversy within the committee will cause further friction and division within the group, and the leader will lose the trust of those members who feel misrepresented.

Leading Group Discussions

Administrative responsibilities of designated leaders precede and follow actual meetings of a small group. Now we turn our attention to what designated leaders are expected to do during actual meetings.

Initiating Discussions: Opening Remarks

The opening remarks by a designated discussion leader should be kept as *brief as possible* while accomplishing the task of creating a positive atmosphere, initiating structure for the meeting, explaining the leader's role (if this is a new group), and getting the discussion underway. Here are some guidelines to consider in planning your opening remarks for the introductory stages of a discussion:

1. *It may be necessary, especially with a new group, to reduce primary tensions.* Members may need to be introduced to each other. An icebreaker activity might be planned, or some brief social activity. Name tents or tags should be provided if members are not acquainted.
2. *The purpose and importance of the meeting must be described and possibly discussed, and the area of freedom (and limitations) made clear.* Sometimes this will take little more than to review the meeting notice with the group.
3. *Some effort to create a climate of trust and informality may be needed.* This might include suggesting norms such as confidentiality of what members say, respectful active listening, and the need for cooperation. When a new group first meets, the discussion leader should briefly describe his or her role and what is expected of other members during discussion. For example, you might explain that your role will be that of a facilitator and coordinator, but not a decision maker for the group, arguing the relative merits of proposals, or trying to get the group to adopt some policy. Rather, your role would be explained as that of a member performing the functions described below, as needed.

Sometimes a ventilation period of a few minutes may help get the discussants acquainted with each other's values, beliefs, backgrounds, and attitudes on the problem. This is a period of totally free, unstructured, unorganized talk usually related to the problem or task facing the group, which serves primarily a socioemotional function. The designated leader who senses a need for ventilation and encourages it may later find the job of keeping talk organized, relevant, and objective much easier than if no ventilation of feelings and positions has occurred. It is important that ventilation not go on so long that members begin to feel that time is wasted, but long enough for them to want order and organization. Any open conflict is a good sign that it is time to get the discussion organized.

4. *Informational and structural handouts may be presented,* such as informational sheets, an agenda, outlines to guide discussions, case problems, copies of things to be discussed, etc.
5. *Supply suggested structure and procedures.* You may want the group to set these up, but be prepared to suggest. You will find it advisable to provide members with an outline for organizing discussion, then ask members to modify or accept it.
6. *See that any special roles needed are established, such as recorder.*
7. *Ask a clear question to focus initial discussion of the first substantive issue on the agenda.*

Structuring Discussions

1. *Keep the group goal oriented.* Be sure the goal is clearly understood and accepted by all members. At times you will find it helpful to ask a question such as "How will this help us achieve our goal?" or to comment "We seem to be losing sight of our objective."
2. *A procedure for problem solving or an outline for learning discussion can be put on a handout, a chalkboard, or a chart.* You may find it helpful to distribute a sheet explaining any procedure with which group members are not well acquainted, such as brainstorming or the Nominal Group Technique. A group that resists following an outline early in the discussion may welcome such structure after some confusion and frustration set in.
3. *Summarize,* or see that a summary is made of each major step in a problem-solving discussion or of each decision reached. Ask if the summary is accepted by all members as accurate and complete. In many discussions a secretary can help summarize. It is important that the group have a complete record of findings, ideas, criteria adopted, and decisions.
4. *Make a clear transition to each new step or agenda item.* A transition can be combined with a summary. For example, "We have heard that time pressure, grade pressure, and inadequate preparation lead to

Figure 9.3   Recording can help structure discussion.

plagiarism on term papers. Are we ready to consider possible solutions for this problem? . . . Well, what might we recommend to reduce such cheating?" When members keep restating the same idea, you might suggest that agreement seems to have been reached, and if so the discussion can move on to the next issue.

5. *Be sure that all needed steps in the problem-solving procedure, items on the agenda, or issues for a learning discussion are adequately dealt with,* if at all possible. Keep track of the time so you can point out to the group what needs to be done and how much time is available. Point out anything of importance that is being overlooked.

6. *Watch for extended digressions,* and for frequent changes of theme. Some digressions will occur in almost every discussion. The leader needs to be constantly on guard for them, and to bring the group back on track before the digression becomes extended. When you notice a digression from the agenda or outline, you can point it out, and perhaps ask the group what to do about it. If a member suggests a solution prematurely, you might ask if he or she would bring it up when the group has finished mapping out the problem. When a change of issue or irrelevant topic creeps in, or a fantasy chain has been spun out, you may suggest returning to the previous issue or step.

7. *Bring the discussion to a definite close.* This should be done not later than the time a meeting has been scheduled to end, or extended only if all members consent. Continuing groups that continually run overtime tend to lose members! The conclusion might include any or all of the following: a summary of all progress made by the group; a statement of how reports of the meeting will be distributed to members and other interested persons; comments about preparations for the next meeting; assignments for follow-up and implementation; commendations to the group for a job well done; or an evaluation of the meeting to improve the group's future discussions.

Equalizing Opportunity to Participate and Influence

1. *Address your comments and questions to the group rather than individuals,* unless you want to elicit a specific item of information or respond directly to what a member has said. Be sure that you are making regular eye contact with everyone when you ask questions, especially with the less talkative members.
2. *See that all members have an equal chance to participate verbally.* While no one should be forced to speak, neither should any member be prevented from speaking by the aggressiveness of others.
    a. You might point out in opening remarks that part of your role will be to see that everyone has an equal opportunity to get the floor, and that you will be primarily a coordinator.
    b. Make a visual survey of all members every minute or two, looking for nonverbal cues that a member wants to speak. If you see such a reaction from a discussant who has had little to say, "gatekeep" the person into the discussion as soon as you can. You might cut in with a comment like, "Joe, did you want to comment on Mary's idea?" Encourage, but do not embarrass the participant if you misinterpreted the nonverbal signals by asking a question such as "Joe, what do you think about that idea?" He might not even be listening! Avoid asking questions such as "Xenia, what do you think of that?" Always leave room for the member to remain silent without losing face.
    c. Sometimes a quiet member can be assigned to investigate and report on needed information.
    d. You might invite a quiet person to speak if you are sure that he or she has special knowledge or interest on an issue: "Belinda, I think you made a special study of that, didn't you?"
3. *Listen with real interest* to what an infrequent participant says, and encourage others to do so if they seem not to be listening. Infrequent speakers in a continuing group may be ignored if the designated leader does not intervene to get some response to their remarks.

4. *Try to control compulsive, dominating, or long-winded speakers.* Occasionally a member so monopolizes the conversation that either others must fight for a chance to speak, or just give up. A few will repeatedly interrupt and drown out the voices of others who are speaking. Such monopolizers must be controlled for the benefit of the group. The techniques for controlling such problem members are listed in the approximate order in which they would be used—less blunt and direct methods first, then those that involve confrontation only if more tactful and subtle techniques do not work. Often highly verbal persons are valuable members of a group, and although you may need to control their aggressive or dominating tendencies, it would possibly weaken the group as much to drive them out as to let them continue putting down others.

   a. When feasible, seat talkative members where you can seem to overlook them naturally when asking questions of the group. Avoid the tendency to look at such a person when you ask a question.

   b. Establish eye contact with those who have spoken infrequently when you ask a question; avoid contact with the talkers.

   c. When a long-winded person has made a point, cut in as tactfully as possible with "How do the *rest* of you feel about that point?" or a similar request for *others* to participate.

   d. Suggest a norm that each person make one point, then allow others the floor, and that persons not interrupt or drown out others.

   e. In private, ask the frequent talker to help get the quiet members to speak up more.

   f. Have one person keep a count or stop-watch on each participant's remarks, then report the findings to the group and discuss them in an evaluation period.

   g. Describe the problem openly, and ask the group to deal with it as a group.

   h. Even more drastic measures may be needed on occasion, to the point of asking the person to leave the group, but only after discussion of the troublesome behavior has failed.

5. *Avoid commenting after each member remark.* Some designated discussion leaders do this, perhaps unaware, producing a wheel network of verbal interaction. Often such leader behavior seems to come from a desire to dominate and control the ideas and decisions of the group. Procedural leaders cannot get involved in the substance of the discussion without losing perspective. Listen, speak when you are really needed, but avoid a question-answer role or becoming the interpreter or repeater of what others say.

6. *Bounce questions of opinion back to the group,* as a rule. There is a tendency in some groups to either accept or reject designated leader opinions, so unless the group is quite well developed, you will be wise to hold your opinions until after others have expressed theirs and then express them as just another point to be considered before making a decision. So if a member asks "What do you think should be done?" you can reply with something like, "Let's see what other members think first. What do . . .?"

7. *Generally remain neutral during the argument over the merits of alternatives.* If you get heavily involved, you will then be in a poor position to see that all have equal opportunity, the discussion remains orderly and relevant, that other structuring services are provided, and— perhaps most important—to seek constructive compromises as a basis for consensus. You can and usually should react with acceptance, showing that you heard and were interested. If evaluation seems needed, encourage others to provide it.

Stimulating Creative Thinking

All too often problem-solving groups create less than imaginative products, settling for "tried and true" solutions. A thorough analysis of the problem is often a rich source of inventive alternatives. A few special techniques may help in some discussions:

1. *Apply the principle of deferred judgment.* Ask "How *might* we . . .?" rather than "How should we . . .?" Suggest waiting to evaluate proposals until no one has any more possible solutions to suggest.

2. *When the flow of thinking seems to have dried up, encourage the group to search for a few more alternatives.* You might use this idea-spurring question: "What else can we think of to . . .?" or "I wonder if we can think of any more possible ways to . . .?"

3. *It sometimes pays to take up various characteristics of components of the problem, one at a time:* "Is there any way to improve the appearance of . . .?" or "the durability of . . .?"

4. *Watch for suggestions that could be used to open up whole new areas of thinking, then pose a general question about the area.* For example, if someone suggests putting up signs in the library that show the cost of losses to the users, you might ask, "How else could we publicize the cost of losses to the library?"

Stimulating Critical Thinking

It is essential that possible solutions be subjected to rigorous evaluation before a group reaches a position or major decision. Sometimes an atmosphere develops in which group members do not feel free to criticize or assess the potential faults of each other's ideas. Some members may be unduly defensive. There may be a tendency to conform to the thinking of high-status members, or to decide quickly without the benefit of thorough scrutiny of the evidence, reasoning, and implications of a proposal. All information and opinions should be subject to critical judgment. Here are a few things you might use to encourage evaluation without evoking undue levels of secondary tension:

1. *If the group gets solution-minded quickly, suggest more analysis of the problem.* As explained in chapter 11, a thorough analysis of a problem can be facilitated with a detailed outline of questions about the problem.
2. *Encourage group members to evaluate information.* For example:

    To check the relevance of evidence, you might ask: "How does this apply to our problem?" or "How is that like the situation we are discussing?"

    To evaluate the source of evidence, you might ask such questions as, "What is the source of that information?" "How well is ＿＿＿ recognized in his field?" "Is this consistent with his other pronouncements on the subject?"

    To check on the credibility of information, you might ask: "Do we have any information that is contradictory?"

    To test a statistic, you might ask how it was derived or how an average was computed.

    Bring in outside experts to challenge the views of the group and its central members.
3. *See that all group members understand and accept all standards, criteria, or assumptions used in making judgments.* For example, you might ask, "Is that criterion clear to us all?" "Is this something we want to insist upon?" or "Do we all accept that as an assumption?"

    There are a number of procedures you can follow to insure that a proposed major policy is thoroughly and critically tested before it is adopted:

    a. Ask all members to discuss tentative solutions or policies with persons outside the group.
    b. One or more members can be asked to take the role of critical evaluator and challenger of all ideas, with high priority in speaking to see that all doubts are aired openly;
    c. Subdivide the larger group into two subgroups under different leaders to evaluate all alternatives, then rejoin to iron out differences;
    d. Before reaching a binding decision on a policy of far-reaching consequence, hold a "second-chance" meeting at which all doubts, moral concerns, or untested assumptions can be explored before a final conclusion is reached by the group.
4. *See that all proposed solutions are given a thorough testing before they are accepted as group decisions.* Encourage the group to apply the

available facts and all the criteria. You may even want to remind the group members of the dangers of "groupthink" explained in chapter 11. Some questions you might ask:

"Do we have any evidence to indicate that this solution would be satisfactory?" "Unsatisfactory?"

"Are there any facts to support this proposal?"

"How well would this idea meet our criteria?"

"Would that proposal get at the basic problem?"

"Is there any way we can test this idea before we decide whether or not to adopt it?"

Promoting Teamwork and Cooperation

Maintenance functions require time that might otherwise be devoted to productive problem-solving or learning discussion. Too much time spent on interpersonal relations will lead to frustration with the lack of goal progress. But neglecting them can often lead to low morale or even group disintegration. The challenge for leaders is to maintain the appropriate balance of task and maintenance work. Every group will vary in the amount of maintenance leadership needed, and the same group will vary in its needs through time. It is vital that someone sense the climate of interpersonal relationships, and work to develop a team spirit in any group that must work together through time. There are many ways to do this, some of which almost any of us can do, and others that require specific personal proclivities.

Here are a few things that may help:

1. *A name for the group, and possibly other symbols can be developed* (e.g., t-shirts, logos, "in" jokes, slogans, etc.).
2. *Speak of "us" and "we," not so much of "I" and "you!"*
3. *Watch for evidence of hidden agendas at variance with group goals,* and bring these to the attention of the group as maintenance problems to be solved by it. Avoiding such matters usually encourages them to grow.
4. *If there are competing groups, a sense of common fate in a larger conflict will often help members pull together.*
5. *Keep argument focused on facts and issues.* Step in at once if any member starts an attack on another's personality or character.
6. *Don't let the discussion get so serious that persons cannot enjoy themselves.* Humor may help reduce the tensions that are generated when persons work hard together at the job of hammering out ideas. Good task leaders may have trouble with humor. Lee observed that many of the most efficient leaders were lacking in human warmth.

When men are driven, they lose spontaneity and the zestful interest in what goes on. . . . There is a very real danger that our concern with improving human communication may lead members to forget the human part of the matter. . . . We need efficiency *and* satisfyingness. One may try to rig a discussion in the image of a belt line; if he succeeds he may find that those who attend become as inert as machines without the capacity (or will) to create. [To maintain a balance in discussion, Lee suggested that designated leaders] listen with lessened tension when the bent to comedy or diversion or personal release is being manifested . . . [and] pick up the problem *after* the camaraderie or tension has been spent.[40]

Secondary tensions build, and they must be released or interpersonal friction will grow. Effective discussion is characterized by a constant shifting between the serious and the playful, the relevant and remote, kidding and criticism. Certainly you will want to let the group chain out fantasies that lead to the establishment of shared beliefs and values. The result of such tension-relieving activity is much more concerted action by group members. If you are not skilled at relieving tensions, welcome the leadership of members who are. Then bring the group back to the task outline when the fantasy chain is completed or secondary tensions have been reduced to a level where productive problem-solving discussion can again resume.

7. *When a group seems to be deadlocked, look for a basis on which to compromise.* Perhaps you can synthesize parts of several ideas into consensus solution. As Tropman says,

Leadership also involves political and intellectual synthesis. The chair participates a bit less than other members because the chair's contribution is more to provide mortar to join different decisional blocks than to provide the blocks themselves. On political grounds, the chair looks for possibilites for bringing about certain types of relationships among members, for suggesting new possibilities of potential compromise. . . . An effective chair hears the ideas that people are communicating—or seeking to communicate—and tries to blend the idea of one member with the idea of another member.[41]

Conferees may represent points of view that they cannot abandon or sell out, but eventually a decision must be made. For example, labor and management negotiators must eventually agree on a contract if the company is to work. To handle the problems presented by conferees representing diverse interests, we can use techniques employed by mediators of bargaining conferences. The mediator seeks to find a common ground, a *compromise* solution that all parties can accept as the *best achievable solution.* Each partisan yields something in order to obtain something. In common parlance, "half a loaf is better than none." A complete surrender by one of two or more partisans will only postpone the settlement of a basic issue.

To encourage compromise, you may first need to point out that compromise need not be a sellout or dirty word. As Edmund Burke put it, "All government,—indeed every human benefit and enjoyment, every virtue and every prudent act,—is founded on compromise and barter."[42] Second, insist that the interests and needs of each participant are clearly understood by all other participants. Find the minimum conditions that are acceptable to every conferee, and then suggest a solution that will meet these minimums. Of course, this may take a great deal of discussion.

8. *Share rewards with the group.* Wise leaders give credit to the group, especially when they, as visible spokespersons, receive praise from parent organizations or power figures. Comments about what a fine job the group has done, pride you have in it as one member, and acknowledgement of outstanding service provided by members can do much to build cohesiveness and team spirit.

Developing the Group

The need for development will vary widely from group to group. A one-meeting discussion group may have no reason to spend any time evaluating the group's process. On the other hand, a continuing group such as a college class, a standing committee, an engineering staff, or a study-discussion group should definitely allow time for feedback and evaluation of meetings. Periodic evaluations of the group's procedures and outputs should be made.

Sometimes the impetus for growth can be given by asking the group, after a discussion has ended, to examine its discussion. For example, a designated leader might ask, "How well did we do in our discussion?" or "What might we do to make our next meeting more profitable than this one?" If a group is having trouble, the leader might interrupt the discussion with some comment such as this: "We seem to be making little headway. What's wrong? How might we get more accomplished (or, relieve this tension, or make the discussion more interesting)?" The specific question should be in reaction to what the leader senses is wrong.

A class studying discussion techniques should have at least one observer for almost every discussion. The observer may break into the conversation to point out what he or she thinks is hampering the group, make a brief report after the discussion, fill out rating forms that the group can discuss, or raise questions pertinent to the group's procedures. Any continuing group will benefit by doing this occasionally. A member can serve the group as an observer by focusing his or her attention for a period of time on the process instead of on the content of the interaction. Interpersonal feedback sessions in which members air any negative or positive feelings not previously cleared up may help a group. Advice on how to do this is provided in the final chapter. However it is done, a leadership service is made to a continuing group when members are made more aware of how they are participating and interacting together. In chapter 13 the role of the observer and procedures for group evaluation are explained in detail.

An ideal discussion leader serves as a *model* of the kind of group-centered (as opposed to self-centered), open-minded, thoughtful, responsible behavior needed from all members. As Tropman says, the chair informs the committee of how he or she perceives the committee and wishes it to function more by actions than by words.[43] Examine your attitudes when a committee or task group you chair is doing poorly—our values and attitudes leak nonverbally despite what we say. Communicate your group-centeredness by dependable service to the group.

The preceding list of leadership services and techniques is at best a partial one. Whatever his or her techniques, the leader must be flexible, adapting to the specific group. The main tools of the discussion leader are carefully laid plans, questions, skillful listening, clarifying comments, effective summaries, tension-relieving humor, and appropriate observations that are fed back to the entire group. Democratic, shared leadership, even when one person has been designated the leader, contributes most to group success and member development.

Summary

Chapter 9 has explored small group leadership, especially of discussions. The first half of the chapter summarized pertinent research and theory; the second half provided prescriptive advice for those in designated leader positions. Productive discussion leadership depends on a thorough understanding of input and process variables of small groups, understanding leadership, and personal attitudes of commitment to both self and group. Insight into self, mastery of a variety of techniques, and development of specific communicative skills all play a part in learning to be a more effective discussion leader.

Leadership, leader, and *designated leader* are similar but different concepts. Leadership was defined as group goal oriented influence, leader as anyone exerting such influence, and designated leader as anyone who is appointed, elected, or who emerges as occupant of a special position or role in a group. Influence rests on power of position, expertise, identification, and the ability to reward or coerce. Leadership implies that power is granted to a person by the freely-given consent of those who follow, and can be shared among all group members. Small groups are most productive when a stable leadership structure has been accepted by all members.

Each of the major approaches to the study of leadership offers some insight into the phenomenon. Trait studies have indicated that certain attitudes, abilities, and skills are characteristic of accepted discussion leaders. The functions approach has indicated what leaders do and how they do it in providing for both task and socioemotional needs of groups. In discussion, the most consistent functions seem to be those of coordinating and verbalizing group positions, but the contingency and systems approach have stressed that style and functions must be adapted to such contextual variables as member expectations and traits, task, and other input variables. Certainly the designated leader needs a high degree of flexibility, and usually will serve as a central member of a leadership team. Sharing in the functions of leadership is vital in all small groups.

Designated discussion leaders are generally expected not only to lead discussions during meetings, but also to perform a variety of administrative duties and help develop the group. Among the major administrative responsibilities one takes on with the position of chair for most committees and task forces are planning and preparing for meetings, following up on group decisions for action, and liaison with executives, other groups, and in some cases the news media. Developing the group into a more efficient system may entail modeling the kinds of behavior needed from members, training sessions, brief statements of expectations and norms, and periodic evaluation sessions. Leading actual discussions during meetings requires planning for initiating the actual discussion, providing both purpose and structure (including agenda-drafting and outlining), encouraging a cooperative and supportive climate, promoting creative thinking, stimulating thorough evaluation of information and ideas, pointing out common ground and bases for compromise, promoting teamwork, and seeing that all phases of the problem-solving procedure or issues of interest to members are explored.

What follows is a personal view of the discussion leader's role written by student Tom Rogers as a summary of what he had learned from assigned leadership experiences in a course using an earlier edition of this book. You may find it helpful as you develop your own personal rules, style, and skills as leader.

⌐I learned nine major rules to help me when leading a group. The first is to lay all the cards on the table and make sure everything is understood. Be sure everyone comprehends and agrees with the established goal or goals. Plan *as a group* how the members are to attain the goals. The second rule is to put all members at ease. Make sure everyone feels relaxed enough to speak up when they don't understand or disagree with something. Third, be sure the group establishes some basic norms and standards to guide the group. The fourth lesson is, if you are designated leader, work hard to stimulate the group into being inventive. The fifth and probably the most important rule is to *LISTEN* at all times. If you as leader get lost or confused because you weren't listening, the group effort is as likely to fail as you are as leader. If one does get into this predicament, be honest and clear it up right away. Another lesson equally as valuable is to be prepared. As a designated leader, one should have a grasp of the situation or problem. Prior to the meeting the leader should construct some thorough and well-thought-out questions. This should not wait until the last minute. The lead question should also be flexible. A leader should try to be aware of possible miscommunication among members. If you see this happening clear it up right away. My advice to future leaders is my ninth rule—take a formal discussion course! ⌐

Exercises

1. Scoring and interpreting the Sargent and Miller Leadership Scale. The scale you filled out on page 220 had ten items. A maximum score of 10 means you are very democratic in your responses to this test; a minimum score of 0 means you are very autocratic. Put a (1) after each item you checked as indicated in the key:

KEY:

1. a	2. b	3. b	4. a	5. b
6. b	7. b	8. a	9. a	10. a

Now read on in the chapter, and you will find some of the research that has been done on this scale. You may want to discuss your choices with several of your classmates.

2. Based on your most recent experiences in group discussions, complete each of the following statements about yourself:

A. My most important strengths as a discussion leader are

B. My most important weaknesses as a discussion leader are

C. I plan to remove or reduce my weaknesses by _____

3. Select a case problem, preferably from your own experience, for which you do not have a solution. Prepare and distribute copies of this case to all members of your discussion group. Be sure you present all information the discussants will need to understand what is wrong in the present situation, and to decide what would be the desired situation. During the discussion a classmate should serve as observer, rating you as a leader. Following the discussion (20–30 minutes as assigned by your instructor), the observer will guide your group in a brief evaluation of the discussion. At the class meeting after the discussion you should hand the following to your instructor: (1) a copy of the case; (2) a copy of your leader's outline; (3) a report of the discussion following the format on page 188; (4) the observer's rating sheet evaluating your leadership; (5) a brief essay in which you evaluate your functioning as leader of the discussion. You may want to make a recording of the discussion for later analysis. As you listen, make a list of:

   a. The functions you performed, how effectively you performed them, and how appropriate each was to the need of the group at the moment;

    b. Points during the discussion where you failed to supply some needed leader intervention, and what happened as a result. Did someone else eventually provide the needed function? If not, how was the group process and productivity hurt?

4. Think of leaders of small groups in which you have been a member:
    A. Who was the *worst* leader? List the characteristics and behaviors of this person (including both what he or she did and failed to do) that led to your selection. Especially list what this leader did in leading discussions;
    B. Who was the *best* leader? List the things that led to your judgment of this person as best small group leader.
    C. Now indicate those characteristics and behaviors that were most important in distinguishing between the two persons as leaders.
    D. Compare your items in step C with those of several classmates.

5. Buzz groups should draw up lists of topics, problems, or value questions about which all members would like to learn more. Select the subject of most interest to the group, and compile a bibliography of pertinent materials. Each discussant should then do the required reading, making study notes and a tentative leader's outline. Then the group can discuss the topic, with the designated leadership rotating every fifteen to twenty minutes. One or more observers should report their findings before each new designated leader takes on his responsibilities. Some possible questions:
    "What can a college student do to keep down the cost of personal transportation?"
    "What should be the requirements for a college degree?"
    "What control should be exercised over the content of textbooks used in public schools?"
    "What can formal religion contribute to our lives?"

6. Select a problem. Then have each class member prepare and deliver a leader's opening remarks for initiating a discussion of the problem. Have the class evaluate each introduction.

7. After a brief discussion, have each participant write a summary of what was said. Compare the summaries. What can you conclude?

8. Role play some problem-solving discussions (preferably using case problems presented by your instructor). Two or three problem members should be planted in each group, doing such things as pleading personal interests, sidetracking and introducing irrelevant issues, making cutting personal criticisms, talking incessantly, remaining silent, and so forth. Experiment with various leader techniques for handling these problem members and evaluate the results.

9. In a project group, plan and conduct an experiment to test the effectiveness of various leader techniques for equalizing opportunity for participation, promoting creative or critical thinking, keeping a discussion organized, and so forth.

10. Engage in four discussions of case problems supplied by your instructor. Alternate between having a designated leader and no designated leader. What differences do you observe? What are some implications of these differences?

11. Each class member should obtain one or more charts of the organization of clubs, businesses, agencies, or schools of which he or she is a member. Compare several of these organizational charts. Invite persons holding positions of headship at several levels in two or more different types of organizations to attend your class. Ask them to describe their concepts and techniques of leadership, and what is expected of them in their positions.

Bibliography

Bormann, Ernest G. *Discussion and Group Methods: Theory and Practice.* 2d ed. New York: Harper & Row, Publishers, 1975, chapter 11.

Cathcart, Robert S., and Samovar, Larry A., eds. *Small Group Communication: A Reader.* 4th ed. Dubuque, Iowa: Wm. C. Brown Company Publishers, 1984, section 6, 367–446.

Hollander, Edwin P. *Leadership Dynamics.* New York: The Free Press, 1978.

Maier, Norman R. F. *Problem-Solving Discussions and Conferences.* New York: McGraw-Hill, 1963.

Paulus, Paul B. *Basic Group Processes.* New York: Springer-Verlag, 1983, chapter 2.

Tropman, John E. *Effective Meetings: Improving Group Decision-Making.* Beverly Hills: Sage Publications, 1980.

References

1. E. P. Hollander, *Leadership Dynamics* (New York: The Free Press, 1978), 13–16.

2. John E. Tropman, *Effective Meetings* (Beverly Hills: Sage Publications, 1980), 14.

3. Robert Tannenbaum, Irving R. Weschler, and Fred Massarik, *Leadership and Organizations: A Behavioral Science Approach* (New York: McGraw-Hill, 1961), 24.

4. John R. P. French and Bertram Raven, "The Bases of Social Power," in *Group Dynamics: Research and Theory,* 3d ed., Dorwin Cartwright and Alvin Zander, eds. (New York: Harper and Row, Publishers, 1968), 259–69.

5. Ernest G. Bormann, *Discussion and Group Methods,* 2d ed. (New York: Harper and Row, Publishers, 1975), 253–69; Nancy L. Harper and Lawrence R. Askling, "Group Communication and Quality of Task Solution in a Media Production Organization," *Communication Monographs* 47 (1980):77–100.

6. Ernest Stech and Sharon A. Ratliffe, *Working in Groups* (Skokie, Ill.: National Textbook Company, 1976), 201.

7. William C. Schutz, "The Leader as Completer," in *Small Group Communication: A Reader,* 3d ed., Robert S. Cathcart and Larry A. Samovar, eds. (Dubuque, Iowa: Wm. C. Brown Company Publishers, 1979), 400.

8. M. L. Chemers, "Leadership Theory and Research: A Systems-Process Integration," in *Basic Group Processes,* P. B. Paulus, ed. (New York: Springer-Verlag, 1983), 9–39.

9. Charles Bird, *Social Psychology* (New York: Appleton-Century-Crofts, 1940).

10. Ralph M. Stogdill, *Handbook of Leadership: A Survey of Theory and Research* (New York: The Free Press, 1974), 63–82; Marvin E. Shaw, *Group Dynamics,* 2d ed. (New York: McGraw-Hill Book Company, 1976), 274–75 and chapter 6.

11. Ralph M. Stogdill, "Personal Factors Associated with Leadership: A Survey of the Literature," *Journal of Psychology* 25 (1948): 64.

12. John C. Geier, "A Trait Approach to the Study of Leadership in Small Groups," *Journal of Communication* 17 (1967):316–23.

13. Robert F. Bales, "Task Roles and Social Roles in Problem Solving Groups," in *Reading in Social Psychology,* 3d ed., E. E. Maccoby, T. M. Newcomb, and E. L. Hartley, eds. (New York: Holt, Rinehart and Winston, 1958), 437–47.

14. Stogdill, *Handbook of Leadership,* p. 30.

15. Norman R. F. Maier, "Assets and Liabilities in Group Problem Solving: The Need for an Integrative Function," in *Problem Solving and Creativity in Individuals and Groups* (Belmont, Calif. Brooks/Cole Publishing Company, 1970), 438–39.

16. Thomas J. Knutson and William E. Holdridge, "Orientation Behavior, Leadership, and Consensus: A Possible Functional Relationship," *Communication Monographs* 42 (1975): 107–14.

17. Barbara F. Sharf, "A Rhetorical Analysis of Leadership Emergence in Small Groups," *Communication Monographs* 45 (1978): 156–72.

18. Ralph K. White and Ronald Lippett, "Leader Behavior and Member Reaction in Three 'Social Climates' " in *Group Dynamics: Research*

and Theory, 2d ed., Dorwin Cartwright and Alvin Zander, eds. (Evanston, Ill.: Row, Peterson and Company, 1960), 527–53.

19. Lawrence B. Rosenfeld and Timothy B. Plax, "Personality Determinants of Autocratic and Democratic Leadership," *Speech Monographs* 42 (1975):203–8.

20. William E. Jurma, "Effects of Leader Structuring Style and Task-Orientation Characteristics of Group Members," *Communication Monographs* 46 (1979):282.

21. Malcolm G. Preston and Roy K. Heintz, "Effectiveness of Participatory versus Supervisory Leadership in Group Judgment," *Journal of Abnormal and Social Psychology* 44 (1949):344–45; George Graen, Fred Dansfereau, and Takao Minami, "Dysfunctional Leadership Styles," *Organizational Behavior and Human Performance* 7 (1972):216–36; Norman R. F. Maier and Ronald A. Maier, "An Experimental Test of the Effects of 'Developmental' vs. 'Free' Discussions on the Quality of Group Decisions," *Journal of Applied Psychology* 41 (1957):320–23; William E. Jurma, "Leadership Structuring Style, Task Ambiguity, and Group Members' Satisfaction," *Small Group Behavior* 9 (1978):124–34.

22. Jurma, "Effects of Leader Structuring Style. . . ," pp. 282–95.

23. Fred E. Fiedler, *A Theory of Leadership Effectiveness* (New York: McGraw-Hill, 1967).

24. James A. Hunt, "Leadership Style Effects at Two Management Levels in a Simulated Organization," *Administrative Science Quarterly* 16 (1971):476–85.

25. Julia T. Wood, "Alternate Portraits of Leaders: A Contingency Approach to Perceptions of Leadership," *Western Journal of Speech Communication* 43 (1979):260–70.

26. R. N. Griffin, "Relationships Among Individual, Task Design, and Leader Behavior Variables," *Academy of Management Journal* 23 (1980):665–683.

27. Cal W. Downs and Terry Pickett, "An Analysis of the Effects of Nine Leadership-Group Compatibility Contingencies upon Productivity and Member Satisfaction," *Communication Monographs* 44 (1977):220–30.

28. Chemers, "Leadership Theory and Research," p. 24.

29. Chemers, p. 28.

30. Charles G. Morris and J. R. Hackman, "Behavioral Correlates of Perceived Leadership," *Journal of Personality and Social Psychology* 13 (1969):350–61.

31. Hugh C. Russell, "Dimensions of the Communicative Behavior of Discussion Leaders," paper presented to Central States Speech Convention, April, 1970.

32. Velma J. Lashbrook, "Gibb's Interaction Theory: The Use of Perceptions in the Discrimination of Leaders from Nonleaders," paper presented to Speech Communication Convention, December, 1975.
33. Norman R. F. Maier and A. R. Solem, "The Contributions of a Discussion Leader to the Quality of Group Thinking: The Effective Use of Minority Opinions," *Human Relations* 5 (1952):277–88.
34. Franklyn S. Haiman, from a paper given at the Annual Convention of the Speech Association of America, December, 1964.
35. Lawrence B. Rosenfeld, *Now That We're All Here . . . Relations in Small Groups* (Columbus, Ohio: Charles E. Merrill Publishing Company, 1976), 76.
36. Rosenfeld, *Now That We're All Here,* p. 76.
37. D. A. Kenny and S. J. Zaccaro, "An Estimate of Variance Due to Traits In Leadership," *Journal of Applied Psychology* 68 (1983):678–685.
38. A. Paul Hare, *Handbook of Small Group Research* (New York: The Free Press, 1962), chapter 11.
39. Julia T. Wood, "Leading in Purposive Discussions: A Study of Adaptive Behavior," *Communication Monographs* 44 (1977): 152–65.
40. Irving J. Lee, *How to Talk with People* (New York: Harper & Row, Publishers, 1952), 158–60.
41. John E. Tropman, *Effective Meetings* (Beverly Hills: Sage Publications, 1980), 39–40.
42. Lee, *How to Talk with People,* pp. 90–91.
43. Tropman, p. 39.

10 which shall it be? decision making in small groups

Study Objectives

As a result of studying chapter 10 you should be able to:

1. Distinguish between the concepts of "problem solving" and "decision making."

2. Describe the relative output advantages of decision making in matters of judgment by individuals and groups.

3. Understand the differences among decision making by a leader, majority vote, and consensus, and be able to list advantages and disadvantages of each procedure.

4. Explain five procedural guidelines for making group decisions by consensus, and reasons for these guidelines.

5. Arrive at true consensus decisions in groups.

6. Guide a group in a three-step procedure for resolving prolonged conflicts over alternatives.

Key Terms

Consensus decision   a choice among alternatives, which all members of a group agree is the best they can make that will be acceptable to all members.

Criterion   a criterion is a standard for judging among alternatives, often stated as a question; plural is *criteria*.

Decision making   choosing among alternatives.

Groupthink   conformity of lower-status members to the beliefs and opinions of a high-status member or majority vote of a group.

Majority decision   decision made by vote, with more than half of the members of a group voting for the winning alternative.

Problem solving   a several stage procedure for moving from some unsatisfactory state to a more satisfying one (or developing a plan for doing so).

Whether we like to acknowledge it or not, the need to make decisions in concert with others is becoming more and more important all the time as our society becomes more complex and interdependent. We Americans have created folk myths about the rugged individualist who does everything alone in his own way. But the reality is that we are constantly becoming more and more interdependent, and must make increasingly larger numbers of decisions in groups, committees, and boards. As Tropman says, "Only when we begin to recognize the importance and necessity of communal decision-making can we begin to prepare ourselves adequately for these roles."[1] It is imperative that we learn to manage collectively if we are to compete successfully in a world of international trade where peoples far more skilled than we at collective decision making are our competitors: the Japanese, Chinese, and others.

Many choices have to be made in concert by members of small groups—when to meet, where to meet, whether or not to accept a statement as truth, whether or not a defendant is guilty, what punishment to mete, what reward to give, which applicant shall receive the scholarship, or which of several proposed solutions to recommend. Some of these decisions are relatively trivial, others highly important. In this chapter we will be concerned with ways in which such decisions are made by groups, the implications of these various procedures, and what to do when deep-seated conflict over a decision seems almost irresolvable.

Decision Making: Choosing an Alternative

Some writers have used the terms "decision making" and "problem solving" as synonyms, creating considerable confusion. There is a major difference between the group procedures denoted by these terms. **Decision making** refers to the act of *choosing* between two or more possible alternatives, whereas problem solving also includes creating alternatives, and usually several other steps.[2] Problem solving is a many-staged procedure through which an individual or group moves from some unsatisfactory state to a plan for arriving at some satisfactory condition. Problem solving usually requires making numerous decisions before the group is ready to choose among several possible solutions to the problem and implement one. In chapter 10 we are concerned with how any decision is made, not with problem-solving procedures *per se*.

Of course some groups are given an assignment or charge to choose one of several alternatives provided them. Their work in choosing is only one major step in the larger process of problem solving which entailed the work of others (probably groups of others) who investigated and created the list of alternatives. An example of a decision-making group without freedom to propose alternatives is a screening committee of students, faculty, and administrators assigned to recommend one of several applicants for the position of college ombudsperson. This is *not* a problem-solving group, but a selection committee.

The entire problem-solving procedure, of which their work is only one step, would include the feeling that something was wrong in the way the college was functioning, some determination of the nature and causes of that problem, the decision that the best possible course of action as a solution was to appoint an ombudsperson, and recruitment of applicants for the job. Our hypothetical screening committee is making only one decision in the lengthy process of problem solving.

Group vs. Individual Decision Making

Before reading further, *rank* the following ways for making decisions in a small group from 1 (most preferred) to 7 (least preferred).

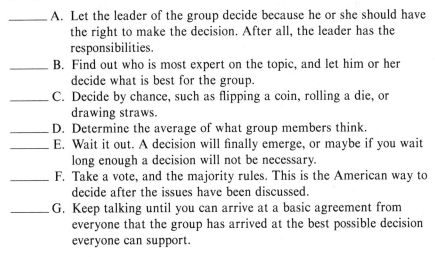

_____ A. Let the leader of the group decide because he or she should have the right to make the decision. After all, the leader has the responsibilities.

_____ B. Find out who is most expert on the topic, and let him or her decide what is best for the group.

_____ C. Decide by chance, such as flipping a coin, rolling a die, or drawing straws.

_____ D. Determine the average of what group members think.

_____ E. Wait it out. A decision will finally emerge, or maybe if you wait long enough a decision will not be necessary.

_____ F. Take a vote, and the majority rules. This is the American way to decide after the issues have been discussed.

_____ G. Keep talking until you can arrive at a basic agreement from everyone that the group has arrived at the best possible decision everyone can support.

If possible to do so, compare your rankings with those of several other persons in a small group of classmates. *Be sure to explain your reasons for your rankings, and listen to understand the reasons of the other persons in your group.*

Deciding among alternatives by a group rather than an individual invariably takes more time. A group of persons must often discuss at great length before making a decision, and time can be quite expensive. Certain types of decisions can be made better by an individual than by a group if the individual is truly expert in the matter and the group members are not, or if there is some clear and unequivocal basis for making the decision. An expert on cleaning agents might make a better decision on how to treat an unusual stain in a carpet than would many persons not so informed. A skilled woodsman could better decide how to fell a tree than could a group of novices. But when it comes to an issue such as how to proceed in coordinating group effort, all members must concur or the decision is not going to work. Most of the major issues confronted by groups have no single best answer, but call for judgments based on a range of information no one member alone possesses. As issues become more and more complex, more people are needed to assemble and interpret the relevant information. When there is not enough information to make a certain decision, groups usually make decisions superior to those made by individuals. Often a major criterion for validating a decision is its acceptance by the persons who must live with it and make it work.

The evidence is clear that in matters where there is no absolute standard of right and wrong groups tend to make decisions superior to those made by individuals, and this is almost invariably true if acceptance of the decision is a factor in its success. Maier developed a formula for evaluating decisions that presents the two major standards for evaluating any solution: (1) its quality (Q), and (2) its acceptance (A) by people who must make it work—ED = Q × A.[3] In the formula ED represents "effectiveness of the decision," Q refers to the technical excellence needed to solve problems, and A refers to the degree to which people responsible for implementing a solution or who are directly affected by a solution try to make it work.

Group decisions tend to be higher in quality than those made by individuals or derived by averaging individual decisions.[4] Examples of quality are the durability of a machine, the measured precision of a rocket flight, or the change in rate of errors in manufacturing. Group decisions tend to be higher in quality than even those made by high-status group members considered especially knowledgeable by other members.[5]

Several studies indicate that supervisors who participate with their subordinates in making decisions when the decision affects the subordinates make more successful decisions than supervisors who decide alone. They also have more satisfied employees.[6] Coch and French demonstrated that when workers have a voice in changing a work procedure they are more productive and loyal than when the change is imposed on them.[7] As Block and Hoffman wrote, ". . . the effectiveness of gaining members' commitment to change through the use of group decision is unquestioned . . .."[8]

At one time it was thought that group decisions were more conservative than those of individuals.[9] Subsequent research first indicated that groups made riskier decisions than individuals when the payoff was high, but later it turned out that groups were more cautious and conservative than individuals when a great deal was at stake (such as the life of a loved one).[10] What has emerged from this long line of research is called the "polarization tendency." This means that after group discussion members tend to make *either* more risky or safe decisions than they did before the discussion. For instance, after discussion they may choose a bet with poorer odds (1 to 4 versus 1 to 2) or choose a less dangerous alternative when health or life are at risk.

Groups frequently achieve an "assembly affect" in which the decision is qualitatively and affectively superior to what could have been achieved by even the most expert member of the group or by adding or averaging the wisdom of the members. The *procedures* that a group employs in making decisions are probably more important than are the sharing of responsibility, individual persuasiveness, or societal norms, but the research evidence is still too sketchy to say this with confidence.

Methods of Decision Making in Small Groups

There are many differences in the ways in which small groups reach decisions, but three of them are most common: by consensus, by majority vote, and by designated leader or head. If you are reading this book for a course in small group communication, discussion, or group dynamics, to get firsthand experience with the differences among these methods you should do the activities explained below for each method.

By Leader

Decision by the leader. The class is first divided into small groups of five or six members each. One person in each group is appointed as leader by the instructor, or elected by the group members to occupy that role. Then each group member should choose from the list below one social activity for your class as a means to getting better acquainted, increasing class cohesiveness, and relaxing.

A. Hold a potluck dinner or picnic at an appropriate location on campus.

B. Attend an intercollegiate sports event together, followed by a dance in the student union building.

C. Arrange a class social hour in a private party room at a nearby bar or lounge.

D. Attend a movie together (selected by leader), followed by an informal discussion of the film over soft drinks and coffee in a comfortable private room on campus.

As soon as each person has made a choice, hold a five-minute discussion of the pros and cons of these social activities. The leader will then *announce* to the rest of the group which of the social activities your group will recommend to the entire class, and explain why it is the best possible decision in his or her judgment. As soon as the leader has made this announcement, complete the Postdecision Reaction Sheet, and tabulate the response.

Postdecision Reaction Sheet. On a sheet of paper record your answers to the following questions; then give the answers to your group's coordinator who will record them on one sheet of paper, compute the averages, and report them to your instructor who may record them on a chalkboard for discussion by the entire class.

1. How much chance to influence the group decision do you feel you had?

| 1 | 2 | 3 | 4 | 5 | 6 | 7 | 8 | 9 |

(none)   (a great deal)

2. How well do you think other members of the group listened to and understood you?

| 1 | 2 | 3 | 4 | 5 | 6 | 7 | 8 | 9 |

(not at all)   (completely)

3. How satisfied or confident are you with the result of your group's decision making?

| 1 | 2 | 3 | 4 | 5 | 6 | 7 | 8 | 9 |

(very dissatisfied)   (very satisfied)

4. What adjective best describes the atmosphere in your group during the discussion? _____

(Note: you will complete this same form after each of the next two exercises.)

Sometimes a designated leader or emergent leader makes a decision and announces it for the group. This may be done after some discussion of the facts, ideas, and issues involved; in other cases, an authoritarian leader will think the problem through alone and simply state his or her decision without discussion. Group members are then given instructions or orders to follow in executing the decision. The resulting solution may or may not be a high quality one, but other outcomes will often be resentment, lowered cohesiveness, halfhearted support for the decision, and a loss of effective influence on later decisions. Indeed, the members may not only "drag their heels," but even work to make the solution fail, as classic studies in management have shown.

By Majority Vote

Majority vote is probably the procedure most used for making decisions in democratic groups. As soon as more than 50 percent of the members vote for one alternative, the decision has been reached. The following activity will give you an experience in this procedure.

Decision making by majority vote. Divide the class into groups different from those used for the previous exercise. Look over the following four alternatives. They are about grading students enrolled in a small group communication course: Should *participation* in the class be evaluated in computing final course grades? Discuss your opinions about these alternatives for not more than 10 minutes. Then vote for the one of your choice by a show of hands. If no one alternative gets a majority, vote again between the two alternatives receiving the most votes. If necessary, discuss these very briefly.

A. The instructor should grade each student on participation during classroom discussions, and make this a major factor when deciding on each person's final course grade.

B. Students should grade each other on class participation, with each receiving the average of all grades received from classmates. This should be a major component of the final grades.

C. Participation should be a major factor in determining final course grades, but both students and instructor should participate in determining this part of the grade. Combine A and B.

D. Grading participation would make competitive relationships among students inevitable. This should not be done. Grades should be based entirely on items other than classroom discussion participation.

Now complete the Postdecision Reaction Sheet for this activity. Voting in a small group can be done by voice ("aye"), a show of hands, or even by ballot (slips of paper). This method of deciding is much easier and faster than consensus as a rule, but all too frequently the members in the minority ("losers") are not satisfied that their ideas have been fully understood and considered or that the best possible decision the group could make has been achieved. Persons in minority positions may not even speak up for fear of being ridiculed. Not only does the quality of the decision frequently suffer, but also the group cohesiveness and commitment to the decision. In some committees the constitution of the parent organization requires that votes be taken and recorded on major issues. If so, the group can discuss until a consensus decision has emerged, then vote to confirm it "legally."

By Consensus

A consensus decision is one that all members agree is the best that ALL can support. It may be, but is not necessarily, the alternative most preferred by all members. When a true consensus has been reached, the result is usually a superior quality decision, a high level of member satisfaction with it, and acceptance of the result. But unless unanimity exists at the beginning of a discussion of alternatives, reaching a consensus may take a great deal more time than other procedures for decision making. Sometimes a true consensus cannot be achieved, regardless of how much time is spent in discussions. Unanimity—the state of perfect consensus in which every group member believes that the decision achieved is the best that could be made—is not at all common. But if all members accept that a consensus may require compromise and collaboration, all will usually support it even though it is not the decision some might have preferred.

The process of arriving at consensus gives all members an opportunity to express how they feel and think about the alternatives, an equitable chance to influence the final decision. Thus consensus depends on active listening so that all important information and points of view are understood similarly by all discussants. A consensual decision is often a synergistic outcome in which the group produces something superior to a summation of individual ideas and thinking. In arriving at a consensus, conflicts and differences of opinion must be viewed as a means for clarification and testing of alternatives, not as interpersonal competition for power. Guidelines for making decisions by consensus were outlined by Hall:

1. Don't argue stubbornly for your own position. Present your position as clearly and logically as possible, being sure you listen to all reactions and consider them carefully.
2. When a stalemate seems to have occurred, avoid looking at it as a situation in which someone must win and someone must lose. Rather, see if you can find a next best alternative that is acceptable to everyone. This may take conscious effort.
3. When an agreement is reached too easily and quickly, be on guard against groupthink. Don't change your position simply to avoid conflict and reach agreement quickly. Through discussion, be certain that everyone accepts the solution for similar or complementary reasons, and really agrees that it is the best possible on which agreement can be reached.
4. Don't use such conflict-suppressing techniques as majority vote, averaging, splitting the difference, coin tossing, or swapping off. These prevent destructive interpersonal conflicts, but at the expense of suppressing constructive conflict which results in the evaluation of ideas on their respective merits.
5. Seek out differences of opinion; they are to be expected and can be most helpful in testing ideas. Get every member involved in the decision-making process. If you have a wide range of information and ideas the group has a better chance of finding a truly excellent solution.

If you are enrolled in a small group class, the activity which follows was designed to give you an opportunity to apply the five rules for making decisions by consensus. Before doing anything else, read the "Lost on the Moon" case, and then rank the items as instructed.

Lost on the Moon

Your spaceship has just crash-landed on the moon. You were scheduled to rendezvous with a mother ship 200 miles away on the lighted surface of the moon, but the rough landing has ruined your ship and destroyed all the equipment on board except for 15 items listed below. Your crew's survival depends on reaching the mother ship, so you must choose the most critical items available for the trip. Your task is to rank the 15 items in terms of their importance for survival. Place number 1 by the most important, number 2 by the second most important, and so on through number 15.

_____ Box of matches

_____ Food concentrate

_____ Fifty feet of nylon rope

_____ Parachute silk

_____ Solar-powered portable heating unit

_____ Two .45-caliber pistols

_____ One case of dehydrated milk

_____ Two 100-pound tanks of oxygen

_____ Stellar map (of the moon's constellations)

_____ Self-inflating life raft

_____ Magnetic compass

_____ Five gallons of water

_____ Signal flares

_____ First-aid kit containing injection needles

_____ Solar-powered FM receiver-transmitter

As soon as everyone has ranked all 15 items without consulting anyone else, your class should be formed into groups of five or six members each. Following the rules for decision making by consensus as closely as possible, arrive at a ranking for your group. As soon as your group has completed a consensus ranking, each member should complete a copy of the "Postdecision Reaction Sheet."

Your instructor may now want you to score your answers to the "Lost on the Moon" items, both as an individual and as a group. Scoring is done by comparing your ranks with those arrived at by a group of experts in the National Aeronautics and Space Administration's Crew Equipment Research Department. Error points for each item are the difference between your rank and that of NASA. Your instructor has a copy of the NASA answers, and will explain how to do the scoring.[11]

Consensus may be superficial when some members give in to other higher status members, such as "experts" who express their opinions with exceptional force, a designated leader, or a large majority. Persons who view human relations as competitive and who play to win may dominate, with less aggressive group members submerging their doubts and conflicting beliefs to avoid the unpleasantness of open conflict. Members regarded as expert on a problem may use name dropping and esoteric jargon to avoid being challenged for specific evidence to substantiate their assertions.

Ideally, conflict over alternatives is totally substantive in nature, as indicated by the five rules for making decisions by consensus. But invariably some personal affect gets involved. We tend to feel defensive when others disagree with us. Submerging one's doubts and misgivings about a proposed solution or course of action amounts to no less than rejecting responsibility for the group, or at least for the quality of its output decisions. The result is probably poor quality decisions. This is most likely to occur when dissenters feel put down by higher ranking group members, or when other members argue without first trying hard to understand the basis of the disagreement. Preventing such a perversion of decision making by consensus requires a high degree of mutual respect and trust that one will not be rejected as a group member for disagreeing. Members also need the ability to empathize and listen actively if some apparent consensus decisions are not to be little more than suppressed conflict, destructive in its effect on the quality of decisions and the cohesiveness of the group. I strongly recommend making major decisions by consensus whenever time permits, but only if they are real consensus choices.

Other Procedures for Making Decisions

Decisions can also be made in small groups by random choice among the available alternatives (coin toss, drawing, etc.), averaging a set of member ranks or ratings, or allowing a subcommittee to decide. All of these have little to favor them except convenience and saving of time. None makes optimum use of information or the reasoning of all members. You can compute the average ranks for members of your class groups in the "Lost on the Moon" exercise (if you did it) and compare them to the group consensus decisions. In groups where I have done this, about 90 percent of the time the group consensus decisions have been superior to the averages.

Managing Extended Conflicts

Conflict is inevitable in the process of group decision making. At times it can be handled productively and easily with no special procedures. Much of this book has been devoted to preventing conflict which is not issue centered by such methods as reducing the ambiguity of messages, asking readers to examine their personal attitudes, providing a group-centered leadership philosophy, presenting problem-solving procedures likely to produce consensus, and distinguishing between discussions in which agreement is and is not necessary. Such information and advice appears under a variety of headings throughout the book. In this chapter it is appropriate to consider how to manage prolonged conflict which results over real differences in value or points of view; note that this is a matter of *managing,* not *eliminating* conflict.

Poor conflict resolution is rampant in everyday life. Friends get into an argument over who is right or what to do, and a physical fight ensues. This leads all too frequently to such consequences as the end of a friendship, enmity, or perhaps physical violence such as assault or even murder. Parents beat their children; spouses hit, kick, bite, stab, and shoot each other. As the cartoon in figure 3.3 (p. 49) indicates, group members all too often acquiesce when they do not agree, producing ideas which have not been tested by critical thinking, and/or resentful group members.

Some persons bring to groups norms for handling conflict that are highly detrimental to the group. Persons who study small group communication must develop ways of managing conflict productively so that they can supply leadership by modeling and by suggesting procedures for managing stubborn conflicts.

Sources of Conflict

Conflict can stem from many sources:

1. Competition for incompatible personal wants and goals. Between spouses with limited resources, conflict may arise from the question of whether to buy a new car or save for a down payment on a house. In a small group, members may compete for the position of leader, or for some hidden agenda item that can only be achieved at the expense of other group members.

2. Competition for the rewards of attention. As Derber said, "Everyone is in a competitive position in a conversation because the amount of attention received depends on the relative success of one's own initiatives to attract and hold the common focus."[12] Conflict over ideas may be a reaction to failure to win a fair share of attention to one's ideas in a competitive group. In cooperative groups, attention is shared according to each person's needs, whereas in competitive relationships powerful persons hog attention.[13] Resentful losers may refuse to agree upon a reasonable alternative.

3. Different beliefs, especially about what is right and wrong. Conflicts over such issues as whether a patch of prairie with an endangered species of wildflower should be protected in its wild state or a developer should be permitted to turn it into a job-producing factory or shopping mall have at their root irreconcilable values and beliefs.

4. A win-lose orientation is at the root of much prolonged conflict. Many people believe that in any conflict there must be a loser and a winner. To seek a resolution in which there are no winners and no losers appears not to have occurred to them. Their concept of conflict management has not advanced since the stone age except in the use of more sophisticated weapons (both physical and psychological) in the effort to win over others. Better discussants place a higher value on maintaining relationships, and seek "win-win" solutions in which there

are no losers. They prize consensus in which everyone is satisfied that the decision is good, the best that group members can agree on. Anyone who sees anything less than total victory as a loss cannot engage in win-win decision making.

As designated leader or other member exerting influence in a small group, you can do much to help resolve a conflict short of using the specific procedure explained below.

1. Try to get all group members to agree on a specific statement of the goal(s), exactly what is to be accomplished.
2. Be sure that the problem has been thoroughly explored and that all participants agree on its nature *before* discussing the relative merits of any proposed solutions.
3. When members begin talking at abstraction levels which leave you confused or uncertain, ask for specifics.
4. Stress the importance of issue-centered clashes as a means of testing ideas and finding the ones most likely to succeed, not as a form of combat.
5. Listen to *everyone's* ideas and arguments supporting them.
6. Do everything possible to see that all group members are treated evenhandedly, given equal access to the floor, and get a good hearing from others.
7. Use a brainstorming procedure to ensure that varied alternatives are considered; an innovative idea may be the only one accepted by all members.

And so on. Throughout *Effective Group Discussion* I have stressed numerous communicative, attitudinal, and role behaviors to prevent irrelevant personal conflicts, reduce the number of non-substantive conflicts which come from misunderstandings, and lead to a critically-tested synthesis all can support.

Despite the best of attitudes toward group work and skilled communicating, sometimes a seemingly irreconcilable conflict emerges over goals or alternatives. Then the group leader (or other member) might suggest the procedure explained below for arriving at win-win resolutions of conflicts. If this procedure fails, probably the group is too divided to arrive at a consensus decision, at least on the issue in conflict. The jury is hung; the committee is hopelessly split on what to recommend so must make two reports.

Procedure for Producing Win-Win Conflict Resolutions

1. Presentation of Alternatives
   a. A proponent of each position, solution, goal, or possible decision presents exactly what the sub-group wants or believes, and why. Other members supporting the position may add clarifying statements, arguments, evidence, and claims. While

this is being done members who disagree can say *nothing*.

b. Those in disagreement can now *ask* for clarification, restatements, explanations, or supporting evidence, but may *not* disagree, argue, or propose any other alternative.

c. A spokesperson for those who disagree is now required to explain the position which has just been presented and clarified to the complete satisfaction of all other group members, both those who agree and disagree with the position originally advanced. Only when this person has restated the first proposal and supporting arguments to everyone's satisfaction is the group ready to advance to the next step.

d. The *second* alternative is now presented by a spokesperson selected by members of the group supporting it. Exactly the same procedural rules are followed as during presentation and clarification of the first alternative.

e. In the event that there are more than two alternatives being supported by sub-groups, all are presented, clarified, paraphrased, and confirmed in exactly the same way.

2. Charting of Alternatives

a. The designated group leader now writes both (or all) positions on a chalkboard or large poster, and underneath each alternative lists PROS (benefits, advantages) claimed by its proponents, and evidence advanced in its support. Under the heading CONS the leader should list any *disadvantages,* possible harmful effects, or evidence advanced against the alternative. An example of such a chart is shown in figure 10.1.

b. When all positions have been charted, the group may want to see if there is unanimity about any of the statements on the chart. What, if anything, do all members of the group agree upon?

3. Search for Creative Alternatives

a. The designated leader reviews all elements of common ground shared by all group members such as shared interest in solving the problem, components shared in the competing alternatives, shared history of the group, etc., and then urges group members to seek a win-win resolution, an alternative all could accept. The leader may propose such a solution if she or he has one in mind, or

b. ask the group members to compromise and create an alternative that meets the "bottom line" or minimum requirements of both (all) sides to the conflict.

4. Resolution occurs when and if a consensus alternative is adopted.

Figure 10.1   Pros and cons of two proposed solutions.

How to Reduce Damage from Lead Inhalation?	
Make reg. gas illegal in city	Eliminate all private cars from central city area
PROS	
1. Inexpensive. 2. Chicago precedent. 3. Could become federal regulation in future.	1. Easy to enforce. 2. Effective in area of greatest problem.
CONS	
1. Difficult to enforce. 2. Owners of older cars will fight it.	1. Politically unpopular. 2. No help to suburbs. 3. Disrupt small companies.

If the procedure is successful, some time should be spent by the group discussing the procedure followed, how they feel about the group and each other as members of it, and how the group can prevent or manage any future conflicts.

Readers who have been involved in successful bargaining sessions may recognize that this procedure is an abbreviated form of a procedure often used by mediators who step into what appears to be a hopelessly deadlocked negotiation. Its essence is to have each side present its best case as objectively as possible, guarantee that everyone listens well enough to understand all positions and all arguments for them, and perceives the "others" as reasonable people, given their desires, interests, beliefs, and knowledge. From such reciprocal empathy a compromise may be possible. If not, the negotiations will end. In labor relations this may mean a strike, in international relations a war, in committees or boards a power decision by majority vote, or decision by fiat from a power figure (such as the "head" of a family).

Alternative Procedures

If the group is so hopelessly deadlocked that the above procedure fails to produce a resolution, the group may want to try some other means of deciding in the future. Chapter 12 presents one such special procedure for settling major issues known as the Nominal Group Technique. This procedure uses an anonymous voting procedure.

Summary

There are numerous ways by which decisions are made in and for small groups. When there is an absolute standard of "correctness" or a formula for decision making, then an individual skilled in the procedure for making the decision should usually make it and explain it to the group. For example, in many groups a skilled mathematician can work out statistics for the group. However, groups far excel individuals—even "experts"—in matters of judgment where no alternative can be confirmed as the "best" when the decision is made. Substantive or task decisions faced by groups are most often of this sort. In such cases the quality of a decision can best be estimated from these process and output criteria: (1) To what degree was the information and thinking of *all* group members used? (2) How satisfied are members with the decision, and how committed are they to working for it? and (3) To what degree has the decision-making procedure improved the cooperativeness and cohesiveness among members?

Group decisions take longer to make than do individual ones, but extensive research shows them to be superior for a number of reasons. Although arriving at a majority takes longer than averaging, and arriving at a consensus takes longer than arriving at a simple majority, the results are usually worth the extra time expended. First, complementary knowledge of members is pooled to provide a better understanding of the situation and the merits of alternatives. Second, persons perform better on many tasks when acting in the presence of others. Discussants often stimulate each other to recall information and invent creative alternatives that could not have been done by working alone. Third, conscientious, confident, and creative persons tend to be more active in decision-making discussions than are less well-prepared persons. Fourth, mistakes in individual thinking are often detected and corrected by other members during honest conflict about alternatives. As a general rule, discussing until consensus emerges among members is the most effective way in the long run to make decisions for small groups. When a group cannot reach a decision, The Procedure for Producing Win-Win Conflict Resolutions may lead to a creative synthesis and reunification of the group.

Bibliography

Coch, Lester, and French, John R. P., Jr. "Overcoming Resistance to Change." *Human Relations* 1 (1948):512–32.

Hall, Jay. "Decisions, Decisions, Decisions." *Psychology Today* 5 (November 1971):51–54, 86–87.

Janis, Irving L. *Victims of Groupthink.* Boston: Houghton Mifflin Company, 1973.

Kline, John A. "Consensus in Small Groups: Deriving Suggestions from Research. *Communication* 10 (1981):73–78.

Shaw, Marvin E. *Group Dynamics.* 2d ed. New York: McGraw-Hill, 1976, especially chapter 3.

References

1. John E. Tropman, *Effective Meetings: Improving Group Decision-Making* (Beverly Hills: Sage Publications, 1980), 11.
2. Norman R. F. Maier, *Problem Solving and Creativity in Individuals and Groups,* (Belmont, Calif.: Brooks/Cole Publishing Company, 1970), 445.
3. Norman R. F. Maier, *Problem Solving Discussions and Conferences* (New York: McGraw-Hill, 1963), 5.
4. Jay Hall, "Decisions, Decisions, Decisions," *Psychology Today* 5 (November 1971):51–54, 86–87.
5. Irving L. Janis, *Victims of Groupthink* (Boston: Houghton Mifflin Company, 1973).
6. M. L. Chemers, "Leadership Theory and Research: A Systems-Process Integration," in *Basic Group Processes,* P. B. Paulus, ed. (New York: Springer-Verlag, 1983), 19–20.
7. Lester Coch and John R. P. French, Jr., "Overcoming Resistance to Change," *Human Relations* 1 (1948):512–32.
8. Myron W. Block and L. R. Hoffman, "The Effects of Valence of Solutions and Group Cohesiveness on Members' Commitment to Group Decisions," in *The Group Problem Solving Process,* L. Richard Hoffman, ed. (New York: Prager, 1979), 121.
9. William H. Whyte, Jr., *The Organization Man* (Garden City, N.Y.: Doubleday, 1957).
10. For a concise summary of this research, see Marvin E. Shaw, *Group Dynamics,* 2d ed. (New York: McGraw-Hill, 1976), 70–77.
11. Both the exercise and the scoring were provided by Hall, p. 51.
12. Charles Derber, *The Pursuit of Attention: Power and Individualism in Everyday Life* (New York: Oxford University Press, 1979), 16.
13. Derber, *The Pursuit of Attention,* 3–19.

11 group problem solving

Study Objectives

As a result of studying chapter 11 you should be able to:

1. Analyze any problem into the three major components of (1) undesirable present situation, (2) obstacles, and (3) goal.

2. List and explain the importance of seven dimensions of a problem when developing a sequence of steps for problem solving.

3. Present a rationale for following a step-by-step procedure during a problem-solving discussion, or at least of determining that no important step in problem solving has been overlooked.

4. List and explain six principles that serve as guidelines for planning specific problem-sovling procedures.

5. List the five steps of the General Procedural Model for Problem Solving in correct order, and be able to adapt this model in outlines for structuring problem-solving discussions of any sort of problem.

Key Terms

Acceptance-technical dimension   characteristic of a problem concerned with the degree to which a solution must be acceptable to affected persons in order to work well, be technically excellent, or both.

Brainstorming   a procedure for releasing the creative potential of a group of discussants in which all criticism is ruled out for a period of time, the group works for a large number of ideas, and building on each other's suggestions is encouraged.

Cooperative requirements   characteristic of a problem, concerned with the degree to which coordinated efforts of group members are essential to satisfactory completion of the group task.

Creative problem-solving sequence   a six-step procedure for problem solving in which brainstorming is used to generate possible solutions prior to any discussion of criteria.

Developmental discussion   specific issues that collectively comprise the problem are thoroughly discussed in order to understand the problem in detail before considering how to solve it.

General Procedural Model for Problem Solving   a general procedural model for structuring problem-solving discussions; involves five major steps which can be adapted to suit the characteristics of any problem.

PERT   acronym for Program Evaluation and Review Technique, a procedure for planning the details involved in implementing the solution to a complex problem in which many persons and resources are coordinated.

Population familiarity   degree to which members of a group (or society) are familiar with the nature of a problem and experienced in solving similar problems or performing similar tasks.

Problem   an existing but undesired state of affairs, a desired state (goal), and obstacles to achieving the goal; difference between what actually happens and what *should* be happening.

Problem question   a question calling the attention of a group to a problem without suggesting any particular type of solution.

Problem solving   procedure followed by an individual or group in the attempt to find a way to move from an unsatisfactory condition to a more satisfactory one (goal).

Intuitive   problem solving that is nonsystematic, impulsive, or not characterized by step-by-step procedure.

Systematic   following a definite series of steps; organized problem solving following a definite sequence.

Reflective thinking   a generic term for systematic thinking when trying to solve a problem; a systematic procedure for organizing group problem-solving discussion that tends to put emphasis on criteria and quality as opposed to quantity and innovativeness in thinking up possible solutions, and in which solutions are frequently evaluated as soon as proposed.

Solution question   formulation of a problem as a question in which a solution to the problem is suggested or implied.

Solution multiplicity   characteristic of a problem; when high, many alternatives are possible as solutions.

Structure   organization; arrangement among parts of a system, steps in a procedure, etc.

Task difficulty   degree to which a problem is characterized by complexity requiring extensive effort, knowledge, and skills for solution.

In chapter 10, *problem solving* was defined as a multi-step procedure beginning with dissatisfaction over an existing situation and ending with a plan of action to produce a more satisfactory state of affairs. Many decisions are made in the process of solving any problem, ideally in a sequence that is both efficient and comprehensive of all issues important to arriving at the best possible solution.

Have you ever noticed how easy it is to overlook some important fact when you tackle a problem alone? Do you find your thoughts often coming in a random, jumbled, helter-skelter fashion? Have you regretted decisions made before all the needed evidence was considered or possible alternatives explored? If individual thinking is often haphazard, consider what can happen when a group of persons try to think together toward a common aim. Each person may have a different way of approaching the subject or problem. If each follows his or her own lead, there will not be a *group* discussion, but individuals talking to themselves. Perhaps you have noticed how often conversation is shallow and vacuous, shifting aimlessly from topic to topic, with nobody appearing to be listening or responding to anyone else. Berg used a content analysis technique to locate the themes in discussions by task-oriented groups. He reported that these groups averaged changing themes or topics every 58 seconds; groups were often unable to complete discussion of these topics. Although his procedure for theme analysis contributed somewhat to the finding that the themes were discussed very briefly, the conclusion that these problem-solving discussions were badly organized is inescapable.[1] It seems apparent that engaging in sustained and organized problem-solving discussion is not easy. If you ask most educated persons how to solve a problem, they will say something like "get the facts, weigh the alternatives, and make a decision." That's not a bad procedure, but extensive observation of both individual and group problem solving reveals all sorts of procedures, mostly haphazard and unsystematic, more intuitive than analytical. Problem solving by groups, if it is to be maximally effective, requires systematic procedures to coordinate the thinking of several persons, just as playing winning football requires systematic coordination of the actions of all players during each play and an overall game plan.

In the all too typical problem-solving discussion, someone outlines a problem, then immediately someone else suggests what to do to solve it, followed by a brief period of discussion evaluating this idea. Then another idea is suggested, discussed, and dropped. Maybe at this point the group goes back to talking about the problem. A third idea for solving the problem is proposed, and possibly forgotten along with the first two. Finally, time begins to run out and a decision is made quickly, usually the last idea discussed, even though the proposals made earlier might have solved the problem more effectively. All too often the group adjourns without making plans for actually getting anything done.

In order to provide a basis for improving problem solving, chapter 11 defines the concept "problem," analyzes the major dimensions and types of problems, provides evidence that problem-solving procedures can be improved by both individuals and groups, reviews research that indicates what can be done to improve it, and provides specific guidelines and sequences for improving the efficiency and effectiveness of problem-solving discussions.

Problem

How a group can proceed most effectively depends on the nature of the problem with which it is concerned. We need to understand the concept "problem," the major variables which comprise any problem, and the major types of problems groups address in order to devise procedures likely to be highly effective for problem solving by groups.

All problems consist of three major components: (1) an *undesirable present situation;* (2) *a goal,* or desired situation; and (3) *obstacles* to the achievement of the goal. Figure 11.1 illustrates these three parts of a problem. Problem solving is the procedure undertaken to overcome obstacles that stand between a present undesirable situation and a goal.

1. A problem does not exist unless someone finds something *undesirable* about a *present situation.* For example, many Americans would feel they had a problem if their residences lacked indoor plumbing, but many people in the world would not consider this a problem. They haven't learned to desire running water and toilets. People with major debts view high interest rates as highly undesirable—a problem to be solved—whereas people with money to lend perceive high interest rates as a very desirable situation.
2. *Goal* refers to the situation desired by a specific person or group. For example, a person's goal might be to reduce heating bills from $2,000 to $500 per year without losing either comfort or housing space, to have indoor plumbing in a Canadian vacation cabin, or to secure a mortgage at 9 percent or less interest.
3. *Obstacles* refers to whatever may be blocking or preventing an easy transition from the present state to the desired one. Obstacles are such items as contributing causes, construction details, lack of a road, economic conditions, or anything else that must be changed, removed, or gotten around in order to reach a goal. A goal to which there are no obstacles does not present a problem. Several persons cannot engage in *group* problem solving until they collectively perceive a problem enough alike that they share perceptions of what needs to be changed, the desired goal, and the obstacles that must be overcome.

Sometimes the process of describing the problem leads to changes in the goal, for effective solutions are those which can succeed in overcoming obstacles. *Unless the group has power to overcome the obstacles it cannot solve*

Figure 11.1   Components of a problem.

Problem Components

Undesirable present situation: we are here	Obstacles	Goal: we want to be here
House heating bills are averaging over $1000 per year	Price of fuel; 40-year-old house with many air leaks; little insulation; limited building skills; doors must be opened frequently; cannot afford new house, etc.	House heating costs of less than $500 per year

Example: appears to the left of the Example row.

Figure 11.2   Kepner-Tregoe model of a problem.

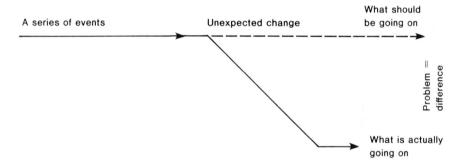

the problem. Unsurmountable obstacles thus necessitate changes in our goals; we can only learn to live with situations we have no power to change. Recognizing what *cannot* be changed (at least for now) and accepting it, as well as recognizing what can be changed and finding ways to change it, are both included in problem-solving behavior. Understanding the details and causes of obstacles lying between the present situation and the goal is essential to the achievement of acceptable solutions.

A similar definition of the concept "problem" as it might be used in the business world is advanced by Kepner and Tregoe: "A problem is a deviation between what *should* be happening and what *actually* is happening that is important enough to make someone think the deviation ought to be corrected."[2] This concept of a problem was diagrammed by Kepner and Tregoe as shown in figure 11.2. The "problem" is the difference between what *should* be going on (desired state of affairs) and what is *actually* going on (present undesired state of affairs). The goal is to get the course of events to lead back to the desired state, "what should be going on." A group using this model of a problem must determine the details of the difference. Then they must decide what produced or caused the unexpected change in order to create an appropriate solution. The Kepner and Tregoe model of a problem may help you to map out such problems as a change in the frequency of accidents, a machine that is not running properly, or even a change in the relationships among members of a family. Regardless of the model, a group does not understand a problem adequately to come up with an effective solution until all members agree on what is the desired situation, what is the actual situation, and the causes or obstacles producing the difference. In one sense, problem solving never ends. Solving one problem often leads to others. For example, if a wood-burning furnace, chain saw, and log splitter were purchased as a solution to the high cost of heating, keeping the chimney free of creosote would likely be one of several new problems the homeowner would encounter growing out of the solution to high heating bills. A high-speed railway to reduce travel time between cities could lead to such problems as dangerous crossings, destruction of communities, and loss of farm land.

Problem Characteristics

Shaw used a complex statistical procedure to determine the major dimensions of tasks used in studies of small group process. This resulted in six task variables or dimensions. Five of these dimensions are characteristics of all problems discussed by problem-solving groups: *difficulty, solution multiplicity, intrinsic interest, cooperative requirements,* and *population familiarity.*[3] To help you analyze the problems facing groups in which you participate we will examine each of these task characteristics, plus two other important characteristics—the *acceptance-technical dimension,* and the *area of freedom of the group.*

   Task difficulty refers to the amount of complexity, effort, knowledge, and skill needed to achieve the goal. The amount and kind of leadership services needed will vary with the difficulty. Group performance on difficult problems was found to be better when members could express their feelings and opinions about possible solutions openly than when such expressions were artificially restricted.[4] Simple problems may be solved quickly with little concern about procedure, whereas complex problems may require many meetings, a highly detailed problem-solving procedure to guide this extended activity, and considerable attention to how well members are cooperating. Only the very general components of the problem-solving procedure will be the same in discussions of simple and complex problems (how to lay out our garden versus developing a differentiated salary schedule for teachers.)

   Solution multiplicity refers to the number of conceivable or feasible alternatives for solving the problem. To illustrate, there are usually only a few ways to obtain potable water for a farmhouse, but innumerable ways to decorate and arrange the living room. Shaw and Blum found that "directive" leadership was more effective when a very low number of alternatives was possible, wereas "nondirective" leadership was more effective with problems for which more alternative solutions were possible.[5] In an unpublished study, I found that the majority of group members preferred a several-step procedure to a simple two-step outline for guiding their discussion when both a limited number (nine) and an unlimited number of alternative solutions were possible. However, nine is still a relatively high number of alternatives compared to the problems used by Shaw and Blum. Several studies of creative problem solving have shown that highly structured brainstorming procedures evoke more possible solutions and more ideas rated good than do simple outlines or no outline to guide the discussions.[6] The procedure for guiding a problem-solving discussion should be selected in part on the basis of the extent to which the problem is characterized by "solution multiplicity."

Intrinsic interest was defined by Shaw as ". . . the degree to which the task in and of itself is interesting, motivating, and attractive to the group members."[7] Discussants' interest is related to (1) how important they perceive a problem to be and (2) the degree to which the solution will directly affect them. Berkowitz found that when members were extremely involved with the task, they preferred sharing in procedural control, whereas strong procedural control of the discussion by a designated leader was preferred when the task was of less direct interest to them.[8] My personal experience and observation of numerous groups supports this finding. If interest is very high, members will not at first want to stick closely to any procedural outline, but will more readily do so when initial feelings and ideas have been expressed ("ventilated").

Ideally, persons in groups would discuss only problems of intrinsic interest to them. But in the world of organizations and committees, persons are assigned to committees that must deal with a variety of problems, some of little interest to them. When intrinsic interest appears to be low, this needs to be discussed by the group, possibly leading to a change of attitude toward the problem, a modification of it, or a request that it be assigned to some other group.

Cooperative requirements refers to the degree to which coordinated efforts are essential to satisfactory completion of a group task. It is obvious that a consensus decision about the solution to a complex problem requires a high level of cooperation when members initially have different perceptions of the problem and different ideas about what ought to be done to solve it. The complexity of a problem and cooperative requirements are thus intertwined variables. Discussions of problems requiring high levels of cooperation usually are inefficient and unproductive unless procedures for problem solving and consensus decision making are understood and accepted by all members. A win-win relationship must be maintained among members.

Population familiarity refers to the degree to which members have previous experience with the task and possess information essential to its successful completion. If other factors are the same, groups with experienced members tend to perform better than groups of inexperienced members.[9] Several writers have stressed the danger that participants experienced in solving problems similar to the one being discussed may be less imaginative or open-minded in thinking of solutions than will less experienced members, even to the extent of squelching creative ideas. A procedure such as brainstorming can be used to offset any such tendency.[10] Shared knowledge about the problem prior to discussing it will facilitate rapid progress toward goal agreement and consensus on a solution. A more extended period of investigation, sharing of information, and developing the details of the problem are required if members are not well informed about it.

The importance of the **acceptance-technical dimension** of problems was stressed by Maier.[11] This dimension concerns the degree to which the solution must be acceptable to persons who will be affected by it, rather than simply being feasible technically. For instance, outlawing the consumption of alcohol and preaching the evils of drunkenness have been tried as solutions to the social problems created by alcoholism. Both failed as solutions. They were not accepted—persons broke the law or refused to believe the preaching—because they did not take into account the importance of the acceptance-technical dimension. Only persons discussing problems that are almost entirely technical in nature can ignore the acceptance factor, such as how to stop the killing of persons by toxic fumes given off by burning plastic in airplanes. The amount of human acceptance necessary for a solution to achieve the goal is always a characteristic of the problem that needs to be considered if a truly effective remedy is to be found.

The **area of freedom of the group** was defined in chapter 4 as the amount of authority given a group, which is related to the type of general question that the group discusses. As mentioned in chapter 7, problem solving groups may seek answers to questions of interpretation ("fact"), value, or policy. Problems of interpretation require the group to assemble a body of information and interpret it with some generalization. Such is the work of the so-called fact finding or investigative committee—for example, a team of detectives working on a bank robbery, a grand jury trying to determine if there is sufficient evidence to prosecute, or a legislative committee trying to decide if there is a need for a statute to control use of ground water. The solution for such a group is a decision about the meaning to be given to the body of relevant data. Their problem-solving procedure entails fewer steps than that of a group dealing with a question of value, which requires not only interpreting data, but also deciding relative worth. A question of policy implies still one more step in the problem-solving procedure, making a decision about what *should* be done, such as "What should be done to reduce the murder rate in our city?" When facing such a problem, a group must locate, select, and interpret a body of information, make value judgments about such matters as rights of suspects versus protection of the innocent, and decide on a general policy to be implemented when dealing with all specific problems of the sort discussed by the group.

All of these types of questions as problems for discussion are more alike than different. Interpreting information often requires making value judgments among conflicting testimony, statistics, and other information. A judgment that a serious problem exists implies that a policy for dealing with it is needed. An answer to a question of value not only depends on interpretation of information, but also implies some alternative that can be considered a general policy. For example, if several makes of trucks are evaluated, obviously the policy implied is to buy the best one, and if a liberal education is truly worthwhile, the policy of encouraging a person to obtain one is indicated. Determining what *ought* to be done is clearly making the value judgment that the policy decided upon is superior to others. In all three types of questions the problem faced by the group entails a "felt difficulty": a body of information is not adequately understood for us to feel comfortable with it, a need to rank or establish priorities among alternatives, or a feeling of need for a general guideline to action in a recurrent type of problem.

Yet none of these questions implies a *complete* problem-solving procedure. Problem solving has not been finished until some definite *action has been taken* to remove obstacles to a desired goal. With that in mind, participants in discussions can formulate their goals clearly not in terms of what "should" be done, but in terms of "what will we do to . . ." or "what action will be taken to . . .." Only *advisory* (or study) groups discuss problems and then terminate their work with a body of interpreted knowledge, value judgments, or statements of policy. Their final action as a group solution is to report, advise, or recommend. A more accurate formulation of their problem would include a question such as this: "What course of action will we recommend to the city council as a means of reducing traffic deaths?" or "What will we report as the relative merits of six makes of cars under consideration as police cruisers?" In the later example, the final action of the group within its area of freedom will be to recommend a specific make of car, not to purchase the cars or even decide that they will be purchased. Groups having the area of freedom to act on a problem are responsible for taking definite action to solve the problem, or see that others do so—they can complete the total process of solving a problem. For instance, a safety committee with authority may shut down a dangerous mine until their solution to the danger has been put into effect. In short, the complete process of problem solving ends with taking action, not merely with a recommendation.

In summary, it is vital to consider all the major dimensions of any problem when seeking to solve it: the degree to which there are few or many possible alternatives, the complexity of the problem, the amount of cooperation required among group members, the familiarity of discussants with the problem, the human acceptance-technical factor, and the charge and area of freedom of the group.

Organizing Problem-Solving Discussions

All thinking involved in problem solving goes on within the nervous system of individual persons; a group does not "think" in some mystical way. How individuals solve problems has been explored by many scholars. This research provides a background to the study of problem solving by groups.

The Need for Structure

Persons have been classified as primarily "intuitive" or "systematic" problem solvers. According to this theory, *intuitive problem solvers* size up a problem, then somehow come up with a solution without consciously following any perceptible procedure. Whatever happens between defining the problem and finding a solution occurs on a pre-conscious level that cannot be observed. Perhaps you have mulled over a problem for sometime, been unable to think of a solution, and then suddenly been aware of a solution at some later time when not consciously working on the problem. This is the so-called "Eureka!" or "Ah-ha!" experience. Quite possibly your subconscious mind continued working on the problem fairly systematically even though you had stopped thinking about it on a conscious level.

Systematic thinkers, on the other extreme, are said to go through a series of mental steps such as those described by John Dewey in his famous book, *How We Think.* Dewey, a philosopher in the early part of the twentieth century, asked his students to recall how they solved various problems. From their descriptions he formulated a five-step model of a systematic problem-solving procedure that he called "reflective thinking." This model did not fit exactly with how his individual students described their mental operations, but was a general pattern that he felt they more or less followed. The result was

. . . a consecutive ordering in such a way that each [step] determines the next as its proper outcome. . . . The successive portions of the reflective thought grow out of one another and support one another; they do not come and go in a medley.[12]

1. *"Awareness of a felt difficulty"* is variously described as "whatever perplexes or challenges the mind" and "an ambiguity to be resolved" such as which fork in the road to take when one has no road map.
2. *"Definition of the difficulty"* is stage 2, involving a detailed exploration of the problem. "The essence of critical thinking is suspended judgment, and the essence of this suspense is inquiry to determine the nature of the problem before proceeding to attempt its solution." Necessary for this step is the ". . . ability to 'turn things over,' to look

at matters deliberately, to judge whether the amount and kind of evidence requisite for decision is at hand, and if not, to tell where and how to seek such evidence."

3. *"Occurrence of a suggested explanation or possible solution"* is the third stage; ". . . *cultivation of a variety of alternative suggestions* is an important factor in good thinking."

4. *"The rational elaboration of an idea"* is stage 4 of Dewey's model. At this point implications of the alternatives discovered during stage 3 are explored. Some ideas might be rejected, some modified, some accepted: "Suggestions at first seemingly remote and wild are frequently so transformed by being elaborated into what follows from them as to become apt and fruitful."

5. *"Corroboration of an idea and formation of a concluding belief"* is the final step. The remaining ideas are evaluated, including an experimental test if that is possible, before making a final decision on a course of action to achieve the goal.[13]

Many writers of books about small group communication use Dewey's sequence of systematic *individual* problem solving as *the* model for organizing problem-solving discussions. However, Dewey was *not* writing about how to organize discussions, but about individual problem solving. He did, however, state emphatically that his model of reflective thinking should be used flexibly.[14]

One of the most common complaints about discussions is that they are *not* organized, but jump back and forth among issues. Two recent studies have shown that perceived quality of discussions is related to how systematically they appear to have been organized. Gouran, Brown, and Henry had students in a group communication course evaluate the quality of audio recorded discussions and the behaviors of the discussants, then later rate these same characteristics of discussions in which they themselves had participated. A major conclusion of the study confirms the importance of procedures that maintain goal orientation and systematic examination of issues:

The results in general indicate that behaviors contributing to the substance of a decision-making discussion, such as introducing relevant issues, amplifying ideas, and documenting assertions, as well as procedural behaviors, such as maintaining goal orientation and pursuing issues systematically, had greater weight on perceptions of quality than the extent of individual member involvement and behaviors focused on maintaining or improving the social-emotional climate . . ..[15]

In the other study, Jurma trained leaders to act both in structuring and nonstructuring roles. The results indicate beneficial outcomes from structuring problem-solving discussions. In the nonstructuring style, the leaders were vague and offered no information, procedural suggestions, or guidance to the group. In the structuring style they offered considerable procedural guidance to see that the issues in the problem were discussed, that goals were set by the group, and that the group was reminded of the passage of time. Independent evaluators rated the discussions led by structuring leaders as significantly better than those led by nonstructuring leaders. Participants low in task orientation were significantly more satisfied with both the leaders and the outputs of the structured discussions. This is an important finding, for persons low in task orientation are likely to be intuitive problem solvers, not high in the need for procedural structure, and inclined to make non-task comments during discussions.[16] I suspect that the more experience a person has in problem-solving discussions that are orderly and follow a structured procedure, the more one prefers to follow a general outline based on some definite problem-solving procedure.

Poole concluded from his studies of discussions by groups of students and groups of physicians that a structured procedure for problem solving served as ". . . a norm or ideal pattern for group decision processes . . ." which groups of knowledgeable persons try to follow. In Poole's opinion, this model often reminds group members to do what they failed to do earlier in a problem-solving discussion (such as analyze the problem thoroughly).[17] As Poole argued in a more recent article, logical time sequences for problem solving do not so much guide the sequence of what is said during an actual problem-solving discussion as they serve as a ". . . specification of logical priorities that shape, but do not determine, group activity." He suggested a model of problem solving that includes ". . . a set of parallel strands or tracks of activity which evolve simultaneously and interlock in different patterns over time."[18]

Previously alluded to was the study by Brilhart and Jochem in which we found that significantly more students participating in experimental problem-solving discussions preferred a complex five-stage problem-solving sequence—the "Creative Problem-Solving Sequence" of problem description and analysis, generation of possible solutions, determination of criteria, evaluation of possible solutions, and decision on final solution—to a simple three-stage process of problem analysis, discussion of solutions, and decision.[19] In a later study I found that when leaders followed a structured problem-solving sequence, the large majority of statements made by participants were relevant to the phase of problem solving announced by the leader and only a small proportion were irrelevant to that phase.[20]

Ability to engage in systematic, step-by-step problem solving seems to be important to being judged an effective contributor to problem-solving discussions.[21] But can one learn to follow a procedure for problem solving which involves distinct steps, or must one be born with such ability? The answer is that one *can* learn, at least to an appreciable degree. It is doubtful that there are purely intuitive or systematic types of thinkers. More important than inherited tendencies is what we have *learned* previously from family members, peers, schooling, and small groups in which we have participated. Nisbett and

Ross have shown that relying on intuitive problem solving and inference making leads to many errors in problem solving. They were able to teach subjects to replace simplistic intuitive strategies with the systematic and statistical procedures of the formal scientist.[22] Further support for this conclusion comes from the work of Sternberg, who found that those who are most successful on mental problems such as are included in IQ tests, follow a definite sequence in which they first set up a procedure for tackling the problem, then routinely follow it step by step. If it does not work, they then try a different approach, but their overall strategy tends to be exhaustive of the possible answers, requiring more steps than are taken by persons who do less well. Small children cannot do some of the steps involved. Expert and beginning chess players likewise are differentiated by the procedures they follow in dealing with a problem. Sternberg believes that impulsive problem solvers can be taught to do better by showing them how their erroneous procedures lead to erroneous solutions, and then how to proceed more systematically and effectively.[23] Certainly one must *learn* how to follow the strict problem-solving procedures of the scientist in attacking research problems. Few individuals naturally or "intuitively" follow a "scientific method" as any of us who has taught a research methods course can testify. Mechanics must learn how to diagnose and correct problems in cars, following a definite sequence akin to that followed by winners of the game "twenty questions." They do not learn this just by developing skills with wrenches and gear pullers. Likewise, the medical student is taught to follow a step-by-step procedure in diagnosing and treating medical problems. I believe strongly that very few persons are so inflexible that they cannot learn to follow systematic procedures or that they are so recalcitrant that they will not do so in a group discussion *if they have seen the benefits from doing so, are guided by norms favoring organized, relevant comments,* and *are following an outline or procedure agreed upon by the group.* Often, of course, groups contain members who do not think systematically in solving problems. Then it may be necessary to accept considerable skipping about among the stages of problem solving, but if a continuing group makes a point to consciously adopt a procedure and follow it, this difficulty can be reduced through time.

General Principles for Structuring Problem-Solving Discussions

I have distilled advice for structuring problem-solving discussions to seven general principles which are described and explained on the following pages. When preparing an outline for problem solving use these principles to guide you. They are criteria for evaluating the adequacy of the problem-solving procedure followed by any group.

1. Focus on the problem before thinking and talking about how to solve it.

What would you think if you drove into a garage with a car that was running poorly and the mechanic almost immediately said, "What you need to fix this buggy is a new carburetor and a set of spark plugs." If your reaction is like mine, you would get out of there as fast as your ailing auto would let you. A competent mechanic, after asking questions about how the car was acting and observing how it ran, might put it on an electronic engine analyzer. After gathering information by these means he or she would make a tentative diagnosis, which would be checked by direct examination of the suspected parts. Only then would the mechanic say something like, "The problem is that two of your valves are burned, and the carburetor is so badly worn that it won't stay adjusted properly."

Our two hypothetical mechanics illustrate one of the most common failings in group (and individual) problem solving: getting solution-centered early in the problem-solving procedure. After observing many problem-solving conferences, Lee said there existed "a deeply held assumption that because the problem was announced it was understood. People seemed too often to consider a complaint equivalent to a description, a charge the same as a specification."[24] Maier, after many years of studying problem-solving discussions in business and industry, stated that "participants as well as discussion leaders focus on the objective of arriving at a solution and fail to give due consideration to an exploration of the problem."[25] Groups tend to act like a surgeon who scheduled an operation when a patient complained of a pain his abdomen, like a judge who handed down a decision as soon as he had read the indictment, or like the hunter who shot at a noise in the bushes and killed his son. This tendency to short-circuit on the analysis and encoding of the problem was the major error found by Sternberg in his studies of how persons tackled IQ test problems.

Hirokawa recently studied differences between procedures of successful and unsuccessful problem-solving groups. His most important finding was that early in the discussion successful groups focused on analysis of the problem and discovery of possible solutions, whereas unsuccessful groups began almost at once to evaluate possible solutions, then got around to problem description and analysis during the middle and later phases of problem solving, if at all. Also, there was significantly more negative socioemotional expression by members of the unsuccessful groups, possibly due to the frustrations of such illogical sequencing.[26]

Time spent on problem analysis often makes achieving consensus much easier than if the group gets quickly into "how to solve it." A thorough description of the problem, discussion of goals, and analysis of the obstacles will in many cases lead to consensus on a solution that appears obvious—after such detailed encoding of the problem. Failure in the beginning to discuss the problem adequately leads to both process and output variables that are undesirable:

   a. *Partisanship is encouraged.* Participants spend a lot of time arguing the merits of their favorite proposals. Often this is a result of having different ideas about the goal, dissimilar information, and varying beliefs about what may have caused the unsatisfactory situation. Only when members first agree on the nature of the problem are they likely to be able to agree on what to do about it; otherwise the group may become hopelessly split or generate interpersonal tensions that hurt future group work.

b. *Time is wasted.* Solution-at-once methods often result in a sort of pinwheel pattern. The problem is mentioned; someone proposes a solution that is argued at length; someone points out that an important aspect of the problem has been neglected; someone then goes back to the problem to see if this is so; another solution is proposed; and so on in a spiral fashion. This problem-solving cycling may be repeated many times, wasting time on solutions that do not fit the facts of the case. First, focus discussion on what has gone wrong rather than on what to do about it.

c. *Ineffectual solutions tend to be adopted.* There is a tendency to spend much time debating the first proposed solutions, which are usually taken bodily from other situations and are not based on the facts of the present case. Innovative ideas are not considered. When a careful analysis of the combination of forces and conditions producing the problem (causes) has not been made, often only symptoms are treated while the basic problem gets worse instead of being solved. To illustrate, think of what will happen if you try to solve the problem of a headache by taking pain killers when the cause is inadequate handling of stress or a brain tumor. Maier and Maier found that a "developmental pattern," while taking more patience and skill on the part of the designated leader, produced a better quality of decision than did a simple "free" pattern.[27] The "developmental pattern" breaks the problem into a series of distinct issues and steps. It forces the group to map out the problem thoroughly and systematically. In a "free" discussion the group tries to find a solution without following any systematic outline to guide the analysis of the problem. In a similar study, Maier and Solem found that a leader technique for delaying the group decision produced solutions to a "change of work procedure" problem superior to those solutions produced when "free" discussion was permitted.[28]

2. *Begin with a single, unambiguous problem question.*

How a problem is formulated into a question by (or to) a group can make a great difference in what happens in the problem-solving process. It is often important to begin with a "problem question" rather than a "solution question." A *problem question* asks what might or should be done to achieve a goal, whereas a *solution question* suggests a solution or type of solution and asks how to put it into effect. Of course a group with its freedom limited to acting upon a policy decided by someone else, or to carrying out a previously decided solution, must begin with an implementation question. But such a group is working through only a small part of the total process of problem solving. If your group has the authority to search for, invent, and decide on a solution, *always* begin with a *problem question*.[29] Differences between the two types of questions are illustrated in figure 11.3, and in the following list.

How can I transfer a man who is popular in his work group but slows down the work of other employees in the group? (a solution-question, the solution being to transfer the man)

versus

How can I increase the work output of the group to the desired level? (a problem-question, focusing on the disparity between present and needed output)

What can be done to reduce complaints about parking space at our college? (a problem question, focusing on the difference between the present state of complaints and a desired state of few or no complaints)

versus

What can be done to get more parking space at our college? (a solution question, asserting indirectly that what ought to be done is create more parking spaces. Maybe more beneficial in the long run would be improved public transit, off-campus classes, or shuttle busing from existing parking space elsewhere.

How will we reduce shoplifting in our stores? (a problem question, if the amount of shoplifting is greater than management finds acceptable)

versus

How can we catch and punish more shoplifters in order to stop the drain on our profits? (a solution question, suggesting that *the* solution to shoplifting is to catch and punish. Maybe some preventive action would be more effective without the negative side effects possible from negative publicity.)

Figure 11.3   Differences between *Problem Questions* and *Solution Questions*.

Solution Questions	Problem Questions
One type of action is suggested.	*Many alternative solutions* implied, none suggested.
Focus is on *what to do*.	Focus is on *what's wrong*.

Once a group has decided on a policy or course of action, then a solution question, as the final phase in problem solving, would be appropriate—"How do we put our agreed-upon solution into effect?"—but never at the beginning of the problem-solving procedure, when attention needs to be focused on fact-finding, analysis, and locating possible alternatives.

3. Map the problem thoroughly.

To help develop an attitude fostering thorough problem analysis, think of the problem as an uncharted area with only vague boundaries. The group needs to know the "who, what, why, when, where, and how" of the problem in order to fill in this map; this is its first step in problem solving. The participants should share all they know about the situation: facts, complaints, conditions, circumstances, factors, details, happenings, relationships, disturbances, effects, etc. In short, what have you heard, read, and observed that bears in any way on the problem? What have other members heard, read, and observed? What does this all add up to?

Such mapping should be as precise and detailed as possible. You might be guided by such examples as the investigation of a murder by a team of trained detectives, the investigation of a plane crash by the Federal Aviation Administration, or the investigation by medical researchers of a series of deaths from Legionnaires' disease. As Kepner and Tregoe pointed out, one of the greatest dangers is that a group will too quickly accept an apparent cause without adequate gathering of facts, analysis, and interpretation of them—"jumping to a conclusion without cause." Instead of being very critical in comparison of possible causative forces, discussants may collect arguments in support of a pet theory, resist other possible explanations of the problem, and pridefully fight to protect their theories of why things are not satisfactory. It is very important to "closely examine each hypothesis, looking for loopholes, for inconsistencies, for exceptions, for partial explanations," even with regard to one's own brainchildren.[30]

Perhaps the greatest obstacle to problem-centered thinking is the leader or member who comes to the group with the problem already solved in his or her mind. The presenter of a problem to a group must therefore set aside any possible solutions she had thought of and focus on the goal she wants to achieve if true discussion is to occur. In advisory groups, where one member brings a problem to the group for advice on how to solve it, the group frequently persuades that person to see the problem very differently. Being willing to explore any and all solutions without favoring one at the start is essential.

Figure 11.4 illustrates the process of gathering and sharing information to map out a problem so that all members have virtually the same understanding of it. The large outer circle represents the entire problem in a context. Each of the four members of the group (A, B, C, D) has some information

Figure 11.4   "Maps" of a problem before and after discussion.

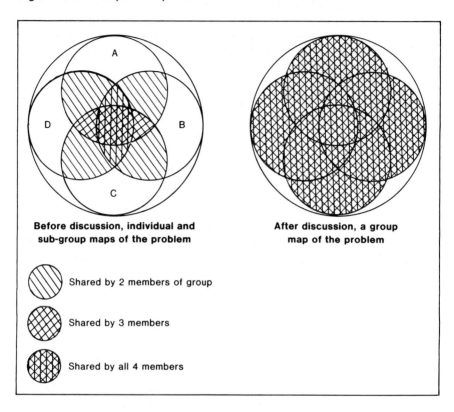

Before discussion, individual and
sub-group maps of the problem

After discussion, a group
map of the problem

Shared by 2 members of group

Shared by 3 members

Shared by all 4 members

about the problem, a unique personal map represented by one of the four inner circles. Some of the information is shared by two members (light shading), some by three members (dark shading), and some by all four members (dark center area), when the discussion gets underway. As the disdussants share their information in a systematic analysis of the problem, they come to have at least very similar images or maps of the problem; no longer do they have four different problems, but a shared problem. This map of the situation facing them is far better than any one or two members could have constructed (indicated by the circle in the right half of figure 11.4).

4. Be sure the group members agree on criteria.
Many times there is a lack of "reality testing" before a decision is made final. Other times, a group cannot agree on which of two or more possible solutions to adopt. If the problem has been fully explored, the most likely source of prolonged conflict is a lack of clear-cut criteria or objectives. In many discussions there is a need for two considerations of criteria: first, when formulating the specific objectives of the group; second, when stating specific

standards to be used in judging among solutions. Until agreement (explicit or intuitive) is reached on criteria, agreement on a solution is unlikely.

Criteria are expressions of values shared by members of a group. Rubenstein gave an example of a problem that brought out very different values from different persons, and thus disagreement over the appropriate course of action (solution). Imagine that a man is in a small boat with his mother, wife, and child. The boat capsizes. The man is the only person in the boat who can swim. He can save only one of the other three persons. Which one should he save? Rubenstein found that all the Arabs he asked would save the mother, explaining that a man can always get another wife and children but not another mother. Of 100 American college freshmen asked this same question, 60 said they would save the wife and 40 the child. These Americans laughed at the idea of saving the mother. Why these great differences in choices? The criteria, based on different values, are different for most Arabs and most Americans. Hence, said Rubenstein: This is the problem of problems, the subjective element of problem solving and decision making. A person's value system or priorities guide behavior manifested in problem solving and decision making. Two people using the same rational tools of problem solving often arrive at different solutions because they operate from different frames of values, and therefore their behavior is different.[31] So a consensus of values relevant to the problem must be arrived at before a group can arrive at a consensus decision. It may take much time for a group to search out common values and beliefs. This is an important function of fantasy chains, the establishment of common frames of values. When a group cannot seem to agree on a solution, look for differences in values, bring these up for discussion, and see if it is possible to agree. It may or may not be possible. Here is a situation in which you can employ the conflict-resolving procedure detailed in chapter 10.

Some highly successful problem-solving groups do not discuss criteria, but readily agree on which of several alternatives to adopt or recommend. In such situations group members have either come from a common culture and thus share values which predispose them to the same alternative solution, or else criteria have previously been established by the group for deciding on a solution to similar problems. In any event, consensus on a choice among two or more alternatives depends on having criteria and values shared by all group members. If conflict over alternatives is prolonged but criteria have *not* been explicitly discussed and agreed upon, you can render invaluable leadership service by pointing out the possible lack of agreement about standards for judgment, and asking the group to describe, discuss, and seek agreement upon criteria by which to evaluate the alternatives.

From the beginning of the discussion, the group needs to be clearly aware of the limitations placed upon its area of freedom. The group that tries to make decisions affecting matters over which it has no authority will be both confused and frustrated. For example, the area of freedom for a group of university students includes recommending changes in teaching methods, but students have no authority to make or enforce policy governing such matters. A committee may be given power to recommend plans for the building, but not to make the final decision and contract for the building. Any policy decision or plan of action must be judged by whether or not it fits into the group's area of freedom. Thus, if a committee is authorized to spend up to $500, it must evaluate all possible ideas by that absolute criterion.

It is important to rank criteria, giving priority to those that must be met. Ideas proposed can be rated *yes* or *no* on whether they meet all the absolute criteria, and from *excellent* to *poor* on how well they measure up to the less important criteria.

Single words, such as *efficient,* are not criteria, but categories of criteria. Such words are so vague that they are meaningless when applied to possible solutions. They can be used to help create specific criteria. Criteria should be worded as questions or absolute statements. For example, the following criteria might be applied to plans for a club's annual banquet:

Absolute—Must not cost over $400 for entertainment.
            Must be enjoyable to both members and their families.
Questions—How convenient is the location for members?
            How comfortable is the room?

The importance of valid facts as criteria is suggested by Maier. Any solution not based on unchallenged facts or interpretations of facts available to the group should be rejected, and any solution based only on challenged information or interpretations should not be given further consideration.[32]

5. Defer judgment when seeking solutions.

Instead of evaluating each possible solution when it is first proposed, it is more efficient to defer judgment until a complete list of possible solutions has been produced. Much of the research already cited indicates that the process of *idea gathering* should be separated from *idea evaluation.* Judgment stifles unusual and novel ideas. It is usually very helpful to list the proposed solutions on a chart or chalkboard. Members should be encouraged to combine, modify, or build upon previous suggestions.

For some types of problems, there are few options open to a group. If so, some discussion of each idea when it is proposed may be appropriate, but no final decision should be made until all alternatives that group members can think of have been recorded. At other times a very thorough exploration of the problem and causes will lead to a sudden insight into a solution. In such a case, the group should still try to think of other ideas with which the first one can be compared—"What *else* might we do?" If nothing is discovered, that solution should still be evaluated very thoroughly, and in the process it may undergo considerable revision and improvement.

Occasionally a problem-solving group may want to engage in full-fledged "brainstorming." Brainstorming depends on deferring of judgment; many auxiliary skills and techniques can be used to advantage. Brainstorming can be applied to any problem if there is a wide range of possible solutions, none of which can in advance be said to be just right. The process of brainstorming can be applied to any phase of the discussion: finding information (What information do we need? How might we get this information?), finding criteria (What criteria might we use to test ideas?), finding alternative solutions (What might we do?), or implementation (How might we put our decision into effect?). The following rules for brainstorming should be explained to the group and enforced by a procedural leader:

a. *All criticism is ruled out while brainstorming.*
b. *The wilder the ideas, the better.* Even offbeat, impractical suggestions may suggest practical ideas to other members.
c. *Quantity is wanted.* The more ideas, the more likelihood of good ones.
d. *Combination and improvement are wanted.* If you see a way to improve on a previous idea, snap your fingers to get attention so it can be recorded at once.

In a brainstorming group it is often advantageous to have persons with experience and persons new to the specific problem—these bring a fresh point of view to it. A full-time recorder is needed to write down ideas as fast as they are suggested, preferably where everyone can see them on a chalkboard or large sheets of paper fastened to the wall with masking tape. Be sure the recorder gets each idea written down in a form acceptable to the person who suggested it.

The flow of possible solutions while brainstorming can often be increased by asking idea-spurring questions. For instance, the leader might ask how to *adapt, modify, rearrange, reverse, combine, minimize,* or *maximize* characteristics of some general solution previously proposed. A concrete suggestion can be used to spur creative thinking in an entire area. For example, someone suggests: "Place a guard at the door." The leader could then ask, "What else might be done to increase security?" When the group seems to have run out of ideas, try reviewing the list rapidly; then ask for a definite number of additional suggestions to see if you can get more ideas. Usually you will get many more, including some very good ones.

A few cautions need to be kept in mind when brainstorming. (1) A thorough job of creating new ideas, based on a thorough mapping of the problem, takes time. If time is short, use a more conventional, simpler procedure. (2) Be sure to stop all criticism, whether stated or suggested by voice or manner. Everyone must feel complete freedom to offer any idea as a solution. Some persons seem to be unable to stop criticizing ideas when they are first uttered. If a few attempts fail to stop such a person, ask the person to follow the rules of brainstorming to the letter, stay quiet, or leave the room. (3) The problem

Figure 11.5   Brainstorming produces lots of ideas.

must be unambiguous, defined, closely limited, and thoroughly analyzed before brainstorming begins. Broad, sweeping problems must be subdivided. (4) Vague generalities cannot be put into action as solutions, so be sure to clarify and elaborate all courses of action before adopting them. (5) Ideas should be evaluated at a later meeting and possibly by a different group.

6. *Use constructive argument and other techniques to avoid groupthink.*

As mentioned earlier, Janis has used the term *groupthink* to refer to conformity to the belief of a head person or a majority in a group. Groupthink sometimes occurs when members begin to think they are infallible, or that the ideas of high status members should not be challenged. Leaders who promote their own solutions invite groupthink, but this phenomenon can occur in any group. Examples of the results of groupthink outcomes are the invasion of the Bay of Pigs, the decision to escalate the United States involvement in South Vietnam, and the Watergate espionage. Contributing to groupthink are pressures for consensus at the price of repressing doubts and contradictory evidence, cohesiveness based on less than open communication, a lack of critical scrutiny of all pros and cons, a failure to look for more alternatives, a failure to examine moral or ethical considerations, stereotyping of opposing groups, pressure from high status members, ignoring of facts and interpretations that do not support a majority view, failure to consult with available experts, and an illusion of unanimity based on suppression of doubts.[33] Manz and Sims found groupthink quite common in autonomous work groups (small groups of workers given considerable authority in planning their work procedures). In most cases the team leader took sides, leading to inadequate consideration of other alternatives because those who disagreed did not get to express their views. The leaders thought they had unanimity, but it was superficial. Other groups failed to consider complaints from outsiders, seeing themselves as so wise and moral that they had no need to consider the opinions of others.[34]

Appropriate norms or rules for arguing can do much to produce constructive argument. Any problem-solving group needs norms such as those that follow. If your group is suffering from groupthink it might be a good idea to make a copy of these for everybody to discuss at one meeting.

   a. Arguments should not lead to some persons being perceived as winners and other members as losers; everyone wins when a more creative, adequate solution is achieved.
   b. Each member of the group should participate openly, expressing feelings, ideas, and positions. Even intuitions and hunches should be expressed and evaluated. A climate in which diversity of opinion is encouraged helps prevent groupthink.
   c. Members should insist on exploring the assumptions and implications of every idea; it is especially important that the person who first suggests a solution ask for such critical evaluation of the idea.

d. Every response to one's ideas should be valued and taken seriously. Every idea deserves an interested hearing.

e. Members should be critical of *all* ideas, but not of the members who express the ideas. Disagreement should not be person-centered but idea-centered. If the best possible thinking is to be done, no one should be put on the defensive. Uptight discussants do not think clearly.

f. Members should frequently state what they think are the positions, feelings, and values of others with whose ideas they disagree. Such active listening and empathic understanding will prevent much bypassing and needless secondary tension.

g. All ideas should be evaluated on their own merits, not on the basis of who suggests them. Insofar as possible, status power should be equalized so all members have the same chance to participate and be listened to, regardless of position or power in the external structure of the group or role in the group—that is the ideal to strive for.

h. The importance of teamwork in striving for consensus decisions that all can support should be stressed, perhaps often.

i. Controversy should be introduced when there is enough time to discuss the point at issue thoroughly, not just before the meeting must adjourn.

j. Trickery, bargaining, manipulation, and deception should be assiduously avoided, pointed out, and rebuked when detected.[35]

7. Plan how to implement and follow-up on solutions.

Many times a group arrives at a policy decision, a solution to a problem, or a resolution all to no avail. No plans are made for putting the decision into effect or seeing how the recommendation is received by the parent organization. Problem solving should always terminate in some plan for action; a task group should not consider its work finished until agreement has been reached on who is to do exactly what, how, and by what time. If a committee is to make recommendations to a parent body, the committee should decide who will make the report, when he or she will make it, and in what form. If this report is to be made at a membership meeting, the committee members may then decide to prepare seconding or supporting speeches, and on a campaign to prepare the general membership to accept their recommendations. A neighborhood group that has decided to turn a vacant lot into a playground would have to plan how to get legal clearance, who to get to do the work, where to get the materials (or at least from whom), and how to check on the use children get from the playground. No good chairperson or leader of a problem-solving group would fail to see that the group worked out details of how to put its decisions into effect.

Phillips suggested the use of PERT (Program Evaluation and Review Technique) as an adjunct to the discussion process for working out the details of a complex solution.[36] It can be very useful for implementing a complex plan of action like constructing a building, conducting a promotional campaign, scheduling the making of a movie, producing a play, etc. PERT involves identifying all events that must take place in sequences, estimating the time and resources needed for each, determining the allocation of personnel and material, and deciding whether a target date can likely be achieved. Although not needed for most plans of action, it is an excellent means for working out a plan based on statistical estimates rather than personal whim or guesswork. You may want to study it in one of the many excellent manuals on the process, but it must be practiced, not merely read about. Regardless of whether or not you study and apply PERT be sure that your decisions will be converted into observable events, that definite actions are taken by designated members of the group, and that some procedure for monitoring is arranged to be sure that the solution is carried out as intended.

Scientific Studies of Group Problem-Solving Procedures

A number of scientific investigations of problem-solving procedures followed by small groups have been made, from which one clear and consistent finding has emerged: ". . . research does not produce unequivocal evidence supporting or disconfirming the utility of reflective thinking models in groups. But it does unequivocally support the advantage of some sort of rational decision making agenda."[37]

Early in the history of research concerned with group problem-solving procedures, Maier and Maier compared a problem-solving sequence they called "developmental" with "free" discussions in which no particular sequence was followed. In a developmental discussion the designated leader posed a series of questions about the details and causes of the problem before permitting discussion of what to do about it. After these questions had been discussed by the group, they could then follow any procedure to arrive at a solution. Blind judgments by experts in the subject matter of the problem showed that the groups following the developmental pattern produced significantly more high quality solutions than did groups involved in free discussions (the leader asked no particular questions to get the group to map out the problem). An important process effect was also found: the developmental outline required more skill and tact on the part of the leader, or an outcome could be resentment by members at having their remarks restricted to one issue at a time. Members of these experimental groups were all managerial personnel in an organizational development program coordinated by Maier, but they were not necessarily trained in the logic and self-restraint required for reflective-type thinking.[38]

Outputs of three procedural patterns for problem-solving discussions were compared experimentally by Brilhart and Jochem. A creative problem-solving procedure produced more possible solutions, and more solutions judged to be good ideas by independent judges than did a simple problem-solving procedure. Participants preferred the complex creative problem-solving outline. Significantly more subjects also preferred a creative problem-solving sequence in which listing possible solutions preceded discussion of criteria to one in which discussion of criteria preceded the search for possible solutions. Subjects indicated that they felt discussing criteria first reduced their feelings of freedom to express novel ideas.[39]

Bayless also reported that subjects in his study of sequences for organizing problem solving felt that following a several-step procedure helped them in reaching a solution.[40] In a subsequent unpublished study, I compared the creative problem-solving sequence (incorporating brainstorming) and a simple reflective thinking sequence in which each idea was evaluated when first mentioned. Discussants in this study made decisions about problems that affected them personally: how to distribute bonus grade points among themselves, and the date for the final examination in their public speaking course. Again, significantly more subjects preferred the detailed creative problem-solving procedure over a simpler problem-solution sequence after using both.

Following up on this line of research, Larson had groups discuss industrial relations problems for which a "best" solution was known. This "best" solution was one of five alternatives supplied to the groups from which they had to choose. Four different problem-solving sequences were compared: the "no pattern," in which the group was given the problem to solve but no outline of steps to follow; the "single question" sequence, which is much like Maier's developmental pattern; the "ideal solution" procedure, which emphasizes the wants and values of persons affected by the decision; and a "reflective thinking" format based on Dewey's model. Any of the three multi-step outlines for guiding group discussion produced significantly more correct solutions than did the "no pattern" discussions. The merit of some structured procedure for a group to follow in problem-solving discussions was again clearly demonstrated.[41]

In the last few years both Poole and Hirokawa have renewed the investigation of whether there is any best procedure for groups to use during problem-solving discussions.[42] Both concluded that there is no *one* sequence or procedure best for problem-solving discussions. In addition to the norm shared by many educated persons that they ought to follow some version of reflective thinking, the specific procedure a group follows depends on many contingencies facing the group. And even though both Poole and Hirokawa found that successful groups follow various procedures, both determined that it was more productive for groups to analyze the problem early in discussion and to delay evaluation of possible solutions until later.

A General Procedural Model for Problem-Solving Discussions

The effectiveness of specific problem-solving procedures is determined by many contingencies facing a group: problem characteristics, member experience and values, involvement with the problem, time available, etc. The demonstrated need not to overlook important phases of problem solving and to structure discussions has led to development of what I choose to call the "General Procedural Model for Problem Solving." This model is flexible enough to allow adjustment to various contingencies. The major steps in the procedure are:

I. Problem description and analysis. (here the group should focus most of its attention and talk on determining the exact details of what is unsatisfactory, what is desired, and obstacles to obtaining the desired state.)
II. Generation and elaboration of possible solutions.
III. Evaluation of possible solutions.
IV. Solution decision. (emergence of a consensus decision)
V. Planning for implementation of the solution decided upon.

When preparing for a problem-solving discussion, the designated leader of the group should write an outline of questions covering all issues she or he can think of that must be considered by the group if no important contingency is to be overlooked. These questions should be arranged in a logical sequence, based on the guidelines presented under the heading "General Principles for Structuring Problem-Solving Discussions." Group members together can construct such an outline, but it is almost always more efficient for the designated discussion leader to present such an outline to the group (usually as a handout) and ask the group to consider it carefully, then modify or adopt it as presented.

Groups will rarely follow such a procedural outline question by question; members will often mention information, ideas, and questions as they occur to them. Scheidel and Crowell found a tendency for groups to spiral considerably from consideration of problem issues to possible solutions, leading to a need for more thorough analysis of some aspect of the problem, then going back to the previously discussed solution or to a new solution that is suggested, etc.[43] The written outline thus becomes a "track" for the group members to follow, or rather to return to when they get off on tangents, and to remind them not to overlook some important step or issue in problem solving.

The following explanation of what is done at each procedural step in problem solving and the examples of sub-issues under each major heading will guide you in writing outlines for organizing problem-solving discussions. However, you must word the actual questions you will ask to fit the specific problem. No general set of questions is suitable for all problems, or even for any specific problem—"one size fits all" does not apply here! You must adapt the General Procedural Model for Problem-Solving Discussions to each specific problem.

I. **What is the nature of the problem facing us?**

Here the group needs to focus most of its talk on determining the details of what is unsatisfactory, what led to this undesirable situation, what is desired, and obstacles to reaching that situation. The leader's outline might contain such "developmental" questions as the following in guiding and focusing description and analysis of the problem. These sub-questions are presented in the approximate order they might be raised, but not all of them fit any one problem. The point is to determine, in advance, as well as is possible the questions that must be answered for the group members to reach a common and thorough understanding of the problem.

What does this problem question mean to us?

What is our area of freedom (or our charge)?

What is unsatisfactory at present?

Who is affected (or what is affected)?

When, where, and how?

How serious do we judge this problem to be?

Do we need additional information to adequately assess the nature and extent of the problem?

What exactly do we hope to accomplish (the desired situation)?

What conditions may have contributed to the problem?

What appear to be the causative conditions?

What precipitated the crisis leading to our discussion?

What obstacles to achieving the desired goal seem to exist?

How can we summarize our understanding of the problem to include the present and desired situations, and causal conditions? (As an alternative, when the problem is very complex and likely to require several meetings, extensive investigation, and perhaps consultations, the designated leader may want the entire group to create a list of sub-issues to be discussed. In that event, the following sorts of questions might be asked:

"What questions must we answer before we can find a satisfactory solution to our problem?"

"What sub-questions do we have sufficient information to answer now?"

"How might we find answers to the other critical sub-questions?"

"What are the most reasonable answers to all sub-questions?"

"Summing up, how do we now perceive the problem we confront?")

II. **What might be done to solve the problem?**

Here the group generates possible alternatives as solutions to the problem. Brainstorming might be used. At this point it is generally advisable *not* to evaluate the merits of ideas—just to list them and make sure everyone understands each. A few sub-questions might be raised about a proposal, such as:

Do we all understand this proposal?

Exactly how would this work?

How is the proposal related to the facts of the problem?

What *can* be changed in the present situation?

Frequently during this phase of problem solving some group member will think of some detail of the problem which ought to be explored more fully. The group will then need to cycle back to further exploration of the problem. Finished with that, the leader should then bring the group back to discussing possible solutions. You can see *how vital it is that each and every proposed solution be recorded* in writing, preferably on chalkboard or chart.

III. What are the relative merits and demerits of the possible solutions?

At this point in the procedure the group evaluates the ideas that have been proposed and elaborated. More detailed explanations of some proposals may be needed here. Additional ideas may be created, or ideas combined. *Before* discussing the pros and cons of the proposed solutions, it may be wise to begin with a period of discussion during which the agenda is to agree upon criteria— standards against which proposed solutions can be evaluated. If the group has previously established criteria while discussing the problem, or in prior discussions, this may not be necessary. If conflict over the relative merits of some ideas is prolonged, it will generally be helpful to ask what criteria the group members are applying. Then discussion might center on trying to agree both on criteria and the rank order in which they should be applied. After that has been settled, the criteria can be systematically applied to the solutions listed in order to determine which best measure up and should be decided upon. Follow-up questions for this step in the problem-solving procedure might include the following:

Are there any ideas we can screen out quickly as being unsupported by uncontested facts?

Is there any way to combine and simplify our list of possible solutions?

What are the *advantages* and *disadvantages* of each idea?

What groups or individuals must accept and support the solution?

From the point of view of each affected group, what would be the most ideal solution?

All things considered, what solution seems most likely to be accepted and supported by all persons involved?

IV. What seems to be the best possible solution which we can all support?

This is the lead question for the phase of problem-solving Fisher called "decision emergence." Sometimes no such question is needed, for the decision will have emerged and been given vocal support by everyone when it was first evaluated. But if several alternatives still remain under consideration, the leader should be prepared with a few follow-up questions like the following:

Which solution seems most likely to be accepted and supported by all persons affected by it?

Is there a compromise solution we can all accept as likely to solve our problem?

Could we combine these ideas, or parts of them, into a solution?

Once the group has agreed on a policy, findings, recommendation, or other product it set out to achieve, the final stage of problem solving—implementation of the solution—should always be discussed until everyone knows exactly what is to take place as a follow-up to the discussion.

V. How will we put our solution into effect?

Who will do what, when, and in what way?

(This might include writing a report, submitting a recommendation, or carrying out other actions.)

Do we need any follow-up to determine how well our solution is working?

Newly formed groups or highly involved members of groups often find it somewhat frustrating to follow an outline of a problem-solving procedure. This will be much less likely to become a problem if the procedure suits the specific problem and if the group as a whole adopts the actual sequence of issues, creating procedural norms. Below is a table of problem characteristics matched with steps needed in the problem-solving sequence. This table may be helpful to you when planning an outline for a group.

Problem Characteristic	Emphasize in Problem Solving
1. Intrinsic interest is high.	1. A period of "ventilation" before systematic problem solving.
2. Task difficulty is high.	2. Detailed problem mapping; many subquestions.
3. Solution multiplicity.	3. Brainstorming.
4. Cooperative requirements high.	4. A "criteria" step, creating and ranking explicit standards.
5. High level of acceptance required for solution.	5. When evaluating solutions, focus on concerns of persons affected.
6. High level of technical quality is required.	6. Focus on evaluating ideas, critical thinking; perhaps invite experts outside the group to testify.
7. One or a few stages of the total problem-solving process.	7. Shorten procedure to only the steps required.

The Discussion Outline

Discussion leaders can get so involved in trying to follow a long, complex outline that they seem unable to adapt to what is actually going on. Such a leader needs a relatively short outline of the procedure the group has decided to follow. An abbreviated outline of the problem-solving sequence of questions can be put on a chart or chalkboard for all members to follow. A longer outline, especially for a procedure likely to extend over many meetings, can be duplicated and a copy given to each member of the group. Notice how the General Procedural Model for Problem Solving had been adapted to the specific problem in each of the examples provided below.

The building in which the Department of Communication is housed may soon be partly remodelled. Up to now, small group communication classes have been taught in typical small classrooms, seating up to 50 students. I recently asked student groups for their advice on what I should recommend to campus planners as a classroom designed to meet the needs of small group communication classes. Other communication courses would also use the room at times. The following outline was prepared by Judy Hartlieb to lead a problem-solving discussion.

Problem question: What facilities will we recommend be created in the Arts and Sciences Hall to accommodate classes in small group communication?

I. What is inadequate about the facilities now available for our small group communication and leadership class, and why?
  A. What is our group concerned with?
    1. How do we understand the problem question?
    2. What do we understand to be our authority in the matter?
  B. What is unsatisfactory about current classroom facilities?
    1. What detracts from the conduct of our class?
      a. Who is affected by these adverse conditions? How?
      b. Under what conditions are these people affected? When? How Often? Specific locations in the room?
    2. How serious do we judge these conditions to be?
    3. Do we know enough about this problem, or do we need to gather more information?
  C. What goal does our group hope to achieve in designing special facilities for small group communication classes?
  D. What obstacles exist to having the facilities we envision?
    1. What obstacles must be removed/overcome?
    Money?
    Space?
    Other?
    2. What may have caused the present situation?

E. How can we sum up our problem in terms of present and desired situations, and obstacles between them?
    1. What consensus do we have in defining this problem?
    2. Should we consider any sub-problems separately?

II. What ideas do we have for improving the classroom facilities for small group communication classes?
  A. What comes to your mind, right of the top, even the wildest of ideas?
  B. What suggestions are triggered in you by the suggestions of other group members? Please associate freely!

III. By what criteria shall we judge our solutions for better accommodating small group communication classes?
  A. Are there any firm criteria which cannot be compromised on?
    1. Space?
    2. Time available?
    3. Money which can be spent?
  B. What other standards do we need? In what order of priority

IV. What are the relative merits of our ideas?
  A. Can we throw out any solutions for lack of solid back-up evidence and arguments?
  B. Can we consolidate and simplify our list of ideas in any way?
  C. How well does each item on our final list mesh with our criteria?
  D. What will we recommend for new classroom facilities?

V. How will we present our recommendations to the Department of Communication?
  A. In what form (written, oral, audio-visual)?
  B. How will we divide responsibilities for preparing and presenting the report among us?
  C. What timetable shall we follow?

In the next example of a leader's outline for a problem-solving discussion, Margie Merken focused on the acceptability dimension of the solution. The problem-question was: "What can be done to improve registration procedures?" Students, faculty members, and staff persons had all been complaining about registration procedures, so our class decided to tackle this issue.

I. What is the nature of the problem with registration?
  A. What exactly is the scope of our concern with registration?
    1. Do we need to clarify any terms?
    2. Do we need to determine the duties of departments involved in registration?
    3. What is our group's area of freedom?
  B. What is unsatisfactory about the present registration procedure?

    1. How do we know that an unsatisfactory registration process exists?
      a. Studies? If so, what conclusions?
      b. Any written complaints from faculty, staff, or students?
      c. Any other type of "feedback" about the registration procedure? If so, what?
  C. What are our goals to be achieved by changes that might be made in registration?
  D. What factors (causes) seem to us to have contributed to the registration problem?
  E. What obstacles stand in the way of solving the problem?
    1. Do we have enough information?
    2. Enough interest expressed from parties involved?
    3. Resources to solve the problem (money, time, personnel)?
    4. Are there any other obstacles to improving registration?
  F. How can the problem best be summarized?
    1. Do we all perceive the problem the same?
    2. In what order should each sub-division of the problem be tackled?

II. What would be an ideal solution to registration problem(s) from the standpoint of each of the interested groups or persons?
  A. Students?
  B. Faculty?
  C. Staff?
  D. Others we ought to consider?

III. What solutions are possible in the present situation at our university?

IV. What solution(s) best fits the problem and desires of parties who must accept it?

V. How will we make our recommendations concerning the registration problem?
  A. Who will do what, when, and how?
    1. To whom will our recommendations be given?
    2. What format will we use to make them?
      a. Writing?
      b. Telephone?
      c. In person—as a group, or representative?
  B. Do we need to plan any follow-up?

Next is a simple leader's outline for a problem on which the possible options were limited, and for which the discussion was brief.

I. What sort of written final exam should we have for our class?
  A. How much authority (area of freedom) do we have?
  B. What facts and feelings should we take into account as we seek to answer this question?

II. What are our objectives (criteria) in deciding on the type of exam?
   A. Learning objectives?
   B. Grades?
   C. Type of preparation and study?
   D. Fairness to all?
III. What types of written final exam might we have?
IV. What are the advantages and disadvantages of each?
 V. What will we recommend as the form of our written exam?

Summary

In this chapter we have considered many process variables of discussions for which the purpose is to solve some problem shared by group members. The concept "problem" was defined as consisting of an unsatisfactory condition, a goal, and obstacles to achievement of that goal. Before embarking on the actual problem-solving process, a group may first need to ventilate feelings and ideas about the problem. Then they should consider the characteristics of the specific problem on seven major variables in order to adopt a procedure suitable to both the problem and the members. It is not always possible to structure problem-solving discussions to follow a specific procedure, but doing so as much as possible will help keep the discussion coherent, goal-oriented, and efficient. Whatever specific procedure is used by a group, it should always begin with a thorough mapping of the details of the problem. It is usually productive to generate a list of possible alternatives before discussing their relative merits unless a solution appears obvious to all members. The group may need to spend time discussing criteria if these are not already clear and accepted by all members from the problem analysis stage. If acceptance is a major factor, a definite stage of discussion should be devoted to it. Every idea should be evaluated until a consensus (or at least a majority) decision emerges. Then the group is ready to work out a specific procedure for putting the solution into effect.

Scientific studies of group problem solving have demonstrated that some multi-step structure such as my General Procedural Model for Problem-Solving Discussion is beneficial to groups. This flexible model can be adapted to specific problem characteristics. A designated leader of a problem-solving discussion needs an outline of questions, adopted or created by the group, to provide the coordination needed to keep a group on the track of this procedure.

Exercises

1. Select two problems you currently are faced with. Write each as a problem question. Then decide what is *unsatisfactory* about the present

state of affairs, the *goal* you hope to achieve, and the *obstacles* that lie in the road to achieving the goal. Write these in the following format:

Problem question—

What is unsatisfactory—

Goal—

Obstacles—

2. As a *class,* select a problem affecting all members of the class—such as the type of final exam for the course, or some campus issue. Now *describe* the problem on each of the seven characteristics (variables) of a problem presented in this chapter.

3. Begin with two problems which differ in their major characteristics: any solution to one requires a high level of acceptance by involved persons, whereas the other needs a high quality solution; one should be characterized by "solution multiplicity," the other should permit few options; one should be of such broad scope that it will probably require extensive investigation and hours of meetings, the other of such limited scope that it can be dealt with in one short meeting. Your instructor may assign these problems, they may be selected by the class as a whole, or a class committee may provide them.

Write a leader's outline for structuring discussion of each of these problems. For each outline adapt the General Procedural Model for Problem-Solving Discussion to the actual problem. Be sure your outlines conform to the General Principles for Structuring Problem-Solving Discussions.

Compare your outlines with those prepared by three or four of your fellow students. Then, as a group, write *one* outline for structuring discussion of each problem, acceptable to each member of your group.

As a group, summarize what you discover from this exercise.

Bibliography

Dewey, John. *How We Think.* Boston: D. C. Health and Company, 1910.

Maier, Norman R.F. *Problem Solving and Creativity in Individuals and Groups.* Belmont, Calif.: Brooks/Cole Publishing Company, 1970.

———. *Problem-Solving Discussions and Conferences,* New York: McGraw-Hill, 1963.

Osborn, Alex F. *Applied Imagination* (rev. ed.). New York: Charles Scribner's Sons, 1957.

Shaw, Marvin E. *Group Dynamics.* 3d ed. New York: McGraw-Hill, 1981. chapter 10.

References

1. David M. Berg, "A Descriptive Analysis of the Distribution and Duration of Themes Discussed by Task-oriented Small Groups," *Speech Monographs* 34 (1967): 172–75.
2. Charles H. Kepner and Benjamin B. Tregoe, *The Rational Manager* (New York: McGraw-Hill, 1965), 20.
3. Marvin E. Shaw, *Group Dynamics,* 3d ed. (New York: McGraw-Hill, 1981), 364.
4. Marvin E. Shaw and J. M. Blum, "Effects of Leadership Style upon Group Performance As a Function of Task Structure," *Journal of Personality and Social Psychology* 3 (1966): 238–42.
5. "Effects of Leadership Style."
6. See, for example, John K. Brilhart and Lurene M. Jochem, "Effects of Different Patterns on Outcomes of Problem-Solving Discussion," *Journal of Applied Psychology* 48 (1964): 175–79; Ovid L. Bayless, "An Alternative Model for Problem Solving Discussion," *Journal of Communication* 17 (1967): 188–97; Sidney J. Parnes and Arnold Meadow, "Effects of 'Brainstorming' Instruction on Creative Problem-Solving by Trained and Untrained Subjects," *Journal of Educational Psychology* 50 (1959): 171–76.
7. Marvin E. Shaw, *Group Dynamics,* 364.
8. Leonard Berkowitz, "Sharing Leadership in Small Decision-Making Groups," *Journal of Abnormal and Social Psychology* 48 (1953): 231–38.
9. James H. Davis, *Group Performance* (Reading, Mass.: Addison-Wesley, 1969).
10. Alex F. Osborn, *Applied Imagination,* rev. ed. (New York: Charles Scribner's Sons, 1957).
11. Norman R. F. Maier, *Problem-Solving Discussions and Conferences* (New York: McGraw-Hill, 1963), 5–15.
12. John Dewey, *How We Think* (Boston: D. C. Heath and Company, 1910), 2–3.
13. Dewey, 9–75.
14. Dewey, 78.
15. Dennis S. Gouran, Candace Brown, and David R. Henry, "Behavioral Correlates of Perceptions of Quality in Decision-Making Discussions," *Communication Monographs* 45 (1978): 62.
16. William E. Jurma, "Effects of Leader Structuring Style and Task-Orientation Characteristics of Group Members," *Communication Monographs* 46 (1979): 282–95.
17. Marshall S. Poole, "Decision Development in Small Groups II: A Study of Multiple Sequences in Decision Making," *Communication Monographs* 50 (1983): 224–225.

18. M. S. Poole, "Decision Development in Small Groups III: A Multiple Sequence Model of Group Decision Development," *Communication Monographs* 50 (1983): 321–341.
19. Brilhart and Jochem, "Effects of Different Patterns."
20. John K. Brilhart, "An Experimental Comparison of Three Techniques for Communicating a Problem-Solving Pattern to Members of a Discussion Group," *Speech Monographs* 33 (1966): 168–77.
21. H. C. Pyron and H. Sharp, "A Quantitative Study of Reflective Thinking and Performance in Problem-Solving Discussion," *Journal of Communication* 13 (1963): 46–53.
22. Richard Nisbett and Lee Ross, *Human Inference: Strategies and Shortcomings of Social Judgment* (Englewood Cliffs, N.J.: Prentice-Hall, 1980).
23. Robert J. Sternberg, "Stalking the IQ Quark," *Psychology Today* 13 (September 1979): 42–54.
24. Irving J. Lee, *How to Talk with People* (New York: Harper & Row, Publishers, 1952), 62.
25. Norman R. F. Maier, *Problem-Solving Discussions and Conferences* (New York: McGraw-Hill, 1963), 123.
26. Randy Y. Hirokawa, "Group Communication and Problem-Solving Effectiveness: An Investigation of Group Phases," *Human Communication Research* 9 (1983): 291–305.
27. N. R. F. Maier and R. A. Maier, "An Experimental Test of the Effects of 'Developmental' vs. 'Free' Discussions on the Quality of Group Decisions," *Journal of Applied Psychology* 41 (1957): 320–23.
28. N. R. F. Maier and A. R. Solem, "The Contribution of a Discussion Leader to the Quality of Group Thinking: The Effective Use of Minority Opinions," *Human Relations* 5 (1952): 277–88.
29. Maier, *Problem Solving Discussions and Conferences,* 62–97, stresses this difference, and gives excellent advice on how to formulate and present problems to a group.
30. Charles H. Kepner and Benjamin B. Tregoe, *The Rational Manager* (New York: McGraw-Hill, 1965), 117–18.
31. Moshe F. Rubenstein, *Patterns of Problem Solving* (Englewood Cliffs, N.J.: Prentice-Hall, 1975), 1–2.
32. Norman R. F. Maier, *Problem Solving and Creativity* (Belmont, Calif.: Brooks Publishing Company, 1970), 453–55.
33. Irving L. Janis, "Groupthink," *Psychology Today* 5 (November 1971): 43–46, 74–76.
34. Charles C. Manz and Henry P. Sims, Jr., "The Potential for 'Groupthink' in Autonomous Work Groups," *Human Relations* 35 (1982): 773–784.

35. David W. Johnson and Frank P. Johnson, *Joining Together: Group Theory and Group Skills* (Englewood Cliffs, N.J.: Prentice-Hall, 1975), 154–55.
36. Gerald M. Phillips, "PERT As a Logical Adjunct to the Discussion Process," *Journal of Communication* 15 (1965): 89–99. Reprinted in Cathcart and Samovar, *Small Group Communication,* 166–76.
37. Edward R. Mabry and Richard E. Barnes, *The Dynamics of Small Group Communication* (Englewood Cliffs, N.J.: Prentice-Hall, 1980), 78.
38. Norman R. F. Maier and Robert A. Maier, "An Experimental Test of the Effects of 'Developmental' vs. 'Free' Discussions on the Quality of Group Decisions," *Journal of Applied Psychology* 41 (1957). 320–23.
39. John K. Brilhart and Lurene M. Jochem, "Effects of Different Patterns on Outcomes of Problem-Solving Discussion," *Journal of Applied Psychology* 48 (1964): 175–79.
40. Ovid L. Bayless, "An Alternative Model for Problem Solving Discussion," *Journal of Communication* 17 (1967): 188–97.
41. Carl E. Larson, "Forms of Analysis and Small Group Problem-Solving," *Speech Monographs* 36 (1969): 452–55.
42. M. S. Poole, "Decision Development in Small Groups II." R. Y. Hirokawa, "Group Communication."
43. Thomas M. Scheidel and L. Crowell, "Developmental Sequences in Small Groups," *Quarterly Journal of Speech* 50 (1964): 140–145.

12 special discussion techniques and methods for learning and organizational settings

Study Objectives

You may choose to read only selected parts of chapter 12, using it as a reference for some special techniques or procedures. If you study the entire chapter carefully, you should be able to:

1. Explain the benefits of cooperative learning discussions.

2. List seven guidelines for conducting learning discussions.

3. Describe a procedure for organizing discussion of a set of related issues, a work of art, a case problem, or of personal feelings and values.

4. Explain the "encounter" concept and list eight guidelines for making the feedback during encounter sessions productive of personal growth.

5. Plan and moderate either a panel or forum discussion for a large group meeting.

6. Conduct buzz groups involving all members of a large gathering.

7. Describe the eight major steps of the nominal Group Technique in chronological order.

8. Explain the purposes, basic procedures, and organizational climate in which quality circles can enhance work outputs.

9. Describe both advantages and disadvantages of teleconferences in comparison to face-to-face meetings, and how both types can best supplement each other for participants scattered geographically.

Key Terms

Affective discussion   members of a small group express and explore their feelings, especially fears, in relation to some topic or concept.

Buzz group session   large group meeting is divided into small groups of approximately six persons each, who discuss a target question for a specified number of minutes, then report their answers to the entire large group.

Case problem discussion   learning discussion beginning with consideration of a specific problem or "case" about which group members exchange perceptions, ideas, and possible solutions.

Comparative outline   a set of questions asking the discussants to compare two or more things, institutions, or other concepts on certain criteria or characteristics.

Encounter discussion   open expression of feelings and reactions of members of a group to each other and the group as a whole.

Feedback   description by member of a group of his or her reaction "here and now" to behavior of another member of the group.

Fine arts discussion format   a sequence for discussing some product of human creativity beginning with examination of the object, discussion of perceived features, interpretation of the whole, evaluation, and ending with reexamination of the object.

Forum   discussion within a large audience, controlled by a moderator, usually following some presentation such as a lecture, panel discussion, or film.

Moderator   designated leader of a public discussion such as a panel, group interview, or forum.

Nominal Group Technique (NGT)   special procedure in which six to nine persons work individually in silence to generate ideas, then interact to pool, clarify, and evaluate these ideas until a plan to solve a major problem has been adopted.

Panel Discussion   informal discussion among members of a small group, coordinated by a moderator, for benefit of a listening audience.

Problem census   technique in which members of a small group are polled for topics and problems that are posted, ranked by voting, and used to create agendas for future meetings.

Quality circle   a group of employees (usually voluntary) meeting on company time to investigate work-related problems and make recommendations to management for solution of these problems.

Teleconference   a conference among participants geographically distant from each other in which signals are carried among them via electronic devices such as television, telephone, and computers.

Up to now this book has been concerned with the dynamics of small groups as open systems, and small group communication processes and procedures. Only decision-making and problem-solving procedures have received detailed treatment as techniques. Chapter 12 shifts the focus from more general principles to special methods and techniques for discussions aimed at learning outcomes, or that are held by small groups embedded in large organizations.

Learning Discussions

Learning discussions can be held for the benefit of the discussants themselves, or primarily for the enlightenment of a listening audience. First, we will consider the reasons for, leadership of, and specific types and techniques of *private* learning discussions. Second, we will examine procedures for two types of *public* learning discussions; panel and forum.

Private Learning Discussions

Learning groups of all types, at all educational levels, formal and informal, sponsored and spontaneous, in and out of classrooms, exist not to reach decisions but for the *personal enlightenment and growth of their members.* There is an old saying to the effect that if two persons each having one idea apiece give them to each other, then each is twice as rich in ideas as before—this is the very gist of learning discussion. In learning groups there is no need to reach accord on values, beliefs, or courses of action. What is sought is a fuller understanding, a wider grasp of information pertinent to a topic, or consideration of a problem from as many points of view as possible. With no need to reach consensus and solution, a pattern of group interaction different from that of problem-solving groups is often needed.

From years of observing learning groups as a researcher, leading various kinds of learning groups, conducting training programs for teachers and study-discussion leaders, and serving as a consultant, I have attempted to distill some principles and techniques for planning and conducting learning discussions.

In addition to classrooms, there are numerous settings in which learning discussions occur. For example, one evening during what was primarily a social gathering of four couples I enjoyed an impromptu discussion of how homes might be made more energy efficient. An engineer, a statistician, a business professor, and I spent nearly two hours sharing our knowledge and ideas about alternative ways to design, insulate, heat, and cool houses. I left with many new ideas for our "dream" house. When members of an informal social gathering discover a common interest, rambling conversation can turn into a deeply satisfying learning exchange.

In recent years much attention has been given to classroom discussion as a means of learning through the sharing of knowledge, beliefs, and feelings. Many schools, colleges, and universities conduct in-service training to help their faculty members learn to lead classroom discussions. In continuing education outside the traditional collegiate structure much learning goes on in discussion groups sponsored by universities, libraries, churches, and other organizations. Encounter and other experiential growth groups can be found in most communities. In these groups members explore new ways of relating and communicating, and how to cope with personal problems. Highly specialized experiential groups exist to help participants cope with problems of alcohol, drugs, weight, and mental health.

Why this great expansion of learning through discussion? For one thing, we have come to view learning as much more than the acquisition of factual information and skills. *Learning* has come to mean any *change* that comes about in a person due to experience, and *education* as the structuring of situations in which change will be facilitated. Learning objectives have been organized and classified into three types: (1) *cognitive* or intellectual, ranging from recognition and recall of specific information to abilities in combining and creating; (2) *affective,* having to do with values and feelings; and (3) *psychomotor,* which are primarily about physical skills. Extensive research has shown that active participation in discussion groups is often more productive of higher mental skills and changes of beliefs and values than is any type of lecture, video, or individualized instruction format.[1] The older person, "largely committed to what he is and what he does" and with extensive experience, needs the opportunity to ". . . *think about what he already knows,"* which the ". . . informal study-discussion process attempts to give him."[2]

Many studies have shown that cooperative group interaction is superior to competitive learning structures for increasing acceptance of people of different types, provided the discussion is not a one-shot affair.[3] That educational innovations such as individualized instruction, computer-assisted instruction, nongraded and open classrooms, team teaching, and "new" math are not helpful if the quality of interaction in the classroom is not given proper consideration was demonstrated by Hunter. The cooperative relationship established in a discussion *group* approach to learning may be essential if many learning objectives are to be achieved.[4] The following quotation from Johnson and Johnson summarizes well the need for cooperative interstudent relationships:

Beyond all doubt, cooperation should be the most frequently used goal structure. The conditions under which it is effective and desirable are almost too many to list. Whenever problem solving is desired, whenever divergent thinking or creativity is desired, whenever quality of performance is expected, whenever the task is complex, when the learning goals are highly important, and when the social development of students is one of the major instructional goals, cooperation should be used. When a teacher wishes to promote positive interaction among students, a facilitative learning climate, a wide range of cognitive and affective outcomes, and positive relations between himself and the students, cooperative goal structures will be used.[5]

Guidelines for Leading Private Learning Discussions

Based on the preceding brief summary of research and philosophy of learning through discussion at all levels of education, some guidelines can be formulated for setting up cooperative learning discussions.

1. *Always establish a cooperative group goal.* The outcome to be achieved should always be presented as a *sharing* of individual knowledge and thinking, never as competing for status by giving "correct" answers. Members should be encouraged to listen to understand, to help each other, and to consider each other as partners rather than as competitors in learning.

2. *Give rewards to the group, not to individual members.* This means that praise for good work is directed to the group, not to individuals. Such comments as "I thought we had a very interesting discussion," "I got a lot from all of you," or "That was a really fine discussion" are group oriented, and stress the cooperative relationship.

3. *Keep the focus on common experience.* Effective learning discussion grows out of a common body of experiences. All participants should be reading the same articles or books, looking at the same painting or movie, observing the same group of children, or studying the same problem. Meaningful, enlightening discussions evolve from differing perceptions of such phenomena, supplemented by events or data experienced by one or a few group members. A secret of productive learning discussion is to focus on what has been observed by all discussants. Members of study-discussion groups are more satisfied when discussion is kept relevant to assigned readings than when it rambles to peripheral topics.[6]

4. *Limit the number of issues or topics.* Greater learning and more satisfaction are found in groups where the average number of distinguishable topics per two-hour session is less than eleven than in groups where the average is more than fourteen per meeting.[7] Jumping rapidly from topic to topic should be avoided. Except with younger children, it is unwise to plan to discuss more than three or four basic issues per hour. Of course several subquestions might be discussed under each of these broader issues.

5. *Plan a variety of open-ended questions.* Open-ended questions encourage a variety of answers from different points of view. The contrast between closed or specific-answer questions and open-ended questions is indicated by the following pairs in which the open-ended question occurs first.

   O—Are there any types of acts now classified as crimes that we think should be decriminalized?

   C—What acts does the chief of police say should be decriminalized?

O—What does the fifth stanza mean to you?

C—What did the poet mean by the fifth stanza?

O—How safe do current nuclear generating plants appear to be?

C—What did the Diablo Canyon power plant cost?

O—What good is membership in the U.N. to the United States?

C—What did the United States pay into the U.N. last year?

This is not to say that no questions asking for specific items of information should be asked, but they should be used to garner evidence and as follow-up questions to the broad issues of the discussion. Memory questions may bring out needed facts, but the answer itself is not discussable if accepted as correct by the group.

Numerous classifications of types of general questions have been developed. This list of types below may help you in planning questions to stimulate and facilitate learning discussion.

Translation—asking the discussants to change information or statements into their own language. Examples: "How else might we say that?" "What does _____ mean to you?"

Interpretation—the question asks the respondent to determine relationships among facts, generalizations, values, and so on. Discussants are challenged to give meaning to a body of information by such questions. Examples. "How serious is the problem of alienation among students at _____ ?" "Why might the settlers have slaughtered the buffalo?" "What might have motivated Luther to defy the Church?"

Analysis—the group is called on to divide an issue or problem into major components or contributing causes. Examples: "What factors determine the total amount of money you earn on a savings account?" "What other things may have contributed to the rate of illiteracy in the United States?" "When do you most enjoy discussing?"

Value—the respondents are asked to make statements of evaluation, judgment of degree of goodness, rightness, or appropriateness. Examples: "What is the best way to respond if someone calls you a honky or nigger?" "Is it ever right to pollute the air?" "Is capital punishment justifiable as a deterrent to murder?"

Prediction—the discussants are called on to use information in predicting some future trend or condition. Examples: "What energy sources do you think we will be using to heat our houses twenty years from now?" "What do you think will happen to Willy if he doesn't change his behavior?"

Synthesis or *problem solving*—discussants are asked to engage in creative thinking that incorporates information, analysis, prediction, and values in arriving at a conclusion. Examples" "What should you do if you discover a close friend has been shoplifting?" "What should we do to reduce drunken driving?"

6. *Be guided by the nature of the subject.* The pattern for a learning discussion is usually inherent in the subject of discussion and the group purpose in discussing it. Thus if a group desired to understand and appreciate poetry, the pattern would emerge from that purpose and the poem. A group discussing a film might well discuss such characteristics as the truthfulness of the theme, the acting, the staging, the photography, and its enjoyment of the film. A group seeking to understand differences in conceptions of God might discuss Catholic beliefs, various Protestant beliefs, and Jewish beliefs. Or, members might compare each major religion by focusing on images of God, beliefs concerning divine purpose, and the individual's relation to God. A group seeking to understand the problems of securing open and fair housing for all citizens might use a problem-solving outline (even though the discussants would not necessarily seek a solution).

7. *Focus on how the subject relates to interests of the members of the group.* To do otherwise, of course, is not to have a *group* goal but an autocratically determined one. One procedure useful for organizing learning discussion of materials previously examined by all members of a group is to poll the group for questions each wants to explore, writing them all on a board or piece of large paper where all can see. Each person can then vote for 3–5 topics of greatest interest. These questions are then discussed in the order of most to least interest (votes).

It is especially important to plan questions relating a topical discussion to personal concerns and experiences of members of a discussion group. For example, compare the following two sets of questions for guiding a discussion of reactions to Arthur Miller's *Death of a Salesman.* The first set is all too typical of what teachers do to turn students off: ask questions reflecting the interests of the teacher, closed questions, and those that have no connection to the personal lives of the students. The second set encourages the student discussants to relate the play to their personal lives.

1. What method of character introduction is used?
2. Which point of view does the author use?
3. What are some figures of speech used by Miller?

versus

1. Does anything seem unhealthy about Willy's inability to face reality?
2. Do we think it was wrong for Biff to quit trying after he surprised Willy in the hotel in Boston? Why?

3. What should we do when someone else fails us, like a teacher we don't like?
4. What does Miller seem to think of the American business world?
5. Should an employee ever take second place to the good of the company?

8. *Don't confuse pseudodiscussion with a cooperative learning discussion.* In a pseudodiscussion the leader has already arrived at an interpretation, value, or solution. Many so-called learning discussion leaders have employed the *form* of discussion, but have used it to disguise lecturing or persuading. The purpose of a learning discussion should never be "to find *the* meaning," "to discover (bring out) the correct interpretation," "to determine the author's meaning," or "find the right way to . . .." If that sort of output is what you have in mind, instead of having a group of people explore and share their differing perceptions, interpretations, and evaluations, *be honest*—present yourself in the role of one who has the answers, a lecturer or persuader instead of discussion leader. If you think a poem has one correct interpretation, that a painting has one meaning and is good or bad, you are not likely to facilitate a group exploration but to steer the group toward your preconceptions. If you do want to promote one interpretation or position, say so. Lecture. Play the dominating teacher role, but do so honestly, not under the guise of facilitator of group discussion. In a discussion approach to learning, each person in the group has perceptions, feelings, interpretations, and ideas about the shared subject matter which should be expressed, understood by other members, elaborated, and perhaps evaluated by the group.

Organizing Learning Discussions

Sometimes there should be no attempt to organize a learning discussion such as an affective discussion or an encounter session. But discussions for many classes and study-discussion groups should be organized, with a designated leader being responsible for developing a set of questions that can be raised to focus and give some order to the group interaction. Many of the same logical patterns used to organize informative public speeches can be applied to discussions.

Topical or Major Issues

This is a common pattern for learning discussions. The group discusses a set of topics or issues, each of which can be phrased as a question. These should be the basic issues that must be understood for members to gain an overall view of the subject matter under study, and to share their differing reactions to it. While a designated leader should prepare a set of questions and subquestions to guide exploration of the major issues, the leader should never insist that the group discuss all of or only the leader's questions. The group must decide what issues will be discussed; the leader can suggest the issues and ask if the discussants want to omit any of them or add others.

Three examples will be presented to show this pattern of organization. The first is from a group that was discussing motion pictures. After seeing each film they used the following outline:

    I. What was the reaction to the theme of the picture?
   II. How good was the acting?
  III. How well was the picture staged and costumed?
  IV. How effective were lighting and photography?
   V. Would we recommend this picture to our friends?

Following a viewing of the movie *The Poseidon Adventure,* a class was divided into small groups for discussion of the following topical outline:

    I. How did Scott establish himself as leader of the group that escaped?
  II. What role did each person play in the group that contributed to their successful escape?
  III. How were these roles established by member and group?
  IV. How does this movie relate to leadership in our class?

Comparison

A *comparative* pattern might be used to compare two or more policies, objectives, organizations, and so forth. The group might begin by discussing criteria and goals, or with the first of the topics to be compared. For example, a group of students could discuss the merits of various teaching-learning approaches they have experienced while using the following outline:

    I. What are the advantages and disadvantages of lecturing?
  II. What are the advantages and disadvantages of discussions?
  III. What are the advantages and disadvantages of seminar or tutorial methods?
  IV. What are the advantages and disadvantages of programmed instruction?

Other Sequences. Other logical sequences can be employed for arranging major questions raised during learning discussions. A leader might propose a chronological sequence of questions for discussing a historical trend or sequence of eras (e.g., being a woman in colonial days, in the early history of the United States, from the Civil War to 1960, and since the recent feminist movement began). A causal sequence might be followed for discussing possible future effects of new technologies which may have contributed to some present conditions. Any logical sequence with which discussants are familiar could be used to structure a discussion, provided it fits the subject matter naturally.

Discussion of a Work of Art

Many learning groups, both in and out of the classroom, have found enlightenment and pleasure in discussing such works of art as poetry, paintings, short stories, pieces of sculpture, or architecture. This format has proven to be helpful in countless discussions: (1) the group examines the work of art together; (2) the group discusses what they perceive in the work of art and what it means to them; (3) the group again examines the work of art. Relatively little time will be spent discussing the artist, the artist's motives, or the artist's life. If artistic techniques are considered, they are left until near the end of the discussion.

Literature. The following set of questions can be used to guide discussion of a poem. With appropriate modifications, a similar sequence of questions could be used to organize discussion of any other art form. With any specific work of art, some questions may be fruitless or meaningless, and others may be needed to open up other avenues of perception and interpretation. Previous beliefs of members about how one *ought* to react to a poem or other work should not be allowed to block discussion.

Introduction: A member of the group reads the poem aloud.

I. What situation occurs in the poem?
   A. What is actually taking place? What do you see in the poem?
   B. What other actions are described by the persons in the poem?
II. How does the speaker in the poem feel about the situation he or she is discussing?
   A. At the beginning of the poem?
   B. In the middle?
   C. At the end?
   D. What is the nature and direction of the change of his or her feelings?
III. What kind of person does the speaker appear to be in the poem?
   A. What kind of person would feel like this?
   B. What kind of person would change in this way (or remain unchanged)?
IV. What broad generalizations underlie the poem?
   A. What ideas does the poet assume to be true?
   B. Does he or she arrive at any insights, answers, or solutions?
   C. How do we feel about these generalizations?

Conclusion: A group member reads the poem aloud.

Some of the questions in the general outline above may not fit a particular poem. You must plan questions for the specific poem, depending on what it is about, how it is written, the reactions it evokes in you, and so on. This adaptation is illustrated in the following poem and outline for a discussion of it by a group of college students.

Invictus
William Ernest Henley

Out of the night that covers me,
  Black as the Pit from pole to pole,
I thank whatever gods may be
  For my unconquerable soul.

In the fell clutch of circumstance
  I have not winced nor cried aloud.
Under the bludgeonings of chance
  My head is bloody, but unbowed.

Beyond this place of wrath and tears
  Looms but the Horror of the shade,
And yet the menace of the years
  Finds, and shall find, me unafraid.

It matters not how strait the gate,
  How charged with punishments the scroll,
I am the master of my fate;
  I am the captain of my soul.

  I. What do you think this poem is about?
    A. What might *night* refer to in the first line?
    B. The black pit?
  II. What sort of person does the speaker appear to be to you?
    A. What does the second stanza tell you about the speaker?
    B. What do you think is his attitude toward dying?
    C. What do you understand about the speaker's view of life and afterlife?
    D. How do you interpret the last two lines?
 III. What beliefs or assumptions underlie the poem?
    A. What does the poet assume to be true?
    B. How do we feel about these beliefs?
 IV. Do you like this poem? Why?

A group might follow a similar outline for discussion of almost any literary work, such as a short story, essay, or even a novel or play.

Visual Objects. An outline of questions for discussing a visual object such as a painting, sculpture, clothing, building, or photograph should focus on various characteristics of features of the object, not the whole. The discussants are led to shift the visual focus in this way, and to describe what they see from each new perspective, such as shape, color, line, texture, area, and so on. As part of her work in one of my classes, a student prepared the next outline to lead discussion of an abstract painting.

Introduction: A painting is hung in front of the group seated in a semi-circle, and the group is asked to examine it silently.

 I. What different elements do you see?
   A. What do you notice about the texture?
   B. What colors do you notice?
   C. What do you notice about the shapes?
   D. Do you observe anything in the lines?
 II. Overall, combining the different elements, what do you perceive?
   A. Does it seem to portray any specific object, idea, or event?
   B. Do your personal experiences or ideas affect your perceptions in any way?
 III. What feelings do you experience from looking at the picture?
   A. What emotions does it arouse?
   B. Does it move you to want to take any action?
   C. What seems to be evoking your reaction or arousal?
 IV. What does the painting seem to say to you?
   A. Does it have any specific message or theme for you?
   B. What might be the purpose of this painting? Strictly aesthetic?
 V. How do you evaluate the painting?
   A. Do you think the artist said what he wanted to say?
   B. Do you feel it was worth saying?
   C. How did the artist achieve this, or what prevented him from achieving it?
   D. Has the painting or our discussion of it revealed anything new or important to you?
   E. Does it have any universality or significance?[8]

Learning Discussions of Case Problems

A group of persons wanting to explore possible ways to cope with some type of problem they may encounter as individuals could structure a discussion around the General Procedural Model for Problem Solving, without needing to come to any decisions or solution as a group. The desired output is for each member to achieve a better understanding of what is involved and to have more options when encountering a problem similar to that discussed. If the members are quite heterogeneous in backgrounds and values, more learning by each is possible than if they all are likely to perceive and handle the problem in the same way.

Often learning discussion is desultory when concerned with a vague, non-specific, general problem such as "What should you do if someone threatens your life?" Rather than begin with such a general question, the leader can usually evoke more interest and involvement by presenting the group with a specific case problem. First, the case problem is discussed as if the group were actually trying to solve it, and then members of the group are invited to generalize from the specific case to similar situations they have faced or may encounter in the future. The following two cases illustrate the type of problem presentation which can be used to stimulate learning discussion following a problem-solving procedure.

The Teacher's Dilemma

An English teacher in a consolidated, rural high school has had extensive dramatic experience, and as a result was chosen by the principal to direct the first play in the new school. The play will be the first major production for the school. Its success may determine whether or not there will be future plays produced at the school, and if well done can bring prestige to both the teacher and the school. As a result, the teacher (a friend of mine) is exhausting every means available to her to make the play an artistic success. She has chosen the cast except for the leading female part. The principal's daughter wants the part, and the principal told the teacher he really wants his daughter to have it. But—she is a poor actress, and would jeopardize the success of the show. Tentatively, the teacher has chosen someone who should do an excellent job in the role, but the principal has implied that if his daughter is not selected, he will appoint another director in the future.

What should I tell my English teacher friend to do?

The Grade Inflation Case

In recent years, a pervasive problem has arisen on many American college and university campuses—grade inflation. Cumulative final averages have never been so high. This problem has hit home at Robert Burns University. Recently, employers who interview graduates have complained to the chancellor, voicing strong objections to grading policies. They claim that it is now impossible to use a student applicant's grades as a basis for comparison with other applicants and for predicting what sort of employee a student might make. Corporate representatives say that almost all students have "above average" grades, and 60 percent have at least a 3.1 average.

A preliminary check of records revealed some eye-opening statistics. In 1962 the average SAT score of freshmen was 1148 and the average final cumulative grade was 2.3 for those students when they graduated. In 1980, the average SAT score of freshmen was 997, but the average final GPA was 3.2 when those students graduated. Prior to 1967 the SAT served as a dependable predictor of a student's academic accomplishments, but it no longer does so.

A survey of teaching practices at Robert Burns University revealed that most professors curve grades on at least half of their assignments in order to raise the class average. Professors say they are reluctant to give below a C grade because low grades are damaging to students' self-concepts and to their chances for employment in desirable jobs. Many said they are reluctant to grade below B.

College textbook publishers report that they are editing for a tenth-grade reading level, because the higher levels at which they used to edit are too difficult for the majority of today's beginning college students. Some publishers say they must edit freshman texts at even lower reading-difficulty levels, or the books are not adopted.

The provost of Robert Burns U. has charged you, as a committee of concerned students from the student senate, to consider whether grade inflation is a serious problem at RBU. If you find that it is, he has asked you to recommend a new grading policy to combat the problem, and to suggest how to implement the policy and make it effective in restoring grades to their former usefulness and credibility.

Techniques for Learning Groups Concerned with Feelings and Interpersonal Relations

The literature of learning discussion contains many special formats, some of which have very limited usefulness. Some are for small children, some for married couples, some for homosexuals, and some for members of a particular church. The two techniques presented here are adaptable to a wide range of situations and types of groups.

Affective Discussion, a term coined by Epstein, was developed to help school children ventilate their feelings, but the technique can be adapted to any learning group at any age level where fears, suspicions, prejudices, and other negative feelings interfere with productive thinking, communicating, and relating to other persons.[9] The purpose of an affective discussion is to help persons express and explore strong feelings (usually negative and based on myths) which interfere with their ability to make objective, rational responses to factual information, mathematics, public speaking, ideas, food habits, cultural practices, or people different from themselves. The group should usually consist of from six to ten persons seated in a tight circle. In a traditional classroom a teacher can seat part of the class in front or back of the room while the other students work at their seats. A college class can be divided into small groups, instructed in the procedure, and each group then allowed to work with one person acting as facilitator to enforce the procedural rules, while the instructor moves from group to group as consultant and observer. I have used this technique very effectively with graduate students in a research methods class before entering the study of statistics or thesis writing, and with beginning public speaking students who have unusually high levels of communication apprehension. The outputs have invariably pleased both me and my students. Affective discussion is also excellent for dealing with racial prejudices, or fears of any new venture.

An affective discussion begins with the beliefs (assumptions) that all persons have feelings and that any feeling is "okay" to have. The technique is based on the assumption that we need to express our feelings without apology and have them accepted without criticism in order for adequate intra- and interpersonal communication to occur.

When conducting an affective discussion the designated leader plays little part except to facilitate expression and empathic listening. Here are some of the types of responses a leader should avoid because they are likely to arouse defensiveness:

That's right.

That's wrong.

Don't you mean . . .?

That's not a nice thing to say.

Gasp.

Look it up in your textbook.

We shouldn't use such language here.

I know you didn't mean that.

The facts are that . . ..

Don't say such things unless you really know.

Comments such as the following may help to facilitate open and honest expression of feelings and values:

What do *you* think?

How do you feel about that?

Let him finish his thought.

It's all right to say what you feel.

I don't know.

I won't answer questions during this discussion.

It's not a matter of right or wrong, but what you feel.

I hope these examples have helped you to understand the nonevaluative, totally accepting responses needed from the leader of an affective discussion. Present the opening question, then *listen,* perhaps making an occasional facilitative comment showing understanding and acceptance, but *no* evaluation, critical arguing or disagreement, weighing, or questioning of any kind. Here the leader is for once advised to be *laissez-faire.* In the classroom this is learner-learner interaction; the teacher is largely an outsider to the affective discussion.

Questions can be on any issue about which group members have shown strong feelings. These issues might come from the problem census, inability to come to consensus on a problem, fantasy chains, or issues raised in a textbook. For example, in a course on small group communication an affective discussion might be generated from such questions as: "How do we feel about members of project groups who are undependable?" or "How do we feel about autocratic leaders?" A lively interchange is likely on any questions involving a subject on which students talk a lot:

"How do we feel about parking penalties on campus?"

"How do we feel about interracial dating?"

"How do we feel about being graded?

Encounter discussion can be a means to personal growth and improving interpersonal relations for the participants. "Encounter" means that members of the learning group explore their reactions to each other, describing openly and honestly what they feel. If done in an honest and caring way, such descriptions by other members of a group of how they are responding to you can be a means for gaining self-insight and self-acceptance. A high degree of interpersonal trust is essential if encounter discussion is to be productive.

Encounter can greatly expand the area of free communication among group members. When a person reveals private information about self he or she previously kept hidden from others, that person will have energy freed up for constructive work. As some of the mask is slipped aside, others can better understand him as he sees himself. If they accept him and find some identification with his feelings, fears and needs, he is likely to achieve a higher level of self-acceptance and constructive assertiveness. He is also free, if he chooses, to adjust his behavior in order to achieve different responses from others. In a full encounter, nothing of import is left hidden—members reactions to each other are shared as fully as possible. Such encounter discussion should be held only in the presence of a trained and experienced facilitator.

Certain types of limited interpersonal feedback and interpersonal encounter can be used by any group studying small group discussion or enrolled in a speech communication, social psychology, group dynamics, or other course concerned with discussion and small group communication. In this context, *feedback* is defined as information given to a person by another (or others) about how the other has perceived and been affected by him or her. This permits the recipient of feedback to compare the responses of others with the responses expected. Feedback lets you compare your self-image with the image others hold of you; others may see you very differently from how you see yourself. Like a mirror, feedback lets one see how he or she is judged on such dimensions as active-passive, agreeable-disagreeable, dependent-independent, warm-cold, and helpful-harmful. You may think of yourself as warm and friendly, but discover that others feel you are cold and aloof, or everyone may perceive you differently. Since self-images are based on what we *think* others think of us, such feedback can modify your self-concept, perhaps increasing your confidence, reducing dogmatism, and so forth. If so, you are more likely to disclose your feelings and responses, making possible still greater openness and trust among the members of your group.

In feedback sessions among members of a class in group discussion or a working group, comments should be limited to what happens among members of the group while it is in session, excluding talking about other situations members have been in, topical issues, or theorizing—a "here and now" focus, excluding talking about "then and there." Participants should state their remarks as *their personal* reactions and feelings, describing how they feel or felt and what they were reacting to. They should avoid any name calling, theorizing about why someone acted as he or she did, accusing, or telling another how he or she should behave.

Any extensive period of feedback or encounter in interpersonal relations should be conducted in the presence of your instructor or some experienced group trainer. If no experienced trainer is available, you can still benefit from limited interpersonal feedback. Many variations are possible. The important thing is for each member of the group to be free to invite or not to invite the reactions of others. Comments should be limited to what has happened in the class.

The following guidelines should make a feedback discussion helpful to the discussants:

1. *Describe rather than pass judgment.* No one should feel condemned as a person. A description of one's own reactions and feelings leaves the receiver of feedback free to react as he or she sees fit. Avoiding the use of evaluative, emotive, or stigma terms reduces the need for the recipient to react defensively. For example, rather than saying, "You were nasty," one might say, "I felt myself growing very angry when you . . .." And don't forget to express positive feelings that are sincere.

2. *Be as specific as possible.* To be told he or she is dominating may do a discussant more harm than good. Rather, the recipient should be told what was perceived as an attempt to dominate. Give details, describing what was done and your reactions to it. For example, "When we were talking about how to proceed, I thought you refused to consider anyone else's ideas, so I felt forced to accept your suggestions, face an attack from you, or leave the group."

3. *Consider the needs of the receiver.* What can the receiver hear, accept, and handle at this time? A lambasting to relieve your own tension may do much harm if the needs of the receiver are not sensed and responded to. Usually you should balance negative reactions with any favorable ones you may have.

4. *Deal only with behavior the receiver can change.* For example, you would not tell a stutterer that such hesitations annoy you, or a person with a tic in his cheek that it drove you nuts! However, you might let him know that you feel he has been sulking and you don't like it when he withdraws after his suggestion has been turned down.

5. *Don't force feedback on another.* Let the recipient invite comments (unless you respond immediately after something is said or done). If she indicates she wants to hear no more, stop. She is not likely to accept what you say anyway.

6. *Check to see if your feedback is understood.* Did the receiver understand what you mean? Watch for reactions, perhaps asking him or her to restate your point.

7. *See if the others agree with you.* You may find that other participants do not respond as you did to a particular participant. Questions like,

"How do the rest of you feel about that?" should be asked often. When no one else agrees, try to find out why!

8. *Expect slow moments.* At times there will be a lot of hesitation and fumbling. A group may be very hesitant to express its feelings openly. It may take a long time for frank feedback to develop.

Feedback can be especially useful after discussion of a problem directly involving the group, such as, "What should be the date and type of our final exam?" or "By what policy should this class be graded?" Feedback can be helpful between friends and within families, sometimes under the heading of a gripe session. Indeed, no close interpersonal relationship can develop without interchange of this sort.

Public Learning Discussions

All public discussion is conducted for the learning of an audience, not primarily for the learning of the discussants in a small group. Thus all public discussion involves public speaking, no matter what format is employed or whether the audience is physically present for a panel presentation or viewing a telecast of it. When a small group of persons discuss for the benefit of an audience, special planning, organization, and procedures must be done for the benefit of all involved. Precise timing is essential when broadcasting and highly advisable for any public presentation. The cycling, restating, and socializing of a private discussion could bore or confuse an audience. Panel discussions must combine elements of spontaneity with planned performance.

The purpose of a public discussion is usually determined by the program committee of some organization, the producer of a broadcasting station, or a group before whom the presentation will be made. A special designated leader called a *moderator* needs to be appointed. To plan and organize the discussion, the moderator would contact the participants and ask each to agree to be a part of the program, telling each the general topic or issue, the purpose of the discussion, the reasons he or she was selected as a participant, who the other participants will be, and who is likely to compose the audience.

Participants in a public discussion should be selected on criteria of expertise, fluency, and diversity. They should be experts on the topic or knowledgeable representatives of special points of view, and able to state their information clearly and concisely. An audience will benefit little from ignorant, misinformed, or incoherent discussants!

A variety of types of public discussion have been developed, but two types are used most frequently: panel and forum.

Panel Discussion

As you will recall, a panel discussion involves a group of specialists interacting informally in front of and for the benefit of an audience. A panel group should

Figure 12.1   A panel discussion is a form of public speaking.

represent a variety of points of view, types of experience, or sides of a major issue. For example, if you were to have a televised panel discussion on how to reduce traffic congestion and air pollution in a city, yet improve transportation, you might want such persons as the following: (1) a city planner who had investigated rapid transit systems; (2) an air pollution control expert; (3) a highway engineer; (4) an urban businessman; and (5) an automotive designer. For a panel on the pros and cons of hunting as recreation before a conservation class you might have: (1) an antihunting lobbyist; (2) a professional game biologist; (3) an articulate sport hunter; and (4) a spokesperson for the National Wildlife Federation. For a panel on opportunities for women in management, you might want to have three or four executive women from different government agencies and corporations.

Public discussions call for special physical arrangements. When staging a public discussion for a live audience, it is important that all discussants be in view of each other and of the audience at all times. Only with this arrangement can a sense of direct interaction occur. To accomplish this, seat the discussants in a semicircle, with the moderator either at one end of the group or at the center. The audience members then face the panelists, and the panelists can alternately establish eye contact both with each other and with members of the audience. When not speaking, most of the time panel members should be looking at and listening to the speaker of the moment.

Panelists should be seated behind a table, preferably with some sort of cover on the front of it. Two small tables in an open V make an excellent arrangement.

A large name card should be placed on the table in front of each panelist. If the room is large and microphones are needed, they should be in sufficient number and so placed that the panelists can largely ignore them. Neck microphones can be used. If a chalkboard or easel is available, display the topic or question being discussed; sometimes the major issues or questions can also be listed. Such visual devices help auditors keep the discussion organized and clear in their minds.

In a very large assembly it may be necessary to have floor microphones for a forum discussion. If so, these should be strategically placed and their use clearly explained to the audience before the forum begins. If not essential, do not use them. They will inhibit some persons, and can lead to much confusion and delay.

The outline for a panel discussion could follow a problem-solving pattern or one of the enlightenment patterns suggested earlier. The moderator should ask each participant in the forthcoming panel to suggest questions for the discussion, then use these in preparing the leader's outline of three to five major questions, each with appropriate follow-up questions or subquestions. This rough draft outline should be sent to each of the participants so that they have a chance to investigate and think of possible answers to each question.

The moderator prepares a special outline with an introduction, the pattern of questions to be raised, and a planned conclusion format. Of course, physical arrangements need to be made by the moderator also, including name cards, possibly a poster with the overall topic or question, seating arrangements, etc. During the panel presentation the moderator asks questions of the group and sees that all panelists have equal opportunity to speak, then clarifies ambiguous remarks or asks panel members to do so. The moderator should encourage participants to react directly and courteously to each other's comments. But the moderator does not participate in the substance of the discussion; rather, moderating means coordinating the discussion by the other group members for the benefit of the listeners. It is also the moderator's job to see that the panel is kept organized when underway, summarizing each major topic or having the participants do so, and keeping it moving so that time is well distributed among the major topics on the outline and among the participants. A moderator's outline might look like this:

Introduction

"What should be the law in the U.S. governing abortions?"

I. "Ladies and gentlemen (to audience), the question of what the law should be governing abortions in the U.S. has been a subject of heated argument, physical confrontation, intensive lobbying, court cases, sermons, and pamphlets—and far too little calm, thoughtful discussion.

II. Today we are fortunate to have a panel of thoughtful experts on this subject representing all major points of view.
  A. Father Jon McClarety has made an intensive study of the Catholic theology and arguments underlying the church's stand against legalizing abortions. He is a member of the Department of Philosophy and Theology of Holy Name Academy.
  B. Robert Byron is an attorney for the Legal Aid Society who has served his society in appeals to the Supreme Court which led to the current legal status of abortions.
  C. Dr. Robert Splando is a specialist in obstetrics and gynecology, and has performed hundreds of therapeutic abortions.
  D. Ms. Dorothy Mankewicz, a social worker and volunteer lecturer for "Zero Population Growth," has assisted many women who wanted abortions.
  E. Professor Maha Kazakrim is historian of ethical and social values at Western State University, and author of two books dealing with the abortion law controversy.
III. Our panelists have agreed to discuss four specific issues which are part of the question you see on the poster before you, "What should be the law in the U.S. governing abortions?"
  A. When does a human life begin?
  B. Who has the right to decide whether or not a woman should be allowed to have an abortion?
  C. What would be the effects of greater restrictions on the right of choice to have an abortion?
  D. Under what conditions, if any, should abortions be legal?
IV. Each panelist will give a brief statement of his or her position on each issue and the reasoning behind it, then the panelists will question and debate their positions informally. After fifty minutes the floor will be opened for questions from you, our listening audience. While the discussion is proceeding, you may want to jot down questions as they occur to you so you can remember them for the forum period."

Body of the Discussion

  I. "When does a human life begin?"
    A. Dr. Splando: _____ .
    B. Father McClarety: _____ .
    C. Ms. Mankewicz: _____ .
      etc.

(All four issues are discussed, with the moderator summarizing, seeing that each panelist gets an opportunity to present a position on each issue and question, support, or argue with the others, and moving the group to the next major question at a pre-arranged time.)

Conclusion

I. "Let's see if we can summarize what we have learned about each other's positions. I'd like each of you to summarize in a minute or less your position and arguments." (Often the moderator does the summing up, with panelists being free to correct or supplement.)

II. "I believe all of us in this room are now better prepared to cope with this vital issue. We now understand each other's positions as well as possible, and the values and beliefs supporting them."

III. "Now I wonder what questions our listeners have for the panel? Please raise your hand if you want to ask a question, and wait for me to recognize you by pointing. I will give each person the floor one time before allowing anyone to ask a second question. Your questions can be directed to a particular panelist, or to the entire group. If you want a particular panel member to answer, state the name of that person. Okay, what's our first question? The lady to my right wearing the maroon blazer—please state your question loudly enough for all present to hear it."

Forum

A forum discussion is often conducted following a speech, panel discussion, educational film, public interview, or symposium. To have a satisfactory forum discussion requires strict procedural control by a moderator who understands the purpose of the forum and has mastered techniques for keeping the discussion interesting and fair to all persons involved. A chairperson or moderator should control the forum following a speech, film, or other presentation; the moderator of a panel, symposium, or public interview also moderates any forum following such a group presentation. Follow these guidelines:

1. During the introduction to the panel (or other program) announce that there will be a forum or question and answer period. This allows listeners to be thinking of questions and remarks.

2. State whether only questions or both questions and comments will be permitted.

3. Just before allowing the audience to participate, announce definite rules to assure equal opportunity for all to speak, and insist that they be followed:
    a. Raise your hand and wait to be recognized before speaking;
    b. No one may speak a second time until each person who wants to speak has had the floor at least once;
    c. Comments or questions should be addressed to either a specific panelist by name or to the entire panel;
    d. Remarks must be limited to not more than _____ seconds;
    e. Speak loudly enough to be heard by everyone (or, go to the floor microphone, if one is available).

4. Tell the audience if there will be a definite length of time for the forum; then end it when scheduled.
5. If the audience is large, recognize persons from various parts of the room in a systematic pattern.
6. Encourage different points of view by asking for them: "Does anyone want to present a *different* point of view from that which we have just heard?"
7. If a questioner cannot be heard by all, restate the question clearly and concisely.
8. If a question is unclear, or lengthy, restate it to the originator's satisfaction.
9. When the alloted time is nearly up, state that there is just enough time for one or two more questions (or comments).
10. If no one seeks the floor, wait a few seconds, then thank the panel and audience for their participation and either dismiss the meeting or go on to the next item on the agenda.

Techniques for Groups within Organizations

There are a large number of special discussion techniques for getting small group involvement into a large group meeting, for facilitating communication within small groups that are part of large organizations, and for increasing "up the line" communication in participatory management. Those selected for inclusion in this chapter are all group centered and discussional in nature, and can be of value in a variety of organizational contexts. Any of these techniques or procedures should be explained carefully by the coordinator of a meeting before it is first tried. Often a sheet of instructions is handed to participants in order to explain the purpose and rules of the procedure to be used.

Buzz Groups (Phillips 66)

This procedure is used to organize a large group meeting into many small groups that work concurrently on the same question. The purpose may be to get questions for a speaker or panel, to identify problems or issues, to compile a list of ideas or possible solutions, to develop a list of techniques for implementing and adapting a general solution to local conditions, to get personal involvement and thinking by members of a large class, etc. For example, I was a participant in a workshop of about 500 local education leaders in Kentucky who met to understand and work out techniques for promoting a "minimum foundation program" for public education in that state. Needed was a favorable vote of taxpayers in a special statewide election that would mean state tax support for local schools based on need. This would mean higher taxes overall and a flow of money from the wealthier districts to the poorer. Several times the entire group used the Phillips 66 technique to identify specific local problems, inexpensive advertising and promotional techniques, arguments for the program, etc.[10] These lists were processed in work groups of fifteen to eighteen members each and the final results distributed to all members. Even though the conference was large, every participant was active in discussions and the sense of enthusiasm and involvement was truly remarkable. The procedure:

1. The chairman presents a "target" question to the entire assembly, which may be seated in rows in an auditorium or at small tables. This question should be very concise, limited, and specific. For example:
    "What techniques could be used to publicize the MFP to citizens of each county or city?"
    "What topics or issues should be dealt with in the next year's convention?"
    "What new projects might local unions undertake to help members with social problems?"
    "What questions would you like to have Dr. Hanson answer about the effects of narcotics?"
    Each question should be written on a card (4″ by 6″ or 5″ by 8″) with one card for each group of six members. It is a good idea to display it also on a large poster or blackboard in front of the assembly.
2. Divide the large group into work groups of six by seating them at small tables, or in an auditorium by counting off by three in each row, then having alternate rows turn to face each other as shown in figure 12.2.
3. Appoint a recorder-spokesperson for each group based on seating, as: "The person sitting in the forward left-hand seat of each group will be its recorder. The recorder should write on the card *all* ideas presented, then have the group put them in rank order." An assistant or assistants then pass out the cards.
4. Next, ask each group to record as many answers to the target question as it can think of in five minutes, then spend one minute evaluating the list to decide if any items should be eliminated and in what order to present them. Thus discussion occurs in groups of six members for six minutes—66!
5. When the five minutes are up, warn the groups and allow an extra minute if all seem involved. Then ask them to evaluate and rank the list.
6. At this point you may do any of several things, depending on the size and plan of the overall meeting.
    a. Collect the cards, which are then edited to eliminate duplications with a tally of the number of times each item was mentioned on cards. The total list is then duplicated and handed to the entire group at a subsequent meeting, presented

Figure 12.2 Buzz group seating in an auditorium.

to some special group for processing or whatever is appropriate; or

b. The chairperson asks each recorder to report orally from his seat one *new* item from his card without explanation, or say "pass" if all his items have been presented. A secretary writes all the items on a chart or chalkboard in front of the room. The list is then processed as above or according to the problem census technique described below.

c. The questions listed are presented in rotation to the speaker or panel.

This technique is also used by teachers in classes studying literature, social problems, political science, psychology, and so on. The buzz groups in a class may have more than six minutes and may even follow a brief outline prepared by the teacher. A number of reports have indicated very little or no difference in the amount of information learned from a more traditional lecture approach, and significantly more creative and critical thinking and modification of values by students involved in discussions. Many variations in the buzz group procedure are possible, limited only by the ingenuity of the chairperson or teacher.

The Problem Census

This "posting" technique is useful for building an agenda for future problem-solving meetings, for program planning by an organization, or to discover problems encountered by a group of employees or students that might not be known by a supervisor or teacher. As examples: a university department in which I was employed conducted a problem census that developed into the agenda for a series of future meetings. Different members of the faculty committed themselves to investigate the various problems and to prepare a presentation of information and an outline for each problem as it came up in turn. A group of salesmen for a feed company scattered over two states met with the sales manager to develop a list of problems and programs for a series of monthly meetings. A class in discussion developed a list of questions about how to handle various problems often encountered in committee leadership, and this became the agenda for a series of eight class meetings that included problem-solving discussions, reports, role-played demonstrations, a film, and some lectures. The graduate teaching assistants in my department frequently use this technique to prepare agendas for a series of weekly seminars.

The problem census technique involves a series of distinct steps to be followed by the supervisor or other designated leader of the group:

1. Seat the group in a semicircle facing a chart or chalkboard.
2. Explain the purpose of the technique, which is to bring out all problems, concerns, questions, or difficulties any member of the group would like to have discussed.
3. The leader then asks each participant to present one problem or question, going around the group clockwise. Anyone not ready to present a new problem says "pass" and the next person has the floor. After one complete round, anyone who said "pass" may now add his or her question or problem. The group continues to do this until all problems have been presented.
4. The leader "posts" each problem as it is presented, writing it clearly on a chart or chalkboard where all can see. Each filled chart page can be fastened to the wall with masking tape. The leader must be totally accepting of whatever is presented, never challenging its validity or disagreeing. He or she may need to ask for clarification or elaboration, but always in a way that does not challenge the concern being expressed by a member. Often the leader will need to "boil down" a long question to the core issue, but should always rephrase it and ask if that is what the speaker intended before posting the rephrased question.
5. The group now evaluates the list for priority by voting, usually with each member voting for his or her top three or four choices. But all problems are included on the agenda—this merely gives order to the list.
6. The group may now find that some of the questions can be answered or solved at once by other members to the satisfaction of the presenter. Such questions are then removed from the list, and the remaining ones are now in order for future treatment.
7. Each problem is dealt with in turn. Some may call for a factual presentation by a consultant. Others may be handled by a brief lecture or other informational technique, some by printed materials. But the core problems should be analyzed and dealt with by the entire group or a subcommittee of it, following on appropriate problem-solving procedure.

The Nominal Group Technique (NGT)

Some of the research into brainstorming showed that persons working individually in the presence of others can generate more ideas for solving problems than will the same number of persons interacting. Interacting groups deciding on a solution by consensus sometimes suppress divergence, producing a group-think outcome. As an outcome of effort to codify the research on small group problem-solving interaction, Delbecq and Van de Ven developed a procedure they call the Nominal Group Technique as an alternative to conventional problem-solving discussions.[11] They found that NGT will usually produce more alternatives and a higher quality solution than will discussion in a conventional group session. A nominal group is one in which people work in each other's presence on the same task, but they do not interact verbally. NGT alternates between interacting verbally and working silently in the presence of others. It is *not* recommended for the typical problems that come up in the operation of any organization, but only for such major problems as planning a long-range program; it is not for routine meetings.[12] Delbecq claimed that the superiority of NGT for major program planning resulted from two things: (1) when a question is asked in a group, as soon as one person starts to answer it all others stop thinking; and (2) most persons do not work hard in interactive meetings, but they will when acting individually in the presence of others.[13] As a result, he claimed that different angles, approaches, and possibilities are either overlooked or not brought up (you will recall that the prescriptive developmental outlines for problem solving were developed to offset this tendency). The NGT helps to reduce secondary tension and control conflict, and it virtually eliminates the chance for some members to make speeches to impress or represent outside constituencies rather than to help the group. On the negative side, NGT is not a complete problem-solving process. It does not enhance cohesiveness (and may reduce it), and it produces far less member satisfaction than does problem-solving discussion.[14]

The essence of NGT is for several persons (six to nine) to work individually in each other's presence by writing their ideas down on paper, then to record these ideas on a chart as a group, clarify them, and evaluate them by a ranking procedure until a decision has been reached. The procedure may be varied somewhat but should always involve members working silently, then discussion, then silent work, more discussion, and so on. Here are the steps for the leader as outlined by Delbecq:

1. State the known problem elements or characteristics of a situation that differ from what is desired. At this point there should be *no* mention of solutions, and no interaction. Members are seated at a table facing a chart easel. A large group can be divided into several small working groups, each with a leader.
2. Ask the participants to generate a list of features of the problem, considering the emotional, personal, and organizational. Then give a clear definition of the problem. (1 and 2 can be one step, with no discussion as in step 2, with leader presenting the problem and moving group at once into step 3.)

3. Allow the group five to fifteen minutes to work silently. Each person is asked to write down all ideas that he or she can think of for solving the problem.
4. In a "round robin" session the results are collected on a sheet of paper (chart) in front of the group where all can see the list.
    a. Ask each person in turn to give *one* item from his or her list. This item is recorded on the chart. No discussion is allowed at this time.
    b. Do not record who suggested the idea, or more than one idea from a person at a time;
    c. Keep going around the group until *all* ideas have been posted on the chart. Additional ideas may occur to members while this is going on; be sure they are stated and listed;
    d. If someone has the same idea as another, put a tally mark by the idea, but don't record it twice;
    e. The leader has also generated a list, and posts his or her ideas in turn just as for the other members.
5. Clarification interaction—anyone may ask another person for clarification of an idea or proposal on the list. Questions such as "What does item 6 mean?" or "Do you understand item 4?" are now in order for discussion. The leader should take the group through the list item by item, but only to clarify and elaborate, *not* to evaluate. At this point allow no lobbying, criticism, or argument for an idea.
6. Each person is now given a set of note cards, on which to write the five or so items (all should have same number of cards, one item per card) he or she most prefers. These cards are now ranked (5 being highest, and 1 being lowest rank) and collected by the leader. Sum the ranks for each item, and divide by the number of persons in the group to get a value weight for each solution.
7. Now engage in an evaluation discussion of the several items having the highest average ranks. This should be a full and free evaluative discussion, with critical thinking, disagreement, and analysis encouraged.
8. If a decision is reached, fine. If not, revote, and then discuss further. This process can be repeated several times if necessary until a clear synthesis of a few ideas or support for one idea has emerged. The end result is submitted to the appropriate planners, executive, or other group for action.

This is a "supergun" technique, to be used only for major issues. Obviously you could use variations of this technique in many discussion sessions, by having quiet periods when discussants think silently and jot down their ideas on paper to enrich the ensuing discussion.

Quality Circles

The name "Quality Circle" has been given to small groups of employees who meet at regular intervals to discuss ways in which to improve their jobs, increase their productivity, or increase the quality of what they produce. Quality circle members share their opinions with management in an attempt to solve all sorts of job-related problems.

The term "quality control circle" originated in Japan, where the technique was developed to help improve the quality of Japanese products and thus make them more successful in the competition for world markets. And successful they were! Participative management was introduced to Japanese executives after World War II by American consultants, and it fitted well into Japanese culture. "Made in Japan" has almost become a synonym for excellent workmanship, and Japanese workers have increased their productivity at a rate many times greater than that of their American counterparts.

The quality circle movement is only part of the reason for Japan's tremendous manufacturing success, but it is the part that is now being studied and applied by U.S. corporations. You may well find yourself in a job permitting you to participate in or lead a quality circle (membership is voluntary). You may be made a part of a "work effectiveness team" (every employee must belong), or a similar procedure under some different name. Among the American corporations using some version of the quality circle are Ford Motor Company, General Motors, Hewlett-Packard, Burlington Industries, Ethyl Corporation, Anchor Hocking, Control Data, Galion, Sheller-Globe, 3M, Dresser Industries, Firestone, W. R. Grace, Sony, Honda, Weyerhauser, Northrup, Smith Kline, American Airlines, and dozens of others.[15] Such nonprofit organizations as Red Cross and Boy Scouts, as well as several cities, have quality circles.

Employees enrolled in a quality circle meet with a team leader on company time to discuss production or problems of which they are aware, or to react to problems presented to them by management. Usually they meet for an hour a week, but the time varies considerably from company to company. All ideas agreed upon in the circle are submitted to management. Management must react to every suggestion, either reporting that it has been adopted, is being investigated (perhaps for cost accounting), has been adopted with modifications, had previously been suggested and adopted, or is rejected for reasons given with the reply. Many corporations reward employees with special bonuses or cash awards for ideas which enhance company profits.

For the quality circle form of consultative management to work, employees must have job security, assuring them that their ideas for increasing their efficiency will not ultimately cost them jobs or earnings. They must know that their ideas are eagerly sought and will be dealt with seriously and thoroughly. They must have a sense both of commitment to the company and of the company's commitment to them. They must truly share in the growth,

Figure 12.3   A quality circle at work.

profits, and future of the company. When employees are treated like machines which can be readily replaced, or if they have no job security other than that provided through a hard-fought union contract, quality circles are not going to work very well.

Everyone must be an integral part of the corporation, sharing in its successes and failures, if participatory management is to be more than an illusion and succeed over the long haul. A corporation in which all personnel are treated as equally important human beings, share the same parking, dining, and recreational facilities, and perhaps even dress alike, maximizes the chance that quality circles will produce the tremendous enhancement in quality and productivity of which they are capable. When they are considered one more ploy to get more production out of workers with no exchange of commitment to those workers, quality circles (by any name) are likely to be a waste of time and soon abandoned (as has already happened in several North American corporations). Pseudodiscussion creates nothing.

If you join a company that has incorporated the quality circle concept and procedures, you will be given special training for this procedure. If you are in a staff position in organizational communication or you are a part of management, you may see a way to improve your corporation by instituting participatory management, possibly in the form of quality circles. Of course you would study thoroughly what has and has not worked for companies with quality circles and go through extensive training before trying the procedure in your plants. Several helpful references are provided in the bibliography for this chapter. Quality circles could be an excellent topic for an instructional unit or panel presentation by a group from your class, or even for a term paper. Meanwhile, all that we have been considering together throughout this book about small group dynamics and leadership will stand you in good stead as an employee involved in any of the many forms of small group participation in management and production.

Electronically Mediated Meetings: Teleconferencing

The many conferences needed among representatives of departments in large corporations, among executives of large universities with several campuses, among staff members of international agencies, and for cooperative ventures among different organizations and nations are highly expensive in time and travel costs. Apart from the tremendous costs, sometimes it is almost impossible to get needed people and resources together in one place. A solution being promoted by telecommunication companies is the electronically mediated "teleconference." Interaction may involve video images of all conferees, listening to each other's spoken words, or messages printed at computer terminals. Since a computer conference is quite unlike small group discussions, I will say no more about it. In some ways the video conference is most like face-to-face meetings of small groups, but the special studio, transmission, and imaging facilities are so expensive and available in so few locations that they are used only infrequently at present. Readily available to almost everyone is the voice conference via telephone lines and satellites or microwave towers.

In recent years there have been well over 100 studies of teleconferencing, including surveys of persons who participate in them, experiments, and field studies of actual conferences.[16] Even though the future of teleconferencing is not at all clear (except that electronic meetings are certain to increase greatly in number), enough is now known to have developed practical guidelines for making electronic meetings productive.

Video conferences are limited by many factors, and likely to continue to be relatively few in number for the foreseeable future. Costs are high for the special imaging and transmission equipment required, and participants must go to studios. Images from different locations cannot be synthesized into anything even remotely resembling what one sees in a face-to-face meeting. Space, body angles, touch, and other nonverbal signals still are not possible regardless of image fidelity. In most cases only two locations can be linked at a time.

Audio teleconferencing is much less expensive than video, speaker phone equipment is relatively inexpensive and readily available to anyone interested in using it, and can be located in any office. Persons in many places can be linked in one conference call. But there are serious drawbacks due to channel limitations. Audio conferences lack what Short, Williams, and Christie call a sense of "social presence."[17] Even when face to face, people vary in awareness of social presence, but when linked only by sound waves of rather low fidelity, the sense of sharing, belonging, and of each other as persons can be very low. On the plus side, the potential for *greater* equality of opportunity to participate lies in control equipment available for conference leaders if group norms permit its use. But all electronic equipment can fail suddenly, ending a meeting right in the middle of a heated conflict, or perhaps leaving the impression that one member has slammed an electronic door in the faces of others.

In order to use teleconferencing equipment to maximum advantage, Johansen, Vallee, and Spangler recommend that *before* any major teleconferencing, persons who must work together repeatedly or on a long term project first hold an extended face-to-face conference in which they can develop a sense of groupness, a functioning system.[18] Group members will need to resolve primary social tensions, learn each other's personal styles of communicating, establish a sense of unity and trust in each other, and come to agreement on goals and procedures for their electronic meetings. With extremely complex tasks (such as writing up a complex solution, or combining several proposals into one on which consensus can be achieved), a face-to-face meeting may again be needed, at least for a working subcommittee. Delicate negotiating when potential for prolonged conflict is high may call for such meetings. Teleconferencing is well suited for dealing with more routine coordination of efforts among groups represented by the conferees, day-to-day matters, and expediting the exchange of information and implementation of policies agreed upon.

The coordinator of a teleconference should be a skilled group-centered leader, or the potential for domination by that person is great. Efforts needed to understand all members' positions and to coordinate them—the "nerve ring" functions—are not qualitatively different from face-to-face group meetings, but are limited by the means available for signal exchange. As in all meetings of interdependent humans, the foundation of effective group discussion continues to be the development of a sense of shared purpose, commitment to the good of the group over self-aggrandizement or a desire for power, listening to understand, a will to achieve win-win resolution of conflicts, and skills in verbalizing.

Summary

Discussion methods and techniques for learning discussions, public discussion, and discussions of small groups that exist within large organizations have been presented in this chapter. Ways to enhance cooperation and the achievement of the common good have been stressed throughout.

Learnings in the affective area are greatly enhanced by cooperative relationships; discussion is uniquely suited to building cooperation. Generally the focus in learning discussion should be on sharing perceptions and interpretations of a limited number of topics emerging from shared experiences. Various formats for learning discussion can be used, depending on the nature of the subject matter and interests of members. Discussion of works of art should be concentrated on the works themselves. Case discussion can be used to explore ways of handling more general problems. Personal feelings and interpersonal relationships can be dealt with through affective discussion or group encounter.

The most common types of public discussion are panel presentations and large group forums. Special procedures for each of these formats were described in detail. Panel and forum discussions require close control of the procedure by a designated moderator.

Small groups that are part of large organizations often have special problems; special techniques can enhance their productivity. Every member of a large group can be involved directly and actively through the buzz-group technique.

A problem census can be done to develop an agenda based on member concerns. Management groups doing long-range planning for organizations can often be more productive if they use the Nominal Group Technique rather than more conventional problem-solving procedures. The creative and problem-solving skills of all employees can be put to work in a large corporate structure through a variety of participative management techniques utilizing problem-solving discussion. Most widely used is the quality circle concept, which can greatly increase both quantity and quality of work outputs if employees are provided with necessary commitments from the company.

Modern electronic developments have made possible conferences among persons distant from one another through telecommunication equipment. Video equipment is highly expensive, rare, and inconvenient to use, whereas audio equipment is inexpensive, readily available, and convenient. But it requires strict coordinating by a group-centered leader, and for long-term groups, some early face-to-face conferencing in order to develop a functioning group system.

You will undoubtedly find many occasions in your life when some of the techniques described in this chapter will serve you well. Many others have also been described in the literature of small groups and management. I urge you to explore them, and use them to facilitate group interaction toward achieving truly shared goals.

Exercises

1. Select a poem, short story, brief essay, painting, sculpture, or other work of art that intrigues you. Your class will be divided into several groups of five to seven members each. If you have selected something written, make a copy for each member of your group. Plan an outline

for leading discussion of the work of art; the discussion will be limited to 15–20 minutes. Each member of your small group will in turn lead discussion, using the outline prepared. You may want to have one member sit out as a critic-observer, then lead a brief evaluation discussion.

2. All members of your group or class may view a film or TV program. Together prepare an outline of questions, then discuss the film or show.

3. Conduct an affective discussion either with a group of classmates or some other group, and report the results in a short essay. The target question might come from a previous problem census, or the following list:
   "How do we feel about classmates who don't speak up?"
   "How do we feel about interracial marriages?"
   "How do we feel about capital punishment?"

4. Conduct a problem census on some question, possibly, "What do we want to know about small group discussion techniques?" or "What would we like to know about different religions?" After the agenda has been completely rank ordered, have a planning committee develop a schedule to deal with each of the questions, topics, or issues recorded.

5. Following a series of discussions, have a feedback session. On a chart or chalkboard write a set of terms for guiding the feedback. These should be selected by the group, possibly including some of the following: attitudes, preparation, speaking, supportiveness, acceptance of others, self-acceptance, personal insight, openness, warmth.

6. Engage in an encounter session or laboratory, with a trained facilitator to conduct the session(s). Use the guidelines on pages 337–38 as a contract for the members of the group.

7. Plan in detail a panel discussion on a topic of national importance. Imagine that you can select whomever you want as panelists. Select them, giving a rationale for each panelist. Then prepare a moderator's outline.

8. The class can be divided into project groups, each of which will research a problem of interest to it and of importance to all the class. Then the group should prepare and present a panel for the benefit of the rest of the class.

9. Conduct a Nominal Group Technique session in your class. Divide the class into small groups of six to eight persons, and seat each group at a table or in a semicircle facing a chart easel or wall on which are taped sheets of large plain paper for recording results. Your instructor will coordinate and time the exercise, but a student should be appointed to

coordinate each working group. Work on some target question such as "How should registration procedures at our college (or university) be revised?" or "How might our highways be made safer?"

10. After receiving the blessing of the instructor, volunteers from a small group communication class could form a quality circle. They would then meet approximately every two weeks to discuss any problems in the class, what might be done to solve them, and any other ways in which the class could be made more interesting or valuable to the students. The circle then gives consensus recommendations to the instructor. The instructor makes some reaction to each suggestion at the next class meeting, incorporating it if possible and advisable, or explaining why the suggestion was declined.

Bibliography

Baird, John E., Jr. *Quality Circles: Leader's Manual.* Prospect Heights, Ill. Waveland Press, 1982.

Beal, George M., Bohlen, J. M., and Raudabaugh, J. N. *Leadership and Dynamic Group Action.* Ames, Iowa: Iowa State University Press, 1962; an anthology of small group techniques and procedures.

Delbecq, Andre L., Van de Ven, A. H., and Gustafson, D. H. *Group Techniques for Program Planning: A Guide to Nominal Group and Delphi Processes.* Glenview, Ill. Scott, Foresman and Company, 1975.

Deming, W. Edwards. "What Top Management Must Do." *Business Week,* no. 2697 (July 20, 1981), 20–21.

Egan, Gerard. *Face to Face: The Small Group Experience and Interpersonal Growth.* Monterey, Calif.: Brooks/Cole Publishing Company, 1973.

Elton, Martin C. J., Lucas, W. A., and Conrath, D. W., eds. *Evaluating New Telecommunications Systems.* New York: Plenum, 1978.

Epstein, Charlotte. *Affective Subjects in the Classroom: Exploring Race, Sex, and Drugs.* Scranton, Pa.: Intext Educational Publishers, 1972.

Hunter, Elizabeth. *Encounter in the Classroom.* New York: Holt, Rinehart and Winston, 1972.

Johansen, Robert, Vallee, J., and Spangler, K. *Electronic Meetings: Technical Alternatives and Social Choices.* Reading, Mass.: Addison-Wesley, 1979.

Johnson, David W., and Johnson, Roger T. *Learning Together and Alone: Cooperation, Competition, and Individualization.* Englewood Cliffs, N.J.: Prentice-Hall, 1975.

"Quality Circles Pay Off Big," *Industry Week* 203 (October 29, 1979), 17–19.

Ruch, William V. *Corporate Communications, A Comparison of Japanese and American Practices*. Westport, Conn.: Quorum Books, 1984.
"Survey Suggests Teleconferencing Guidelines," *Communication World* 1 (August 1982): 10.
"What Happens When Workers Manage Themselves?" *Fortune* 105 (June 27, 1981), 64.

References

1. See D. W. and R. T. Johnson, *Learning Together and Alone,* (Englewood Cliffs, N.J.: Prentice-Hall, 1975), 191–92, for a summary of some of this research. See also W. J. McKeachie, "Recitation and Discussion," in *Achieve Learning Objectives,* 3d ed., O. E. Lancaster, ed. (University Park, Pa.: The Pennsylvania State University, 1963), section F.
2. John W. Powell, *Research in Adult Group Learning in the Liberal Arts* (White Plains, N.Y.: Fund for Adult Education, 1960), 3.
3. P. H. Witte, "The Effects of Group Reward Structures on Interracial Acceptance, Peer Tutoring, and Academic Performance" (Unpublished doctoral dissertation, Washington University, 1972); Johnson and Johnson, *Together and Alone,* 193–96.
4. Elizabeth Hunter, *Encounter in the Classroom* (New York: Holt, Rinehart and Winston, 1972), 1–15.
5. Johnson and Johnson, *Together and Alone,* 66.
6. John K. Brilhart, "An Exploratory Study of Relationships between the Evaluating Process and Associated Behaviors of Participants in Six Study-Discussion Groups" (Ph.D. dissertation, Pennsylvania State University, 1962), 283–93.
7. Brilhart, "An Exploratory Study," 275–82.
8. Adapted from outline of Connie Chatwood; April, 1973.
9. Charlotte Epstein, *Affective Subjects in the Classroom: Exploring Race, Sex, and Drugs* (Scranton, Pa.: Intext Educational Publishers, 1972), 12–13.
10. This procedure was developed and popularized by J. Donald Phillips, President of Hillsdale College in Michigan, who served as consultant for the Kentucky Conference. The Conference was held in 1954 at Eastern Kentucky State College.
11. Andre L. Delbecq, Andrew H. Van de Ven, and David H. Gustafson, *Group Techniques for Program Planning: A Guide to Nominal Group and Delphi Processes* (Glenview, Ill.: Scott Foresman and Company, 1975), 7–16.
12. Delbecq et al., *Group Techniques,* 3–4.
13. Andre L. Delbecq, "Techniques for Achieving Innovative Changes in Programming," a presentation at the Midwest Regional Conference of

the Family Service Association of America; Omaha, Neb.; April 20, 1971.

14. Delbecq, "Innovative Changes."

15. William V. Ruch, *Corporate Communications* (Westport, Conn.: Quorum Books, 1984), 205–219.

16. Robert Johansen, J. Vallee, and K. Spangler, *Electronic Meetings: Technical Alternatives and Social Choices* (Reading, Mass.: Addison-Wesley 1979), 2.

17. John A. Short, E. Williams, and B. Christie, *The Social Psychology of Telecommunications* (London: John Wiley and Sons, 1976).

18. Johansen et al., *Electronic Meetings,* 113–115.

13

observing and evaluating small group discussions

Study Objectives

As a result of studying chapter 13, you should be able to:

1. Explain the benefits of having nonparticipating observers for small groups, and the roles of both reminder and critic observers.

2. Prepare a set of questions to guide your observations of any small group discussion.

3. Explain ways to make the report of your observations both acceptable and helpful to group members.

4. Devise instruments for obtaining postmeeting reactions from group members, to chart the flow and frequency of verbal participation, and to rate groups, individual members, and designated leaders.

5. Make, record, and report actual observations of discussion inputs, processes, and outputs.

Key Terms

Consultant-observer   a nonparticipant observer whose primary responsibility is to give assistance and advice to a discussion group or a designated small group discussion leader, based on observations of group input, process, and output characteristics.

Critic-observer   a nonparticipant observer of a small group discussion who evaluates the functioning of the members and group as a whole.

Interaction diagram   a diagram showing the seating arrangement of a discussion group, how often each member speaks, and to whom.

Postmeeting Reaction Sheet, or PMR   a form completed by group members following a discussion, on which they evaluate the discussion, the group, and the leader; the responses are usually tabulated and reported back to the group.

Rating scale   a pencil-and-paper instrument, usually completed by a critic-observer, to render an evaluation of some factor involved in the discussion.

Reminder-observer   a nonparticipant observer of a small group discussion selected from the regular membership of the group, who tries to determine what is missing that might be helpful to the group (information, roles, procedures, techniques, etc.), then suggests to the group what has been overlooked.

Student-observer   a nonparticipating observer whose only purpose is to learn about groups by observing, usually to develop skills in small group communication or as a researcher investigating questions about the nature of small groups.

Throughout this book the importance of developing a participant-observer focus is stressed. Through reading the book, classroom discussions, and the guidance of your instructor you are developing such an orientation. Even while you have been participating in discussions, part of your attention and energy have been given to observing group inputs and processes. But, as you are undoubtedly aware, one cannot both observe and participate in the substance of a discussion at the same instant, so you have had to shift attention back and forth from the content of the discussion to the processes of the group. You have been able to supply functional behaviors appropriate to the group based on your observations of its processes, and to supply some feedback to reinforce what is going well and to modify what is not so productive. But no matter how skilled you may be as a participant-observer, there are times when you have missed something of importance, and perhaps been puzzled at what happened or frustrated by a lack of goal achievement and member satisfaction. Sometimes the most skillful of us becomes so engrossed in the interaction over an important issue that we lose perspective.

Thus a nonparticipating observer can be of real assistance in helping the group perceive what is going on. Any group of persons trying to understand group dynamics and develop skills as discussion participants and leaders will benefit from the feedback observations of a nonparticipating observer. When serving as a nonparticipant observer, the student of small group communication can see and learn a great deal that would be missed while actively participating. Consultants can often help problem-solving groups and leaders, provided their advice is based on careful observation of the group's discussions. Critic-observers are a regular feature of education in small group communication. This chapter describes roles taken by nonparticipating observers, offers guidelines for such observers, supplies a variety of types of forms for recording observations and evaluations of both individual participants and groups, and provides instruments for gathering data directly from participants in discussions. Many of these instruments can be used by groups even when a nonparticipating observer is not available.

The Role of the Observer

Every student of discussion and group processes needs the experience of observing discussion groups at work. As students have remarked countless times, "It looks different when you are sitting outside the discussion." The observer can see clearly what he or she was only vaguely aware of while discussing. After observing other discussants, the observer may be motivated to change his or her own conduct as a discussant. It is therefore suggested that you observe as many discussions as possible. In the classroom, it is wise for you to change frequently from being a discussant in one group to being an observer of another.

When serving as a group observer, there are many things you might want to look for. Considering the group as a system, you will certainly want to be aware of a variety of input, process, and output variables. Although you will be able to pay close attention to only one or a few variables at any one time, you may want to prepare and occasionally scan a mental checklist of items to help you select those that seem most important to the group. Here is a list that you can use as a general guide to observing. You can also use it when preparing more limited lists of questions to answer as observer.

1. Are there clear and accepted group goals? Has the committee a clear understanding of its charge? Is there an understanding of the type of output needed?
2. Are all members aware and accepting of limits on their area of freedom?
3. Are any hidden agenda items interfering with group progress?
4. Are any environmental problems disrupting the group, such as poor seating arrangements, noise, or other distractions?
5. What attitudes toward themselves, each other, and the substance of the discussion are members manifesting?
6. To what degree does the group climate seem to be one of open communication, trust, and cooperation?
7. How well are members listening and trying to understand each other?
8. Are there any communication problems due to the way members encode their ideas verbally and nonverbally?
9. Are any norms interfering with progress and cohesiveness?
10. Do members seem to be adequately prepared with information?
11. Are information and ideas being evaluated, or accepted at face value? Is there any tendency to groupthink and conform to high-status persons?
12. Has some procedure, or agenda for the discussion been provided or developed by the group? If so, how well is this being followed? Does it serve the group's needs?
13. If a problem-solving discussion, has the group defined and clarified the problem thoroughly, or has it become solution-centered too soon?
14. How creative is the group in generating potential solutions to its problem? In interpreting information?
15. Has judgment been deferred until solutions have been listed and understood by all members?
16. Do members seem to share the same values and criteria in making decisions, or do they need to clarify their criteria?
17. When evaluating ideas and opinions, is the group making use of the information brought out during earlier discussion?
18. How are decisions being made?
19. If needed, has the group made adequate plans to implement its decisions, including member responsibilities, future meetings, etc.?

20. Are periodic summaries needed to help members recall and maintain perspective on the discussion and move the group to new issues without undue redundancy?
21. If needed, is the discussion being adequately recorded (and possibly charted)?
22. How well is verbal participation spread among all members? Is the pattern of verbal interaction all-channel or unduly restricted?
23. If there is a designated leader, what style of leadership is he or she providing? Does this seem appropriate to the group?
24. Does the role structure provide optimal inputs from all members? Are any needed behavioral functions missing?
25. Are special procedural techniques such as brainstorming or parliamentary procedure being used in ways that are productive? Could procedural changes benefit the group?

Do not try to observe everything at once. Limit your focus to a few aspects of the discussion, perhaps at first to only one. Later, with experience, confidence, and increased awareness of the dynamics of a group, you will be ready to observe without a definite focus. You will then be able to decide as you watch which characteristics of the group are most important to assess in detail. No observer can simultaneously chronicle the content and flow of interaction, take notice of various group and individual objectives, judge the information and logic of remarks, assess the atmosphere, and note the organization of the discussion. If the observer tries to do so, the result is sure to be confusion that will reduce both personal learning and ability to give feedback to the group.

The nonparticipating observer can do four types of things as a result of what is observed: (1) learn from the example of others; (2) remind the group of techniques or principles of discussion it has overlooked; (3) give advice to improve the group's communication and procedures; or (4) supply critical evaluations of the discussion. We will examine the role of observers who do each of these types of things.

The Student Observer

The primary purpose of a "student-observer" is to learn from observing and evaluating the functioning of small groups. Such an observer does not normally make a report of observations to the group, although a report might be given when observing a group which is part of a small group communication class. Small group researchers, many of whose studies have been cited in this book, frequently gather data by observing small groups in their natural settings. Such student-observers seek to establish valid generalizations about small groups.

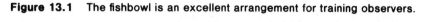
Figure 13.1   The fishbowl is an excellent arrangement for training observers.

You are free to observe any small group meeting legally declared open to the public, such as most meetings of boards, councils, and committees of governments where a "sunshine" law has been passed. You can obtain permission to observe many other small groups by describing your purpose as a learner and promising to maintain the confidentiality of details which are the business of the group and no one else. Of course it is *imperative* that you keep this promise.

A very useful technique is the *fishbowl* arrangement in which a discussion group is surrounded by a circle of nonparticipating observers. These observers may all be focusing on the same aspects of group process and content, or may be assigned to observe, evaluate, and report on different factors (e.g., leadership, process of group problem solving, use of information, roles of members, verbal and nonverbal communication). Observers can be assigned on a one-to-one basis to participants as *alter egos* who make whispered suggestions to the discussant behind whom they sit, or when asked to do so indicate how they think their discussant feels or what he or she means by some action or comment. Observers can learn a great deal by comparing their perceptions and evaluations of the same meeting.

The Reminder Observer

Often group members just need to be reminded of principles and techniques with which they are familiar, but have not thought of in the heat of a lively discussion of substantive or procedural issues. The reminder-observer focuses attention on group interaction and procedures while other members of the group are deeply involved with the content of the discussion. When the observer notices some difficulty with the way the group is proceeding, he or she speaks up to "remind" the group members of communication principles and techniques which they appear to have momentarily overlooked. Many of your classroom discussions can be improved by having one group member act as a reminder-observer. This role assignment should be changed frequently (at least from meeting to meeting) in order to give everyone a chance to remind without depriving anyone for long of the chance to contribute to the discussions. When you have become very skilled as a participant-observer, you may be able to act as an unappointed "reminder" to nonclassroom groups in which you are a participant. Usually other members will begin to do likewise when one group member models the reminding function.

A few guidelines may help you serve your group as a reminder:

1. Focus on group processes rather than on content and issues of the discussion.
2. Realizing that all authority for change rests with the group, put most of your remarks in the form of questions and suggestions for group consideration. This way you will remain completely neutral on any content issue. For example: "I wonder if the group realizes that we have discussed _____ , _____ , and _____ in the space of only five minutes?" "Are we ready to list possible solutions, or do we need to explore the problem in more detail?" "I think the group has forgotten to record ideas as they are being proposed." "I wonder if Jake and Marita understand each other's proposals." "We sound as if agreement has been reached. I wonder if a vote would confirm that we have arrived at a consensus?" "Some members do not appear to have much chance to be heard. Does the group want to do more gatekeeping to equalize opportunity to be heard?" Such comments and questions can remind the group of principles of effective discussion without leveling criticisms at any specific member of a group.
3. Focus on trends; avoid singling out individual members.
4. Interrupt the discussion only when you believe the group is unlikely to become aware of what is troubling it without wasting a lot of time or creating disunity, tension, and frustration. Usually you should give the group some time to correct itself.

The Consultant Observer

Many designated leaders and groups will benefit from the advice and coaching of a consultant-observer. This role is becoming increasingly more important as more and more organizations institute autonomous work group procedures or such participative management techniques as quality circles. Workers who select their coordinator-leaders from among their own ranks and decide as groups how to manage much of their work routines must become proficient in group discussion and able to serve as problem-solving discussion leaders. Quality circle participants and leaders, whether from the ranks of production employees or supervisors, must know how to participate in order to make a success of this small group technique. Managers new to the problem census procedure or the Nominal Group Technique often need advice and assistance when conducting such a long-range type of planning meeting. Committees and task forces may need someone to help them resolve communication, relational, and procedural difficulties. Hence the need for small group communication consultants. The consultant is often a member of a communication or training department. Any organizational communication specialist should be prepared to serve as a consultant-observer to small groups in the organization.

Appointed or elected task group leaders of discussion groups will especially benefit from the coaching of a consultant-observer. The role of consultant-observer is analogous to that of the parliamentarian, who is consultant and advisor to the presiding officer of a large group, and sometimes to the entire assembly. As a small group consultant, you will, of course, need a thorough grasp of small group dynamics and techniques. Probably you will need at times to use a variety of types of observation, feedback, and evaluation instruments such as those presented in the next section of the chapter.

Here are a few guidelines for making your performance as a consultant-observer more helpful to a group and satisfying to you:

1. *Begin* your post-discussion remarks *by stressing the positive,* pointing out what a leader or group is doing well.
2. *Emphasize what you think matters most,* what most needs to be improved upon, rather than overwhelming the person(s) receiving your advice with more suggestions than she or he can accept and handle at any one time. Most coaches and speech teachers can provide role models of this guideline.
3. *Avoid arguing.* Present your observations, opinions, and advice, make sure they are understood, and then leave the group members free to decide if your evaluations and advice will be used in any way.
4. If you *advise a leader* during the actual meeting, do so—as often as possible—*without interrupting the meeting,* by using whispered or written suggestions.
5. When group members ask your advice, *give it clearly, precisely, and as briefly as possible.* If the group asks for a presentation or demonstration of some technique, prepare and present it at a time agreed upon.
6. *Critical comments* to a leader should usually be *made in private* where that person will not appear to be under attack before the rest of the group. The duties of consultant may often require considerable evaluating. That leads us to the final type of observer role, the "critic-observer."

The Critic Observer

A critic-observer may do considerable consulting, but the primary function is to evaluate and render judgments. Such an observer belongs primarily in a classroom or training program. The critic-observer may also act as an advisor. For example, your instructor may interrupt a discussion of a student group to point out what he or she thinks is going wrong and to suggest a different procedure or technique. After you have become a proficient observer, you might take on the role of critic-observer for a small group in another speech class or some other course in your school. The critic usually makes a detailed report after observing a discussion. In addition to describing and interpreting selected aspects of the discussion, the critic expresses opinions about the strong and weak points. He or she may compliment the group, point out where and how the group got into trouble, and even place blame or take a member to task. This must be done with tact. Many persons balk at accepting criticism leveled at them. Discussants can be helped to accept criticisms by applying two guidelines: (1) all criticism should be constructive, meaning that when you point out a problem you also suggest what to do to correct it, and do so in a spirit of helpfulness; (2) all critiques should include positive comments before pointing out what needs to be changed.

In general, a critic-observer's postmeeting judgments should cover at least four aspects of a discussion: (1) the group product, including how well it has been evaluated by the group, how appropriate it seems to be to the problem described by the group, and how likely members are to support it; (2) the group process, including patterns of interaction, communication, decision making, and problem solving as a whole; (3) contributions and functional roles of members; and (4) leadership, especially the role of the procedural leader. Of course different criteria for evaluation will be needed by observers of public and private, learning and problem-solving, advisory and action groups.

Instruments for Observing and Evaluating Discussions

Whether or not a consultant or critic-observer is available, any discussion group can improve its processes and outputs by taking time for some evaluation. Most groups will benefit from evaluation sessions scheduled at regular intervals, perhaps at the end of each meeting. There is a danger of not getting to such assessment if it is not scheduled. For this reason, regular times for assessment have been built into the operations of many business, government, and military groups. Hill's *Learning Thru Discussion* procedure includes evaluation of the meeting as the last stage of each learning discussion.[1] However, if group evaluation is limited only to scheduled periods following meetings, much of importance may be forgotten. Taking a break for an unplanned evaluation may correct a dangerous pattern of behaviors or procedure before a serious breakdown occurs in a group. Continuing groups need both routine and spontaneous evaluation sessions.

The remaining section of chapter 13 is devoted to instruments for observing and evaluating both groups and individual members. Many of these forms were developed especially for classes in small group communication, discussion, and leadership. They can be used as is, or as models to be adapted to fit specific situations in your class or in ongoing groups to which you belong or serve as observer.

Postmeeting Reaction Forms

Postmeeting Reaction Forms, or PMRs as they are called for convenience, are used to get objective feedback from group members. Since PMRs are anonymous, a participant can report personal evaluations without any threat to self. A PMR may be planned by a chairperson or other designated leader, by an instructor, by a consultant, by a group, or by the organizers of a large conference. The PMRs are distributed, completed and collected immediately following the discussion.

A PMR sheet is a simple questionnaire designated to elicit frank comments about important aspects of the group and the discussion. *Questions should be tailored to fit the purposes and needs of the person preparing the questionnaire.* Sometimes the questions concern substantive items, sometimes interpersonal matters, and sometimes matters of technique and procedure. Two or more types of questions may be mixed on a PMR. Three illustrative PMR sheets are shown in figures 13.2, 13.3, and 13.4. These can be used for almost any type of discussion.

Figure 13.2   Postmeeting Reaction Form.

Instructions: Check the point on each scale that best represents your honest judgment. Add any comments you wish to make that are not covered by the questionnaire. Do *not* sign your name.

1. How clear were the *goals* of the discussion to you?

| very clear | somewhat vague | muddled |

2. The *atmosphere* was

| cooperative and cohesive | apathetic | competitive |

3. How well *organized and systematic* was the discussion?

| disorderly | just right | too rigid |

4. How effective was the *style of leadership* supplied by the chairperson?

| too autocratic | democratic | weak |

Figure 13.2—*Continued*

5. *Preparation for this meeting* was

---

thorough   adequate   poor

6. Did you find yourself *wanting to speak* when you didn't get a chance?

---

almost never   occasionally   often

7. How satisfied are you with the *results* of the discussion?

---

very satisfied   moderately satisfied   very dissatisfied

8. How do you feel about *working again* with this same group?

---

eager   I will   reluctant

Comments:

Figure 13.3   Postmeeting Reaction Form.

1. How do you feel about today's discussion?

   excellent _____ good _____ all right _____ so-so _____ bad _____

2. What were the strong points of the discussion?

3. What were the weaknesses?

4. What changes would you suggest for future meetings?

(you need not sign your name)

Figure 13.4　　Reaction Questionnaire.

Instruction: Circle the number that best indicates your reactions to the following questions about the discussion in which you participated:

1. *Adequacy of Communication*: To what extent do you feel members were understanding each others' statements and positions?

   0　　1　　2　　3　　4　　5　　6　　7　　8　　9　　10

   Much talking past each　　　　　　　Communicated directly with
   other, misunderstanding　　　　　　each other, understanding well

2. *Opportunity to Speak*: To what extent did you feel free to speak?

   0　　1　　2　　3　　4　　5　　6　　7　　8　　9　　10

   Never had a　　　　　　　　　　All the opportunity to
   chance to speak　　　　　　　　　　talk I wanted

3. *Climate of Acceptance*: How well did members support each other, show acceptance of individuals?

   0　　1　　2　　3　　4　　5　　6　　7　　8　　9　　10

   Highly critical　　　　　　　　　Supportive and receptive
   and punishing

4. *Interpersonal relations*: How pleasant and concerned with interpersonal relations?

   0　　1　　2　　3　　4　　5　　6　　7　　8　　9　　10

   Quarrelsome, status　　　　　　　　Pleasant, empathic,
   differences emphasized　　　　　　　concerned with persons

5. *Leadership*: How adequate was the leader (or leadership) of the group?

   0　　1　　2　　3　　4　　5　　6　　7　　8　　9　　10

   Too weak ( ) or　　　　　　　　　Shared, group-centered,
   dominating ( )　　　　　　　　　　and sufficient

6. *Satisfaction with role*: How satisfied are you with your personal participation in the discussion?

   0　　1　　2　　3　　4　　5　　6　　7　　8　　9　　10

   Very dissatisfied　　　　　　　　　Very satisfied

7. *Quality of product*: How satisfied are you with the discussions, solutions, or learnings that came out of this discussion?

   0　　1　　2　　3　　4　　5　　6　　7　　8　　9　　10

   Very displeased　　　　　　　　　Very satisfied

8. *Overall*: How do you rate the discussion as a whole apart from any specific aspect of it?

   0　　1　　2　　3　　4　　5　　6　　7　　8　　9　　10

   Awful, waste of time　　　　　　　Superb, time well spent

Specialized PMR forms for learning discussions are presented in figures 13.5, 13.6, and 13.7. The first of these was developed to give evaluative reactions to the leader of a group discussing such products of human creativity as poetry, stories, music, painting, or sculpture. The second can be used to get feedback for almost any learning group; it can be modified quite readily to elicit any kind of responses you might want. Figure 13.7 is designed to be used after an encounter session or during a recess by an encounter group.

Figure 13.5 Postmeeting Reactions for Learning Discussion Leader.

Leader's Name _____

Instruction: Circle number on each scale that best indicates your reaction.

1. *Preparation* for leading the discussion seemed:

   thorough and appropriate   very inadequate

7	6	5	4	3	2	1

2. *Organizing and guiding* the discussion were:

   clear and orderly   rigid or haphazard

7	6	5	4	3	2	1

3. *Spreading of participation* was:

   just right   completely neglected

7	6	5	4	3	2	1

4. The *style* or philosophy of the leader was:

   group centered stimulator   autocratic ("expert")

7	6	5	4	3	2	1

5. *Participating* in the discussion was:

   satisfying and enjoyable   boring or frustrating

7	6	5	4	3	2	1

Comments:

Figure 13.6   Learning Group PMR Form.

1. What did you especially *like* or *dislike* about the discussion?

2. What, if anything, do you believe you learned?

3. What do you most *approve* and *disapprove* of in the leader's behavior?

Figure 13.7   PMR Sheet for Encounter Sessions.

Instructions: Circle number indicating your reaction on each scale.

1. How well was discussion focused on the "here and now" experience of the group?

1	2	3	4	5	6	7

   little;   totally on
   mostly   here-and-now
   story telling

2. How open were members in describing feelings and reactions?

1	2	3	4	5	6	7

   no self-disclosure   open, much self-disclosure

3. How descriptive and supportive were members?

1	2	3	4	5	6	7

   evaluative and critical,   neutral   entirely descriptive
   a "hatchet job"   of reactions and
                                                                 others' behaviors

4. How specific and clear were comments?

1	2	3	4	5	6	7

   vague, general and   clear, specific
   theoretical   and focussed

5. How much responsibility did members assume for the session?

1	2	3	4	5	6	7

   leader dominated, much   members assumed responsibility
   dependency behavior   for success of session

   Comments:

Figure 13.8   PMR sheets can help diagnose problem groups.

PMR responses should be tallied and reported back to the group as soon as possible, either on a duplicated summary sheet or by posting on a chart or chalkboard. The results then become the grist for an evaluation discussion and for planning changes in group procedure.

Verbal Interaction Diagrams

A diagram of verbal interaction made by an observer will reveal a lot about the relationships among members of a group. The diagram can reveal who is talking to whom, how often each member participates orally, and any dominating persons. A model interaction diagram is shown in figure 13.9. Notice the data at the top of the sheet; the names of all participants are located around the circle in the same order in which they sat during the discussion. Each time a person speaks an arrow is drawn from his or her position toward the person to whom the remark was addressed. If a member speaks to the entire group, a longer arrow points towards the center of the circle. Subsequent remarks in the same direction are indicated by short cross marks on the base of the arrow.

Figure 13.9   Verbal interaction diagram.

Group _____

Time _____

Begin _____

End _____

Place _____

Observer _____

Frequency and direction of
participation

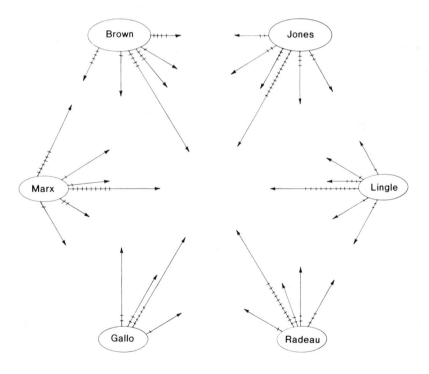

Scales for Rating Group Inputs, Process, and Outputs

Rating scales can be used by critic-observers to record their judgments about any aspect of the group and its discussion, including group climate, cohesiveness, efficiency, satisfaction, degree of mutual respect, organization of discussion, adequacy of information, and the like. A five or seven point scale is sufficiently detailed for most purposes. Members of a class in small group communication can learn much by preparing their own scales to rate both groups and participants on various characteristics; deciding what to emphasize and rate will force you to think through many issues on group process. A sample of the type of instrument you might develop for rating a small group discussion is shown in figure 13.10.

Figure 13.11 is a scale for evaluating the problem-solving procedure of a group, adapted from a similar scale developed by Patton and Giffin.[2] A problem-solving group will need to discuss any deficiencies pointed out on this scale by the evaluator, and how to overcome the deficiencies in future discussions.

Figure 13.10   Discussion Rating Scale.

Date _____   Group _____

Time _____   Observer _____

Group characteristic	5 excellent	4 good	3 average	2 fair	1 poor
Organization of discussion					
Equality of opportunity to speak					
Cooperative group orientation					
Listening to understand					
Evaluation of ideas					

Comments:

Figure 13.11   Problem-Solving Process Scale.

Instructions: On each scale indicate the degree to which the group accomplished each identified behavior. Use the following scale for your evaluations:

Poor	Fair	Average	Good	Excellent
1	2	3	4	5

Circle the appropriate number in front of each item.

1 2 3 4 5   1. The concern of each member was identified regarding the problem the group attempted to solve.

1 2 3 4 5   2. This concern was identified *before* the problem was analyzed.

1 2 3 4 5   3. In problem analysis, the present condition was carefully compared with the specific condition desired.

1 2 3 4 5   4. The goal was carefully defined and agreed to by all members.

1 2 3 4 5   5. Valid (and relevant) information was secured when needed.

1 2 3 4 5   6. Possible solutions were listed and clarified before they were evaluated.

1 2 3 4 5   7. Criteria for evaluating proposed solutions were clearly identified and accepted by the group.

1 2 3 4 5   8. Predictions were made regarding the probable effectiveness of each proposed solution, using the available information and criteria.

1 2 3 4 5   9. Consensus was achieved on the most desirable solution.

1 2 3 4 5   10. A detailed plan to implement the solution was developed.

1 2 3 4 5   11. The problem-solving process was systematic and orderly.

Forms for Evaluating Individual Participants

Almost any aspect of individual participation can be evaluated by preparing appropriate forms. An analysis of roles of members can be made by listing the names of all members in separate columns on a sheet on which the various functions described in chapter 5 are listed in a vertical column at the left side of the sheet (figure 13.12). Each time a participant speaks, a tally is made in the column after the role function just performed. If a member performs more

Figure 13.12   Behavioral functions of discussants.

Date _____   Group _____

Time _____   Observer _____

Participants' Names

Behavioral Functions						
1. Initiating and orienting						
2. Information giving						
3. Information seeking						
4. Opinion giving						
5. Opinion seeking						
6. Clarifying and elaborating						
7. Evaluating						
8. Summarizing						
9. Coordinating						
10. Consensus testing						
11. Recording						
12. Suggesting procedure						
13. Gatekeeping						
14. Supporting						
15. Harmonizing						
16. Tension relieving						
17. Dramatizing						
18. Norming						
19. Withdrawing						
20. Blocking						
21. Status and recognition seeking						

than one function in a single speech, two or more tallies are made. The completed observation form will indicate what functions were supplied adequately, the absence of any needed participant functions, the degree of role flexibility of each member of the group, and the kind of role each took.

Figure 13.13 shows a simple rating form that can be completed and given to each participant by a critic-observer. The forms should be filled out toward the end of the discussion so the group does not have to wait while the observer completes them. This form was written by a group of students and has been used extensively to rate students engaged in practice discussions. Although only illustrative of many types of scales and forms that could be used, it has the virtue of being simple and brief, yet focuses on some of the most important aspects of participation. A somewhat more detailed rating scale for individual participants is shown in figure 13.14. This form could be used by a critic-observer, or each participant in a small group might prepare one for each other member of the group.

Figure 13.13   Participant Rating Scale.

For _____   Date _____

_____   Observer _____
         (Name)

1. Contributions to the *content of the discussion?* (well prepared, supplied information, adequate reasoning, etc.)

5	4	3	2	1
Outstanding in quality and quantity		Fair share		Few or none

2. Contributions to *efficient group procedures?* (agenda planning, relevant comments, summaries, keeping on track)

5	4	3	2	1
Always relevant, aided organization		Relevant, no aid in order		Sidetracked, confused group

3. Degree of *cooperating* (listening to understand, responsible, agreeable, group centered, open-minded)

5	4	3	2	1
Very responsible and constructive				Self-centered

4. *Speaking.* (clear, to group, one point at a time, concise)

5	4	3	2	1
Brief, clear, to group				Vague, indirect, wordy

Figure 13.13—*Continued*

5. *Value* to the group? (overall rating)

5	4	3	2	1

Most valuable   Least valuable

Suggestions:

Figure 13.14   Discussion Participation Evaluation Scale.

For _____

Instructions: Circle the number that best reflects your evaluation of the discussant's participation on each scale.

Superior   Poor

1	2	3	4	5	1. Was prepared and informed.
1	2	3	4	5	2. Contributions were brief and clear.
1	2	3	4	5	3. Comments relevant and well timed.
1	2	3	4	5	4. Spoke distinctly and audibly to all.
1	2	3	4	5	5. Contributions made readily and voluntarily.
1	2	3	4	5	6. Frequency of participation (if poor, too low ( ) or high ( ).
1	2	3	4	5	7. Nonverbal responses were clear and constant.
1	2	3	4	5	8. Listened to understand and follow discussion.
1	2	3	4	5	9. Openminded.
1	2	3	4	5	10. Cooperative and constructive.
1	2	3	4	5	11. Helped keep discussion organized, following outline.
1	2	3	4	5	12. Contributed to evaluation of information and ideas.
1	2	3	4	5	13. Respectful and tactful with others.
1	2	3	4	5	14. Encouraged others to participate.
1	2	3	4	5	15. Overall rating in relation to other discussants.

Comments: Evaluator _____

Figure 13.15 is an observer form for assessing the assertiveness of members of a small group. The observer completes one of these scales for each participant in the discussion. This instrument is different from the other scales in that "Assertive," the optimal position on each scale, is located at the center instead of at one end. A check toward either end of a scale indicates that the participant was either less assertive or more aggressive than seemed desirable to the observer.

Figure 13.15   Assertiveness Rating Scale.

Discussant _____   Date _____

Observer _____   Time _____

The check mark on each scale indicates my best judgment of your degree of assertiveness as a participant in the discussion.

Behavior	Nonassertive	Assertive	Aggressive
Getting the floor			
	yielded easily	usually refused to let other take over or dominate	interrupted and cut others off
Expressing opinions			
	never expressed personal opinion	stated opinions, but open to others' opinions	insisted others should agree with you
Expressing personal desires (for meeting times, procedures, etc.)			
	never, or did so in a pleading way	stated openly, but willing to compromise	insisted on having own way
Sharing information			
	none, or only if asked to do so	whenever info was relevant, concisely	whether relevant or not; long-winded, rambling

Personal Manner			
Voice			
	weak, unduly soft	strong and clear	loud, strident
Posture and movements			
	withdrawn, restricted	animated, often leaning forward	unduly forceful, "table pounding"

Figure 13.15—*Continued*

Eye contact			
	rare, even when speaking	direct but not staring or glaring	stared others down
Overall manner			
	nonassertive	assertive	aggressive

All of the previously described observation forms and rating scales can be used to analyze and appraise functional leadership. However, because most discussion groups have a designated leader and because his or her participation is so vital to the group, many special forms have been developed for recording and evaluating the behaviors of designated leaders. The form shown in figure 13.16 is one of the most comprehensive available for evaluating leaders.

Figure 13.16   Leader Rating Scale

Date _____   Leader _____

Time _____   Observer _____

Instructions: Rate the leader on all items that are applicable; draw a line through all items that do not apply. Use the following scale to indicate how well you evaluate his or her performance:

5—superior
4—above average
3—average
2—below average
1—poor

Personal Style

To what degree did the leader:

_____ Show poise and confidence in speaking?

_____ Show enthusiasm and interest in the problem?

_____ Listen well to understand *all* participants?

_____ Manifest personal warmth and a sense of humor?

_____ Show an open mind toward all new information and ideas?

_____ Create a supportive, cooperative atmosphere?

_____ Share functional leadership with other members?

_____ Behave democratically?

_____ Maintain perspective on problem and group process?

Preparation

To what degree:

_____ Were all needed physical arrangements cared for?

_____ Were members notified and given guidance in preparing to meet?

_____ Was the leader prepared on the problem or subject?

_____ Was a procedural sequence of questions prepared to guide discussion?

Procedural and Interpersonal Leadership Techniques

To what degree did the leader:

_____ Put members at ease with each other?

_____ Equalize opportunity to speak?

_____ Control aggressive or dominant members, with tact?

_____ Present an agenda and procedure for group problem solving?

_____ Encourage members to modify the procedural outline?

_____ State questions clearly to the group?

_____ Introduce and explain the charge or problem so it was clear to all?

_____ Guide the group through a thorough analysis of problem before discussing solutions?

_____ Stimulate imaginative and creative thinking about solutions?

_____ Encourage the group to evaluate all ideas and proposals thoroughly before accepting or rejecting them?

_____ See that plans were made to implement and follow-up on all decisions?

_____ Keep discussion on one point at a time?

_____ Rebound questions asking for a personal opinion or solution to the group?

_____ Provide summaries needed to clarify, remind, and move group forward to next issue or agenda item?

_____ Test for consensus before moving to a new phase of problem solving?

Figure 13.16—*Continued*

_____ Keep complete and accurate records, especially of all proposals and decisions?

_____ If needed, suggest compromise or integrative solutions to resolve conflict?

_____ (Other—name the technique or procedure _____)

It often pays to have two observers filling in the same rating scale independently of one another; you could even use a fishbowl arrangement with several observers. The observers can learn by comparing their ratings, and discussing those on which they differ by more than one point.

Critic-observers are not often available outside the classroom. As a means to self-improvement, designated discussion leaders can evaluate their own functioning. The questionnaire in figure 13.17 may be used to evaluate how well you led a discussion. Many students of small group leadership have found it helpful to complete this form after leading a discussion.

Figure 13.17 Self-Rating Scale for Problem-Solving Discussion Leaders.

Instructions: Rate yourself on each item by putting a check mark in the "Yes" or "No" column. Your score is five times the number of items marked "Yes." Rating: *excellent*, 90 or higher; *good*, 80–85; *fair*, 70–75; *inadequate*, 65 or lower.

	Yes	No
1. I prepared all needed facilities.	_____	_____
2. I started the meeting promptly and ended on time.	_____	_____
3. I established an atmosphere of permissiveness and informality; I was open and responsive to all ideas.	_____	_____
4. I clearly oriented the group to its purpose and area of freedom.	_____	_____
5. I encouraged all members to participate and maintained equal opportunity for all to speak.	_____	_____
6. I used a plan for leading the group in an organized consideration of all major phases of the problem.	_____	_____
7. I listened actively, and (if needed) encouraged all members to do so.	_____	_____
8. I saw to it that the problem was discussed thoroughly before solutions were considered.	_____	_____

9. I integrated related ideas or suggestions, and urged the group to arrive at consensus on a solution. ⎯⎯⎯⎯ ⎯⎯⎯⎯

10. My questions were clear and brief. ⎯⎯⎯⎯ ⎯⎯⎯⎯

11. I saw to it that unclear statements were paraphrased or otherwise clarified. ⎯⎯⎯⎯ ⎯⎯⎯⎯

12. I prompted open discussion of substantive conflicts. ⎯⎯⎯⎯ ⎯⎯⎯⎯

13. I maintained order and organization, promptly pointing out tangents, making transitions, and keeping track of the passage of time. ⎯⎯⎯⎯ ⎯⎯⎯⎯

14. I saw to it that the meeting produced definite assignments or plans for action, and that any subsequent meeting was arranged. ⎯⎯⎯⎯ ⎯⎯⎯⎯

15. All important information, ideas and decisions were promptly and accurately recorded. ⎯⎯⎯⎯ ⎯⎯⎯⎯

16. I actively encouraged creative thinking. ⎯⎯⎯⎯ ⎯⎯⎯⎯

17. I encouraged thorough evaluation of information and all ideas for solutions. ⎯⎯⎯⎯ ⎯⎯⎯⎯

18. I was able to remain neutral during constructive arguments, and otherwise encourage teamwork. ⎯⎯⎯⎯ ⎯⎯⎯⎯

19. I suggested or urged establishment of needed norms and standards. ⎯⎯⎯⎯ ⎯⎯⎯⎯

20. I encouraged members to discuss how they felt about the group process and resolve any blocks to progress. ⎯⎯⎯⎯ ⎯⎯⎯⎯

Summary

In chapter 13 we have examined the role of the nonparticipant observer whether acting as a learner, reminder, consultant, or critic. The student of small group communication can hasten development of insights and skills by observing numerous small group discussions. The student may be called on to assist discussion groups in such roles as reminder or consultant. As a professional, the observer may function as a researcher, consultant, or critic. No one can comprehend all that is happening during any group discussion, so it is necessary to focus one's observations on selected group variables. Preplanned questions and observation forms can assist one to do so.

Numerous forms were provided to help you function as an observer of discussions or to get responses from group members that can be tabulated and used to improve future meetings of the group. You can use any of these forms as provided, but they may serve you best as models for forms you create to accomplish specific objectives as observer or group facilitator. After extensive observing there will be times when you will prefer to use no observation forms; that which focuses attention also limits perceptions.

Enough reading! You must *observe* to develop the insights and skills required to make valid and useful ratings and observations, whether you are learner, consultant, reminder, or critic of small groups.

Exercises

1. Divide your class into project groups of five or six members each. If there are both men and women in your class, draw them separately so that no group contains just one man or one woman.

   Each group should select a major term project that it will undertake. These can be limited to questions about small group communication and discussion, or your instructor may permit the groups to undertake any projects selected by the groups. For instance, groups from my classes have planned and held a party for the entire class; studied leadership in various campus groups and reported their findings in a panel discussion and paper; conducted studies of group counseling in area high schools; undertaken experiments in group interaction; participated in the National Contest in Public Discussion; evaluated learning discussion leadership in college classes; developed manuals; studied the jury system; prepared and presented instructional units to the rest of the class; served as advisory committees to campus and city administrators; and even written and produced short training films. The purpose and procedures for each project should be approved in advance by your instructor who may be able to assist you with resources, ideas, and techniques.

   The project groups will need a limited amount of time for meeting in regular class hours, but may need to conduct additional meetings outside of class.

   The major purpose is to develop insights and skills as participant-observers. The project group exercise provides an opportunity to study how a group develops from a collection of persons who at first lack any group goal, role structure, or norms. Each student should write an essay describing the group and evaluating its functioning, using for an outline a set of questions such as those below.

Guidelines for Evaluating Your Project Group

The questions below are only suggestions: there may be other issues of importance in examining your particular group, some of these questions may be inappropriate or in need of modification for your essay, and you will need to decide what topics to raise in describing and evaluating your unique small group.

1. What was the *goal* of the group? How did the group develop this as its objective? How adequately did this goal represent the interests and concerns of the members (individual goals)? What *hidden* agendas existed, and how did these contribute to or interfere with the surface agenda?

2. What *phases* were there in the emergence of a group structure? How could you tell when the group had progressed from one stage of development into another?

3. What do you perceive to be the *role* of each member? How did members come to have their roles? Were any needed behavioral functions missing? If so, what was the impact on the group?

4. Did a procedural *leader* emerge in your group? Who? *How* did this person come to be acknowledged by others as leader? What responsibilities did the leader perform? What leadership functions did others perform? If no leader emerged, how were necessary leadership services provided (or were they?)?

5. What *communication network* seems to exist in the group (i.e., who talks to whom)? How well do members listen to each other? Have there been problems in communicating, such as ambiguity, bypassing, stoppers, or the mood of dismissal? How did the group handle these? Have adequate records been kept and reports made from meeting to meeting?

6. What *norms* governing individual and group behavior emerged? How did these come about? What effects do they have on group productivity and maintenance? If there were counterproductive norms, were these changed? How? Did you have any problem members? If so, who, and how were these persons handled?

7. How were discussions *structured?* What overall procedure did the group follow for its problem solving? How adequate was this procedure? How well were all members' resources of knowledge, creativity, reasoning, and evaluating used? Did each meeting have a clear objective and an agenda to follow?

8. How well were *decisions* made? What decision-making techniques were employed? If any prolonged conflicts occurred, how were they resolved?

9. What *climate* or atmosphere existed and now exists among the members? How have tensions been handled? Are members committed? Task oriented? Accepting and supportive of each other? Appropriately flexible?

10. *Overall,* how do you evaluate your group and your personal contribution to it? What changes would you make if you could? How, and why?

2. You may be assigned to serve in various observer roles of discussions both within your class and of groups that exist in the outside world. Use forms supplied in this chapter, or appropriate adaptations of them, to guide your observations and reports.

References

1. W. Fawcett Hill, *Learning Thru Discussion* (Beverly Hills: Sage Publications, 1977), 30–31.
2. Bobby R. Patton and Kim Giffin, *Problem-Solving Group Interaction* (New York: Harper & Row, Publishers, 1973), 213–14.

author index

subject index